Higher Education and the Civil Rights Movement

SOUTHERN DISSENT

UNIVERSITY PRESS OF FLORIDA

Florida A&M University, Tallahassee
Florida Atlantic University, Boca Raton
Florida Gulf Coast University, Ft. Myers
Florida International University, Miami
Florida State University, Tallahassee
New College of Florida, Sarasota
University of Central Florida, Orlando
University of Florida, Gainesville
University of North Florida, Jacksonville
University of South Florida, Tampa
University of West Florida, Pensacola

Higher Education and the Civil Rights Movement

White Supremacy, Black Southerners, and College Campuses

Edited by Peter Wallenstein

Foreword by Stanley Harrold and Randall M. Miller

University Press of Florida
Gainesville/Tallahassee/Tampa/Boca Raton
Pensacola/Orlando/Miami/Jacksonville/Ft. Myers/Sarasota

Copyright 2008 by Peter Wallenstein
Published in the United States of America
All rights reserved

25 24 23 22 21 20   7 6 5 4 3 2

First cloth printing, 2007
First paperback printing, 2009

Library of Congress Cataloging-in-Publication Data:
Higher education and the civil rights movement: white supremacy,
black Southerners, and college campuses/edited by Peter
Wallenstein; foreword by Stanley Harrold and Randall M. Miller.
p. cm.—(Southern dissent)
Includes index.
ISBN 978-0-8130-3162-0 (cloth)
ISBN 978-0-8130-3444-7 (pbk)
1. College integration—Southern States—History. 2. Civil rights
movements—Southern States—History. 3. Social change—
Southern States—History. I. Wallenstein, Peter.
LC214.22.S68H54 2007
379.2'6309759—dc22   2007027406

The University Press of Florida is the scholarly publishing agency
for the State University System of Florida, comprising Florida
A&M University, Florida Atlantic University, Florida Gulf Coast
University, Florida International University, Florida State University, New College of Florida, University of Central Florida,
University of Florida, University of North Florida, University of
South Florida, and University of West Florida.

University Press of Florida
2046 NE Waldo Road
Suite 2100
Gainesville, FL 32609
http://upress.ufl.edu

For

Thomas Hocutt, not of the University of North Carolina

Alice Jackson, not of the University of Virginia

Pauli Murray, not of the University of North Carolina

Lucile Bluford, not of the University of Missouri

Virgil D. Hawkins, not of the University of Florida

Horace Ward, not of the University of Georgia

Alexander Pierre Tureaud Jr., not of Louisiana State University

Medgar Evers, not of the University of Mississippi

Autherine Lucy, not of the University of Alabama

Clyde Kennard, not of the University of Southern Mississippi

And the many other failed applicants in the era of Jim Crow who did what they could to blaze the way, together with those who followed their lead and pioneered an African American presence on campuses that had historically barred any black enrollment

Contents

Foreword ix

Preface xi

Introduction: Higher Education, Black Access, and the Civil Rights Movement 1

1. Black Southerners and Nonblack Universities: The Process of Desegregating Southern Higher Education, 1935–1965
   PETER WALLENSTEIN 17

2. Four Who Would: *Constantine v. Southwestern Louisiana Institute* (1954) and the Desegregation of Louisiana's State Colleges
   MICHAEL G. WADE 60

3. The Long Journey from LaGrange to Atlanta: Horace Ward and the Desegregation of the University of Georgia
   ROBERT A. PRATT 92

4. Black Colleges and Civil Rights: Organizing and Mobilizing in Jackson, Mississippi
   JOY ANN WILLIAMSON 116

5. Prying the Door Farther Open: A Memoir of Black Student Protest at the University of Maryland at College Park, 1966–1970
   HAYWARD "WOODY" FARRAR 137

6. Hold That (Color) Line! Black Exclusion and Southeastern Conference Football
   CHARLES H. MARTIN 166

7. African American Women Pioneers in Desegregating Higher Education
   MARCIA G. SYNNOTT 199

Afterword: Unfinished Business 229

Appendix 1. Federal Initiatives on Race and Higher Education, 1890–1965 239

Appendix 2. *University of Maryland v. Murray* (Maryland, 1936) 242

Appendix 3. The U.S. Supreme Court and Segregation in Missouri (1938) 249

Appendix 4. President Truman's Commission on Higher Education (1946–1948) 253

Appendix 5. *McCready v. Byrd* (Maryland, 1950) 257

Appendix 6. *Sweatt v. Painter* (1950) 262

Appendix 7. "Desegregation" at the University of Missouri (1950) 266

Appendix 8. *Frasier v. Board of Trustees of the University of North Carolina* (1955) 270

Appendix 9. Interview with Theotis Robinson Jr., of the University of Tennessee 275

Appendix 10. Model Universities and Racial Diversity 280

List of Contributors 283

Index 285

Foreword

The story of desegregating southern schools is long. Much of it, in the popular mind at least, centers on several key moments or incidents in law or protest that affected, and eventually effected, the official desegregation of public elementary and secondary schools. There was great drama in the Supreme Court's decision in *Brown v. Board of Education* (1954) and in white southern "massive resistance," epitomized by the confrontation at Central High School, in Little Rock, Arkansas, in 1957. Efforts to desegregate southern colleges and universities also produced mythic moments. Mississippi governor Ross Barnett's defiance of a federal court order to admit James Meredith to Ole Miss and the violence that met Meredith there in 1962, for example, became a centerpiece in the desegregation narrative. For a time, desegregation played out almost as a Kabuki of a white official barring a black student from the schoolhouse door before yielding to federal power. Such confrontations made good copy for newspapers and striking visual shots for the television evening news. In a fuller story of desegregation, however, they distort the dynamics and direction of the process. They make it seem that only through direct public encounters could desegregation happen or become possible.

Peter Wallenstein's collection of original essays, *Higher Education and the Civil Rights Movement: White Supremacy, Black Southerners, and College Campuses*, shows that the desegregation of higher education in the South was more complicated and widespread, if also often less dramatic and more incremental, than the standard accounts have it. The collection includes a very useful chapter on the role of "black" colleges in the desegregation effort. But its major contribution lies in studying a variety of "white"—or at least "non-black"—colleges and universities. The authors analyze the educational settings and circumstances that influenced African Americans' efforts to seek admission to southern institutions of higher learning and gain an education in them.

The different terms by which the federal government established land-grant colleges affected the curriculum and character of these institutions. The Morrill Land-Grant College Act of 1890, for example, offered federal support for colleges, so long as black students also benefited from the money, though a state might extend such benefits by maintaining racially segregated institutions. As students' programmatic needs changed in a more complex economy and society, black students excluded from "white" colleges and unable to get needed coursework at "black" colleges challenged Jim Crow by demanding admission to "white" colleges on the principle of equal access to public resources. The struggle existed on many fronts. African Americans sought entrance to "white" schools of law, schools of medicine, and graduate schools. They sought to enroll as undergraduates in the South's "white" colleges and universities. As the authors illustrate, desegregation succeeded by dint of individual courage and resolve, as well as institutional acceptance, however grudging, of the new realities of law and social change. Black dissent increasingly forced white assent. Once admitted to "white" schools, black students asserted their rights to use campus space and attend events. They forced faculty, administration, and other students to respect their purpose, presence, and persons. Success in one place encouraged challenges in others. The desegregation of higher education was thus at once episodic and evolutionary.

Through a series of case studies of individual black dissenters, as litigants and as students in institutions of higher education across the South, *Higher Education and the Civil Rights Movement* tracks the long process whereby, from the 1930s through the 1970s, the desegregation of "white" colleges and universities merged with, and reinforced, the modern civil rights movement. In doing so, the authors demonstrate that any honest telling of the desegregation narrative must recognize the persistence of black dissent and the importance of breaching racial barriers in higher education. Their work is a welcome addition to the Southern Dissent series.

Stanley Harrold and Randall M. Miller
Series Editors

Preface

This book has many origins, many points of entry that had to go right for it to be completed. One could say that it began when I embarked in 1997 on a history of my own school, Virginia Polytechnic Institute and State University (Virginia Tech), whose 125th anniversary was coming up. When reconstructing the beginnings of desegregation there, I found virtually no literature that could help me place the Virginia Tech story in a regional context—although a graduate student of mine, Anthony Deel, had begun the story several years earlier with a master's thesis on the desegregation of higher education in Virginia, and Elaine Dowe Carter, a graduate student at Tech at the time, had been developing the early history of black women at the school.

The work that Anthony Deel and Elaine Carter had done helped me sketch the Tech story, but to place that story with certainty in the context of the entire South, I knew I would have to do what I could to redress a serious deficiency I encountered in the historical writing on the region. At any rate, I found the topic the most challenging one in the book—the most difficult to contextualize and the most intriguing and important. The book on Virginia Tech came out in August 1997, as accurate and finished as possible.

For the fall 1997 issue of the Virginia Tech alumni magazine, I wrote a short essay I called "Not Fast, But First: The Desegregation of Virginia Tech." In it, I claimed (with requisite modifiers) that Tech was the first historically white public four-year institution in the former Confederacy to enroll a black undergraduate—in 1953. The editor, Su Clausen-Wicker, queried her counterparts at other institutions, people in information and public relations units, by means of a to-whom-it-may-concern e-mail, regarding the validity of the assertion as to Tech's primacy. From Texas and assorted other venues came rebuttals. Each competing claim proved short-lived, but that sortie also led me to the story of Southwestern Louisiana Institute (now the University of Louisiana at Lafayette), and through it to the research of Michael Wade, and then Mike himself, whose work appears in this book.

During the fall semester of 1997, occurrences at Tech generated a continuing need to pursue the story. While poking around old student yearbooks, several of my students discovered that Claudius Lee, the longtime professor for whom a large campus residence hall is named, had represented himself in the 1896 yearbook (which he edited) as a member and former "right hand of terror" of a campus group he called the "K.K.K." The discovery became an event after one of my students, Cordel Faulk (a writer for the student newspaper, the *Collegiate Times*), published an op-ed piece, and other newspapers, from across the country, picked up the story.

University president Paul Torgersen appointed me to chair a committee, along with Joyce Williams-Green and Michael K. Herndon, to investigate the factual basis for the characterization, assess its significance, and suggest actions that he and the university might consider to redress the past and render the present campus a more warmly inclusive one. In that context, my statement that Tech in fact seemed to have an alternative past—that it was the first public institution of higher education across the states of the former Confederacy to enroll a black undergraduate in the twentieth century—led to a rebuttal from an alumnus whose wife, he said, remembered that there had been one or more black students at her school, now the University of North Carolina at Greensboro, even earlier. I was fairly certain that no such thing could have happened before 1956. My wife and I drove to Greensboro, where a day in the university archives confirmed that 1956 was the correct date for the enrollment of the first African Americans, and where I acquired a treasure trove of interviews and other materials that I used immediately for a report and later for a conference paper.

The project took two tracks. One developed the story at Virginia Tech; the other explored the broader regional context of desegregating public higher education across the South. I published a number of pieces on Virginia Tech in *Diversity News* (edited then at Tech by Michele Clark Holmes), thus reaching an interested local audience and at the same time refining my ideas. Essays that first appeared there, between 1997 and 2000, included "The First Black Students at Virginia Tech" and "Asians and Asian-Americans at Virginia Tech: The Early Years, 1920–1950." In addition, the university archivist, Tamara Kennelly, continued her own strong interest in reconstructing black history at Virginia Tech, interviewing early black graduates, especially the pioneer black women, and posting much of the resulting material on the library's Web site.

The trip to Greensboro became part of an ever-growing project that took me to other institutions. Mounting evidence seemed to confirm my original statement. Working within the seventeen segregated states of the first half of the twentieth century, I defined my universe as all the flagship university campuses, together with the historically white land-grant institutions in each of these states. Ten states combined the two institutions into one—Florida, Missouri, Maryland, and Kentucky are examples—so this definition gave me twenty-four schools to examine, although I was tempted to know more about some other schools, too, among them Virginia Military Institute, the College of William and Mary, Florida State University, and the University of North Carolina at Greensboro.

In November 1998, at the annual meeting of the Southern Historical Association, in Birmingham, Alabama, Randall Miller asked me what I was working on, and I mentioned my project on the desegregation of higher education—on which I had in fact just spent several days in Starkville, Tuscaloosa, Tallahassee, and Auburn before I arrived at the conference. Great, he said. While you are working toward your big book, why not edit a collection of other people's essays on the subject for my University Press of Florida series, Southern Dissent? Doing so would, he observed, help propel the process along. And that's more or less what happened, although the process took longer than he or I had anticipated, and also my conception of the single-authored book changed course.

As I did my preliminary exploration of the project in 1997 and 1998, I met more people who were working on one aspect of the story or another. I already knew that Hayward "Woody" Farrar, a colleague of mine in the history department at Virginia Tech, had given a conference paper some years earlier, based on his own experiences at the University of Maryland. Robert A. Pratt, whom I had met years earlier at the Virginia Center for the Humanities, was involved in writing about the beginnings of desegregation at the University of Georgia, where he was teaching. On my visit to Auburn University, I met the archivist there then, Martin T. Olliff, at about the time he gave a conference paper on that school's desegregation, in which he focused on the Auburn administration. Among other historians I met who had been working in the field of higher education, Charles H. Martin had been developing the story of desegregation of southern college sports. In 1999, at the annual meeting of the American Historical Association, Marjorie Julian Spruill told me a riveting story about Clyde Kennard's catastrophic attempt to enroll in what is now the University of Southern Mississippi, although to my regret she was unavailable to produce an essay on the subject.

Over the years, I have tried out my ideas and my materials in many conference papers. Bernard Timberg connected me with Marianne Bumgarner-Davis, who was organizing a conference at Johnson C. Smith University on the civil rights movement in North Carolina, at which I introduced the story of a black high school's senior class project in 1957 to push the desegregation of the University of North Carolina along. Some days later, at the annual meeting of the History of Education Society in Atlanta, Roger L. Geiger invited me to revise my conference paper for a special volume, on higher education in the South, of the *History of Higher Education Annual*, and thus there emerged, far faster than might otherwise have been the case, an early version of this book's opening essay, which frames the entire project. At the same conference, Marcia G. Synnott mentioned to me the interviews she had conducted with pioneer black female students on various southern campuses.

Other conference papers led me to develop additional parts of the story and also led to new conversations, new contacts, and a renovated conception of the book, to focus not on the desegregating institutions but, rather, on the black pioneers who forced the changes at those schools. A paper I gave at a conference that Elna C. Green organized at Florida State University in 2000 occasioned my recounting the story for Florida. A paper I presented at the 2000 Citadel Conference, on the desegregation of the University of North Carolina, occasioned my more explicitly linking higher education's desegregation with the civil rights movement. At the 2000 conference of the Southern Association of Women Historians, I presented a paper that, as part of the battle over Claudius Lee, I had originally researched and drafted on the University of North Carolina at Greensboro. A paper for the American Historical Association, presented in 2001, occasioned new writing that sharpened my focus on black voices and made its way into the introduction here.

Over the years, subsequent papers clarified the ideas and applied them to new materials. Among these were a paper on South Carolina, presented at the 2003 Citadel Conference on the civil rights movement in South Carolina and subsequently published in the *History of Higher Education Annual*; "Brown v. Board of Education and Segregated Universities: From Kluger to Klarman—Toward Creating a Literature on King Color, Federal Courts, and Undergraduate Admissions," at the 2004 meeting of the Organization of American Historians; "Desegregating Higher Education in the Upper South: Delaware and Maryland, 1935–1970," at the 2005 meeting of the History of Education Society; and "Segregation, Desegregation, and Higher Education in Virginia," at the 2006 Virginia Forum and again at the 2006 Policy History Conference. I am grateful to the organizers of these and other conferences and sessions, and also to the numerous scholars who offered counsel on those occasions. All of these experiences helped shape and strengthen this book.

At Virginia Tech, the College of Arts and Sciences and also the Department of History provided travel funds that facilitated my attendance at some of those conferences—and research funds that financed portions of my travel to university archives in all seventeen states that had maintained segregated institutions of higher education in the first half of the twentieth century. A Summer Humanities Stipend from Tech also facilitated work on the book. A fellowship from the North Caroliniana Society helped me pursue the North Carolina story, about which I plan to complete a book that details the century-long history of segregation and desegregation in the higher education of a single state—a scaled-back version of the project I first outlined to Randall Miller.

Speaking of Randall Miller, he would not let me go. From time to time, I would receive from him an e-mail or a letter calling my attention to an additional recent publication or yet another possible contributor to my book. He and series coeditor Stanley Harrold were patient as I worked by indirection toward the book. Meredith Morris-Babb, too, director of the University Press of Florida, expressed keen interest in my work and how it was coming along. All three were vital to my work, even aside from their excellent suggestions, for I had confidence that the project—as soon as I and the other contributors could complete it—had an excellent home.

Often (I fear) to the dismay of Marcia, Woody, and Bob, the other contributors and I stayed far too busy at far too many things to move the volume to a quick completion. I needed, for example, to complete the two books—one on interracial marriage, the other on twentieth-century Virginia—that I had put aside to write the 1997 book about Virginia Tech that had launched this big project in the first place; one came out in 2002, the other in 2004. But there were advantages to the delay. Charles and Mike and I all knew far more by the end of that time than we had at the beginning. Over the months, extending into years, as I narrowed the focus to black southerners, I found it necessary to drop Marty Olliff's fine essay, but with pleasure I added one by Joy Ann Williamson. I met Joy at the 2003 History of Education Society conference in Chicago, discovered her new project on Mississippi, and was fortunate to be able to add her to the roster of contributors, thus including an essay about black students at black colleges in the civil rights era.

My thanks to all who have contributed to the project and nudged it along. These include my editor, the series editors, and my fellow contributors. They surely also include the two outside readers for the Press in 2006, Stephanie Y. Evans of the University of Florida and Amy Thompson McCandless of the College of Charleston, each of whom exemplified the model outside reader, enthusiastic about the project but offering great advice on how to improve a good product. Certainly also to be included are Lindsay Cherry, Essex Finney, Irving Peddrew, Matthew Winston, and Charlie Yates, five men who were crucial to helping me reconstruct the story at Virginia Tech in the 1950s and thus launch the larger study. Without them and their stories, this project would never have been conceived.

I speak for all the writers in this volume in saluting the people whose stories we tell. Black southerners in general lived these stories a generation or two ago. We focus on two groups—those who tried but failed to break through the Jim Crow barriers, and the pioneer black students on historically white campuses. We as writers have tried to get the stories right in our retelling of them and, bringing these stories together, to share them with a wider audience.

Peter Wallenstein
Blacksburg, Virginia

Introduction

Higher Education, Black Access, and the Civil Rights Movement

Vivian Malone started college in 1961 at Alabama Agricultural and Mechanical Institute (A&M), the state's black land-grant school in Huntsville. But A&M did not offer the program that she wanted, and she could not afford to go out of state to a school that did, so she applied to enter the University of Alabama as a transfer student. She was not accepted. She later recalled that, as she exclaimed, "the University of Alabama had a reasonable fee, it had the major that I was interested in, and [yet] here they were telling me, a citizen of Alabama, that the only reason that I couldn't attend was because I happened to be black."[1] In the end, under a federal court order, she enrolled in June 1963. She graduated in May 1965.

Black Voices, Higher Education, and Southern History

A century after the end of the Civil War, it could be a momentous occasion when a solitary African American took a class, let alone a degree, at an institution that had long rejected all black applicants. Once enrolled, Vivian Malone was permitted to stay—unlike James Hood, who also enrolled in 1963, or Autherine Lucy, the one earlier black student at Alabama, who enrolled briefly in 1956 and then was expelled. In addition to Vivian Malone, the former Confederacy's college class of 1965 included a young black woman at the University of South Carolina, Henrie Monteith, and a young black man at Clemson, Harvey Gantt.[2]

Across the South, during a turbulent time, tremendous changes were taking place. In the first half of the 1960s, events like these in Alabama and South Carolina—and similar ones in Georgia and Mississippi—could be front-page news, and historians continue to emphasize those late, dramatic events from the Deep South. In the thirteen other historically segregated states, however, the beginnings of change dated back to the 1950s, the 1940s, or even the 1930s, and other voices, too, have much to tell us about desegregation of higher education across the South.

Henrie Montieth, when she graduated in August 1965, became the first black student to do so at the University of South Carolina since 1877, the last year of Republican political power during Reconstruction in that state.[3] When Donald Murray broke the color line at the University of Maryland's law school in 1935, he became the first black student there in the twentieth century, but a few black students had earned degrees at the Maryland law school in the 1880s, before the school slammed the door to black enrollment.[4] Thus, although these two schools were exceptional in having admitted—and graduated—black students at an earlier time, it is often necessary to qualify statements about the "first black student" by adding the phrase "in the twentieth century." The era of Jim Crow was at its height of power—and permitted no exceptions in public higher education anywhere in the South—between 1890 and 1935.

Black voices from the struggle to achieve the twentieth-century desegregation of higher education in the South can be those of people, like Vivian Malone, whose pluck and timing combined to achieve success in one challenge to Jim Crow policies and practices. Other black applicants, by contrast, failed in their bids to break the racial barrier; yet their stories, too, are revealing, as they struggled through what remained—despite their effort—the "prehistory" of desegregation. Still others, not necessarily the first African American to enter or graduate from their particular institution, encountered other barriers and played other roles in pushing back the shadows from the past.

This book listens primarily to black voices. Other people also participated in the drama of desegregation—or there would have been scant drama. School presidents, state governors, and federal judges frequently appear on stage, as do white faculty and white students. Here, however, the major roles are assigned to the people who forced the changes, who made things happen, whether as lawyers or litigants, whether as applicants for admission or matriculated students. Other books may focus on the activities and attitudes, the experiences and memories, of other players. Here the chief agents of change are black southerners—applicants, litigants, lawyers, students, parents, teachers, communities. They forced the questions to which answers had to be found. They initiated the actions that made the history that the writers in this volume seek to reconstruct.

A Dual Tradition of Dissent

Southern history regarding race can best be understood as consisting of two competing streams of dissent, and the stories in this book reflect this dual tradition. Since the colonial period, southerners had contested matters of racial identity and racial privilege, and the essays in this book pick up that history and retell some major developments of the middle third of the twentieth century. On the one hand were the white southerners—among them state governors and legislators, school faculty and administrators, students and voters—most of whom dissented from desegregation, resisted change on the racial front, fought judicial decrees that promoted change, in sum did all they could to prevent, delay, or minimize the desegregation of public institutions of higher education. On the other hand were the black southerners who raised the issues in the first place, who applied for admission in the face of exclusionary policies and practices, and who brought the court cases that sometimes led—eventually did lead—to changes in those policies and practices.

Black southerners dissented from the racial orthodoxy of the twentieth-century South. They sometimes found sympathetic white southerners who, in one fashion or another, pushed the process of change along. As they challenged the discrimination and segregation that Jim Crow imposed, they contested both the "separate" and the "unequal" in the operation of the doctrine of "separate but equal." Sometimes they secured support from a court of law, whether a state court or a federal court—and it was usually a federal court—that fostered their success in resisting policies that perpetuated segregation, prevented black access, and curtailed black opportunity. Risking much—and sometimes paying much—they sometimes succeeded in their efforts. They sometimes failed. In failure, they often nonetheless nudged change along—they showed that black southerners were not content with the way things were and propelled a process that led to success for others in breaking down the old rules of a caste society. The history of higher education during the last generation of the Age of Segregation puts on display a variety of efforts that black southerners undertook in their dissent from the rule of Jim Crow.

An additional facet of the emergence of desegregation is the way in which institutions of higher education—in particular, their leaders—fashioned a path, navigated a way, between the two main currents of dissent. Not all members of university communities fully subscribed to the one true faith of maintaining a caste society. Regardless, the people in those communities—in particular, key administrators—tended to maintain as their highest priority what they saw as the good of the school, not the degree to which it remained segregated or commenced desegregation. School administrators worked within a framework of law and policy that emanated in part from state authority and in part from federal, and as federal authorities intervened, state authorities often stiffened their resistance, for a time.

As the forces of change grew in strength, school presidents tended to seek ways to accommodate the agents of change while appeasing the forces of resistance to change. They tried to accommodate the forces of dissent against segregation while not alienating the forces of dissent from new rules being imposed by agents of federal policy. Bending but not breaking, they might—as the University of Mississippi did—accept a black student, but only under court order, and then accept another solitary black student, again under court order. In pursuing this minimalist approach to change, they sought to navigate between antithetical forces of dissent, and in doing so they managed to blunt calls that schools be shut down rather than desegregated.

Race and Region in Public Policy

The song of black and white—according to the music of "separate but equal"—was long sung in many states of the nation. The "South" is a malleable concept and can itself bring confusion. The eleven states of the former Confederacy all maintained fully segregated educational institutions in the 1920s, whether in such Upper South states as Virginia and North Carolina or in such Deep South states as Alabama and Mississippi. So did the Border South states of Delaware, Maryland, West Virginia, Kentucky, Missouri, and Oklahoma.

At all points beginning with Reconstruction, black southerners had some possibility, and white southerners some need, to take into account federal policies regarding higher education. Each set of possibilities, state and federal, placed limits on what the other level of government could do. The interplay of the three forces, black and white citizens within each state, the federal government from outside, dynamically shaped the changing policy outputs at every step of the way.[5] The white South's leaders did everything within their power to control federal power and prevent its reach into southern race relations, but the dynamic relationship could play out in various ways. At some points, congressional action did more to spur changes in policy; at some points federal judicial decisions did more to shape it (see appendix 1).

In all, seventeen states maintained segregated public education—from elementary school (everywhere) through doctoral and professional programs (if available), without exception between at least 1890 and 1935. In most such states, policy was governed by statutes and in some cases even by provisions of the state constitution. Regardless of its legal foundation, the practice was consistently segregationist. Moreover, what an occasional federal court characterized as "a tacit policy" of black exclusion proved, when the issue arose, to have the full force of state authority behind it. As for the formula "separate but equal," the range of opportunities was far more restricted for black southerners than for their white neighbors and cousins.

The "colleges of 1862" and the "colleges of 1890," although themselves subject to misapprehension, are useful terms often associated with this regime. The "colleges of 1862" were those institutions associated with a federal law, the Morrill Land-Grant College Act of 1862, conferring an endowment for each state to support an institution that, whatever else it offered, provided a curriculum in "agriculture and the mechanic arts."[6] Eleven states were out of the Union in 1862 and warring against the United States, but during Reconstruction they, too, benefited from the legislation. Thus there originated such schools as today's Auburn University, Clemson University, Mississippi State University, Texas A&M University, and Virginia Polytechnic Institute and State University.

Even after emancipation and during Reconstruction, however, few southern states made much—or any—provision for black students to attend any public institutions of higher education; Mississippi and Virginia were among the few that did. When Congress enacted the Morrill Land-Grant College Act of 1890, providing states with substantially increased funding for land-grant schools, it required that black students also benefit from the money. The 1890 act offered states the option, though, of maintaining segregation, provided the state's fund was "equitably divided" between "a college for white students" and an "institution for colored students." The statute thus embodied the separate but equal doctrine to which the U.S. Supreme Court gave broader currency six years later in *Plessy v. Ferguson*.[7]

Every one of the seventeen states soon had a "college of 1890," though well into the twentieth century such schools offered a radically narrower curriculum than did their 1862 counterparts. By the 1920s, the "colleges of 1890" were increasingly offering baccalaureate degrees; beginning generally in the late 1930s, master's degrees became available, too, particularly in education. Yet the curricular offerings at the black schools remained very restricted, even for undergraduates and especially at the graduate level. Into the 1930s, nowhere in the seventeen states was there a law school, for example, at any of the "colleges of 1890." This was the institutional backdrop to the efforts that, beginning in the 1930s, led black southerners to seek admission to various programs in "white" schools. The white schools excluded black students, and the black schools failed to offer programs that growing numbers of black residents—like Vivian Malone in Alabama—sought to enter.

The establishment of the "colleges of 1890" represented a substantial improvement over the previous regime. In the words of historian Howard N. Rabinowitz, the move "from exclusion to segregation" in education constituted almost everywhere a change toward greater opportunity, not a new restriction.[8] Yet, though such an observation has great conceptual merit, Rabinowitz applied it primarily to elementary schooling, and in fact "exclusion" continued to be the prevailing practice in higher education with regard to law schools, medical schools, graduate programs, and many undergraduate programs.

In short, public higher education across the South was born segregated and with few episodic exceptions remained that way well into the twentieth century. Black exclusion from white institutions persisted for generations after the general emancipation that came in the 1860s, but over the years a parallel universe of black schools came on stream. Congress and the Supreme Court alike approved the Jim Crow world of segregated higher education. "Separate but equal" was, everywhere and at all times, a sham—that is, the "separate" was absolute everywhere, but the "equal" could be found nowhere. Not only the separateness but also the inequality was deeply entrenched, and black southerners, when they attacked either or both dimensions of policy and practice, were swimming against a very strong current. Yet the "separate but equal" formula, though used effectively by states to defend against efforts to achieve desegregation, could be deployed as well by black southerners to extract more of the "equal," even when the "separate" remained more or less intact. So the meaning of segregation changed even as efforts to achieve desegregation continued.

Black, White, Other: The Rhetoric of Racial Identity

During the era of Jim Crow, racial identity determined which groups of residents went where in public institutions of higher education in all seventeen segregated states. But the narrative cannot be restricted solely to "black" and "white" students. In part, that is true because the boundary that separated the two was itself in flux—in the 1920s, for example, Georgia, Virginia, and Alabama all changed the legal definition of "white," so that some individuals who had been legally white found themselves newly black. Even more, it is true because there were other people to be accommodated in that binary scheme. From early on, for example, Native Americans enrolled at Oklahoma and at Oklahoma State. In Oklahoma, people were classified as "white" unless they had some African ancestry, and therefore, under Oklahoma law, Native Americans were "white" unless they were part black.[9]

People of recent Asian ancestry, whether immigrants or Asian Americans, posed other problems of racial definition and institutional practice. They were not Caucasian, but neither were they "of African ancestry." Since they were nonwhite, the "white" schools they attended cannot be characterized as "all-white" in the sense that only people of undiluted European ancestry attended them. The shorthand term "historically white"—like the conventional distinction between "white" universities and "nonwhite" schools—can be profoundly misleading, for at most (perhaps all) so-called white institutions of higher education across the South, African Americans comprised the only "nonwhite" group to be categorically excluded during the era of Jim Crow. By the 1920s, cadets from China drilled on the campus of Virginia Polytechnic Institute, among them Cato Lee, as well as at The Citadel. Also in the 1920s, Texas A&M

sported a football player, Taro Kishi, who had immigrated from his native Japan, and Art Matsu, a student whose father was Japanese, played varsity football at the College of William and Mary.[10]

Asians and Asian Americans were likely to be found at other schools, too, long before the first African Americans could attend. By the 1970s, three generations of the Wen family had attended the Virginia Military Institute (VMI). The first, a member of the class of 1907, transferred to the U.S. Military Academy, where he became that school's first ethnic Chinese student to graduate. The second was in the VMI class of 1944, and the third graduated from VMI in 1977. At the University of Maryland at College Park, Chunjin C. Chen enrolled as a freshman in 1915 and earned a master's degree in 1922. He had traveled from his home in China, to which he returned until the Communist takeover in 1949. His four sons all graduated from the University of Maryland. Chen came to the United States, rather than moving to Taiwan, in part because he had a son attending Maryland at the time, and Chen himself taught Chinese language courses at College Park from 1956 until he retired in 1967.[11]

Chinese Mississippians long shared a nonwhite racial classification with black Mississippians. Through the 1930s and 1940s, however, for one family after another, or in one elementary or high school after another, Chinese Mississippians managed to migrate across the racial divide, from nonwhite to nonblack. Soon after World War II, the reclassification reached into institutions of higher education. In 1945–46, Dong Jung Gong enrolled as a freshman at Mississippi State College, and the following year, Hin Luck Wingo was a freshman at the University of Mississippi. Dozens of other Chinese Mississippians followed them. Into the 1960s, most Chinese Mississippians at the state university studied pharmacy, and most of those at the "white" land-grant school studied engineering. At the same time that white Mississippians were insisting on the absolute exclusion of black Mississippians from "white" schools, Chinese Mississippians enrolled at and graduated from both schools. By 1960, Chinese Mississippians were attending Southern Mississippi College. In 1961–62, they included a freshman from Greenville, Jefferson D. Hong, whose parents had evidently sought to help their son, who was born during World War II, navigate from a nonwhite racial identity to a white one by naming him after the onetime president of the Confederate States of America.[12]

Ethnic Asians, though they forged identities that distinguished themselves from black southerners, should not be assumed to have taken on all-purpose white identities. In 1924, during the time that Cato Lee was running track and playing tennis at Virginia Polytechnic Institute and Art Matsu was playing quarterback and kicking punts at William and Mary, the Virginia legislature enacted a law that made it a felony for either of them to marry a white classmate. Nonetheless, across the South, Asians or Asian Americans took undergraduate and graduate degrees at various schools—among them the University of Missouri, the University of Tennessee, North Carolina State, the University of Florida, and the University of Alabama—before the first African American could enroll there.[13] Rather than "all-white," though they may have started out that way, these institutions are better understood on the eve of "desegregation" to have been "nonblack." The breakthroughs of the 1950s and 1960s did not bring nonwhite students to white campuses so much as they brought black students to nonblack campuses. Whatever hurdles other racial or ethnic groups may have encountered, the pioneer black students broke through the most intractable twentieth-century barriers.

Racial identity is rooted far more in the realms of culture and policy than in biology. Scholars—natural scientists and social scientists—tell us that "race" is a legal and social construct.[14] But it is very real when it dictates policy and governs opportunity, when it declares what group of people can participate in a given realm of life or a given set of institutions and what group cannot. Some collection of racial terms must be employed to talk about the phenomena described in this book. But the conventional terms of "black" and "white" will hardly suffice, and not only or even primarily because people with "black" racial identities could—often did—have multiracial ancestry.

In two ways, "nonblack" becomes the term of choice. The binary world of "black" and "white" leaves out people who are neither, and if they are accommodated in the binary world, then it can only be because people in the third group have been reclassified as either "black" or "white" and not because they actually are of African ancestry and therefore "black," or of undisputed European ancestry and therefore "white." Moreover, many twenty-first-century readers are at risk of misreading "white institutions" as "predominantly white" (consistent with new language that addresses more current realities) and "black institutions" as "predominantly black."

Racial identity—whether adopted or imposed, agreed upon or disputed—was, after all, the absolutely central feature of the practices and policies of race in the Age of Segregation. We need some language that will serve the purpose of analyzing the experiences of individuals and the histories of institutions. The absolute exclusion from so-called white institutions of African Americans—typically the sole group identified for exclusion—can better be conveyed if these schools are instead termed "nonblack."

Southern schools were not so much "all-white," then, as "nonblack." Rather, they were "antiblack." Instruments of white supremacy, they represented more than sensibilities of aversion, though that too. A spokesman for the medical school of the University of Georgia declared in 1906: "There are no niggers in this school and there never have been and there never will be as long as one stone of this building remains upon another."[15] Not for another six decades, in

1967, did the stones at the medical school finally fall apart. Against this backdrop of behavior and attitudes, reinforced with legal bans, black prospective students waged their assault.

During the last of those six decades, other declarations from Georgia urged closing the state university rather than integrating it. And when a court order in January 1961 pointed toward the enrollment of two black undergraduates, a student group distributed a proclamation that African Americans' gaining admission, if such were to occur, would result in no softening of white attitudes of resistance, even if some whites might betray the cause: "We will NOT welcome these intruders. We will NOT associate with them. We will NOT associate with white students who welcome them."[16]

Higher Education and the Civil Rights Struggle

One of the iconic moments of the civil rights movement came when the Reverend Dr. Martin Luther King Jr. gave his "I have a dream" speech at the Lincoln Memorial in Washington, D.C., on August 28, 1963. At the time of King's birth in Georgia thirty-four years earlier, in 1929, not a solitary black student could enroll at a public "white" institution of higher education anywhere across the South. Jim Crow ruled everywhere. By the time he greeted his fellow marchers at the close of the great March on Washington for Jobs and Freedom, at least one black student had enrolled in at least one such school in every state.

In the twelve months preceding King's speech, James Meredith had enrolled at the University of Mississippi in September 1962, and Harvey Gantt had done the same at Clemson College in January 1963—albeit both admissions had taken place only because of a federal court order. Just weeks before King went to Washington, Vivian Malone had begun summer classes at the University of Alabama, also under a federal court order. Under the duress of federal authority, King's "dream" was coming true, bit by bit. There might even come a time when it flourished. In the meantime, black applicants—and litigants—became black students, and, as they did so, the walls of segregation were again and again breached.

The National Association for the Advancement of Colored People (NAACP), established in 1909, brought litigation to enhance African Americans' opportunities in areas ranging from voting rights to housing to transportation to education. In the mid-1930s, litigation attacked black exclusion from public institutions of higher education in North Carolina, Maryland, and Missouri, and similar court action soon emerged in other states. Black plaintiffs brought these suits, black lawyers argued them, and black families and communities supported them and watched with great interest as they unfolded. In the late 1940s, culminating in two Supreme Court decisions in June 1950, the NAACP won Supreme Court cases in higher education that laid the foundation for a direct assault on segregated schools at the elementary and secondary levels.

That assault on segregation led to the decisions in *Brown v. Board of Education* in 1954 and 1955. The civil rights movement is often understood as dating from the mid-1950s—originating with *Brown*; launched by the Montgomery bus boycott in 1955–56; propelled by the sit-ins that began in Greensboro, North Carolina, in 1960; and culminating in the March on Washington in 1963, Freedom Summer, and the Civil Rights Act of 1964 and the Voting Rights Act of 1965.[17] Higher education plays little or no role in most accounts. But the civil rights struggle had been under way long before 1954 and 1955; it continued on past 1964; and as the essays in this book reveal, it related in profound ways to higher education. The earlier litigation from the 1930s and 1940s—during Martin Luther King Jr.'s childhood and college years—demonstrates both the longer period of the civil rights struggle and the significance of higher education as one of the great issues at stake.

Another of the great iconic moments of the civil rights movement came on February 1, 1960, when four freshmen at North Carolina A&T—Ezell Blair Jr., Franklin McCain, Joseph McNeil, and David Richmond—began their sit-in at a Woolworth's lunch counter not far from their campus in Greensboro. Black students at various black institutions of higher education played central roles in the sit-in movement at lunch counters and other public facilities. Many of these students, like the Greensboro Four, were enrolled in one or another of the "colleges of 1890." They now attacked the very segregation that had led to the establishment of the segregated colleges and universities they were attending.

The nation's attention often focused on black students at black schools. Just as significant were the black students for the first time attending "white" schools. A handful of students—black and white—from "white" schools in Greensboro joined the black students from North Carolina A&T who had launched the sit-in in that city. Among the white students was Ann Dearsley, from Woman's College (today's University of North Carolina at Greensboro). Among the black students was Claudette Graves, who had graduated from all-black Dudley High School in Greensboro in 1957 before enrolling at Woman's College.[18]

Before the sit-ins began, black North Carolinians had already become part of the civil rights struggle. They did so when they applied to nonblack institutions of higher education. They did so when they went to court if necessary—and again and again it was necessary. They did so when they gained admission at some point in the 1950s and took classes on historically nonblack campuses—when they did what had never been done until their time at Chapel Hill, Raleigh, and Greensboro. Among the college seniors in February 1960, preparing to graduate that year from "historically white" institutions of higher education in North Carolina, were black students, the first cohort of black undergraduates to enroll at their school, whose enrollment resulted directly from successful litigation brought in 1955 by three black high school seniors to enroll at the University of North Carolina.

As for Claudette Graves, she entered Woman's College in the second cohort. She did so as part of a senior class project at Greensboro's Dudley High School, a project designed to propel North Carolina's public nonblack institutions of higher education farther along the process of desegregation, a process only just beginning at that time. Richard H. Bowling was her classmate who went to North Carolina State, and David Mozart Dansby Jr. the one who went to Chapel Hill. All three graduated.[19] Meanwhile, what's more, having enrolled at Woman's College, Claudette Graves and some classmates, white and black, went downtown to participate in the Greensboro sit-ins.

At black schools and white ones alike, higher education and the civil rights movement continued to merge, to flow together. Studies of the two phenomena should also converge. Histories of the civil rights movement routinely tell the dramatic story of James Meredith at the University of Mississippi in 1962, but other pioneers, including the Frasier brothers in North Carolina, have remained invisible. The dominant visual image of the civil rights movement from 1960, a photograph of the four North Carolina A&T freshmen at that Greensboro lunch counter, captures the significance for the movement of black students at black schools. Yet the graduation that year of black students from historically nonblack schools—Manuel Crockett and Irwin Holmes at North Carolina State in Raleigh, Elizabeth JoAnne Smart and Bettye Anne Davis Tillman at Woman's College in Greensboro—displays another facet of the civil rights movement.

The civil rights struggle proceeded on many interrelated fronts. One of those, a very important one, was the desegregation of higher education, at both the graduate and undergraduate levels, in state after state, at school after school, in program after program, from the 1930s through the 1960s.

Civil Rights and Southern Dissent: Seven Essays

Higher education should become integral to our understanding of the civil rights struggle. Moreover, higher education wonderfully serves to illustrate the dual traditions of southern dissent. Across the South, public policy displayed a commitment to retain traditional ways and to deflect calls for change in racial affairs. Across the South, too, however, black citizens challenged those traditional ways, sought allies, and persisted in their various quests to bring to an end the exclusion of African Americans from "white" public institutions—whether absolute, as it long was, or partial, as it typically became for a time. Viewed from the perspective of higher education, the modern civil rights movement—sustained efforts, eventually successful, to dismantle legally mandated obstacles to equal opportunity, laws that restricted African Americans' behavior on the basis of their racial identity—can be dated from about 1935 to about 1968.

Black southerners were attempting to enter "white" institutions of higher education years before *Brown v. Board of Education*. At many schools, some number of them had gained admittance before the Supreme Court decided *Brown*. By the time the *Brown* decision was handed down in 1954, only five states—Alabama, Florida, Georgia, South Carolina, and Mississippi—had yet to enroll at least one black student in a previously nonblack public institution of higher education. All twelve of the other southern states had begun enrolling black students in at least some programs. But the decisions in *Brown* proved crucial in spurring the process along in some states, and the Civil Rights Act of 1964 brought a new constellation of changes.

The essays in this book detail various dimensions of the story of black southerners and their efforts to desegregate public higher education across the South. In their various efforts, successful and unsuccessful, they embodied the spirit of dissent from the reign of Jim Crow, whose authority they rejected. They refused to worship at the altar of white supremacy. They rejected the notion that racial segregation—in particular, black exclusion from "white" institutions of higher education—had to persist just because it had been in place so thoroughly and for so long.

The first essay, by Peter Wallenstein, adds texture to the notion that attacking Jim Crow in higher education was a "process." Wallenstein distinguishes a series of steps in the process, and he further situates the story of higher education in the civil rights struggle. His essay surveys the entire South between the mid-1930s and the mid-1960s, and it recounts in some detail the main developments in such states as the Deep South's Florida, the Upper South's Virginia, and the Border South's Delaware. Among the themes he emphasizes, one is that black southerners' use of the courts provided a crucial means of gaining access to campuses that had in the past absolutely barred black enrollment. Another is that key changes were under way in the early post–World War II years, during Harry S. Truman's presidency. Yet a third is that the Supreme Court's 1954 and 1955 rulings in *Brown v. Board of Education*, although focusing on elementary and secondary schools, proved particularly potent in fostering further desegregation of public higher education across much of the South.

Chapters 2 and 3 explore the process of desegregation in Louisiana and Georgia, and while each emphasizes the 1950s, each sweeps across half a century of change down to the recent past. Michael G. Wade tells of developments in Louisiana—in particular the stutter-step desegregation at Southwestern Louisiana Institute, in Lafayette, where a federal court order in spring 1954, shortly before *Brown*, led to the enrollment that fall, under "separate but equal," of scores of black undergraduates at a historically nonblack school. Emphasizing one community, Wade tells how black citizens of Louisiana went to court, won, enrolled at nonblack institutions, but, when the forces of white supremacy and racial segregation rallied, were turned out again and had largely to start over, which they did.

Robert A. Pratt also emphasizes a single institution, in his case the University of Georgia, but he recounts the story through a biographical study of one participant. Pratt details the efforts by Horace Ward, year after year in the 1950s, to enter the University of Georgia law school. He tells, too, how, after Ward gave up on being admitted there, he earned a law degree at Northwestern University, then returned to Georgia and participated on the legal team that obtained a court order that launched the university's desegregation in 1961. Demonstrating why the state and the university might wish to forestall the kind of training Ward sought, he was able to use his professional training to break open the University of Georgia to black undergraduates and graduate and professional students alike.

Rather than focus on segregated white campuses, Joy Ann Williamson reconsiders the roles of black southerners on segregated black campuses, as she explores student-led developments in the early 1960s at two black institutions in Jackson, Mississippi. Rather than focus solely on public institutions, she compares a public school, Jackson State College, with a private one, Tougaloo College. Her work examines how black institutions of higher education provided movement centers, institutional spaces and bases from which black southerners could plan and carry out attacks on segregation beyond their campuses.

The next two essays, which mostly detail developments in the late 1960s, examine the process and significance of university desegregation after the first steps had been achieved. In an essay that is more memoir than monograph, Hayward "Woody" Farrar recounts developments in which he was centrally involved as a black undergraduate at the University of Maryland between 1966 and 1970. Years after the first black enrollment at College Park, Farrar perceived the school as remaining segregated. He reflects on how he and other black undergraduates pushed the process of desegregation along—how their actions fostered a viable and effective Black Student Union, a substantial increase in black enrollment, the hiring of black faculty, and the beginnings of a black studies program.

In Chapter 6, Charles H. Martin—taking the story back to such Deep South states as Mississippi and Georgia—focuses on the desegregation of college sports. He recounts developments on the racial front in the varsity football programs of the Southeastern Conference (SEC) in the late 1960s and early 1970s, ending with the University of Mississippi. If college campuses provided a key site for contesting whether black southerners were to be excluded from or included in public spaces, varsity football fields supplied a key symbolic frontier after the issue of black access had moved beyond undergraduate enrollment.

Finally, Marcia G. Synnott revisits the entire process through a series of vignettes of black female pioneers, among them Vivian Malone at Alabama, in forging the desegregation of southern higher education. Seven of her pioneers depict either the era of predesegregation—the failed early efforts—or the experiences of the very first cohort of black students on various campuses. With her final vignette, Synnott takes the story into the mid-1970s, when the process of desegregation had advanced far enough that a student could perceive that her being female was more significant, in terms of obstacles and of triumphs over them, than that she was African American. Each of the last four essays takes the story substantially beyond the enrollment of the first black student at a nonblack school, and each shows that, by the early 1970s, remarkable—albeit finite—change had occurred.

After that last essay, an afterword sums up our collective major findings. More than that, it speaks of unfinished business of two sorts. The essays in this book tell important parts of the story of the years between the mid-1930s and the early 1970s, and they make occasional connections to the more recent past, but much remains untold. Moreover, the process of desegregation itself remains unfinished. The essays presented here point toward diminishing the degree to which both the historical process of desegregation and the historical reconstruction of that process remain unfinished. Citizens, educators, students, historians—white, black, and other—all have more to do, miles to go.

Notes

1. Quoted in Howell Raines, ed., *My Soul Is Rested: The Story of the Civil Rights Movement in the Deep South* (New York: G. P. Putnam's Sons, 1977), 332–33. The tale of the battle of Tuscaloosa is recounted in E. Culpepper Clark, *The Schoolhouse Door: Segregation's Last Stand at the University of Alabama* (New York: Oxford University Press, 1993).

2. "Clemson Negro Graduates; Joining Architectural Firm," *New York Times*, May 30, 1965; "Coed Is First Negro Graduated by Alabama U. in Its 134 Years," *New York Times*, May 31, 1965; "Clemson [actually, the University of South Carolina] Graduates First Negro since '77," *New York Times*, August 22, 1965.

3. Regarding black enrollment at the University of South Carolina during Reconstruction—the one time and place that black undergraduates attended a historically

white public college or university anywhere in the South before the mid-twentieth century—see Daniel Walker Hollis, *University of South Carolina*, vol. 2, *College to University* (Columbia: University of South Carolina Press, 1956), 61–79; Pamela Mercedes White, "'Free and Open': The Radical University of South Carolina, 1873–1877" (Master's thesis, University of South Carolina, 1975); Peter Wallenstein, "Higher Education and Civil Rights: South Carolina, 1860s–1960s," *History of Higher Education Annual* 23 (2003–4): 1–22; W. Lewis Burke Jr., "The Radical Law School: The University of South Carolina School of Law and Its African American Graduates, 1873–1877," in *At Freedom's Door: African American Founding Fathers and Lawyers in Reconstruction South Carolina*, ed. James Lowell Underwood and W. Lewis Burke Jr. (Columbia: University of South Carolina Press, 2000), 90–115.

4. David Skillen Bogen, "The Transformation of the Fourteenth Amendment: Reflections from the Admission of Maryland's First Black Lawyers," *Maryland Law Review* 44 (1985): 939–1046 (especially 939–41 and 1029–46); David Skillen Bogen, "The First Integration of the University of Maryland School of Law," *Maryland Historical Magazine* 84 (Spring 1989): 39–49.

5. Wallenstein, "Higher Education and Civil Rights."

6. Harold M. Hyman, *American Singularity: The 1787 Northwest Ordinance, the 1862 Homestead and Morrill Acts, and the 1944 G.I. Bill* (Athens: University of Georgia Press, 1986), 35–61; Peter Wallenstein, *Virginia Tech, Land-Grant University, 1872–1997: History of a School, a State, a Nation* (Blacksburg, Va.: Pocahontas Press, 1997), chapters 1–3.

7. Jean L. Preer, *Lawyers v. Educators: Black Colleges and Desegregation in Public Higher Education* (Westport, Conn.: Greenwood Press, 1982); Joel Schor, *Agriculture in the Black Land-Grant System to 1930* (Tallahassee: Florida A&M University, 1982); John A. Munroe, *The University of Delaware: A History* (Newark: University of Delaware, 1986), 162, 361; Peter Wallenstein, *From Slave South to New South: Public Policy in Nineteenth-Century Georgia* (Chapel Hill: University of North Carolina Press, 1987), chapter 15.

8. Howard N. Rabinowitz, *Race Relations in the Urban South, 1865–1890* (New York: Oxford University Press, 1978).

9. Pauline W. Kopecky, *A History of Equal Opportunity at Oklahoma State University* (Stillwater: Oklahoma State University, 1990), 233–42; Peter Wallenstein, *Tell the Court I Love My Wife: Race, Marriage, and Law—An American History* (New York: Palgrave Macmillan/St. Martin's Press, 2002), chapter 9.

10. Wallenstein, *Virginia Tech*, 173–75; "Asians and Asian-Americans at Virginia Tech: The Early Years, 1920–1950," *Diversity News* 4 (Fall 1997): 8–9, 11; Jian Li, "A History of the Chinese in Charleston," *South Carolina Historical Magazine* 99 (January 1998), 58–64; "Taro Kishi" vertical file, University Archives, Memorial Library, Texas A&M University, College Station (my thanks to Texas A&M University archivist Angus Martin for bringing this file to my attention); Matt Gottlieb, "Nippon QB," *Virginia Living* 3 (October 2005): 46–47.

11. William Couper, "Chinese Students at the Virginia Military Institute since Its Foundation in 1839" (1934) and other materials in a folder, "Chinese Cadets at VMI," VMI Archives, Preston Library, Lexington, Va.; "UMCP's First Chinese Student: Chun-

jin C. Chen," *College Park International* (September 1995), 9 (together with other materials in a folder on "Students, International," Special Collections, the McKeldin Library, University of Maryland at College Park).

12. *Gong Lum v. Rice*, 275 U.S. 78 (1927); the schools' student directories and student yearbooks.

13. *A Survey of Chinese Students in American Universities and Colleges in the Past One Hundred Years* (New York: China Institute in America, 1954), 40–50. Given all the evidence it supplies regarding Chinese students at southern schools, it is striking that this little book was published the same year as the *Brown* decision. Many of the students from China who studied at southern institutions in the 1910s, 1920s, and 1930s—including Chunjin Chen at the University of Maryland and the Chinese cadets at The Citadel—were financed through the partial remission of an indemnity that China was required to pay other nations dating from the Boxer Rebellion. Regarding that program, see Carrol B. Malone, "The First Remission of the Boxer Indemnity," *American Historical Review* 32 (October 1926): 64–68; and Michael H. Hunt, "The American Remission of the Boxer Indemnity: A Reappraisal," *Journal of Asian Studies* 31 (May 1972): 539–59.

14. Lee D. Baker, *From Savage to Negro: Anthropology and the Construction of Race, 1896–1954* (Berkeley: University of California Press, 1998); Wallenstein, *Tell the Court I Love My Wife*.

15. Thomas J. Ward Jr., *Black Physicians in the Jim Crow South* (Fayetteville: University of Arkansas Press, 2003), 31, 57.

16. Robert A. Pratt, "The Rhetoric of Hate: The Demosthenian Literary Society and Its Opposition to the Desegregation of the University of Georgia, 1950–1964," *Georgia Historical Quarterly* 90 (Summer 2006): 246.

17. Examples are Harvard Sitkoff, *The Struggle for Black Equality, 1954–1992*, rev. ed. (New York: Hill and Wang, 1993), beginning the narrative in 1954, and Anthony Lewis, *Portrait of a Decade: The Second American Revolution* (New York: Random House, 1964), ending it ten years later.

18. Peter Wallenstein, "Color, Courts, and Coeds: The Desegregation of the Woman's College of the University of North Carolina, Greensboro, 1956–1960" (paper presented at the Fifth Southern Conference on Women's History, Richmond, Va., June 2000); Anne Dearsley-Vernon, "A White at the Woolworth Sit-in," *UNCG Alumni News* 68 (Spring 1980): 7–8, 29; Allen W. Trelease, *Making North Carolina Literate: The University of North Carolina at Greensboro, from Normal School to Metropolitan University* (Durham, N.C.: Carolina Academic Press, 2004), 270.

19. Peter Wallenstein, "Higher Education and the Civil Rights Movement: Desegregating the University of North Carolina," in *Warm Ashes: Issues in Southern History at the Dawn of the Twenty-first Century*, ed. Winfred B. Moore Jr., Kyle S. Sinisi, and David H. White Jr. (Columbia: University of South Carolina Press, 2003), 280–300; Claudette Graves Burroughs-White, interview by Cheryl Junk, February 25, 1991, unpaginated transcript, University of North Carolina at Greensboro Centennial Oral History Project, University Archives, University of North Carolina at Greensboro.

1

Black Southerners and Nonblack Universities

The Process of Desegregating Southern Higher Education, 1935–1965

PETER WALLENSTEIN

On July 19, 1965, Douglas L. Conner, an African American medical doctor in the town of Starkville, Mississippi, drove his car onto the campus of nearby Mississippi State University. When he came to a stop, his passenger and foster son, Richard E. Holmes, stepped out. Dr. Conner's final words of advice, before driving back to town, were: "Keep your head up."[1] It was the beginning of second summer session, and Holmes wanted to take two nonscience courses—psychology and American government—before returning in the fall to Wiley College, in Marshall, Texas, where he had completed two years as a premedical student. If successful in making his way through the formalities that day, Holmes would be the first African American ever to enroll at Mississippi State.

Holmes registered that day for his classes and paid his fees. He completed his courses, and then he continued at Mississippi State rather than return to Wiley. Although he had very much liked Wiley—and in fact had occasion to wish that he could bring his friends and school life from Texas to Mississippi—he decided to stay in Starkville because it was his home; costs of attending a state school at home were far lower than a private school far away; and he learned that another black youth from Starkville wanted to attend State that fall, but only if Holmes would be there too. Holmes completed his bachelor's degree at Mississippi State, and a master's there, and later he earned an M.D. at Michigan State University. Then he returned to the South and worked as a doctor, for a time in nearby Columbus, not far from where he had grown up, not far from where his mentor and foster father, Dr. Conner, continued to practice.[2]

Meanwhile, the black student presence at Mississippi State University continued to grow. By the late 1990s, African Americans comprised about 16 percent of all undergraduates enrolled there. Across the years, Dr. Holmes continued a medical practice, either in Alabama or Mississippi, and in 1991 he returned to his alma mater when Mississippi State dedicated the Holmes Cultural Diversity Center, named in his honor as the school's first African American student.[3] How representative, we might ask, is the story of Richard Holmes?

This essay seeks to introduce a research area regarding the desegregation of higher education in the seventeen states of the Jim Crow South. Emphasized are the experiences of the people who most directly pursued desegregation and made it happen—the black applicants, often plaintiffs in court cases, and, if successfully enrolled, pioneer black students on previously nonblack campuses. Desegregation is portrayed here as a process rather than an event at each school, for all doors did not open at the same time, as undergraduate programs remained segregated at many schools even after black graduate students enrolled there. The essay has the dual intent of outlining the chronology of desegregation between the 1930s and the 1960s and situating major schools within that framework.

Various schools have been declared, by one writer or another, to be the "first" to "desegregate." Yet absent a literature that supplies some context, such statements are shots in the dark. Close attention to the process of desegregation in southern public higher education has the potential to reshape our understanding of the history of individual institutions and, more generally, the course of higher education in the South and the nation. In addition, much remains to be clarified regarding the development of judicial responses to segregated higher education and much, too, regarding racial identity and the structure of opportunity in American educational and professional life. Moreover, a significant dimension of the modern civil rights movement is missing from the literature and from our understanding as long as higher education gets little attention. This essay offers a down payment on reconsidering old questions and opening up new ones.

Throughout, the dual dimensions of dissent in southern history emerge in bold relief. Increasingly, black southerners expressed their dissent from the racial orthodoxy that mandated their exclusion from "white" institutions. White southerners, as a rule, did not budge. Increasingly, however, federal authorities, when called upon, sided with black citizens. In particular, federal judges sided with black plaintiffs in undermining Jim Crow practices and policies in higher education. At many times and places, white southerners—politicians and their constituents—nonetheless continued to resist any relaxation of the old order. In 1962, Mississippi offered an extraordinary instance of white insurrection. Even in the face of danger, black southerners pushed ahead in their quest for change in racial policies.

Georgia, Mississippi, and Alabama

The events in Starkville in summer 1965 did not make front-page headlines across the state, the nation, or the world. The lack of notice stood in stark contrast to the coverage of the traumatic events associated with the enrollment at the University of Mississippi nearly three years earlier, in October 1962, of the man who became known in the media as "Negro James Meredith." Developments at Mississippi State contrasted, too, with the drama associated with the enrollment of the first African Americans at the University of Alabama and the University of Georgia.

Much took place behind the scenes before and during the summer of 1965. Holmes's low-keyed enrollment at Mississippi State—and the similarly low-keyed coverage of that event—depended on a changing political context in the mid-1960s; the determined efforts of school president Dean W. Colvard; and an understanding by 1965 that the institution's continued receipt of federal funding would be in grave jeopardy if it continued to exclude all African Americans.[4]

The particularly dramatic episodes at the state universities of Georgia, Mississippi, and Alabama have each generated at least one fine book.[5] The events at these three Deep South schools highlighted the greatest resistance to the drive for desegregation and equal access to higher education. Under a court order, graduate student Autherine Lucy gained entrance to the University of Alabama in January 1956, but threats of violence swirled all around her, and she was there only briefly before being expelled. In Georgia, the governor spoke of ordering the University of Georgia closed down, rather than permit undergraduates Hamilton Holmes and Charlayne Hunter to register and begin attending classes in January 1961, and an ominous crowd gathered one night the first week of Hunter's time on campus and threw bricks through her dormitory window.[6]

The events of 1962 and 1963 echoed, even amplified, the earlier strife. So great was the confrontation over enrolling transfer student James Meredith at the University of Mississippi in fall 1962 that two men died in the violence. The dominant image from the entire history of the struggle over desegregation in southern higher education came when Alabama governor George C. Wallace took his symbolic stand "in the schoolhouse door" at the University of Alabama in June 1963, before he stepped aside and undergraduates Vivian Malone and James Hood registered for classes.[7]

The story at Mississippi State, though far less well known, is more representative of the experience, by people and institutions, of the beginnings of desegregation of public institutions of higher education across the South in the 1950s and 1960s. This essay explores the contours of desegregation at a number of schools where—again, in contrast to the headline-grabbing stories broadcast from Athens, Georgia; Oxford, Mississippi; and Tuscaloosa, Alabama—the end of black exclusion, when (and to the extent that) it finally came, went fairly smoothly.

True enough, each school's faculty, administration, students, alumni, and trustees displayed their own personalities, and each school took its own trajectory through the general process of desegregation. Each school's unique story deserves to be told. Cumulatively, these stories about race and higher education in America may do much to illuminate these important developments from the still-recent past.

The pioneer black students, as they sought and secured access to campuses from which African Americans had long been categorically excluded, demonstrated a determination to delete the "separate" from "separate but equal," the mendacious old formula in public facilities. They often had to resort to the courts to pursue their objectives. State legislatures and governors had more direct control over public institutions than they did over private institutions, but the federal courts, too, had more of a direct say over public institutions. The contest between state and federal authority, when it came, focused on public institutions.

Although this essay sometimes mentions additional schools, its primary frame of reference includes just twenty-four institutions, all historically white, in the seventeen segregated states. The seventeen states—extending from Delaware and Maryland to Missouri and Oklahoma as well as from Virginia and Georgia to Texas and Arkansas—each maintained a "black" land-grant school as well as a "white" one. In Maryland, Kentucky, Florida, Georgia, Louisiana, and five other states, the flagship state university is also a land-grant institution. Seven states supported separate institutions: Texas and Texas A&M, Oklahoma and Oklahoma State, Mississippi and Mississippi State, Alabama and Auburn, South Carolina and Clemson, North Carolina and North Carolina State, and Virginia and Virginia Tech.

Five states in the Deep South proved to be the most resistant to desegregation. In these states, whites constituted the nation's smallest majorities of the population and had, they believed, the most at stake in preserving total segregation. In 1950, the figures ranged from Mississippi's 55 percent white and South Carolina's 61 percent to Louisiana's 67 percent, Alabama's 68 percent, and Georgia's 69 percent. Four of these states were the only ones to support South Carolina's Strom Thurmond, the Dixiecrat candidate for the presidency in 1948. All five voted for Barry Goldwater (the only other state he won was his home state, Arizona) against Lyndon B. Johnson in 1964, in a contest that pitted a senator who had opposed the Civil Rights Act of 1964 against a sitting president who had championed it.[8]

By 1970, the heroic age of the civil rights movement had about run its course in higher education. Where victories for civil rights were defined in terms of the very first African Americans to enter a state university or other public institution, by 1965 the major frontiers had been crossed, the major defenses of racial privilege breached. The late 1960s brought new struggles over institutional practices and cultural climate.

Among the twenty-four schools, Mississippi State was dead last in admitting its first African American student. The fact that Richard Holmes decided to enroll in the summer of 1965, rather than at some earlier point, surely had something to do with his easy time gaining entrance. At Ole Miss, James Meredith had graduated in August 1963. But, even after that, it took federal court orders to secure the enrollment of Cleve McDowell to the law school in June 1963 and transfer student Cleveland Donald Jr. in June 1964. Less than a year before Holmes enrolled in Starkville, the University of Mississippi had finally enrolled a black student (freshman Irvin Walker) without first requiring a court order.[9] Just as Alabama had reverted to nonblack after expelling Autherine Lucy in early 1956, Ole Miss reverted to nonblack when it expelled Cleve McDowell in September 1963. Each school had been "desegregated" in the sense of having admitted at least one black student, yet it had no black students and continued for some time to resist letting any in.

The most dangerous and dramatic events took place not at the beginning, nor at the very end, but toward the end of the time line along which the twenty-four schools began to desegregate. Only when the federal government put its full resources into backing up federal court orders did the governor and the University of Mississippi finally concede the beginnings of desegregation in 1962, and the governor and the University of Alabama went through a similar exercise the following year.

Litigation—Won and Lost, Federal and State

Richard Holmes did not have to go to court to force his admission. Nor did many of the other pioneer African American students on white campuses. Yet they, like Holmes, benefited from litigation elsewhere.

Court cases framed the timing of the first steps toward desegregation, beginning with rulings by the Maryland courts in 1935–36. Decisions by the U.S. Supreme Court in 1938, 1948–50, and 1954–55 transformed the law of the land for every state. A case from Missouri, brought by Lloyd Gaines, led to a 1938 ruling (see appendix 3) that—though no state need offer a law school education—if it chose to offer one to white residents, it could not constitutionally require black residents to go out of state to obtain similar training. A series of cases from Oklahoma and Texas between 1948 and 1950, brought by Ada Lois Sipuel Fisher, George W. McLaurin, and Heman Marion Sweatt, reinforced the 1938 ruling, demanded a greater measure of equality within "separate but equal," and banned segregation of black students in classrooms and libraries once they had gained admittance to an institution. The two decisions in *Brown v. Board of Education* in 1954 and 1955, one rejecting the old formula of "separate but equal" in public elementary and secondary education and the other addressing the problems of implementing the first decision, narrowed still more the discretion state governments had, narrowed still more the arguments they could mount against desegregating their public institutions of higher education.[10]

In most states, a state or federal court directed that an institution desist from rejecting students on the basis of their race. Three states—West Virginia, Delaware, and Arkansas—began admitting African Americans as graduate students without awaiting court orders. Yet state and school officials in these states knew about, and were responding to, court rulings elsewhere, West Virginia to the 1938 decision in Lloyd Gaines's case from Missouri, and Delaware and Arkansas in 1948 to court action regarding Ada Lois Sipuel Fisher in Oklahoma (see appendix 1). Though permitting black applicants into some programs in the 1940s, all three opened only selected doors and waited until subsequent court action led them to adopt broad-based nondiscriminatory admissions policies.

A single suit developed in Delaware, and another in Virginia, Delaware's in state court regarding undergraduates, Virginia's in federal court regarding an applicant to law school, both in 1950. At the other end of the range, some states—among them Florida and Louisiana—seemed always to be in litigation in the 1950s. In the middle of the range, such states as North Carolina and Maryland each generated several cases in federal court. In two Border South states—Delaware and Missouri—state courts forced desegregation, but in both of these instances the decisions were handed down in the summer of 1950, within weeks following decisions in which the U.S. Supreme Court greatly narrowed the basis on which racial discrimination could survive constitutional challenge. In Missouri, the 1950 decision forced the very beginnings of desegregation (see appendix 7), and Gus T. Ridgel, who brought the suit, enrolled that fall and earned a master's degree in economics in 1951.[11]

In a broad pattern, though not a universal one, each of the seventeen segregated states required a court order at one school before "voluntarily" adopting a less exclusive racial policy at other schools. Mississippi State fits this pattern, as black enrollment there followed litigation that had targeted persistent black exclusion at Ole Miss. In South Carolina, the litigation dance focused on Clemson; in Virginia, on the University of Virginia; in Oklahoma, on the University of Oklahoma.

Some of the litigation proved protracted and tied up litigants for years. Two examples are Virgil D. Hawkins, who sought admission into the University of Florida law school from 1949 to 1958, and Horace Ward, who did the same at the University of Georgia from 1950 to 1957 (see Robert Pratt's essay in this volume). Plaintiffs could find that there was nothing certain about victory. Virgil Hawkins, for one, seemed more than once to have won in court and still did not gain admission. That is, states might insist on the ritual of a trial in court, but that did not ensure compliance by the state and the school if the plaintiff prevailed. At times in Louisiana, a court victory was overturned, either on appeal to a higher court, as in the case of Alexander Pierre Tureaud Jr., a prospective undergraduate at Louisiana State University who actually attended classes for several weeks during fall 1953, or by legislative creativity, as was the case for a time at other public institutions in Louisiana, especially Southwestern Louisiana Institute in Lafayette, after initial court victories in 1954 (see Michael Wade's essay in this volume).[12]

Other litigation was episodic—it was traversed, implemented, and over with. Virginia, for example, insisted on going through the formalities of a federal court decision before admitting an African American, Gregory Swanson, to the University of Virginia law school, in September 1950, but then permitted occasional black applicants, depending on what programs they wanted, into graduate or professional programs there or elsewhere.[13]

The litigation involved countless individuals, among them willing plaintiffs, committed attorneys, resistant public officials, and troubled judges. Actions in the courts framed the possibilities of what might happen on campuses to alter traditional ways. Rather than emphasize the many figures who played roles in establishing the political, judicial, and administrative context within which desegregation took place, this essay focuses on the African Americans who applied if they chose; sued if they found it necessary; forced the question time and again; and then, though hardly in all cases, won the right to attend and enrolled and took classes. A sampling of pioneer black students' experiences from a variety of schools—including the state universities in the Border South's Maryland and Delaware, the Upper South's Virginia Tech and University of Arkansas, and the Deep South's University of Florida—will illustrate and illuminate the process of desegregation in southern public higher education.

Arkansas

At the University of Arkansas, Silas Hunt sought admission to the law school. The state of Arkansas had long maintained a fully segregated system of education, but it had no statute or constitutional provision that mandated black exclusion at the university. Without waiting to go through the ritual of a court battle, state and school officials adopted a policy according to which qualified black applicants would be admitted, provided they were seeking entry to graduate programs unavailable at the black land-grant school at Pine Bluff.[14]

Silas Hunt entered the law school in February 1948—the first African American to enroll in the twentieth century in a historically white public institution of higher education anywhere in the former Confederacy. A veteran of World War II, his health had been severely compromised in the war, and he died in 1949. Today on the Fayetteville campus a prominent sign identifies Silas H. Hunt Hall, dedicated in his memory in February 1993 on the forty-fifth anniversary of his enrollment.[15]

Already by the time Hunt died, other black students had enrolled at the university. Among the other students who gained entry in 1948, Jackie L. Shropshire went on to complete a degree in law in 1951. Two hundred miles to the southeast, in Little Rock, where the University of Arkansas has its medical school, Edith Irby also enrolled in 1948, and she earned an M.D. in 1952. She was the first African American to be admitted to a historically nonblack medical school anywhere in the seventeen segregated states, and the first to graduate.

Edith Mae Irby—born poor, black, and female in central Arkansas—went to college, the first person in her family to do so. Among the medical schools to which she applied for admission in 1948 was Arkansas. "It didn't even occur to me that the school didn't accept Blacks," she once explained. "I just knew that I wanted to become a doctor, so I decided that going to the University of Arkansas was the most sensible and economical thing."[16]

She had, then—almost surely—never heard of Silas Hunt, never heard that the university had just begun to admit black students, but she applied and, given the Silas Hunt precedent earlier that year, was admitted. "There was no struggle, no fight, no court battle," she says. Yet she exemplified the process of desegregation, and she rode with the current of the civil rights struggle.[17]

Although subject to the kinds of restrictions that typically awaited the midcentury black pioneers at the South's state universities, Irby, having enrolled, changed the world by her mere presence. According to school authorities, she had to have her own restroom—which the two other female students in her class found more convenient than their own, so the facility became desegregated. She had to have her own dining area—and it was so quiet, so conducive to study, that she was soon joined by white students.[18]

Edith Mae Irby Jones did not set out to be a pioneer, but she pressed against barriers at the very moment that they could be brought down, and she helped take them down. After graduation, Dr. Jones joined the National Medical Association, the black equivalent of the American Medical Association, and a third of a century later she was chosen its first female president. An oil portrait of Dr. Jones hangs in a building at the university medical center in Little Rock.

Oklahoma

Arkansas behaved much as it might have had it been a Border South state. Oklahoma, which was a Border South state, put up more resistance and appeared in national headlines between 1946 and 1950 regarding litigation by Ada Lois Sipuel Fisher and George W. McLaurin to enroll at the University of Oklahoma in Norman. Fisher, a former classmate of Silas Hunt's when both were undergraduates, wanted to study law, and McLaurin, a professor at all-black Langston University, wanted to pursue a doctorate in education.[19]

In the wake of that litigation, various students sought admission to Oklahoma Agricultural and Mechanical College (later Oklahoma State University) in Stillwater. In February 1949, two students at Langston University, Oklahoma's black land-grant school, sought admission as undergraduates at Oklahoma State, the nonblack land-grant school twenty-five miles away. Jane Ellison wanted to study textiles, and Henry W. Floyd wanted to pursue a degree in political science. Both were denied admission on the grounds that the courses they desired could be obtained at Langston.[20]

Graduate students were another matter. Nancy Randolph Davis, a graduate of Langston, was teaching home economics and, like many teachers, wanted to work on a master's degree during summers. She overcame a series of obstacles to enroll during summer 1949. Davis earned her degree in 1952. Years later, she recalled how she had been segregated at first when she took classes at Oklahoma State. Reflecting the kind of experience that Silas Hunt had experienced at Arkansas, and the kind that led George McLaurin to go to court and obtain a ruling from the Supreme Court against segregation within the institution at the University of Oklahoma, Davis spent her first few weeks of class time sitting just outside the classroom so the institution would be in compliance with a state law prohibiting black students and white students from sitting together in the same classroom. Moreover, she lived off campus because, at first, black students were not permitted to room on campus.[21]

Five new black graduate students enrolled at the Stillwater school for fall semester 1949, and two continued through the spring. In June 1950, Phail Winn earned a master's degree in mechanical arts, and Melvin B. Tolson Jr. earned a master's in French. Tolson, a graduate of Wiley College in Texas, went on to earn a Ph.D. from the University of Oklahoma. Other early black graduates of Oklahoma State were Tolson's brother, Arthur Lincoln Tolson, who earned a master's in history in 1952 with a thesis titled "A History of Langston, Oklahoma, 1890–1950," and Huey Jefferson Battle, who earned a Ph.D. in agricultural economics in 1954.[22]

Stillwater's first black undergraduates enrolled in 1953. They came in under an exemption for students wanting to study in fields unavailable at Langston, as two studied electrical engineering and one pursued a degree in veterinary medicine.[23] Dolphin Al Wharton Jr. and Glenn Bernarr Wharton, from Guthrie, entered the Oklahoma State engineering program in 1953 as juniors, and both returned the following year. Each took time away from school after that point, but Glenn Wharton earned his degree in electrical engineering in 1959.

The Supreme Court's first ruling in *Brown v. Board of Education* (*Brown I*, in 1954) resulted in no changes in racial policy on enrollment at Oklahoma State, though a decision was made at that time that black students there ought to have access to all campus facilities. After the second ruling in *Brown* (*Brown II*, in 1955), the state of Oklahoma took the next step in desegregating higher education. Beginning in fall 1955, black students, undergraduate and graduate alike, could enroll at Oklahoma's historically nonblack public campuses regardless of whether the programs of study that they desired were available at Langston University.[24]

By the time Glenn Wharton earned his degree in 1959, some students who came in after the 1955 change in policy had also completed their undergraduate work. Tycine Marie Lyons, for example, transferred to Oklahoma State in 1955 as a junior, earned a bachelor's degree in home economics in May 1958 and a master's in home economics education in August 1959, and retired years later from the San Diego, California, public schools. Both students had lived on campus.

Maryland

Thurgood Marshall grew up in Baltimore. After completing his undergraduate degree in 1930, he wanted to attend law school, and there, in his hometown, was the University of Maryland's college of law. The school refused to admit black students, however, and Marshall enrolled instead at Howard University. For the next three years he made his way to Washington, D.C., for classes. Half a century later—remembering with bitterness the initial slight, the daily cost, the unremitting discrimination—he would growl, "The sonsabitches turned away the guy who finished number one at a better law school—Howard."[25] Had Marshall been admitted to Maryland, he might not have had the bitter experiences that did so much to make him one of the great leaders of the civil rights movement, that drove him to make things right.

Marshall nourished a compelling need to change the Maryland law school's evil ways. And he soon succeeded. He played a central role in taking a case to state court on behalf of Donald Murray, another black citizen of Baltimore and a recent graduate of Amherst College who sought admission to Maryland's law school. At trial, Marshall and his team—it included his mentor at Howard, Charles Hamilton Houston—won in June 1935. The university appealed, but the trial judge made it clear that he intended that Murray be admitted in September even if an appeal was pending. In January 1936, indeed, the Maryland Court of Appeals upheld the trial court verdict (see appendix 2). Marshall later harrumphed, "The first thing I did when I got out [of Howard] was to get even."[26]

At Howard, Marshall learned his craft well, and he learned it in an environment in which apprentice attorneys were trained—by the likes of Charles Hamilton Houston—to function as social engineers in the civil rights struggle. Well prepared, Marshall welcomed Donald Murray's case, and, under court order, the law school ended its practice of excluding black students. Murray played a similar role in subsequent attacks on segregation at other branches of the University of Maryland, including the main campus, at College Park. He, like Thurgood Marshall, left tracks all over the story of race and higher education in Maryland between the 1930s and the 1950s.[27]

In April 1950, for example, with Thurgood Marshall and Donald Murray at the helm, Esther McCready won a court order to be admitted to the University of Maryland School of Nursing, located in Baltimore. The McCready case illuminates many facets of the struggle over opening public institutions of higher education to black citizens. University of Maryland president Harry C. Byrd thwarted his own board's 1948 decision to permit otherwise qualified black Marylanders to enroll in graduate and professional programs unavailable at a black school in Maryland. The school put up sustained resistance to change, matching McCready's persistence in seeking to overcome that resistance. Having been rejected in her bid for admission, McCready sued for admission and lost at trial in Baltimore. She appealed the decision and won in the state's highest court (*McCready v. Byrd*; see appendix 5); the state then appealed that ruling to the U.S. Supreme Court, which refused to hear it and left the state appeals court ruling in place.[28]

By midcentury, a dozen years had passed since the Supreme Court's 1938 decision in *Missouri ex rel. Gaines v. Canada* (see appendix 3) regarding access to a law school education, and black lawyers and black plaintiffs were still trying to make the limited case that a state had to offer opportunities to blacks that it offered whites—to obtain, that is, implementation of what they understood to be the import of the Court's 1938 ruling. "Separate but equal" remained the working premise—operating, however, in a manner to exclude black citizens from in-state programs—and into 1950 Marshall and Murray were still working at retail regarding graduate and professional curricula not available at a black school in Maryland.

Maryland argued that state and federal rulings in law school cases should not govern the outcome in the *McCready* case, for nursing (or dentistry or medicine) and law were different kinds of curricula—according to the Maryland argument, the need to study law within the state where one would be practicing made it a special case, but nursing learned in Nashville at Meharry would be pretty much identical to the training at Maryland in Baltimore. Maryland tried to use an interstate arrangement dating from 1948, through the Board of Control for Southern Regional Education, as the basis for offering McCready a place in the Meharry Medical College's school of nursing, but she had rejected the offer and insisted on a place in the Maryland nursing school in her hometown, Baltimore. The Maryland Court of Appeals determined that the offer did not satisfy McCready's constitutional right to attend a school within the state—that if whites could attend an in-state school, blacks could not constitutionally be forced to go outside the state for similar training.[29] Having won her case, McCready entered the Maryland school in 1950, graduated in 1953, and went on to a career in teaching and nursing.

Murray and Marshall teamed up in another case, too, in a Maryland court, one that led to the admission of Parren J. Mitchell to the University of Maryland's main campus, at College Park, to pursue a master's degree in sociology. The university offered Mitchell assistance in attending an out-of-state institution, but he declined that opportunity; it offered him off-campus work as the sole student in a graduate program in Baltimore (at Frederick Douglass High School, where he had graduated in 1940, before his service in World War II and his undergraduate degree at Morgan State College in 1950), but he rejected that option as well. Mitchell took his case to city court in Baltimore, where, unlike McCready the year earlier, he prevailed. In early October 1950, the judge directed the university to admit him to the College Park program. Attending College Park was not an easy experience, Mitchell later recalled. For one thing, whereas the Baltimore residents were seeking to take law or nursing courses in Baltimore, he had to commute by bus all the way to College Park, much as Thurgood Marshall had had to take the train to Washington, D.C.—except, of course, that Marshall was forced to go to Howard because of segregation, and Mitchell was participating in an adventure that was bringing down segregation. Of his first day in particular, he said: "No one smiled at me. No one talked to me."[30] But he completed the degree in 1952, returned to Morgan to teach, and later served eight terms in Congress (1971–87).

Hiram Whittle, another black resident of Baltimore, entered historically black Morgan State College in 1948. But he wanted to study electrical engineering, and he wanted to do it at College Park, so he brought suit against the school after it rejected him on racial grounds. Here was a campus where one program was formally desegregated by October 1950, but the other units continued to exclude black applicants. As in the case of Parren Mitchell, Hiram Whittle's lead lawyer was Donald Murray, and Thurgood Marshall was on the team as well. In January 1951, just before Whittle's case was due to come to trial, the University of Maryland's board of regents—recognizing no doubt that the university was almost surely about to lose yet again—determined to admit him. During spring 1951, Whittle lived off campus, but then, for the semester beginning September 1951, he asked for a dorm room, and the state attorney general advised university officials: "You must make dormitory space available to Negro students under the same conditions and on the same terms as those accommodations are made available to white students." Whittle found the academic work far more challenging than he had been used to. But the social side was easier for Whittle than it had been for Mitchell. "No problems," he says. For one thing, Whittle grew up in a family of Jehovah's Witnesses, so, as he recalled, "I have pretty much always operated in an interracial environment."[31]

In 1951, the University of Maryland also admitted two black applicants to the medical school—Donald W. Stewart, a senior at Morgan State College in Baltimore, and Roderick E. Charles, a Howard University senior from Baltimore.[32] These were only the beginnings, to be sure, and they had been a long time coming, but—in Maryland, at least—the process of desegregation was ever so much farther along in the early 1950s than it had been in the early 1930s. All of these examples of pioneer black students at the University of Maryland—like those at the University of Arkansas and at Oklahoma Agricultural and Mechanical College—took place during an era of "protodesegregation," an early form of desegregation.

Delaware

On January 12, 1948, the U.S. Supreme Court decided a case in favor of Ada Lois Sipuel Fisher and against the University of Oklahoma law school's refusal to admit her. Before the end of the month, without waiting for further court action, the University of Arkansas and then, the next day, the University of Delaware announced that each would open its graduate and professional programs to black enrollment. Neither school acted in a vacuum, for not only were administrators' eyes on the Supreme Court, but also black applicants were seeking admission to the officials' own programs. In 1947, for example, three black prospective students applied for admission as undergraduates at Delaware—two of them in engineering—and another to a graduate program there. A committee of Delaware citizens supporting the black applicants met with the university president, William S. Carlson, on January 20, 1948; and the state's sole black attorney, Louis L. Redding, wrote him a nudging letter on January 28, three days before the university's board of trustees met in special session and made its decision.[33]

That decision, voicing what proved to be routine restrictions accompanying a breakthrough, limited its effect to black bona fide residents of Delaware who sought courses unavailable at the state's black school, Delaware State College. The dean of the Howard University Graduate School, Charles H. Thompson, wrote a congratulatory letter to President Carlson, but he expressed the hope that, before long, the restriction about course availability at Delaware State would be lifted. The first graduates under the 1948 policy were Catherine J. Young (later Hazeur) and Cora Berry (later Saunders), each in 1951 with a master's degree. Elbert C. Whisner earned a bachelor's degree in electrical engineering in 1952, and John Henry Taylor earned a Ph.D. in 1953.

In the meantime, word came in late 1949 and early 1950 that Delaware State had lost its accreditation, and dozens of students at the black school initiated applications to transfer to the University of Delaware. Never having been accredited by the Association of American Universities, Delaware State had lost its accreditation by the Middle States Association of Colleges and Secondary Schools. Hoping to derive some good from a bad situation, proponents of change looked for admission of black students to the state university's programs, which were all accredited. Beyond that, they saw the situation, as one wrote, as "an excellent opportunity to seek the elimination of the segregated schools upon the accreditation issue."

Soon, attorney Redding was writing the board of trustees to protest recent rejections of several black students who had tried to transfer to the University of Delaware from the unaccredited black school. He quoted at length from the accreditation report, which had observed, for one thing: "The quality of instructional work falls short of acceptable standards." In fact, the report stated: "One might well question the initial accreditation of Delaware State College. The deficiencies in the educational program are not of recent origin." Moreover, the report made reference to "the new policy of the University"—that is, permitting some black citizens of Delaware to enroll in Newark—suggesting that the black school was an "anomaly," and Delaware's entire system of public higher education should be reconceived.

In the months between January and June 1950, the effort grew. The board of trustees, at a special meeting on February 18, refused to modify its decision from January 1948, denied the black applicants their request for admission, and thus forced the issue into the courts. Redding and his allies, together with the student plaintiffs (among them Brooks M. Parker), took their challenge to state court. Early that June—in two decisions, one from Oklahoma and one from Texas—the U.S. Supreme Court greatly narrowed the basis on which racial discrimination in higher education could survive constitutional challenge. During the voluminous testimony in mid-June in *Parker v. University of Delaware*, each plaintiff was asked questions designed to demonstrate that he or she was a resident of Delaware and was, except for his or her racial identity, qualified for admission to the university. And the judge made his way out to Dover to see for himself the kinds of facilities at Delaware State College.

On August 9—two months after the Supreme Court decisions and the Delaware trial—the state court decided the case in favor of Redding, the National Association for the Advancement of Colored People (NAACP), and the black applicants for admission to the University of Delaware. The court's understanding of equal protection did not yet require abandonment of the old principle of "separate but equal," but it did require substantial equality of opportunity, and in Delaware that included access to the state university regardless of racial identity. The presiding judge, Collins J. Seitz, observed: "Although the facilities at the College are even inadequate in most respects when judged by any reasonable educational standards, it must be remembered that the test here is whether they are equal to those provided at the University. Defendants' counsel, in seeking to justify the adequacy of many of the facilities at the College, overlook this important fact." The judge went on: "The College is woefully inferior to the University in the physical facilities available to and in the educational opportunities offered its undergraduates in the School of Arts and Sciences." The trustees decided not to appeal the ruling, which went into effect in time for fall enrollment.[34]

The NAACP, anxious that "full advantage be taken" of the court victory "in the fall term," called a meeting in Wilmington on August 28, as the organization sought "to implement the recent court decision opening up the facilities of the University of Delaware to qualified Negro undergraduate students." Hoping to see more than the ten victorious plaintiffs enter the University of Delaware, the NAACP declared that "other qualified students should be encouraged to enroll at the University." Undergraduates who enrolled under the 1950 order included Helen Handy (later Powell), one of the original plaintiffs as well as one of first black undergraduates at Delaware to earn a degree, in June 1952; Homer W. Minus, another plaintiff, who graduated in 1953 and subsequently became a dentist; and Roy E. Holland Jr., yet another plaintiff, who participated on the wrestling team, graduated in 1958, and later became a school principal. They had brought the case that permitted their enrollment, and they had stayed the course to graduation. The numbers of black students at the University of Delaware remained small across the 1950s, but those numbers far exceeded the traditional quota of zero.

Roy J. Deferrari, a professor of Greek and Latin at Catholic University in

Washington, D.C., had chaired the Middle States Association of Colleges and Secondary Schools group that had denied Delaware State's bid to retain its accreditation, and he had testified as an expert witness on behalf of the plaintiffs in the case that followed. Writing in August from Catholic University, he exclaimed to Jack Greenberg, at NAACP headquarters in New York: "You should get after my neighbor the University of Maryland next." By that point, Delaware, having begun the process of desegregation long after Maryland did, had—as a consequence of the initiative of black plaintiffs and the decision of a state judge—moved well beyond it. Delaware could now provide a model for Maryland—in fact, for the entire South. No longer so fully focused on graduate and professional programs, especially law schools, the NAACP had won its first case seeking to bring down racial barriers in undergraduate programs.

As the stories from Maryland and Delaware reveal, the "desegregation" of higher education is a concept that makes far more sense when understood as a process than as a single event. This is just one of the ways in which the very language employed to understand the phenomenon requires renovation before we can fully reconstruct the transition that had to take place for the world of Jim Crow in higher education to recede. Jim Crow had a long career in college. In one small realm after another, Jim Crow was suspended from school. But he lingered on campus a long time after the first challenges to his enrollment. Segregation did not end when the first black student enrolled. Desegregation had not yet been achieved, even though that "first" was a tremendously important marker of change. Change had only begun, and continuing it required constant pressure from civil rights organizations and black applicants. Breaking through the color barrier to one program at a school did not automatically bring down the color line elsewhere at the same institution.

In this view, the University of Maryland remained segregated for many years after 1935. Alternatively, while few black students attended either Delaware or Maryland between 1950 and 1954, Delaware was officially desegregated; Maryland remained in the stage of protodesegregation.

The series of court cases that led to token black enrollment in one program, then another, all came under the rubric of "separate but equal." Victories by black litigants and black lawyers did not entirely overcome the "separate"; but within the "separate," they did achieve a fuller measure of the "equal." Certainly it made a difference of some significance that the enhanced "equal" was achieved by opening a program at the "white" school to black students rather than inaugurating a counterpart program at the black school. Either way, however, the change had come within the old constitutional framework. That old framework continued to govern black access to higher education, in Maryland and across the South. Black southerners continued to challenge black exclusion, whether from all programs or from any particular program. And once having gained admission, they challenged white proprietary claims on residence halls, sports teams, faculty and administration, or any other aspect of campus life.

Border South, Upper South, Deep South—and *Brown v. Board of Education*

The Border South states—Delaware, Maryland, West Virginia, Kentucky, Missouri, and Oklahoma—retained fully segregated systems of education, from elementary schools through higher education, into the 1930s. The University of Maryland began admitting black students to the law school in Baltimore after a court order in 1935. After the Supreme Court's 1938 decision in the *Gaines* case, West Virginia University began admitting black graduate students; and earning master's degrees in education were Kenneth James in 1941, W. O. Armstrong in 1942, and Victorine Louistall in 1945.[35] Elsewhere in the Border South, however, all schools, including Maryland's main campus at College Park, remained absolutely nonblack into the late 1940s.

By 1950, historically "white" schools in all the states of the Border South began admitting black students under certain conditions. Oklahoma State University exemplified the pattern of gradual change through its first decade of "desegregation," from 1949 to 1959. At the University of Kentucky, Lyman T. Johnson, who won a suit in federal court in March 1949, enrolled as a graduate student that year. Holloway Fields, an undergraduate, transferred there in January 1950 and received a bachelor's degree in electrical engineering in 1951, the same year that Susie Jones Elster and Betty Richardson Newby earned graduate degrees in education.[36] Though the process at schools like Maryland, West Virginia, Kentucky, and Oklahoma State unfolded too fast for many people, it seemed slow to many others, and it certainly was gradual.

The Supreme Court's 1954 and 1955 decisions in *Brown v. Board of Education* had an immediate impact in some states, at some schools. As a result of the original 1954 decision, the state universities of Maryland, West Virginia, Kentucky, and Missouri changed their policies on admitting black undergraduates (or at least in-state applicants, though any distinction soon vanished). Race vanished as an official criterion for excluding applicants.[37]

The implementing decision in *Brown* the next year led to similar actions in Oklahoma and Arkansas. In 1955, therefore, Oklahoma State University, the University of Oklahoma, and the University of Arkansas each began admitting small numbers of black undergraduates without curricular restrictions. Moreover, the University of Texas decided in July 1955 to begin admitting black undergraduates in September 1956 and actually admitted small numbers of black architecture and engineering undergraduates in June and September 1955.[38]

Thus the decisions in *Brown* led directly to the dismantling of racial barriers to undergraduate admissions in five of the six Border South states (Delaware had already made the shift in 1950) as well as at the state institutions in Arkansas and the leading state institution in Texas.

North Carolina was another matter. After Floyd McKissick and other black applicants brought a successful suit in federal court, black students enrolled in law school and medical school at the University of North Carolina beginning in 1951, and two black graduate students began classes at North Carolina State in 1953. Yet undergraduate programs in the "white" schools of the North Carolina system remained closed to black applicants. Then three black high school seniors in Durham—Leroy Benjamin Frasier Jr.; his brother, Ralph Frasier; and John Lewis Brandon—sought admission to Chapel Hill in 1955. Turned down, they went to federal court, where their lawyers argued that the logic of the *Brown* decisions ought to apply to undergraduate education as well as to elementary and secondary schooling, and the court agreed (see appendix 8). The three students enrolled in September 1955, although the state and the university appealed the decision to the U.S. Supreme Court.[39]

In March 1956, the nation's high court upheld the lower court. Therefore, desegregation also came to North Carolina State, where two black undergraduates—Edward Carson and Manuel Crockett—enrolled that summer, were joined by others that fall, and graduated a few years later. Much the same was true at the third institution in the University of North Carolina system, the Woman's College in Greensboro, where the first black students—JoAnne Smart and Bettye Tillman—registered for fall classes in 1956 and graduated in 1960.[40]

By fall 1955, black students—undergraduates as well as graduate students—had enrolled at all the historically nonblack state universities and land-grant schools of the Border South: Delaware, Maryland, West Virginia, Kentucky, Missouri, Oklahoma, and Oklahoma State. A few black students—including black undergraduates—were also attending several historically nonblack schools in the former Confederate states, among them the University of Virginia, Virginia Polytechnic Institute, the University of North Carolina, the University of Arkansas, and the University of Texas.

By fall 1956, black undergraduates had also enrolled at North Carolina State and at the Woman's College of the University of North Carolina. Almost everywhere else, black enrollment had yet to take place, though federal court orders had ended the exclusion of black graduate students at Louisiana State University, where Lutrill Amos Payne enrolled in June 1951, and at the University of Tennessee, where Gene Mitchell Gray enrolled in January 1952.[41]

At most schools in the Deep South, and at some schools elsewhere, the 1950s ended before the process of desegregation began. In the core states of the Deep South, in contrast to the Border South, the *Brown* decisions regarding K–12 schools demonstrated that more was at stake than whether a few black students might be admitted to universities, and, if anything, resistance stiffened as a consequence. As late as 1960, prospective black undergraduates could not yet gain admission to the main Louisiana State University campus at Baton Rouge, nor had any surmounted the racial barrier at the University of Tennessee, and no black student had yet enrolled at Texas A&M. The University of Alabama had briefly conceded graduate student Autherine Lucy's enrollment in 1956, but then it expelled her, and it, like Alabama's white land-grant school, Alabama Polytechnic Institute (later Auburn University), remained, if not lily-white, absolutely nonblack. So did the historically nonblack public institutions of higher education in South Carolina, Georgia, and Mississippi.

Their time came, too, as federal authority grew more forceful. The first African Americans enrolled in the final four states between 1961 and 1963, and the land-grant schools as well as the state universities had all admitted black students by 1965. Charlayne Hunter and Hamilton Holmes enrolled as transfer undergraduates at the University of Georgia in January 1961. Transfer student James Meredith began undergraduate classes at the University of Mississippi in October 1962. Harvey Gantt enrolled at Clemson College (Clemson University) in January 1963. The University of Alabama enrolled undergraduates Vivian Malone and James Hood in June 1963, seven years after graduate student Autherine Lucy's aborted bid to enter the Tuscaloosa school. Transfer students Henrie Dobbins Monteith and Robert G. Anderson Jr., as well as graduate student James Solomon, enrolled at the University of South Carolina in Columbia in September 1963. When graduate student Harold A. Franklin enrolled in January 1964 at Auburn University, that institution joined the list of desegregating schools, as did Mississippi State University in July 1965 when Richard Holmes registered for two summer classes.[42]

Much the same time line in the 1960s can track movement among other laggard schools, including institutions that had enrolled black graduate students a few years earlier but held the line at undergraduate admissions, especially at the main campus. The University of Tennessee enrolled its first black undergraduate students, Theotis Robinson Jr. (for an interview with him, see appendix 9) and Charles Edgar Blair, in January 1961, the same month that Harvey Gantt finally gained admission to Clemson. The University of Florida enrolled its first black undergraduates in September 1962, a few weeks before James Meredith enrolled at the University of Mississippi. Texas A&M enrolled its first black students, graduate and undergraduate alike, in June 1963, the same month Vivian Malone and James Hood began classes at Alabama. Under court order, Louisiana State University finally admitted black undergraduates to its Baton Rouge campus in June 1964.[43]

By summer 1965, all twenty-four institutions that are the primary focus of this essay had enrolled at least one black student, and many other public institutions had as well. For example, The Citadel enrolled its first black cadets in 1966. At Auburn, though Harold Franklin left the school and completed his degree elsewhere, other black students carried on where he left off. Josetta B. Matthews began graduate school there in 1965, became Auburn's first black graduate with a master's in education in 1966, became Auburn's first black faculty member when she began teaching classes there in 1971, and earned an Ed.D. there in 1975. Meanwhile, Anthony Tilford Lee, Auburn's first black undergraduate, enrolled in 1965 and graduated in 1968, and Samuel Lamar Pettijohn Jr. became the school's first black undergraduate to earn a degree when he finished in December 1967.[44]

Jim Crow had not abandoned school, had not dropped out of college, but his absolute power to control the admissions process, to bar all black applicants, had vanished in all seventeen southern states. "White" schools—though they did not recruit black students, or seek to make them feel particularly welcome, as if they had a right to be there too—could no longer, on grounds of policy and race, turn away all black prospective students, or even all black prospective undergraduates, or all black prospective undergraduates in programs available in-state in some form at a black school.

The Upper South state of Virginia was both early and late in undergraduate desegregation, after desegregation began in some graduate programs in 1950. Virginia Military Institute, established in the Shenandoah Valley in 1839, did not matriculate its first black students until 1968. By the time Philip L. Wilkerson and two other African American cadets earned degrees there in 1972, Longwood College, a white women's public institution in Farmville, also enrolled a few black students. Yet Virginia displayed another variation, too, one that began the long process of desegregation by admitting a black undergraduate as an engineering student at Virginia Polytechnic Institute as early as 1953, the same year Glenn Wharton began his studies at Oklahoma State.[45]

Virginia Polytechnic Institute: The 1950s

In the 1950s, white schools across the South continued to reject black applicants when they could, but for the first time some accepted a few black students. Everett Pierce Raney applied in 1951 to Virginia Polytechnic Institute (VPI) to study business but was rejected on the basis that he could study business at Virginia State College, the black land-grant school near Petersburg. In 1953, however, Irving L. Peddrew III enrolled to study electrical engineering, a subject unavailable at Virginia State. During his first year, Peddrew was the only African American among 3,322 students. The special circumstances under which Peddrew gained admittance were clear from the low-key press coverage. Rather than chance being taken to court, where it would surely lose, the school admitted Peddrew on the basis of a new policy approved by "the majority" of the Board of Visitors:

> The Board is advised and informed that the educational facilities and offerings sought by the applicant and offered by the Institute are not to be had or found in comparable form and substance at any State supported institution of higher learning maintained and operated by the State of Virginia exclusively for members of the Negro race.
>
> Whereupon, the Board having been [apprised] by the Attorney General of Virginia of the nature of the decision and precedents laid down by the Supreme Court of the United States, which have taken precedent over Virginia laws, is of the opinion that the applicant is legally entitled to admission under the particular and specific facts and circumstance which in this instance it has found to exist.[46]

VPI (better known by the 1970s as Virginia Tech) thus became the first historically white four-year public institution in any of the eleven states of the former Confederacy to admit a black undergraduate in the twentieth century—and the first "college of 1862" in the former Confederacy to admit a black undergraduate ever. In that sense, Irving Peddrew was for black undergraduates what Silas Hunt had been for black graduate students. VPI was unusual in admitting black undergraduates before black graduate students, but it fell in the mainstream in admitting black students only into a specialized program.

Permitted to take classes, and required to be in the Corps of Cadets, Peddrew was not admitted to all the school's facilities. He was defined, the news release announcing his enrollment made clear, as a "military day student." Day cadets were typically students who had obtained permission to marry and live off campus, not, as Peddrew was, a single student who was told he had to live and eat off campus. Peddrew had been advised of the potentially difficult situation awaiting him in Blacksburg, and he assured VPI officials that he could cope. He did, for a time, though he paid a high price. He bore by himself the full burden of desegregating a school, and he left late in his third year without graduating, although he continued his education elsewhere and applied his coursework throughout his professional career.

Meantime, in 1954 VPI admitted Lindsay Cherry, Floyd Wilson, and Charlie L. Yates to the engineering school and the Corps of Cadets. All three were 1954 graduates of Booker T. Washington High School in Norfolk, Virginia. Floyd Wilson left after a year in electrical engineering to join the U.S. Air

Force. After three years in mechanical engineering, Lindsay Cherry withdrew because of bad vision, but he, like Irving Peddrew, put his training to good effect.

Charlie L. Yates was one of six honors graduates in mechanical engineering at VPI in 1958. He not only graduated with honors in four years but also served as an officer in two engineering groups on campus, Tau Beta Pi and Pi Tau Sigma. In addition, like Irving Peddrew, he was active in the Young Men's Christian Association (YMCA), which welcomed black students and provided them something of a sanctuary. Yates was the first African American to graduate from VPI. In fact, nowhere in the former Confederacy during the twentieth century did a black undergraduate earn a degree at a flagship state university or at a historically nonblack land-grant school before Yates did. He graduated without ever being permitted to room on campus, and he recalls the one time an exception was made to allow him to eat on campus. He was in the Corps of Cadets, and once when he pulled guard duty at mealtime, "There I was in the dining hall," he says, "off to myself, eating a meal."

Charlie Yates exemplified the trials, and he highlights the successes, of the pioneer black students at Virginia Polytechnic Institute. He later earned a master's degree from the California Institute of Technology and a Ph.D. from Johns Hopkins University. From 1987 until his retirement in 2000, he taught aerospace engineering at Virginia Tech, after first returning to Blacksburg in 1979 to teach mechanical engineering and then leaving for four years to teach at Hampton Institute (during those four years, he served a term on the Virginia Tech Board of Visitors). His continuing pride in his undergraduate accomplishment is evident on his automobile license plates, which read "CLY 58."

VPI admitted a fifth black freshman, Matthew M. Winston Sr., in 1955, and a transfer student from Virginia State, Essex E. Finney Jr., in 1956, but no new black students enrolled in 1957 or 1958. Tech's total black enrollment in the 1950s peaked at four in 1954–55, 1955–56 (Winston took Wilson's place), and 1956–57 (Finney took Peddrew's place). Finney was transferring from one land-grant school to another, from the black school, Virginia State College, to the historically white one, where he could study engineering. Finney and Winston both completed their studies at VPI in 1959. Finney soon earned a master's and a doctorate, and then he went on to a distinguished career with the U.S. Department of Agriculture.

Unlike many schools, VPI did not wait until a federal court order forced a first step in integration. The process of racial desegregation at Tech, though slow and grudging, was quicker and smoother than in Virginia's public elementary and secondary schools (none of which began to desegregate before 1959), and it was far more peaceful than were the first steps toward desegregation at various Deep South universities, colleges, and junior colleges.

Yet the top administrators at Virginia's nonblack public institutions feared for their appropriations from the state legislature. They were fearful enough between 1950 and 1954, before the Supreme Court decision in *Brown* threw out the "separate but equal" formula. After *Brown*, they saw the Virginia legislature adopt "massive resistance," a policy reflecting the state's determination—not abated before court decisions threw out that policy, too, in 1959—to close elementary and secondary schools rather than permit any integration.[47] Leaders of higher education, in Virginia and elsewhere, were not about to take the lead in desegregating their own institutions.

During the school's first six years of "desegregation," VPI admitted six black students, all undergraduates in engineering, and three of them graduated. The pioneer black students there understood that they did not have an option their white classmates had—to switch out of engineering yet remain at the school. They took the language of their acceptance letters literally when they were told, as Essex Finney was, "We have decided that we can accept you at VPI . . . to take our course in agricultural engineering."

Matthew Winston has no recollection of hostile treatment from his classmates. To the contrary, he recalls that some were shocked when, if they invited him to go out for food or coffee, he explained why he could not accompany them; he was officially excluded from on-campus facilities and legally segregated at off-campus establishments. The sit-ins of February 1960—in Greensboro, North Carolina, and in other cities across the South—occurred after Winston had completed his studies, moved back to Tidewater Virginia, and gone to work as an engineer. So did the enrollment of the first black students, graduate or undergraduate, at such schools as Mississippi and Mississippi State, Clemson and South Carolina, Georgia, Auburn, and Texas A&M.

Virginia Polytechnic Institute: The 1960s

In 1959, Virginia Polytechnic Institute enrolled its seventh and eighth black students, James L. Whitehurst and Robert G. Wells. Wells graduated in metallurgical engineering, Whitehurst in electrical engineering. Intent on obtaining the best possible education, James Whitehurst picked VPI over Virginia State because, he explained years later, VPI had "better laboratories, better professors, and better equipment." He chose VPI even though he understood that he would have to major in electrical engineering instead of physics (which he had wanted to study), since Virginia State offered physics. Like the other black pioneers, Whitehurst had been admitted only to classes, not to the full run of student activities and facilities. When he went to the snack bar in Squires student center, he was asked to leave. He had been a football star in high school, but the VPI coach kept him off the college team. For his third year at VPI,

Cadet Whitehurst demanded a room in the barracks and was at last given one.[48] After that year, black students could live in residence halls, just as other students did, and eat on campus.

Black student enrollment at Virginia Polytechnic Institute remained in the single digits into the mid-1960s, but the school changed many of its ways during the administration of T. Marshall Hahn Jr., who became president in 1962. Beginning in 1964, male freshmen and sophomores were no longer required to belong to the Corps of Cadets, and soon, too, the institution began to admit women in much larger numbers than ever before. The College of Arts and Sciences was formed, together with the inauguration of a host of new majors outside the traditional areas of engineering, agriculture, and business administration. Moreover, VPI began to recruit black students, not just passively await applications. A grant from the Rockefeller Foundation funded an effort that took recruiters from Blacksburg to Virginia's black high schools. Rockefeller scholarships that targeted black undergraduates enticed a larger number of black students than ever before.[49] The cohorts of black students entering in 1966 and 1967 reflected the nation's transformed social and political environment of the mid-1960s and completed the early stages in the process of desegregation at VPI.

Robert Wells and James Whitehurst, like the six earlier black students, majored in engineering. Unlike the first eight, subsequent black students could choose other majors. Six black female undergraduates enrolled in 1966, and all six lived on campus. Linda Adams, who came to Blacksburg as a junior, graduated in 1968 in statistics and began a career with the U.S. Census Bureau. Linda Edmonds majored in home economics, went on to earn a master's and a doctorate, and later served as dean of one college in New England and then president of another one. In 1970, Marguerite Harper graduated in history and Jackie Butler in sociology. During their time in Blacksburg, Harper and Butler challenged other vestiges of the past, like flying the Confederate battle flag and playing "Dixie" at football games, and they recall that all their black classmates joined with them in their campaign.[50]

Other hurdles fell, too, during the time the first contingent of black women studied in Blacksburg. Jerry Gaines entered VPI in 1967, the first black student there to be awarded a sports scholarship, indeed the school's first black athlete. An excellent student as well as a track star, Gaines earned his degree in 1971 in foreign languages and went on to win awards as a high school Spanish teacher.[51]

The school that James Whitehurst and Robert Wells graduated from in the 1960s had changed since Irving Peddrew and Charlie Yates applied for admission in the 1950s. The pioneers had made a difference, and their successors did so as well. Racial desegregation on college campuses across the South—not just at VPI—is best understood as a process, not a single event. Enrollment in classes did not necessarily carry with it the privileges of eating on campus, rooming on campus, joining sports teams, or even changing majors. At Virginia Polytechnic Institute, the first hurdle fell in the 1950s; the others fell in the 1960s.

University of Florida: Graduate Education

The struggle for desegregation at the University of Florida reveals several facets that appear typical. First, there is what I have termed the prehistory of desegregation, or the era of predesegregation. Not the first black applicant to be turned away on racial grounds, though certainly the most persistent, was Virgil D. Hawkins, who, beginning in 1949, tried until 1958 to crack the Jim Crow barrier at the University of Florida law school. Despite court victories, he was deflected and never managed to enroll. Second, the first African Americans to gain admittance to white campuses in the 1950s were in most cases, like Virgil Hawkins, trying to enroll in graduate or professional programs. When Florida finally permitted the door to be edged open, black students entered the law school in September 1958 and a master's program in education in February 1959. No black undergraduate enrolled until 1962.

Virgil Hawkins spent nine years in the courts. The Florida Supreme Court routinely held against him, and, though appearing to take a very different stance, the U.S. Supreme Court did not prove much more helpful. One week after handing down the 1954 school desegregation decision in *Brown v. Board of Education*, the nation's high court sent Hawkins's case back to the Florida Supreme Court with instructions that it be reconsidered in light of *Brown*. Two years later, Hawkins having persisted in his efforts against an entirely obstructionist Florida establishment, the case was back in the nation's capital. In March 1956, the Supreme Court insisted that, whatever language it may have used about "deliberate" speed in its May 1955 implementing decision in *Brown*, higher education did not require a period of adjustment that might support a claimed need for further delay. There was, the Court insisted, "no reason for delay" in admitting Hawkins to "a graduate professional school."[52]

Yet the Florida Supreme Court refused to order his admission to the University of Florida. Hawkins returned to the U.S. Supreme Court, which in October 1957 directed him to the lower federal courts. District Judge Dozier A. DeVane balked, but Hawkins took his case to the Fifth Circuit Court of Appeals, which agreed with Hawkins and, in April 1958, sent the case back to Judge DeVane for action. This time, on June 18, 1958, the judge issued an order directing the University of Florida to cease using race as a basis on which to deny admission to its graduate programs. The breakthrough was clear; so were the limits. The school could no longer maintain a policy "limiting admission to the *graduate* schools and the graduate *professional* schools of the University of Florida to white persons only."[53]

At the same time, Judge DeVane noted that Hawkins himself could not benefit from the ruling. The University of Florida had raised its entrance requirements sufficiently to bar Hawkins from enrolling. Having obtained yet another victory in federal court, Hawkins nonetheless failed once again to gain admission. Finally giving up, he eventually enrolled in a small unaccredited institution, the New England School of Law, where he earned a law degree in 1964.[54]

As a direct consequence of Hawkins's persistence, black Floridians finally did gain admission to the Gainesville school. George H. Starke Jr. entered the law school in September 1958. As in many cases of pioneer black students on white campuses, Starke, excluded from on-campus housing, lived off campus. In contrast to the experience of pioneers in Oklahoma a decade earlier, however, his classrooms did not have "colored" sections, nor did the library have a "colored" table. Starke did not complete the degree, but by the time he left, other black students had enrolled at the university. In February 1959, Daphne Duval, a teacher at Lincoln High School in Gainesville, began taking night classes. During summer 1959, four other African Americans took classes in conjunction with summer institutes sponsored by the National Science Foundation, and in September 1959 the medical school admitted a black student.[55]

W. George Allen was the University of Florida's second African American law student. His participation in the Reserve Officers' Training Corps (ROTC), as an undergraduate at Florida A&M University, led to his being commissioned as an officer in army intelligence. For two years after his graduation, from 1958 to 1960, he served in the army, first in Maryland and later in California. He gained some social polish, and he learned that "I was just as smart as any white person." Before he left the army, he took the Law School Admission Test (LSAT) and applied for admission to law school at Harvard, the University of California at Berkeley, Florida, and Florida A&M. Though accepted everywhere, he was determined to return to Florida—because, as he told his wife, "that is where the action is"—and to attend the University of Florida.[56]

Allen was, as he later said, "never a quiet person." During his first two years at the Gainesville campus, he was "the only black student there." "Everybody knew me because I was everywhere. I went to the football games and sat on the fifty-yard line with the lawyers. I did not like football. I went there because I heard a cracker say, 'I ain't going to no game with no nigger.'" That did it. "I said, 'I want you to know, you are not going to a goddamn game as long as I am here because I am going. I do not normally go to football games. I will only go to keep your white ass from going to the game.'"[57]

Years later, George Allen insisted that Virgil Hawkins had made his own accomplishments possible. Allen met Hawkins a number of times in the 1960s, and "I had always talked to Virgil and said how he had made it all possible, because without Virgil none of us would have been admitted to the University of Florida. . . . We were only admitted because Virgil had opened the door. If Virgil had not filed the lawsuit, we would never have been admitted to the University of Florida."[58]

University of Florida: Undergraduate Education

George Allen wanted to leave his mark on the University of Florida. According to his account, the arrival of the first black undergraduates at the University of Florida resulted from his efforts. During summer 1962, he was "getting ready to graduate in December," and he "started recruiting blacks to go to the school"; in fact, he "begged them to come in." Regarding Stephan Mickle in particular, Allen has said, "I recruited Stephan to go, begged his daddy to let him leave Bethune and come as an undergraduate."[59]

Stephan Mickle graduated in 1961 from all-black Lincoln High School in Gainesville and then attended Bethune-Cookman College. Summer 1962 came, and he returned to Gainesville to live at home and work as a lifeguard and swimming instructor at the city's black swimming pool. And he met George Allen, whom his father had met through their fraternity, Alpha Phi Alpha.[60]

Mickle later recounted some of the events of that summer. Allen "suggested one evening that I should apply and go to the University of Florida. I said, 'There are no black students there. Why should I want to go there?' He said, 'Well I am there.' I said, 'But you are way over in the law school stuck over in the corner somewhere. There are no undergraduates there.'" But they "talked for a while. I guess that is what planted the seed. At some point during the summer, I got an application, filled it out, and sent it in. To my surprise, dismay, and trepidation it came back as an acceptance." Mickle had "thoroughly enjoyed the year at Bethune-Cookman," and now it looked like he must leave there for a very different environment.[61] He was a far gentler soul than Allen, far less confrontational, and he would have to make a different kind of peace with the place.

Stephan Mickle was the first black undergraduate to earn a degree from the University of Florida, but six other black undergraduates also entered the school in 1962. Mickle, a political science major, was a transfer student, and

Oliver Gordon, an engineering student, transferred from Florida A&M. The other five were freshmen. Two, Johncyna Williams and Rose Green, lived on campus, where they shared a dormitory room, the first black students to secure that privilege. Among the seven, Stephan Mickle graduated in 1965, Johncyna Williams completed the degree requirements in 1966, and Jesse James Dean did so in 1967.[62]

Did black students have classes together? Not according to Mickle, who declared, "I never had a class with another black student" after transferring to Gainesville. Mickle is one of the pioneer black students who have expressed a sense that there were decided benefits to living at home rather than on campus. "One of the reasons I was able to survive and eventually graduate was because I could withdraw from that University setting and go back home every day. I could revive my spirit, if you will, get some words of consolation, get cheered up the next morning, and go back out there and deal with that very hostile and frightening environment." It was not so much a matter of overt abuse or a sense of physical danger as "a wall of silence. Nobody spoke to you all day long. You did not talk to anybody. You went to class. You went and sat on a park bench. You went to class. You went back home." In short, "We were there and ignored."[63]

University of Texas and Texas A&M

The University of Texas began admitting black graduate and professional students to one program or another in 1949 and 1950 and black undergraduates in 1955. The saga began in February 1946, when Heman Marion Sweatt applied to the law school and was turned down because he was black. After a great deal of jockeying in the courts, in June 1950 the U.S. Supreme Court ruled in his favor, and he registered that fall for classes, though he did not complete the degree. As a result of Sweatt's victory, John S. Chase enrolled in 1950 and earned a master's degree in architecture in 1952.[64]

The Supreme Court's 1954 *Brown* decision led to a statement by the university president that black students would continue to be admitted only to graduate and professional programs unavailable at a black school in Texas. Yet the school quietly admitted three black undergraduates in June 1955, among them John W. Hargis, who insisted that he wanted to study engineering there. Soon after the second *Brown* decision, moreover, the school announced a policy change and declared that the doors would be open to black applicants for all undergraduate programs for fall 1956. That semester, the University of Texas enrolled 104 black students: 55 graduate students, 19 transfer students, and 30 freshmen. Hargis earned a bachelor's degree in chemical engineering in 1959.[65]

As elsewhere, admission to take classes left many other questions to be determined. Students at the University of Texas could eat on campus and attend university functions without any segregated access or seating, but campus housing and varsity athletics were something else. As the chairman of the board of regents explained in a letter to the campus newspaper, such a distinction was "entirely in accordance with the Regents' basic policy . . . that Negro students will be integrated at the University of Texas at the undergraduate level for educational purposes but will be segregated for residential purposes."[66]

Unlike the University of Texas, Texas A&M University enrolled no African Americans until summer school 1963, when they numbered eight in all. Two graduate students—Vernell Jackson and George Douglas Sutton, public school teachers in Texas—attended A&M during the first summer term under a National Science Foundation fellowship. A. Leroy Sterling, A&M's first black undergraduate, enrolled both the first and second summer sessions. During the second summer session, Sterling was joined by five new black students. Two were graduate students—Edward Elliott Jr. and the first black female graduate student, Edessie V. McClendon. Barbara Searcy, A&M's first black female undergraduate, also attended that term. The other black undergraduate students during the second summer session of 1963, Bernest Charles Evans and Arthur Lee Dunn, both eventually earned degrees at A&M, Evans in economics in 1967 and Dunn in sociology in 1970. Also in 1967, Leon James Greene and James Louis Courtney earned undergraduate degrees, and Ernest J. Jones and Clarence Dixon Jr. completed graduate programs. Courtney went on to complete a doctoral degree in veterinary medicine there in 1970, the year that Dunn earned his bachelor's degree.[67]

Brown v. Board and Higher Education in the 1950s

Florida and North Carolina acted as though *Brown v. Board of Education*, both the original decision in May 1954 (*Brown I*) and the implementing decision in May 1955 (*Brown II*), had no bearing on higher education, but a number of states acted as though they did. By fall 1955, every state university in the six states of the Border South—from Delaware to Oklahoma—had begun to admit black undergraduates without restriction as to their major. Delaware had done so after a ruling in state court in 1950, but the others had all acted in response to either *Brown I* or *Brown II*. In 1954, *Brown I* led directly to policy changes in Maryland, West Virginia, Kentucky, and Missouri. In 1955, *Brown II* did the same in Oklahoma—the last among the Border South states—as well as in Texas and Arkansas among the states of the former Confederacy. In each instance, without litigation to obtain a ruling that segregation in undergraduate programs must go, modest black enrollment quickly took place.

In the remaining eight states of the former Confederacy, *Brown* led to no immediate change in policy, no immediate movement toward desegregation. In Virginia, for example, neither *Brown I* nor *Brown II* led to a change in policy or practice, unless the University of Virginia's admission of its first three black undergraduate engineering students in 1955 can be attributed to *Brown*. After enrolling one black engineering undergraduate in 1953, VPI enrolled three more such students in 1954. Total black enrollment there never exceeded four at one time in the 1950s, and none of the black students was allowed to live on campus. Neither the University of Virginia nor VPI enrolled a black undergraduate in any program other than engineering before the early 1960s; nor could a black engineering undergraduate switch to a major available at Virginia State College. The University of Virginia continued to admit a few black law and medical students, as it had since a federal court order in 1950, though the state also continued to pay for black Virginians to attend graduate programs at out-of-state schools. In short, the post-*Sweatt* world (actually, the post-*Gaines* world; or even the pre-*Gaines* world)—certainly also the pre-*Brown* and pre-*Frasier* world—persisted in Virginia through the 1950s. Virginia continued through the 1950s to fund scholarships to out-of-state schools for black citizens seeking programs available within the state only at nonblack institutions; black applicants continued to be turned away from historically white institutions if Virginia State could supply the program they sought. The first evidence of change in Virginia, at any level, as a consequence of *Brown* came at the high school level, when a few black students began attending previously nonblack high schools, such as in the city of Norfolk, in 1959.[68]

In eight states, undergraduate programs at public nonblack universities continued to resist all desegregation, and the mantra "separate but equal" continued alive and well, in K–12 and in higher education alike. In most of those eight states, protracted litigation proved necessary before undergraduate programs were opened to black enrollment. And yet at least one black undergraduate earned a degree at Florida, Mississippi, Georgia, South Carolina, and Alabama in 1965, the flagship campuses in the states that had put up the greatest resistance to any desegregation. By 1968, few historically nonblack public institutions could be found that had yet to enroll a black undergraduate, although as late as that year black enrollment at many such schools remained small—in triple, double, or even single digits. Everywhere, change had come, in some instances with states and institutions responding to the original 1954 decision in *Brown*, in others responding to the 1955 implementation decree, and in still others after protracted legal struggles in the courts.

Without *Brown*, there would have been no *Frasier*, and in declaring an end to the constitutionality of segregated public undergraduate education, *Frasier* went farther than *Brown* or *Hawkins* did. Regarding *Frasier* and its interpretation of *Brown*, the North Carolina story reveals what could happen in court, not necessarily what usually did happen. But as a result of the *Frasier* litigation, the Supreme Court's 1954 decision in *Brown* moved the timing up when one state system began to admit black undergraduates into programs from which they had always before been categorically excluded. *Frasier* demonstrated that *Brown* could be called upon to obtain decisions in federal court designed to break down barriers to black admission into undergraduate programs. And if we count the seven states that responded directly to *Brown* as well as Florida and North Carolina, *Brown* led directly to change in nine of the seventeen southern states, eight of them by fall 1955.

Far more than before *Brown*, citizens soon had the freedom, regardless of their racial identities, to attend the school of their choice. State governments had lost the ability to determine otherwise, and citizens of any racial identity had lost the ability to demand that their state do so. *Plessy v. Ferguson* (1896) did not inaugurate school segregation, and *Brown* did not produce wholesale desegregation. But each of the two decisions is, with good reason, a symbol of a regime, if not a marker of sudden historical transformation.

From Kluger to Klarman: Toward Creating a Literature on Desegregation and Higher Education

In the past generation, many schools have reassessed the past. Institutions, having done all they could to prevent desegregation at the time, subsequently embraced as positive the limited change that did occur. Whether the facts are right about the process of desegregation at any given school is one problem in the historiography. Moreover, any of a number of schools, in one manner or another, have claimed to be, or have been said to have been, the "first" to "desegregate." As long as no literature could be consulted that might either rebut or confirm such assertions, they tended to go unchallenged. Having set out a cluster of concepts and terms, as well as some stories, about desegregating undergraduate education in the 1950s, we can relate these stories to such literature as there is on the desegregation of higher education as well as to the wider literature on *Brown v. Board of Education*. The literature relating *Brown* to subsequent changes in higher education remains notably scant.

Three institutional studies published between the 1960s and the 1990s can represent the state of the literature on individual schools that was long available for scholars to draw on regarding desegregation. A history of the University of Maryland misleads both as to the timing of the school's admission of its first black undergraduate and as to situating Maryland in the context of the region's history: whether we have in mind the first black individual, an engineering student who enrolled in 1951, or the more general policy, which came in 1954, directly after *Brown*, Maryland was not the first southern university to desegregate its undergraduate programs. A history of the University of Arkansas recounts the beginnings of black enrollment in the law school in 1948—and then skips directly to the presence of black players on the varsity football team two decades later, as if undergraduate education did not have to be desegregated in the meantime, a change that was directly linked to *Brown*. A history of the University of North Carolina recounts the federal court ruling in 1951 that brought the beginnings of black enrollment in the University of North Carolina's law school (and led to similar change in some other programs, starting with the medical school); but that book nowhere mentions the litigation that took place a few years later—on the basis of *Brown*—so that black undergraduates could take classes at the university.[69]

That the literature is maturing is seen in a few recent books on one state or another. One of these, by Robert Pratt, recounts the struggle for black access at the University of Georgia, summarized in an essay in this book, and another, by Culpepper Clark, does so for the University of Alabama. Amilcar Shabazz has recently published an impressive analysis of racial identity and higher education in Texas since the Civil War. Just as the books by Clark and Pratt each provide model reconstructions of the story of segregation and desegregation at one major southern state university, Shabazz supplies a model history of developments in higher education on the racial front in one state across the entire century after emancipation—in black schools as well as nonblack institutions; in the legislature as well as the courts; and in community colleges, four-year institutions, and graduate and professional programs. Each of these three books makes available work of high quality for scholars who seek to synthesize such state and institutional studies into region-wide analyses. Shabazz's has the added value of focusing scholarly attention on a state that—unlike Alabama, Mississippi, and Georgia—displayed no notable violence at the time and thus escaped much attention in the press then or by historians since.

Two magisterial accounts of segregation and the beginnings of desegregation offer glimpses into the state of the literature on racial identity and higher education. In *Simple Justice* (1976), Richard Kluger told, in considerable detail, the stories of Lloyd Gaines in Missouri, Ada Lois Sipuel Fisher and George W. McLaurin in Oklahoma, and Heman Marion Sweatt in Texas. In doing so, he set the stage for his treatment of the K–12 cases—how they arose, how the NAACP chose to address them, and how the federal courts ruled in them along the road to *Brown*. In his epilogue, Kluger referred briefly to a single person, a single incident regarding higher education, the court-ordered admission of graduate student Autherine Lucy at the University of Alabama in January 1956 and her expulsion the next month.

Michael Klarman's similarly magisterial *From Jim Crow to Civil Rights*

(2004) supplies astute treatments of the Supreme Court's pre-*Brown* decisions—regarding Lloyd Gaines, for example, and Ada Lois Sipuel Fisher. Published nearly thirty years after the Kluger book, and half a century after the *Brown* decision, Klarman's book explores the full range of topics dealing directly with race that the Supreme Court ruled on between the 1890s and the 1950s, from *Plessy* to *Brown*. Education is only a portion of that story, higher education only a subset of that portion, and undergraduate education only a fragment of that subset, before, let alone after, *Brown*. But we can work from the premise that what Klarman offers about post-*Brown* higher education summarizes the current scholarly knowledge, or at least those dimensions of it that have made their way into broad understanding and synthetic studies.

For the immediate post-*Brown* years, Klarman supplies but a single paragraph, and its topic sentence declares in full: "*Brown* also retarded progress in university desegregation." Following this sentence are statements that appear factually unreliable or conceptually uncertain, not to mention ruthlessly selective. "By 1955," Klarman writes, evidently intending to provide a pre-*Brown* baseline for calibrating a post-*Brown* pullback, "roughly 2,000 blacks attended desegregated universities in southern and border states."[70] Yet however we might use the term "desegregated" to describe previously nonblack institutions that had begun to admit black students, Klarman's marker of 1955 came after at least one of the rulings in *Brown*. As to whether *Brown* produced a backlash that slowed the process of desegregation, Virgil Hawkins in Florida and Horace Ward in Georgia, both of them candidates for admission to law school, might have been startled at the implication that the decisions in *Brown* in 1954 or 1955 had anything of consequence to do with explaining their lengthy and futile travails in the courts from midcentury on. The Frasier brothers, for their part, might be surprised to find no mention of their court victory or their enrollment as undergraduates at the University of North Carolina.

Black southerners continued, in the years after *Brown*, to do what so many had been doing in the years preceding *Brown*—the years that made *Brown* possible. In every segregated state, they applied to enter programs that had always barred black enrollment, and they often went to court if rejected. *Brown* made it easier for them to gain admission without litigation, and easier to win in the courts if that proved necessary. We need to acknowledge—not deny, not skip over—the state actions to which *Brown I* or *Brown II* led more or less immediately in seven states: Maryland, Missouri, Kentucky, Oklahoma, West Virginia, Texas, and Arkansas. And we must include—not ignore—the immediate response, through the federal courts, in North Carolina. Delaware had already, in effect, made the change before *Brown*. And in eight among the remaining sixteen historically segregated states, as a direct result of *Brown*, black undergraduates could and did suddenly find themselves eligible for, rather than categorically excluded from, admission to programs in any undergraduate area of study at the state university.

As for the other eight states, change consistent with *Brown* began in 1958 at the graduate or professional level at the University of Florida—and by 1963 at the undergraduate level even on the main campuses at Georgia, Mississippi, Alabama, South Carolina, Florida, Virginia, and Tennessee. Black undergraduate enrollment soon began at Louisiana State University main campus at Baton Rouge. Auburn and Mississippi State each admitted a black undergraduate in 1965, the last of the historically nonblack land-grant institutions—the South's "colleges of 1862"—to do so. Also by 1965, at least one black undergraduate had earned a degree at the state university in Georgia (Charlayne Hunter and Hamilton Holmes), at Mississippi (James Meredith), at South Carolina (Henrie Monteith), at Alabama (Vivian Malone), and at Florida (Stephan Mickle).

Even if, in higher education, *Brown* "retarded progress" (as Klarman puts it) on the racial front in several states, the worst we come away with appears to be a split decision, according to which the rulings in *Brown* impelled change at universities in half the segregated states and stiffened white resistance in Louisiana (as Michael Wade shows in his essay in this volume) and perhaps some others. Moreover, whether because of *Brown* or in spite of *Brown*, continued categorical black exclusion persisted for only a few more years at even the most resistant universities in even the most recalcitrant states. At every flagship campus across the South except Louisiana State University, at least one black undergraduate received a degree by about the tenth anniversary of *Brown II*. One might readily conclude, in short, that *Brown* caused a tremendous break in historical continuity, even if not everywhere or all at once. It strengthened the ability of black southerners to break through barriers that so many white southerners had long desired and sought to maintain.

Desegregating Higher Education: Process and Timing

Even at the end of the twentieth century, most institutions of higher education across the South clearly retained their historical identities as black or nonblack, though the boundaries between the two sets of schools had blurred. Absolutes had disappeared, but the past lived on. Mississippi State University's black undergraduate enrollment had climbed from zero to 16 percent since the summer of 1965, but the state's population was 36 percent African American; the figures were 97 percent at Alcorn State University, the historically black land-grant school, and 11 percent at Ole Miss.[71]

All but two of the twenty-four schools in this study began to desegregate at some point during a span of seventeen years, from 1948 through 1965, and the other two had begun to admit African Americans into one or more programs a few years earlier. Within a briefer period, around the late 1960s, all the schools also began to hire black faculty and recruit black athletes, if they had not already done so. It was, by then, already a far cry from the very recent time when some nonblack schools refused to play opposing teams that had even one black player (see Charles H. Martin's essay in this volume).[72] Each school continued to change, as various implications of desegregation worked their way through the faculty, the curriculum, and extracurricular activities. Previously nonblack schools had African American players on their football and basketball teams—by the 1980s and 1990s, even black quarterbacks and Heisman Trophy winners—and, on occasion, a black homecoming queen or student body president.

By 1965, desegregation was under way at most southern institutions of higher education. Not only had all twenty-four of the schools emphasized in this essay begun to admit black students, most of the schools—even the relative latecomers—had acquired one or more black alumni. The beginnings of desegregation, at one school or another, can be dated at any point from 1935 through about 1970, but the enrollment of a school's first African American opened a range of new questions, among them whether another black applicant could gain admission, whether all curricula would be open to black enrollment, whether black students could room and dine on campus, and whether they could represent their schools on varsity sports teams. At many universities (among them Maryland, Arkansas, Tennessee, and Florida), the enrollment of black students in graduate and professional programs predated, by at least four years, a policy that permitted the enrollment of black undergraduates across the curriculum, so "desegregation" began at different times even on a single campus.

Court cases framed the timing of the first steps toward desegregation, though states and institutions varied as to whether litigation was necessary, and how much was required. Every one of the seventeen states put up resistance to desegregated higher education. Yet the degree of tenacity they showed varied, with the Border South states most prepared to adopt new policies and practices, the Upper South states next, and the Dixiecrat states of 1948 or the South's Goldwater states of 1964 most determined to resist.

Only three of the twenty-four schools experienced notable violence associated with the enrollment of the first black students. The University of Alabama, together with its counterparts in Georgia and Mississippi, displayed the travails of desegregation in far starker ways than did any of the other twenty-one schools, including the historically white land-grant institutions in Alabama and Mississippi.

As a rule, the drama was of a far more subtle sort, as individual black applicants pushed ahead with their plans, plans that often involved court cases that might well take years—and might or might not succeed in eventually securing their enrollment as pioneer black students on historically nonblack campuses. The drama continued, as the pioneer black students worked out such questions as whether—on account of their racial identity—they would be shunned by the sea of white students, whether they could live and eat on campus, whether they could join sports teams, even whether they were subject to curricular restrictions. By 1965, in every southern state, the process of desegregation had clearly begun. It was clearly also still under way.

Notes

Portions of this chapter previously appeared in *History of Higher Education Annual* 19 (1999): 121–48 and are used here with permission of Transaction Publishers.

1. Sammy McDavid, "Thank You, Mrs. Hunter," *Alumnus* 58 (Spring 1982): 2–5; see also Douglas L. Conner, with John F. Marszalek, *A Black Physician's Story: Bringing Hope to Mississippi* (Jackson: University Press of Mississippi, 1985); Thomas J. Ward Jr., *Black Physicians in the Jim Crow South* (Fayetteville: University of Arkansas Press, 2003).

2. Vertical File, "MSU Alumni—Richard E. Holmes," Special Collections, Mitchell Memorial Library, Mississippi State University, Starkville.

3. *Peterson's Guide to Four-Year Colleges*, 29th ed. (Princeton, N.J.: Peterson's, 1999), 689; Vertical File, "Diversity Center," Special Collections, Mitchell Memorial Library, Mississippi State University.

4. Dean W. Colvard, *Mixed Emotions: As Racial Barriers Fell—A University President Remembers* (Danville, Ill.: Interstate Printers, 1985).

5. Calvin Trillin, *An Education in Georgia: Charlayne Hunter, Hamilton Holmes, and the Integration of the University of Georgia* (1964; reprint, Athens: University of Georgia Press, 1991); Robert A. Pratt, *We Shall Not Be Moved: The Desegregation of the University of Georgia* (Athens: University of Georgia Press, 2002); Maurice C. Daniels, *Horace T. Ward: Desegregation of the University of Georgia, Civil Rights Advocacy, and Jurisprudence* (Atlanta: Clark Atlanta University, 2001); E. Culpepper Clark, *The Schoolhouse Door: Segregation's Last Stand at the University of Alabama* (New York: Oxford University Press, 1993); David G. Sansing, *Making Haste Slowly: The Troubled History of Higher Education in Mississippi* (Jackson: University Press of Mississippi, 1990), 140–214; Nadine Cohodas, *The Band Played Dixie: Race and the Liberal Conscience at Ole Miss* (New York: Free Press, 1997); William Doyle, *An American Insurrection: The Battle of Oxford, Mississippi, 1962* (New York: Doubleday, 2001). Charles Eagles has a book under way about the desegregation of Ole Miss.

6. Clark, *Schoolhouse Door*, 5–113; Trillin, *Education in Georgia*, 50–54; Charlayne Hunter-Gault, *In My Place* (New York: Farrar Strauss Giroux, 1992), 181–85; Robert Cohen, "'Two, Four, Six, Eight, We Don't Want to Integrate': White Student Attitudes toward the University of Georgia's Desegregation," *Georgia Historical Quarterly* 79 (Fall 1996): 616–45. For the experiences of several black female pioneers, including Autherine Lucy and Charlayne Hunter, see the essay in this volume by Marcia G. Synnott.

7. Cohodas, *Band Played Dixie*, 57–106; Doyle, *American Insurrection*; James Meredith, *Three Years in Mississippi* (Bloomington: Indiana University Press, 1966); Clark, *Schoolhouse Door*, 147–233.

8. U.S. Census Bureau, *Census of Population: 1950*, Vol. 2, *Characteristics of the Population* (Washington, D.C.: Government Printing Office, 1952), 2–30, 11–39, 18–26, 24–22, 40–26; Arthur M. Schlesinger, ed., *History of American Presidential Elections, 1789–1984*, 5 vols. (New York: Chelsea House, 1971–86), 4:3211, 3702.

9. Cohodas, *Band Played Dixie*, 104–15.

10. *Missouri ex rel. Gaines v. Canada*, 305 U.S. 337 (1938); *Sipuel v. Board of Regents of the University of Oklahoma*, 332 U.S. 631 (1948); *Sweatt v. Painter*, 339 U.S. 629 (1950); *McLaurin v. Oklahoma State Regents*, 339 U.S. 637 (1950); *Brown v. Board of Education*, 347 U.S. 483 (1954) and 349 U.S. 294 (1955). Surveys of the legal history include Richard Kluger, *Simple Justice: The History of* Brown v. Board of Education *and Black America's Struggle for Equality* (New York: Random House, 1976); Jean L. Preer, *Lawyers v. Educators: Black Colleges and Desegregation in Public Higher Education* (Westport, Conn.: Greenwood Press, 1982), 63–156; Richard Paul Chait, "The Desegregation of Higher Education: A Legal History" (Ph.D. diss., University of Wisconsin, 1972), 124–250; and Mark V. Tushnet, *The NAACP's Legal Strategy against Segregated Education, 1925–1950* (Chapel Hill: University of North Carolina Press, 1987), 82–166. A recent history of developments on the constitutional front is Michael J. Klarman, *From Jim Crow to Civil Rights: The Supreme Court and the Struggle for Racial Equality* (New York: Oxford University Press, 2004).

11. Kluger, *Simple Justice*, 186–95; *University v. Murray*, 169 Md. 478 (1936); Rita Sutter, "When Yesterday's Traditions Are Thankfully Past," *Outlook* (University of Maryland at College Park faculty and staff weekly newspaper) February 7, 1994, 1, 6; John A. Munroe, *The University of Delaware: A History* (Newark: University of Delaware, 1986), 361–64; *Parker v. University of Delaware*, 75 A.2d 225 (1950); various materials in University Archives, University of Delaware, Newark; Delia Crutchfield Cook, "Shadows across the Columns: The Bittersweet Legacy of African Americans at the University of Missouri" (Ph.D. diss., University of Missouri–Columbia, 1996), 41–75.

12. Thomas G. Dyer, *The University of Georgia: A Bicentennial History, 1785–1985* (Athens: University of Georgia Press, 1985), 304–13; Barbara A. Worthy, "The Travail and Triumph of a Southern Black Civil Rights Lawyer: The Legal Career of Alexander Pierre Tureaud, 1899–1972" (Ph.D. diss., Tulane University, 1984), 83–103; see also the essay by Michael G. Wade in this volume.

13. Peter Wallenstein, *Blue Laws and Black Codes: Conflict, Courts, and Change in Twentieth-Century Virginia* (Charlottesville: University of Virginia Press, 2004), 107–8; Anthony Blaine Deel, "Virginia's Minimal Resistance: The Desegregation of Public Graduate and Professional Education, 1935–1955" (Master's thesis, Virginia Polytechnic Institute and State University, 1990), 75–123; Peter Wallenstein, "Segregation, Desegregation, and Higher Education in Virginia" (paper presented at the Virginia Forum, Winchester, Va., April 2006, and at the Policy History Conference, Charlottesville, Va., June 2006).

14. Robert A. Leflar, *The First 100 Years: Centennial History of the University of Arkansas* (Fayetteville: University of Arkansas Foundation, 1972), 276–82.

15. A. Stephen Stephan, "Desegregation of Higher Education in Arkansas," *Journal of Negro Education* 27 (Summer 1958): 243–52; Leflar, *First 100 Years*, 281–84; "Silas Hunt" Vertical File, Special Collections Division, Mullins Library, University of Arkansas Libraries, Fayetteville.

16. This material is drawn from the "Edith Irby Jones" Vertical File, Special Collections Division, Mullins Library, University of Arkansas. The quotation is from Charles Whitaker, "Breakthroughs Are Her Business," *Ebony* (June 1986), 94. See also John Egerton, *Speak Now against the Day: The Generation before the Civil Rights Movement in the South* (Chapel Hill: University of North Carolina Press, 1994), 489–90, more or less replicated in Ward, *Black Physicians*, 54. Dr. Jones is mentioned in Gordon D. Morgan and Izola Preston, *The Edge of Campus: A Journal of the Black Experience at the University of Arkansas* (Fayetteville: University of Arkansas Press, 1990), 11, 172, 185.

17. Martha Anne Tudor, "Dr. Jones Encourages Students," *Augusta (Georgia) Herald*, August 2, 1986. Learning of Irby's acceptance into the program, Arkansas civil rights leader Daisy Bates for one made sure that Irby had the money she needed to pay the tuition in Little Rock, and that area black doctors saw to it that her rent was paid. Irene Wassell, "Pioneering Doctor," *Arkansas Gazette*, May 5, 1985.

18. When she was riding with friends on Little Rock's segregated buses, they all simply stood rather than sitting in a segregated pattern in the designated areas. As one of her white classmates, another female doctor in Houston, later said, the segregation "didn't seem to bother her as much as it did us." The quotation, by Dr. Mary Arthur, is from Wassell, "Pioneering Doctor."

19. Ada Lois Sipuel Fisher, with Danney Goble, *A Matter of Black and White: The Autobiography of Ada Lois Sipuel Fisher* (Norman: University of Oklahoma Press, 1996); George Lynn Cross, *Blacks in White Colleges: Oklahoma's Landmark Cases* (Norman: University of Oklahoma Press, 1975).

20. Kopecky, *History of Equal Opportunity*, 271–73.

21. Ibid., 273–75; "Black Students" Vertical File, University Archives, Low Library, Oklahoma State University, Stillwater.

22. Kopecky, *History of Equal Opportunity*, 275–77.

23. Ibid., 279–80. The notes to this essay do not include citations to student directories, student yearbooks, commencement programs, and alumni directories, though such materials have been used extensively.

24. Kopecky, *History of Equal Opportunity*, 281–82.

25. Quoted in Carl T. Rowan, *Dream Makers, Dream Breakers: The World of Justice Thurgood Marshall* (Boston: Little, Brown, 1993), 50.

26. *University v. Murray*, 169 Md. 478 (1936). The story can be found in George H. Callcott, *Maryland and America, 1940–1980* (Baltimore: Johns Hopkins University Press, 1985), 147 (source of the quotation); Rowan, *Dream Makers*, 50–57; Sally Seawright, "Desegregation at Maryland: The NAACP and the Murray Case in the 1930s," *Maryland Historian* 1 (Spring 1970): 59–73; Edward J. Kuebler, "The Desegregation of

the University of Maryland," *Maryland Historical Magazine* 71 (Spring 1976): 37–49; and Kluger, *Simple Justice*, 179–94.

27. An interview with Donald Murray when he was in his early sixties (July 7, 1976, Oral History 8139, Maryland Historical Society, Baltimore) is disappointing. He had suffered a stroke, and he revealed little about his experiences.

28. "Maryland Rejects Negro's Study Suit," *New York Times*, October 11, 1949; *McCready v. Byrd*, 195 Md. 131, 73 A.2d 8 (1950); *Byrd v. McCready*, 340 U.S. 827 (1950); and various materials in the NAACP Papers at the Library of Congress, available in the microfilm version, Part 3, Series B, Reel 12. In articulating the 1938 ruling in the *Gaines* case from Missouri, the U.S. Supreme Court had drawn on the Maryland state court's 1936 ruling in *University of Maryland v. Murray*; the Maryland appeals court in 1950, for its reversal of the trial court in *McCready*, drew directly upon *Gaines* as well as on the Oklahoma case of *Sipuel*, decided in 1948.

29. The Compact was designed to address two perceived needs—one, distinctly racial, would operate successfully the way Maryland hoped it would regarding McCready; the other, not racial in nature, would permit states to benefit from each other's strengths in areas like dentistry and veterinary medicine, and the University of Maryland served as a regional provider in dentistry. As to the first of these two strategies—as Thurgood Marshall pointed out in letters to black editors in Pittsburgh and Norfolk, as well as in Baltimore, after they characterized the appeals court victory as a civil rights triumph over the Compact—the Control Board for Southern Regional Education itself opposed Maryland's attempt to use the Compact in support of segregation in this case. Rather, as the Court of Appeals observed, a number of white residents of Maryland were attending an out-of-state veterinarian school through the Compact, in view of there being no veterinarian school in Maryland; the state would apparently offer black Marylanders a comparable opportunity, the court went on, and such an arrangement would be consistent with the Compact and with the Constitution. But with regard to racial identity and higher education, the Maryland appeals court asserted, in an apparent jab at southern states' constricted view of states' rights, that the "separate responsibility of each State within its own sphere is of the essence of statehood maintained under our dual system." For a contemporary assessment of the Southern Regional Board, or Regional Compact, see Pauli Murray, comp., *States' Laws on Race and Color* (1951; reprint, Athens: University of Georgia Press, 1997), 201–5 (the Maryland statute), 666–71. Thurgood Marshall had been confident he could beat the state's argument about the uniqueness of legal training, but for a moment he had fun in court and conceded the point, declaring that he could prove there was a difference—he had gone to law school and not come out a nurse.

30. Sutter, "When Yesterday's Traditions Are Thankfully Past," 1, 6; "Maryland U. Opens Doors to First Negro," *New York Times*, February 1, 1951. The account in Callcott, *History of the University of Maryland*, 352–53, reports misleadingly that Mitchell was admitted to College Park "without court action."

31. Sutter, "Yesterday's Traditions," 6.

32. "Break in Maryland Bias," *New York Times*, May 7, 1951.

33. The materials drawn on in this and the next few paragraphs for the account of developments in Delaware, from the NAACP Papers at the Library of Congress, can be found in the microfilm version, Part 3, Series B, Reel 11. For a sketch of Redding, see J. Clay Smith Jr., *Emancipation: The Making of the Black Lawyer, 1844–1944* (Philadelphia: University of Pennsylvania Press, 1993), 128–29.

34. Munroe, *University of Delaware*, 362–64; *Parker v. University of Delaware*, 75 A.2d 225 (1950); and materials in University Archives, University of Delaware. Kluger, *Simple Justice*, 429–33, gives the *Parker* case a brief treatment on the way to a more sustained treatment of the public school case in Delaware that became one of the cluster known as *Brown v. Board of Education*. Largely derivative of Kluger are James T. Patterson, Brown v. Board of Education*: A Civil Rights Milestone and Its Troubled Legacy* (New York: Oxford University Press, 2001), 30–31; and Peter Irons, *Jim Crow's Children: The Broken Promise of the* Brown *Decision* (New York: Viking, 2002), 109–11.

35. Connie Park Rice, *Our Monongalia: A History of African Americans in Monongalia County, West Virginia* (Terra Alta, W.Va.: Headline Books, 1999), 130.

36. *Lexington (Kentucky) Herald-Leader*, October 29, 1992; Wade H. Hall, *The Rest of the Dream: The Black Odyssey of Lyman Johnson* (Lexington: University Press of Kentucky, 1988).

37. Callcott, *History of the University of Maryland*, 353; William T. Doherty Jr. and Festus P. Summers, *West Virginia University: Symbol of Unity in a Sectionalized State* (Morgantown: West Virginia University Press, 1982), 212; Cook, "Shadows," 74–75.

38. Morgan and Preston, *Edge of Campus*, 13–15; Richard B. McCaslin, "Steadfast in His Intent: John W. Hargis and the Integration of the University of Texas at Austin," *Southwestern Historical Quarterly* 95 (July 1991): 20–41.

40. Peter Wallenstein, "Higher Education and the Civil Rights Movement: Desegregating the University of North Carolina," in *Warm Ashes: Issues in Southern History at the Dawn of the Twenty-first Century*, ed. Winfred B. Moore Jr., Kyle S. Sinisi, and David H. White Jr. (Columbia: University of South Carolina Press, 2003), 280–300; William D. Snider, *Light on the Hill: A History of the University of North Carolina at Chapel Hill* (Chapel Hill: University of North Carolina Press, 1992), 246–48; *McKissick v. Carmichael*, 187 F.2d 949 (1951); Neal King Cheek, "An Historical Study of the Administrative Actions in the Racial Desegregation of the University of North Carolina at Chapel Hill, 1930–1955" (Ph.D. diss., University of North Carolina at Chapel Hill, 1973).

40. *Board of Trustees v. Frasier*, 350 U.S. 979 (1956); Wallenstein, "Higher Education and the Civil Rights Movement"; Allen W. Trelease, *Making North Carolina Literate: The University of North Carolina at Greensboro, from Normal School to Metropolitan University* (Durham, N.C.: Carolina Academic Press, 2004), 241, 277–81.

41. Worthy, "Travail and Triumph," 71–83; James Riley Montgomery, Stanley J. Folmsbee, and Lee Seifert Greene, *To Foster Knowledge: A History of the University of Tennessee, 1794–1970* (Knoxville: University of Tennessee Press, 1984), 228–29; *Wilson v. Board of Supervisors*, 92 F.Supp. 986 (1950); *Gray v. University of Tennessee*, 97 F.Supp. 463 (1951).

42. Maxie Myron Cox Jr., "1963—The Year of Decision: Desegregation in South Carolina" (Ph.D. diss., University of South Carolina, 1996), 14–143; Martin T. Olliff,

"'Just Another Day on the Plains': The Desegregation of Auburn University," *Alabama Review* 54 (April 2001): 101–44.

43. Montgomery et al., *To Foster Knowledge*, 267–68; "Desegregation—Undergraduate Experience—1961" Vertical File, University Archives, Hoskins Library, University of Tennessee, Knoxville; "Negro Is Enrolled in Louisiana School," *New York Times*, June 9, 1964.

44. "South Carolina Segregation in State Universities Ends," *New York Times*, June 16, 1965; "Desegregation—Auburn" and "Civil Rights—*Franklin v. Parker*" Vertical Files, University Archives, Draughon Library, Auburn University, Auburn, Ala.

45. Peter Wallenstein, "King Color Goes to College—The Waning Years: Desegregating Public Higher Education in Virginia, 1950–1972," *Diversity News* 5 (Spring 1999): 5–7.

46. Wallenstein, *Virginia Tech*, 185–87; "Virginia Tech Admits First Negro, Student from Hampton," *Roanoke Times*, September 11, 1953.

47. Peter Wallenstein, *Cradle of America: Four Centuries of Virginia History* (Lawrence: University Press of Kansas, 2007), chapter 23.

48. Michael Ollove, "Fighter Broke Racial Barriers at Virginia Tech," *Roanoke Times and World News*, May 13, 1979.

49. Wallenstein, *Virginia Tech*, 195–207; Warren I. Strother and Peter Wallenstein, *From VPI to State University: President T. Marshall Hahn Jr. and the Transformation of Virginia Tech, 1962–1974* (Macon, Ga.: Mercer University Press, 2004), 60, 111–15, 153–67, 295–96, 379–85.

50. Strother and Wallenstein, *From VPI to State University*, 294–95; the essay in this volume by Marcia G. Synnott; and Su Clausen-Wicker, "Breaking the Double Barrier: The First Black Women at Tech," *Diversity News* 4 (Fall 1997): 5–8.

51. Strother and Wallenstein, *From VPI to State University*, 315.

52. Algia R. Cooper, "*Brown v. Board of Education* and Virgil Darnell Hawkins: Twenty-eight Years and Six Petitions to Justice," *Journal of Negro History* 64 (Winter 1979): 1–15; *Florida ex rel. Hawkins v. Board of Control of Florida*, 347 U.S. 971 (1954); *Hawkins v. Board of Control of Florida*, 350 U.S. 413 (1956), quotes from 414.

53. Cooper, "*Brown*," 8–11; *Florida ex rel. Hawkins v. Board of Control*, 355 U.S. 839 (1957); *Hawkins v. Board of Control of Florida*, 162 F.Supp. 851 (1958), quote from 853; Peter Wallenstein, "Black Gators, Black Seminoles: Black Floridians and the Desegregation of Higher Education, 1946–1966" (paper presented at the First Biennial Allen Morris Conference on the History of Florida and the Atlantic World, Florida State University, Tallahassee, February 13, 2000).

54. Cooper, "*Brown*," 10–11; *Hawkins v. Board of Control of Florida*, 162 F.Supp. 851, 853 (1958).

55. Samuel Proctor and Wright Langley, *Gator History: A Pictorial History of the University of Florida* (Gainesville: South Star, 1986), 48; Stephanie Y. Evans, "'I Was One of the First to See Daylight': Black Women at Predominantly White Colleges and Universities in Florida since 1959," *Florida Historical Quarterly* 85 (Summer 2006): 47–48.

56. W. George Allen, interview by Joel Buchanan, July 22, 1996, Fort Lauderdale, Fla., in the University of Florida Oral History Program, 9–14.

57. Ibid., 21–22.

58. Ibid., 24–25.

59. Ibid., 23–24.

60. Stephan P. Mickle, interview by Joel Buchanan, October 3, 1995, Tallahassee, Fla., in the University of Florida Oral History Program, 15–16.

61. Ibid., 17–18.

62. "Black Enrollment" Vertical File, University Archives, Smathers Library, University of Florida, Gainesville; Proctor and Langley, *Gator History*, 48.

63. Mickle, interview, 23–25, 27.

64. Tracy Shuford, "John Chase," *Texas Alcade* (March–April 1996): 20–25. Another black applicant, Horace Lincoln Heath, was also admitted into a Ph.D. program in government. At the same time, the university reportedly rejected two other candidates on the grounds that the programs of study they sought could be had at a black school ("Texas University Enrolls 2 Negroes," *New York Times*, June 8, 1950; "First Negro Enters University of Texas," *New York Times*, June 9, 1950). Even earlier—while the Sweatt case was still in litigation—the university's Medical Branch, at Galveston, admitted a black applicant, Herman A. Barnett, although technically he was enrolled in a black school, pending development of a medical program there. No such new program ever came on stream, and by July 1955 the Medical Branch had enrolled fourteen black medical and graduated two of them ("Texas Medical School Accepts Negro Student," *New York Times*, August 15, 1949; "Integration Test in Texas Studies," *New York Times*, July 24, 1955). Another pioneer black student at the University of Texas was W. Astor Kirk, a teacher at Tillotson College who attended a single class on February 6, 1950, and then quit; he and his teacher met alone in a segregated venue across the street from the main campus, and "after fifty minutes Mr. Kirk issued a statement saying he could not accept the arrangements" ("Negro Enters, Quits Texas U.," *New York Times*, February 7, 1950). For an extended treatment, see Amilcar Shabazz, *Advancing Democracy: African Americans and the Struggle for Access and Equity in Higher Education in Texas* (Chapel Hill: University of North Carolina Press, 2004), 75, 78–89.

65. Almetris Marsh Duren, *Overcoming: A History of Black Integration at the University of Texas at Austin* (Austin: University of Texas at Austin, 1979), 4–5; McCaslin, "Steadfast," 36; Shabazz, *Advancing Democracy*, 155–59.

66. Duren, *Overcoming*, 6; Joe B. Frantz, *The Forty-Acre Follies* (Austin: Texas Monthly Press, 1983), 199–214; Dwonna Goldstone, *Integrating the 40 Acres: The Fifty-Year Struggle for Racial Equality at the University of Texas* (Athens: University of Georgia Press, 2006).

67. Shabazz, *Advancing Democracy*, 208–9; "African Americans at TAMU" Vertical File, University Archives, Memorial Library, Texas A&M University, College Station.

68. Matthew D. Lassiter and Andrew B. Lewis, eds., *The Moderates' Dilemma: Massive Resistance to School Desegregation in Virginia* (Charlottesville: University of Virginia Press, 1998).

69. Callcott, *History of the University of Maryland*, 353; Leflar, *First 100 Years*, 276–82, 287; Snider, *Light on the Hill*, 246–48.

70. Klarman, *From Jim Crow to Civil Rights*, 393.

71. See afterword and appendix 10.

72. See the essay in this volume by Charles H. Martin. See also Russell L. Henderson, "The 1963 Mississippi State University Basketball Controversy and the Repeal of the Unwritten Law: 'Something More than the Game Will Be Lost,'" *Journal of Southern History* 63 (November 1997): 827–54; and Frank Fitzpatrick, *And the Walls Came Tumbling Down: Kentucky, Texas Western, and the Game That Changed American Sports* (New York: Simon and Schuster, 1999).

2

Four Who Would

Constantine v. Southwestern Louisiana Institute (1954) and the Desegregation of Louisiana's State Colleges

MICHAEL G. WADE

"Oh, that all started with the Paul Breaux strike." Thus did Helma Constantine—a bright-eyed, tan-complexioned, active ninety-year-old—explain what led her to sue Southwestern Louisiana Institute (SLI) in 1954 after the college, citing its whites-only charter, had denied her daughter admission. Historic old Paul Breaux was the black community's school in Lafayette, slated to be demolished. When parents learned that the new, relocated Paul Breaux would open in 1953 with hand-me-down furniture, old books, and still no bus service, their patience with years of educational deprivation and school system condescension snapped. Outraged mothers launched a highly effective, weeklong boycott of classes in February 1953. It garnered national attention, wrung concessions from the school board, and emboldened some parents to try breaching the walls of segregation at the local state college. That second effort produced perhaps the most significant episode of undergraduate desegregation in southern higher education. As with much of the civil rights movement, it was locally inspired and owed much to determined black women.[1]

Helma Constantine, secretary of the local chapter of the National Association for the Advancement of Colored People (NAACP), was one of the leaders of the Paul Breaux movement. A struggling seamstress and insurance agent, she faced the considerable expense of sending her daughter, Clara Dell, away to Southern University in Scotlandville—or getting her admitted to SLI. At that juncture, no public four-year college in the Deep South had a desegregated undergraduate population.[2] Coming in April 1954, the month before the U.S. Supreme Court's decision in *Brown v. Board of Education*, the federal district court ruling in *Constantine et al. v. Southwestern Louisiana Institute et al.* was the final and perhaps crowning success of an older NAACP Legal Defense Fund campaign to achieve educational desegregation by insisting on the "equality" in the "separate but equal" formula of *Plessy v. Ferguson* (1896).

It was a victory for a strategy four years retired, after two decades of faithful and successful, but ultimately limited service in that each case had to be pursued individually rather than on a class action basis. The NAACP had already decided in 1950 to try to overturn *Plessy*. Nonetheless, *Constantine* exemplified local initiative as a driving force in the civil rights movement, and the case was the precedent for successful desegregation suits at McNeese State University (Lake Charles) in 1954 and at Southeastern Louisiana College (Hammond) in 1955.[3] These later cases were decided in the time between the issuance of *Brown I* in May 1954 and *Brown II*, the enforcement decree, the following May. During this period, segregationist-organized "massive resistance" gained a substantial measure of control of state politics, thereby forestalling additional campus desegregations.

SLI administrators and Lafayette's community leaders provided McNeese and Southeastern with a model for minimizing publicity and tensions. They cooperated to make the September 1954 desegregation of classes as low-key, carefully structured, and unpublicized an event as it could possibly be. Their insistence on good order and little publicity minimized tensions, but it also ensured that the historic episode would go unremembered, as the civil rights battlefront in higher education moved on to highly publicized confrontations at places like Ole Miss and Alabama, replete with chaos and histrionics recorded for posterity by national news networks and international reporting services.

The earlier history of the NAACP's campaign to desegregate higher education is better known. Though its goal was undergraduate desegregation, *Constantine* marked the culmination of the NAACP's lengthy struggle to desegregate graduate and professional schools at historically white southern colleges and universities. That campaign had begun in 1933, when Thomas Hocutt sued unsuccessfully for admission to the University of North Carolina's pharmacy school because the state had provided no such school for African Americans. Two years later, Donald Murray won admission to the University of Maryland's law school. He graduated in 1938, and some months later, despite the U.S. Supreme Court's decision that year in the *Gaines* case, the Louisiana State University (LSU) law school refused an application by Hurchail Jackson for admission.[4]

In 1946, the LSU law school denied Charles Hatfield's request for admission. The LSU board of supervisors and the State Board of Education suggested that he attend law school on an out-of-state scholarship until a separate school could be established at Southern University, as had recently been promised for the 1947–48 academic year. In the same year, LSU rejected New Iberia resident Viola Johnson's application to the School of Medicine. Hatfield and Johnson each sued in state court for admission, but Judge G. Caldwell Hegert dismissed the suits, saying that the plaintiffs should demand that Southern

University provide the appropriate professional schools. Both pursued their education outside the state.[5]

In two decisions in 1950, the Supreme Court weakened *Plessy*. In *McLaurin v. Oklahoma Board of Regents*, the Court ruled that the University of Oklahoma's efforts to restrict George McLaurin's court-ordered participation in its doctoral program in education by segregating him from his classmates constituted unequal treatment. In *Sweatt v. Painter*, it ordered Heman Marion Sweatt admitted to the University of Texas law school, even though historically black Texas Southern had recently inaugurated a law school. The court reasoned that Texas Southern, whatever its positive attributes might be, could not hope to match the law school in Austin in terms of its prestige, influential alumni, and professional contacts. It therefore could not satisfy the requirement of separate equality mandated in *Plessy*. Thus, by 1950, at least as regarded law schools, the Court appeared but a short step from declaring that segregation itself constituted discriminatory treatment. Yet in 1950, when eight more African Americans applied to LSU—most of them to study law, medicine, or engineering—they, too, were rejected.[6]

The events were closely watched by the *Louisiana Weekly* (the state's premier black newspaper) and by local NAACP chapters. With some misgivings, the NAACP had already begun to shift its legal strategy from stressing the inequitable results of the "separate but equal" doctrine to challenging the constitutionality of segregation itself. In *Wilson v. Board of Supervisors of Louisiana State University* (1950), Thurgood Marshall sought to have LSU remove race from its consideration of applicants. His co-counsel, New Orleans civil rights lawyer Alexander Pierre (A. P.) Tureaud, easily refuted the defense contention that Southern provided substantially equal facilities in its three-year-old law school. Agreeing that Southern could not supply Roy S. Wilson an equal educational opportunity, the three-judge federal court ruled that he must be admitted to LSU's law school. After LSU investigated Wilson's personal background, however, he withdrew his application. Nonetheless, in summer 1951, following another successful suit against the university, Lutrill Amos Payne enrolled in the graduate school, the first person acknowledged to be African American to attend LSU.[7]

The battle to gain access to graduate schools was important, but as Richard Kluger has rightly observed, "The handful of graduate-school victories affected only a fraction of the black elite, and new ones were slow in coming as the state courts declined to fall in line automatically behind the *Sweatt* and *McLaurin* decisions, which on their face did nothing to tamper with the separate-but-equal principle of *Plessy*." Black undergraduates in the southern states remained relegated to schools that were markedly inferior in facilities, funding, and faculty, places that Kluger called "academic shanties." In the Border South, this situation began to end when a Delaware state court ruled in 1950 that, because of the glaring inequalities between Delaware's white and black colleges, black undergraduates must be admitted to the University of Delaware.[8]

In 1953, Alexander Pierre Tureaud Jr. applied for admission to the undergraduate division at LSU, was rejected, and sued the board of supervisors. Donating their services to the defense were eighteen LSU law school graduates, including Leander Perez, the notorious political boss of watery Plaquemines Parish. Despite the display of school spirit, Judge J. Skelly Wright ruled that, because of tangible inequalities between LSU and Southern, LSU must admit blacks to its combined arts and science and law program. LSU lost on appeal, and the younger Tureaud registered on September 18, 1953. On October 28, the Fifth U.S. Circuit Court of Appeals reversed the decision on a technicality. On November 9, Judge Wright vacated his order. The next day, LSU canceled Tureaud's registration. On November 16, Tureaud's attorneys successfully applied to the U.S. Supreme Court for a stay of the Fifth Circuit's judgment, but by then Tureaud had transferred to Xavier University. The following year, *Constantine v. Southwestern Louisiana Institute* resulted in the first broad-based undergraduate desegregation of a historically white state-supported four-year college or university in any state that had been in the Confederacy.[9]

Constantine v. Southwestern Louisiana Institute

On September 15, 1953, Lafayette Parish residents Clara Dell Constantine, Martha Jane Conway, Charles Vincent Singleton, and Shirley Taylor sought admission to segregated SLI. A local civil rights activist, Velma Hollier, described these lower-middle-class kids, and by implication their parents, as "four who would" agree to pursue this risky venture. When their applications were denied, they appealed to the State Board of Education, but to no avail. On January 4, 1954, their attorneys filed a class action complaint in the U.S. District Court for the Western District of Louisiana, seeking to permanently enjoin SLI's governing authorities from refusing them admittance.[10]

A. P. Tureaud, a member of Thurgood Marshall's team of NAACP attorneys since 1939, headed the plaintiffs' legal team, which also included Marshall, Robert L. Carter of New York, and U. Simpson Tate of Dallas, who authored the complaint. The plaintiffs asserted that, by virtue of its admissions policy of excluding all African Americans, SLI was in violation of the Fourteenth Amendment and of the Ku Klux Klan Act of 1870 (Chapter 114, Sec. 16), which provided for the equal rights of all citizens. They based their argument on the

Ku Klux Klan Act of 1871 (Chapter 22, Sec. 1), which authorized legal action by any citizen to redress state-sponsored deprivation of rights secured by the Constitution and laws of the United States.[11]

In this case, the plaintiffs were being prohibited from attending "the sole and only publicly-supported institution of higher learning . . . at which Plaintiffs and other qualified Negro applicants can receive equal or substantially equal educational advantages, facilities or opportunities [equal] to those provided and afforded . . . all qualified non-Negro applicants." There was no college in southwest Louisiana that black students could attend. Louisiana had established regional colleges for the convenience of white students, but none for blacks. Because SLI had refused Constantine and her coplaintiffs the opportunity to attend college while living at home—the least expensive option for any college student—they would have to bear the extra cost of room, board, and transportation to attend Grambling or Southern, the two nearest historically black institutions, or else forego their dreams of a college education.[12]

Martha Jane Conway, who wanted to major in business education, could not afford to go to an out-of-town school. Shirley Taylor was interested in a law enforcement career with a focus on juvenile delinquents, and if she graduated from SLI, she wanted to do graduate work at Atlanta University. Clara Dell Constantine wanted to major in business in order to teach students how to handle their financial affairs more effectively. Charles Vincent Singleton, planning to major in elementary education, believed that attending SLI would make him more competitive in his chosen field. Taylor and Singleton said they thought that this opportunity would make them more effective citizens, better able to contribute something to the country. Constantine thought education would allow her to contribute to her race's tradition of progress. In addition to their personal goals, each of the prospective students believed that their suit would benefit, as Shirley Taylor put it, "all people, Black, White, or what have you."[13]

To hear the case, Chief Judge Edward Hutcheson appointed three judges—Wayne G. Borah of the Fifth Circuit Court of Appeals (New Orleans) and federal district court judges Benjamin C. Dawkins Jr. (Shreveport) and Edwin F. Hunter Jr. (Lake Charles).[14] This was standard procedure when the constitutionality of state laws was in question. Initially, Tureaud and his colleagues had intended to emphasize the advantages that SLI offered over Southern. They considered arguing that, in terms of facilities and programs, Southern was not a substantially equal alternative for their clients, by then a proven tactic. However, they also wanted a speedy trial, one that would enable their students to register for the fall term. In fact, U. Simpson Tate had hopes of getting a hearing in time for the students to be admitted for the spring 1954 term, and Judge Hunter shared his desire for a speedy trial, but delays in serving summons on the defendants in various parts of the state made this impossible. Since arguing educational inequality could require numerous witnesses and much time, Tureaud and his colleagues agreed to Judge Borah's suggestion that the parties stipulate the facts and argue the case on the law, because neither Borah nor Hunter saw anything in the facts that required sworn testimony. Judge Hunter, despite a request by the state attorney general for a delay until after the Supreme Court ruled on the *Brown* case, fixed the trial for January 29, 1954, in New Orleans.[15]

A pretrial conference was held on January 28 to hear the motions and begin negotiations on the stipulations. At Tate's insistence, a defense stipulation that segregation per se was not an issue in the case and that the only issue was "equality of facilities, advantages and opportunities" was deleted, and the parties reached agreement on the facts in time for trial. By agreement of all parties, Judge Hunter set the new trial date for February 19. At trial, the court denied a defense motion to dismiss the case. On April 23, the court granted the plaintiffs' petition for relief.[16]

Judge Hunter authored the decision. Louisiana's six white state colleges had been geographically located to serve their white clienteles, he wrote, "the purpose obviously being to make education available to more people and to make it possible for more people to stay at home and go to college at less expense." The same opportunity had not been provided to Lafayette Parish's black students, who had no college to which they could commute daily. The resultant burden and the loss of time and money imposed on black students and their parents were thus real and substantial. Hunter said the state could not constitutionally make available to prospective white students the kind of access that SLI provided and deny black residents a similar opportunity.[17]

Well aware that the Supreme Court would soon rule on five cases challenging the constitutionality of *Plessy*, Hunter ruled that the question of the constitutionality of the Louisiana statute was irrelevant:

> The entire theory of the Fourteenth Amendment is that where an officer or other representative of a State, in the exercise of authority with which he is clothed, so uses the power possessed to deny a right given by the Fourteenth Amendment, inquiry concerning whether the State has authorized the wrong is irrelevant. The federal judicial power is competent to afford redress for the wrong by dealing with the officer and the result of his exertion of power.

The court thus granted the plaintiffs' petition for relief because Louisiana law—as interpreted and administered by state officials—violated guarantees provided by the U.S. Constitution.[18] The terms of the decree were settled after official notice to all parties.

The state accepted the trial court's decision. Neither the State Board of Education nor other state officials ever publicly explained the decision not to appeal the *Constantine* ruling, but several factors appear to have deterred further action. In light of the *Sweatt* decision, meeting the standard of equality in a new, separate regional college for black undergraduates was quite unlikely. Moreover, separate campuses probably would have to be built in the vicinity of each of the state colleges for whites, draining resources from an already underfunded state college system. In addition, state officials feared that the *Brown* decision, issued the following month, might be interpreted to apply to colleges as well as to the elementary and secondary public school systems—as indeed it later was. For his part, SLI president Joel Lafayette Fletcher always credited the story told him in Ruston by supporters of then-governor Robert Kennon: "It's not because of you, Joel, that Southwestern was integrated. The Governor just had to make some move in that direction on account of President Eisenhower—and he knew the d_ _m [*sic*] Cajuns wouldn't mind."[19]

On July 16, 1954, the court permanently enjoined President Fletcher and his registrar, James Stewart Bonnet, from refusing to admit the plaintiffs, "or any other Negro citizen of the state, residing in Southwest Louisiana, and similarly qualified and situated," on the basis of race or color. This narrowly drawn language, intended to restrict applications from black students outside the college's service region, may have come from the defense, which logically could have argued that since the plaintiffs had made the case for regional racial discrimination, the remedy should be restricted to the geographic area in question. Certainly the attorney general's office intended to interpret the ruling literally. Assistant Attorney General W. C. Perrault defined for State Superintendent of Public Instruction Shelby M. Jackson the thirteen parishes his office considered "Southwest Louisiana." He said that "this office will advise President Fletcher not to admit Negroes to Southwestern except from the 13 parishes named herein."[20] There is no evidence that this particular issue was a matter of subsequent controversy, no doubt because the *Brown* decisions enormously broadened the scope of the school desegregation issue.

Lafayette—Vive la Différence

On the face of it, Lafayette, a market town in rural south Louisiana, seemed an unlikely locale for leadership in a civil rights movement that had yet to achieve the momentum and support that would define it by the early 1960s. Sympathy for experiments in racial justice, insofar as it existed south of the Mason-Dixon Line, was more a feature of such Border South states as Kentucky and Maryland. Less than fifty miles from the Gulf of Mexico, Lafayette was about as far south as a town in Dixie could be. But Lafayette was Deep South with a difference.

Many of Lafayette's early settlers were descendants of the Acadian exiles who peopled southwest Louisiana after 1755. Founded in 1824 as Vermilionville, the village became Lafayette sixty years later. Enriched by infusions of Germans, Irish, "foreign" French, *les Américains*, and later Lebanese and Syrian immigrants, the region centered upon Lafayette developed a "Cajun" culture that included the French language, Roman Catholicism, tightly knit families, and a much-admired cuisine that included not only their adaptations of local foods to French cooking, but also African, French, Native American, and Spanish culinary practices. A substantial Jewish community further enlivened this rich admixture of cultures. In 1900, the rapidly growing town acquired a fledgling college, Southwestern Louisiana Industrial Institute. That institution, its name shortened to Southwestern Louisiana Institute in 1921, made the town a focal point for National Youth Administration programs in the 1930s and for the navy's V-12 program during World War II. After the war, Lafayette emerged as one of the chief beneficiaries of the offshore oil boom when local merchant Maurice Heymann developed the Oil Center, a large complex of office buildings that made the town the logical administrative center for the oil business between Houston and New Orleans, further broadening an already substantial middle class.[21]

African Americans saw World War II not only as a crusade against fascism but also as an opportunity to undermine institutionalized racism at home. Unsurprisingly, then, many black Americans emerged from the wartime experience newly determined to insist on fuller and more equitable participation in the benefits of American citizenship. That resolve produced some of the century's nastier episodes of white violence, but there were signs that whites were less approving of race-based murder and mayhem than in the prewar period. In Louisiana in 1947, Lafayette attorney Bertrand DeBlanc labored mightily on Willie Francis's unsuccessful appeal to escape a second date with the electric chair after a failed first effort to execute him for a robbery-murder conviction by an all-white jury. Southern military bases, such as Chennault Air Base in nearby Lake Charles, racially integrated after 1948, inspired local blacks to resist discrimination while suggesting that the world would not come to an end if the Constitution was respected. Moreover, for many south Louisianans, the Catholic Church's clear admonition that racism was un-Christian would have increased meaning as many clerics actively sought to turn preachment into practice. Just to the north of Lafayette, in Grand Coteau, the College of the Sacred Heart's president, Mother Odile Lapeyre, desegregated her all-girls student body in fall 1953.[22]

Another factor, too, though ultimately unquantifiable, influenced residents of SLI's southwest Louisiana service area as their college's policy and practice of black exclusion came to an end. Acknowledged or not, there were blood ties across the color line. Lafayette's middle class contained a "black" minority, not a few of whom were descendants of Louisiana's *gens de couleur libres* (free people of color), the offspring of antebellum interracial liaisons and relationships. Not a few white planters in the region had sired offspring by both white wives and black or mixed-race mistresses. As one New Iberian of African American and French ancestry told the late Glenn Conrad, founder of the Center for Louisiana Studies, "We *all* know who our white ancestors are." Historian Vaughan Burdin Baker, whose family can trace its roots to antebellum plantation owners in the Cane River country near Natchitoches, has written of Charlotte Broutin, a New Orleans woman of Afro-French parentage who moved to St. Martinville in the old Attakapas District in the late eighteenth century. Broutin bore French royal engineer Marin LeNormand six children prior to marrying him just months before his death in 1812. A substantial property owner in her own right, she and her legitimized children then "passed" into the white population. One of her daughters married the son of a prominent Cajun family; the groom subsequently produced one family with his Broutin wife and another with a mistress of color.[23] Some family names in the old "Mouton Addition" and other African American neighborhoods in Lafayette bear witness to the fact of shared black-white ancestries. This awareness of a shared genealogy was likely a factor in the negotiating of racial boundaries that was to come; certainly many of the African American students who matriculated in 1954 were products of that shared ancestry.

Fall 1954—Law and Order

Preregistration for the fall 1954 term at SLI began just five days after the injunction was issued. The first black student to register for classes was John Harold Taylor of Arnaudville, Louisiana, an engineering student who registered without incident on July 22, 1954. Claudette Arceneaux, who wanted to major in elementary education, had applied to SLI in early June for summer school, before the final judgment was rendered, but was denied on the grounds that J. Stewart Bonnet could not register her without prior authorization from the State Board of Education. She successfully preregistered for the fall term in July. In the final ten days of July, sixty-eight black students registered at SLI, fifty-five of them on or after July 27, as word of the success of the first dozen or so students undoubtedly spread throughout black communities around Lafayette. Five or six appear to have changed their minds before classes began, but a few more black students registered at the start of the fall semester, bringing the total to eighty, with female registrants outnumbering their male classmates by about two to one.[24]

The entire registration line at Martin Hall that fall—fronting on University Avenue, one of the town's busiest streets, and fully visible to passersby—was managed by Dean of Students Glynn Abel and one campus police officer. According to Abel he refused to allow *Life* magazine photographers to take pictures of the black students and persuaded the *Lafayette Daily Advertiser* not to publish the pictures its reporter had taken. Apparently there were no subsequent incidents of a magnitude sufficient to attract journalists. Dean Joseph A. Riehl observed that the registration was incident free, "and our students and faculty seem to be accepting the situation without fanfare or excitement. I suppose this is one of those periods in the life of an institution which tests its mettle, and I feel confident that we will stand the shock and come through without appreciable change. The passing of one era and the beginning of another does have its painful and unpleasant moments, however."[25]

According to one SLI professor and Catholic activist, Julius Gassner, preliminary reactions to the court decision were mixed. Some SLI faculty members were appalled; others were frightened (the government professor predicted violence and bloodshed); and still others welcomed the opportunity to work for racial justice. The public reaction was similarly mixed. One mother of an SLI coed wrote President Fletcher that she thought African Americans were untrustworthy: "you don't know when they might stab you, and . . . there is too many things that can happen." However, a local gas station operator said that he ate, worked, and hunted with blacks, so why not attend classes with them?[26]

Joseph Hardy of Lafayette said that in the public interest, the issues involved in the desegregation case should be clarified "before the barber shop pedagogues and the pool-room professors who are clacking about socialization, miscegenation, etc. thoroughly muddle up public understanding." In Hardy's mind, the desegregation of SLI was something of a moot point:

Segregation at S. L. I. has never been based on color but on accent. Black, brown, and yellow people have always attended S. L. I. but they either have had a Spanish or Asiatic accent. Their people, incidentally, have never paid a penny of tax money to support this institution. Further, if the president and other qualified members of the faculty are proud to act as government consultants for the betterment of conditions in Asia and Africa, the group as a whole should not object to practicing a little charity at home.

Furthermore, the students in question were qualified. They were graduates of Paul Breaux High School, which the school board assured the public was a highly rated institution.[27]

Hardy's letter came precariously close to raising one aspect of the issue that historians would later describe as "whiteness." Louisiana law adhered to the "one drop" rule, defining as black any person with any black ancestry. Black citizens were thus black even if seven of their eight great-grandparents were white, or fifteen of their sixteen great-great forebears. But what about "white" people with a black ancestor? Were they passing for white? When segregationists raised the Stars and Bars in defense of legalized racial barriers, they inevitably invited a discussion of Louisiana's much-mixed racial heritage and the social construction of whiteness and blackness. It was probably fortunate for the course of events in Lafayette that Joseph Hardy did not go there. However, in New Orleans, poet-historian Marcus Christian leaped at the opportunity to hoist segregationists on their own racist petards.[28]

In a series of essays for the *Louisiana Weekly*, Christian detailed the many contributions of black people and Creoles of color to Louisiana's history and challenged segregationist conceptions of exactly who was white and who was black based upon Louisiana's legal definition of blackness. Christian, undoubtedly the leading authority in the country on black Louisiana, noted that some people in New Orleans with some African ancestry, thought to be white, had been asked to join the Citizens' Council. So he wondered:

> If the Citizens Councils cannot differentiate between white and black in soliciting prospective member of admitted Negro blood, the question naturally arises as to their mode of determining the racial backgrounds of their present membership. What is the criteria by which is established the "purity" of their blood? With literally thousands of whites in Louisiana married to persons of some Negro blood or connected by marriage to persons of "tainted ancestry," how is it possible to separate the sheep from the goats?[29]

This issue was hardly unknown in Lafayette, and, by Louisiana's own measure, it is quite likely that those intrepid students of various colors who registered for SLI's fall session were not the first with some African ancestry to attend the school.

The first desegregated classes met on September 10, 1954, and the semester progressed without incident, although ten of the original total of eighty students—including two of the five young men who signed up for the Reserve Officers' Training Corps (ROTC)—had left school by early October. President Fletcher's top dean, Joseph A. Riehl, reported that white students and faculty had "taken this shock very calmly," but there is little to suggest that the new

SLI Bulldogs were welcomed with open arms. In the main, white and black students made little effort to notice each other. Black students attended classes, but were otherwise on the margins of campus life. President Fletcher's administrative team made clear their determination to provide quality education for SLI's newest students; Dean Riehl declared that they were "determined to avoid all incidents if possible. We are also going to give these students the best academic training of which we are capable." Beyond that, however, the commitment was limited. Black students did not live in the dormitories and did not eat in the dining hall. Not welcome in the campus student center, they sat in the commuter buses parked next to Earl Long gymnasium or congregated at the Catholic Student Center's Library Annex across the street. Detractors quickly dubbed this tree-shaded facility the "Liberian Annex."[30]

Several white parents withdrew their children from SLI, and at least two met with Registrar Bonnet to make certain that he understood the reason for their departure. According to Bonnet, "Everyone was afraid. . . . Everyone's afraid that you're going to intermarry. That's the big thing." That first year, a black Lake Charles brick mason met with Bonnet to ask if SLI would allow his son to live in the dormitory. Bonnet's response was that he was entitled to live on campus, but would probably be happier if he found housing in Lafayette's black community. "Let this thing develop a little bit," he said, "and maybe next year . . . people will become accustomed to it and it will be different then." Bonnet thought that a low profile was the best way for SLI's new African American students to deal with what Hamilton Holmes and Charlayne Hunter later experienced at the University of Georgia, what writer Calvin Trillin characterized as "an atmosphere of uncordiality." As for the integration of SLI's dormitories, the legislature's Joint Committee on Segregation delayed it indefinitely by including dormitories in state statutes forbidding the races to live together under the same roof.[31]

Acceptance, though grudging, came more easily because of the intellectual abilities of that first group of African American students. Longtime geography professor Robert Crisler characterized the experience for the first African American students as "traumatic": "But they weren't average. They were generally better qualified. They were from better-educated black homes and top students. . . . They wanted an education. They were willing to put themselves on the line to come here and be the pioneers." Gradually, some black and white students began speaking, especially at the Catholic Student Center. Another positive factor in this adjustment period was the attitude of the college's president, Joel Fletcher.[32]

Prior to becoming president in 1940, Fletcher's career as a professor and administrator had centered around programs that attracted deserving students and built the college. While he harbored mixed feelings about integration, his ambitions for students and SLI remained his focus. If desegregation was the law, then the college must achieve it in ways that advanced the larger mission of educational excellence and institutional growth. A modest but significant core of faculty and administrators shared this commitment, as can readily be detected in the interviews with faculty and administrators conducted by the University of Southwestern Louisiana (USL) Oral History Program in the early 1980s. They included younger professors who arrived in the middle of the decade, notably Milton Rickels and Patricia Rickels in the English department and Amos Simpson in history, as well as continuing faculty like Julius Gassner. Fletcher was particularly fortunate that Joe Riehl became dean of the college in 1955. Born in Washington, Louisiana, Riehl graduated from Lafayette's Cathedral High School and SLI, and worked for five years as an aide to U.S. senator Joseph E. Ransdell, before completing an M.A. in political science at Georgetown in 1933. Riehl came to SLI as an assistant professor of history in 1933 and rose through the ranks, serving as registrar, dean of Liberal Arts, and director of SLI's navy V-12 program during World War II. Loyal, unselfish, and an exceptionally capable administrator, Riehl saw to it that Fletcher's views were reflected in the day-to-day operation of the college.[33]

Tactically, the administration solicited cooperation and discouraged publicity. Fletcher had "no comment" on the court decision. Before black enrollment began at SLI, he traveled the state, informing influential people of his plans and asking their assistance. A campus human relations council composed of faculty and students was established to discuss the problems that black students faced and to work toward solutions. That fall, the registration situation was so well managed that the *New Orleans Times-Picayune* reported only that the presence of black students "apparently did not create unusual interest or action on the part of other students." Despite Bonnet's spirited insistence, Fletcher refused to allow him to note any student's race on the registration cards, and was then able to say that he had no figures on the number of black students who had entered.[34]

Geography also worked in SLI's favor. Louisiana's predominantly Catholic Cajun minority had some understanding of what it meant to be outside the mainstream. Cajun children could go to segregated white schools, but their culture could not. After World War I especially, Cajun schoolchildren were humiliated and otherwise punished if they spoke French at school. Thus did the dominant Anglo-Protestant culture disparage both Cajuns and African Americans who had, if not common cause, at least a common enemy. Though by no means racially liberal, Cajun culture, noted for its joie de vivre, exhibited more of a laissez faire attitude toward change than did its Anglo-Protestant counterpart. Lafayette's ethnic and religious diversity thus worked to produce a kind of tolerance. Desegregation would test that tolerance, and not all would pass the examination, but, as Missouri native Robert Crisler remarked: "the people here in south Louisiana as opposed to people in Alabama or north Louisiana are a little bit more willing to accept that sort of change, [they have] a live and let live sort of philosophy . . . perhaps because they themselves feel that being Catholic and speaking French they are different from the rest of the people in the South themselves."[35] Finally, there was also a critical mass of people of goodwill—including businessmen like Herbert Heymann and Catholic clergy like Bishop Jules Jeanmard and Father Alexander Sigur—who used their influence wisely and well. There were no spitting, cursing crowds as in Little Rock or New Orleans.

On campus, it was easier to control events. In that much different era in college life, in loco parentis was still an omnipresent reality, complete with dress codes for women and rigorous dormitory supervision. Many of the commuters arrived by school bus, as if they were still going to high school. If Fletcher's paternalistic appeals to their better instincts did not work, sterner measures would follow. Faculty and administrators knew what, at a minimum, was expected of them. Louisiana state college presidents answered to the State Board of Education and the legislature, but to few others. If they were visibly successful, as Joel Fletcher was, they were lords of their respective realms, and only the foolish or terribly naive would fail to realize that.

There were problems, of course. That first year, four black couples attended a student dance, further stressing already frayed administrative nerves; there were no incidents, but there were also no more dances for some time. Swimming classes were discontinued because the local pool would not allow African American students to use its facility. When a class in audiovisual education was going to see movie projectors in operation at a local theater, the teacher advised the lone black student in the class to seek individual instruction at one of the theaters for blacks. One student, C. S. Trotter, complained in September 1955 that black students were unable to do practice teaching, thus delaying or preventing them from completing degree requirements. As a married, working student with four children, the delay threatened to impose a considerable hardship on Trotter. SLI's explanation was that the State Department of Education had made no arrangements and that something would be done at some future date.[36]

Desegregation Spreads, Then Stalls

As SLI wrestled with desegregation, suits against three other Louisiana state colleges—McNeese State (Lake Charles), Southeastern Louisiana (Hammond), and Northwestern State (Natchitoches)—proceeded. Judge Edwin F. Hunter Jr.'s December 1954 ruling in *Hilda V. Combre v. John McNeese State College* led to the desegregation of McNeese in spring semester 1955, when twenty-four African American students enrolled without incident; black enrollment there more than tripled that fall. Judge Herbert Christenberry's ruling in *Thomas C. Wells v. Luther H. Dyson* did much the same at Southeastern that summer, with a similar increase in the fall. Both decisions cited the *Constantine* ruling as precedent. McNeese's president, Lethar Frazier, and Southeastern's leader, Luther Dyson, each capably employed Joel Fletcher's minimalist approach to handling the desegregation process.[37]

At none of the three south Louisiana campuses did quiescence signify welcome. Smoldering resentment of these new students at all levels of campus life meant that these desegregation pioneers, the majority of them female, endured persistent stress, reinforced periodically by calculated efforts to hurt and humiliate. Many, if not most, whites associated with the campuses understood that, while they were required to respect the letter of the law, they could not be made to embrace its spirit. After fifty years, a number of these early African American students at SLI remain convinced that they were "graded down" because of their color. Some spoke, with a depth of feeling that made the events described seem as though they had occurred yesterday, of slights and studied insults. Such incidents were by no means universal, nor were they necessarily constant. But the wounds were deep, and they endured.

The nineteen students suing to enter Northwestern State College in north Louisiana's Cane River country did not fare even this well. Filed on April 22, 1955, the suit was a victim of A. P. Tureaud's overburdened caseload; an unsympathetic judge, Benjamin C. Dawkins Jr.; and increasingly well organized white resistance to any threatened breaches in the wall of segregation. By October 1956, sixteen of the plaintiffs, citing "circumstances beyond their control," had withdrawn from the suit, which in 1962 was finally dismissed for want of prosecution.[38]

The failure in Natchitoches, at Northwestern State, crippled the movement to desegregate the remainder of the state colleges. Ruston, home to Louisiana Tech, and Monroe, the site of Northeast Louisiana College, were, if anything, even less hospitable to desegregation. Furthermore, in 1956 Louisiana secured a permanent injunction against NAACP activity because the organization refused to provide membership lists so that the state could search for suspected Communists. That ban lasted until 1961, when the U.S. Supreme Court invalidated Louisiana's laws against the NAACP. Save for the court-ordered desegregation in 1958 of Louisiana State University's new branch at New Orleans, there was not another breach of the racial barrier in Louisiana's public system of higher education until *Edward Baker v. Francis T. Nicholls State College* in 1963.[39]

Even as the white resistance marshaled its forces, the 1955–56 term brought SLI more African American students, many of them transfers. In all, 125 black students were enrolled in fall 1955, 87 of them in the College of Education. The Lafayette campus seemed to be accepting desegregation as a fait accompli and, according to an optimistic Julius Gassner, "interracial fellowship was coming into existence." ROTC dances had been desegregated, and an interracial meeting of the Gulf States Newman Clubs at the SLI Catholic Student Center in April 1956 was a resounding success. SLI's first black graduate, Christiana G. Smith, received her diploma on May 19, 1956, even though she marched without a partner when the young white woman paired with her refused to march next to a person of color. Smith was a forty-year-old teacher who had graduated in 1937 from the Sacred Heart Normal School and had since pieced together enough college credits that she completed the degree requirements during fall 1955.[40]

In 1956, the state legislature undermined this progress when it passed Bill No. 15, which required that all students submit a certificate of good moral character signed by their high school principal and the local superintendent. A companion act made it a crime punishable by dismissal for any teacher or school official to advocate integration. State Senator Willie Rainach, chairman of the Joint Legislative Committee on Segregation, made it clear that signing a certificate of good moral character for a black student applying to a traditionally white college constituted advocacy of integration.[41]

This new legislation was clearly designed to end the integration already accomplished at Southwestern Louisiana, McNeese State, and Southeastern Louisiana. Not only did the new laws cause consternation among Louisiana blacks who hoped soon to be studying at SLI and other such schools in the state, but also just how these provisions applied to current students was by no means clear. The uncertainty derived from Louisiana attorney general J. P. F. "Jack" Gremillion's successive interpretations of Bill No. 15. First he ruled that the requirement for certificates of good moral character applied to all students, new and returning. Then, in response to a query from the president of Louisiana Tech, he declared that it applied only to new students. That in turn produced vigorous protest from State Senator Willie Rainach, leader of the legislature's segregation forces, and considerable uncertainty among students about which rule would apply. Lafayette District Attorney Bertrand DeBlanc warned President Fletcher that it applied to all students and that he would file charges if SLI violated the law as he understood it.[42]

These laws, part of a segregationist package of legislation designed to thwart the *Brown* decision, were vociferously opposed by the Catholic Church and a few intrepid legislators. Whatever his own beliefs, DeBlanc's interpretation reflected the powerful segregationist influences in the legislature and in emergent segregationist organizations around the state.[43]

Federal judges Herbert Christenberry and J. Skelly Wright declared both acts unconstitutional in 1957, rulings that the Fifth U.S. Circuit Court of Appeals upheld the next year. But in the short run, the uncertainties and tensions generated by the acts caused a sharp drop in black enrollment. At SLI, McNeese, Southeastern, and LSU, black enrollment dropped by half, from a total of about 400 students to approximately 200. Clayton Arceneaux, a GI mustered out of the service after the Korean War, attended Grambling instead of SLI because Paul Breaux High School principal W. D. Smith could not sign a certificate of good moral character for him without jeopardizing his job. Another SLI student who transferred to Grambling said that he couldn't take a chance about his studies in Lafayette. One applicant in 1956, Thaddus Wilson, was unaffected by the new legislation—he was a graduate that year from Lincoln High School in Port Arthur, Texas. Julius Gassner said that in September 1956, there were so few African American students at SLI "that the campus all but lost the right to be called integrated."[44] In the long run, of course, SLI remained desegregated, its minority enrollment recovered after the offending laws were struck down, and the remaining state colleges were also desegregated in the early 1960s.

Desegregation and Institutional Development

In 1960, the year that SLI became the University of Southwestern Louisiana (USL), some twenty outstanding graduates of Paul Breaux High School, inspired by the growing strength of the civil rights movement and determined to broaden African American participation in campus life, turned down academic and athletic scholarships at other institutions to go to college in Lafayette. They did not win their battles immediately. When the new male African American students decided to shave their heads and wear beanies, as other male freshmen did, the tradition was discontinued. They pressed for access to the dormitories and the dining halls, for participation in intramural sports, and, in 1963, for recognition for a chapter of Alpha Phi Alpha, a national black fraternity. Their chapter had to remain off-campus when they refused to sign an agreement not to admit white students.[45] Their insistent courage inspired others and led to the gradual opening up of campus facilities and activities.

When the dormitories were opened to black students in the early 1960s, it seemed only natural to housing officials that black students would have black roommates. Natural, that is, until Thetis Simpson came along. A self-described "faculty brat," she was the daughter of historian Amos Simpson and Anne Simpson of the School of Music. In 1964, she lived in Foster Hall, then the freshman women's dormitory, and joined the Young Ambassadors, an interracial group whose purpose was to promote integration in Lafayette and improve race relations on campus. At that point, all black coeds who resided on campus were housed in one wing of Bonin Hall. That separation ended in 1965 when Thetis Simpson and a black Ambassador, Gwen Sigur from Alexandria, announced that they wanted to be roommates in Bonin Hall. The dean of women, fearing that they would be harassed, tried unsuccessfully to dissuade them. Save for one ugly note shoved under their door, Simpson and Sigur roomed together without incident.[46]

Thetis Simpson left Lafayette following her graduation in 1968. When she returned in 1974, she was unable to believe the changes, especially the much larger percentage of black students and the degree to which they participated in campus life. Perhaps the key factor in this change was the university's leadership in desegregating college basketball in Louisiana. On the surface, this seems an odd assertion, but coach Beryl Shipley's courageous decision to break the color barrier by recruiting three black high school all-Americans for his 1966 team had far-reaching consequences. First, it attracted the wrath of the State Board of Education, which refused athletic scholarships to the recruits and then invited a National Collegiate Athletic Association (NCAA) investigation, and probation, when Shipley found scholarship money for the players in Lafayette's black community. Shipley had already drawn the board's ire the previous year when he accepted an invitation to have his all-white team participate in the National Association of Intercollegiate Athletes (NAIA) playoffs, where they would have to face integrated teams, in violation of a moribund segregationist statute (it had already been overturned in the courts) forbidding interracial sports competition by Louisianans.[47]

Second, the advent of highly talented black players fueled the meteoric rise to prominence of Ragin' Cajun basketball. Following a two-year probation during which the school was ineligible for postseason competition, and a rebuilding season in 1969–70, the 1970–71 Cajuns posted a 24–4 record, and their sophomore guard, Dwight Lamar, led the college division in scoring with a 36–point average. The following year, competing at the major college level for the first time, the 25–4 Cajuns won a bid to the sixteen-team NCAA tournament, becoming the first Louisiana team in fourteen years to participate. Lamar led the nation in scoring again with a 36.3–point average, becoming the only player ever to win both small college and major college scoring titles. Lamar was named first team all-American, and sophomore center Roy Ebron garnered honorable mention. The team was selected to the NCAA tournament for the second consecutive year, at one point ranking as high as number four in the national polls.[48] Their success filled Blackham Coliseum to capacity, and more, with delighted community members and students who came to cheer "their" team. It greatly widened the acceptance of black students on campus while providing all students with a source of shared pride.

Another, less well known development in the greater inclusion of African Americans in the school's life was in academics. By the mid-1960s, USL's history department boasted three professors publishing in the field of what was then called black history. Two of them, James Dormon and Robert R. Jones, secured a National Defense Education Act (NDEA) grant for a Summer Institute in Afro-American History and Culture to be held on the Lafayette campus. The institute's purpose was to help high school teachers better understand black history and culture as they confronted integration of the public schools. The theme of the conference was Jim Dormon's idea that black history was tied to a unique black culture. Thirty participants—black and white—from all over the country came to Lafayette that summer; they listened to music in rural black nightclubs and saw the Dashiki Players from New Orleans perform Jean Genet's play *The Blacks*. They heard then-Marxist historian Eugene Genovese hold forth on black religion. Alex Haley came to talk about Malcolm X, though in his briefcase was what later became *Roots*, and he also lectured on his ancestry, and Kunta Kinte. In addition, participants attended a public meeting of the Lafayette Parish School Board on school integration, where they heard a prominent white local insurance agency owner say that he didn't want his children in school with people who, he thought, carried knives. Two of the black participants, imposing former athletes, played softball with history and English department members in a city recreation league that was just beginning to be integrated. Quite a few of the participants, black and white, went on to earn master's degrees in history. One, former Kansas State basketball player Ken Hamilton, earned a doctorate and embarked on a teaching career in St. Louis.[49]

As the 1960s gave way to the 1970s, there was continued resistance as well. Faced with looming public school integration, Lafayette segregationists founded W. B. Vennard Academy to promote racial purity and other Christian principles as they understood them. South Louisiana voters warmed to the Republican Party's "Southern Strategy" in 1968. At Modern Music recording studio and music shop in Crowley, half an hour or so west of Lafayette, three solo artists—Johnny Rebel, Happy Fats, and Son of Mississippi—recorded a series of segregationist anthems for Reb Rebel Records in the late 1960s. Collected on an album titled "For Segregationists Only," the songs ranged in content from Johnny Rebel's epithet-laced "Move Them Niggers North" to the subtler, more coded protests found in Happy Fats's "Dear Mr. President." Rebel had a substantial underground hit with "Kajun Klu Klux Klan," which apparently sold more than 100,000 copies, primarily through Klan publications and most notably at the Klan's booth at the annual North Carolina State Fair.[50] Leroy

"Happy Fats" Leblanc, a Cajun music pioneer, became a kind of conservative celebrity in south Louisiana, developing a local television variety show that showcased his folksy manner, and appealing especially to those discovering that they were conservatives rather than simply racists.

A Community and a School—A Case Study from the Deep South

Meanwhile, public attention, never very much focused on this important episode in the desegregation of southern state colleges and universities, shifted first to other fronts in the civil rights revolution and then to the Vietnam War. Mirroring media coverage of the most visible features of the movement at places well known to viewers and listeners, scholars understandably focused on the most active battlefronts and the generals who led the competing forces. Writing on the legal campaign against segregation in higher education invariably leapfrogs from the *Sweatt* and *McLaurin* cases to *Brown* and the rise of "massive resistance." Scholars of the struggle to translate *Brown* into more fully integrated higher education typically move from that point to Autherine Lucy and James Meredith and other highly publicized desegregation episodes, with due emphasis on the resultant turmoil.

SLI's desegregation attracted so little media attention that this historic event appears in almost none of the scholarship on civil rights.[51] The result has been an incomplete and even skewed portrait of desegregation, one that unduly emphasizes the sensational and flagship universities. *Constantine* marked a further erosion of *Plessy*'s enshrinement of injustice. It produced the first undergraduate desegregation of a state-supported four-year college in the Deep South and led directly, if not entirely expeditiously, to the end of segregation at other colleges in Louisiana. Unlike the initial black enrollments of one or two students elsewhere, SLI's was a large-scale desegregation. It was participated in by men but largely led by women. It measured the leadership and character of the community in which it occurred. Able campus leadership notwithstanding, the process was traumatic, especially for that historically large, but institutionally small, cohort of African American students who led the way. The relatively positive view of desegregation at SLI is based largely on interviews with whites who were present and involved in the process. Geography professor Robert Crisler suggested that the trauma associated with desegregation was substantial, and Patricia Rickels and others have emphasized that, because the process was relatively peaceful, a myth quickly developed, especially among whites, that the experience was not a painful or costly one.

The outward peace of the occasion led many whites to later remember the event as evidence of their magnanimity. While it was not that simple, the fact that it happened at a small state college in Lafayette, Louisiana, favored its success, as did the deliberately low-key approach of school leaders. Mary Dichmann, whose career included stints as English department head and dean of the College of Arts and Sciences, thought that Fletcher's careful groundwork was crucial: "I think that this accounts for everything going as well as it did at USL. In fact, it went so well that people away from Lafayette, I think even people in Louisiana, didn't know for ten or fifteen years that USL was integrated."[52]

In some respects the desegregation of SLI is unavoidably a story of narrow-mindedness and of bigotry. But it is also a human saga of individual courage, magnanimity, and the leadership of a community pulling together to do what the law required, peaceably and with a small measure of equanimity. They did so reluctantly and imperfectly. But they did it. Most of all, the magnitude of the contribution of "black" people of all hues, and especially their courage, should not be underestimated. Following a 1953 Lafayette Parish school board meeting where those resolute mothers made known what was already known, that is, what the parents of students at the Paul Breaux School were demanding for their children, the parish school superintendent, looking for leverage, confronted Helma Constantine. "Who do you work for?" he demanded. "Not you," she retorted. His was the white-collar version of pressure on quietly heroic people across the South who, each in his or her own way, were risking their livelihoods and their psyches in the struggle for recognition of their humanity and full citizenship.[53]

In 1956, the Southern Manifesto made "massive resistance" to desegregation regional policy, and Dixie's politicians devoted themselves to a twentieth-century, working- and middle-class version of what historian Albert D. Kirwan termed Mississippi's 1890s "revolt of the rednecks." Louisiana was not immune to this plague; indeed it was a leader. The ignominious 1956 legislative session produced segregationist statutes that were models for other racist rebels. But by then, SLI had been demonstrating the possibility of interracial cooperation for two years, an achievement that stands in stark contrast to the failures in Little Rock, in New Orleans, and later in Oxford, Mississippi. The racists slowed this tide of history but, like King Canute in the old English legend, they could not forestall it.[54]

It is now a truism that the civil rights revolution liberated not just black southerners but the entire region. As was the case with the South itself, SLI's desegregation proved to be a liberating force that opened up new possibilities for a historically ambitious school that had begun its existence as the smallest of the white state colleges. SLI's desegregation and the racist response to it in the legislature and other parts of state government produced something of a siege mentality that imbued SLI with an emergent new identity and a desire to be something more than a regional teacher's college. Most of SLI's early African American students were from its immediate service region. Nonetheless, these students were a major factor in the erosion of SLI's insularity. Desegregation made its competition for state funds and favors decidedly more difficult, but it also enabled SLI, for the first time, to compete for newly minted Ph.D.s from well outside the region. While substantially enhancing its academic reputation, especially in the humanities, the addition of ambitious, talented, and sometimes renowned scholars to an already solid core of faculty made the university more attractive to top students beyond the state. Importantly, the other state colleges had similar experiences of what might be termed material and moral growth following their desegregations.

There were shortcomings and setbacks to be sure. The USL basketball program suffered yet another round of NCAA penalties, first because of its own failures of oversight and control, but partly because it had upset the balance of power in college basketball, especially in the South. While black students came to feel considerably more at home on campus, and the university developed significant strengths in black history and literature, black students remained unwelcome in traditionally white student enclaves such as "The Strip," an off-campus conglomeration of nightspots and restaurants. This remained true even in the 1980s. At one point, in the 1990s, there was controversy over the school's distinctive Ragin' Cajun moniker, as some black students questioned whether that logo could really include them comfortably.

Even in 2004, half a century after the breakthrough 1954 court case that opened the school to black enrollment, there continued to exist the clannishness, the separation that observers of race relations can find on almost any college campus. But there was by then also abundant evidence of students of different colors comfortable with each other, on campus and off. Jim Caillier, one of those Paul Breaux students who matriculated in 1960, had a remarkable career in Louisiana higher education, one that culminated with his presidency of the Louisiana system of state colleges and universities. Approximately one of every six students on the Lafayette campus was of African American heritage. There was a vibrant Christiana G. Smith Alumni Chapter for black alumni. Shawn Wilson, a former Smith Chapter president, became president of the university's alumni association. Renamed yet again, the University of Louisiana at Lafayette's distinguished doctoral program in English long featured one of the country's greatest writers, Louisianan Ernest J. Gaines, as its writer in residence.

Shawn Wilson and University of Louisiana at Lafayette assistant professor of history Michael Martin were key figures in organizing a fiftieth-anniversary commemoration of SLI's desegregation. It included a two-day academic conference featuring scholars from an impressive range of universities on both sides of the Atlantic, the hosting of desegregation pioneers and their families by President Raymond Authement, and the installation of campus historical markers acknowledging their sizable contribution to the university's history and to the civil rights movement in American higher education. Though the academic presentations were certainly worthwhile, easily the highlight of the event was the opportunity to hear Helen Reaux Gordon, Helma Constantine, Juanita Jackson Thibeaux, and others talk movingly about the intense inner stress of those days when desegregation was new and alarming. Making it an important episode in civil rights history were the way in which they met that challenge, the magnitude of this experiment in racial justice, and its long-term success.

Historians Armstead Robinson and Patricia Sullivan have argued that "more attention must be concentrated on the origins, process, and outcome of civil rights struggles in local communities before the movement and its consequences can be fully understood," for "all too often, scholars emphasize the interracialism of the *Brown* decade and the role of the federal government instead of focusing on the vital and essential role played by black initiative before, during, and after the *Brown* decade."[55] In southern higher education, this is a clear call for a case-by-case examination of the desegregation experience on individual campuses, not least to determine the degree to which the well-documented experiences at Alabama and Ole Miss, or even at Georgia and Clemson, are representative of college desegregation generally, but also to determine the role played by local communities in the process. Fortunately, this challenge is to some extent now being met.

Case studies of other schools and regions also will inspire questions about the oft-supposed homogeneity of the Deep South on the verge of the civil rights revolution; south Louisiana certainly raises that issue. Evidence that local citizens initiated their own civil rights challenges may make it more difficult for unreconstructed segregationists to interpret the efforts of earlier confederates as resistance to government tyranny and outside agitators. Proponents of civil rights will discover a new, larger cast of heroes whose stories richly merit telling, even as neo-confederates continue their enshrinement of the James Eastlands and Lester Maddoxes. These issues should be of considerable interest not only to scholars but also to policy makers in a period of growing environmental, population, and resource limits when issues of race, education, and opportunity will become more, rather than less, important.[56]

Notes

1. Helma Constantine, interview by author, September 15, 2004, Lafayette, La., tapes/notes in author's possession; "400 Students Stage Strike in Lafayette," *Lafayette Daily Advertiser*, February 25, 1953; "Equal Facilities Asked in Local School Strike,"

Lafayette Daily Advertiser, February 26, 1953; "Students Return to Paul Breaux Monday," *Lafayette Daily Advertiser*, February 27, 1953; "School Strike Nears End," *New York Times*, February 28, 1953; "Local Parents Demand Paul Breaux Changes," *Lafayette Daily Advertiser*, March 1, 1953; "School Board Answers Questions on Strike Termed 'Unwarranted,'" *Lafayette Daily Advertiser*, March 5, 1953. Paul Breaux High School was named in honor of the leading figure in education for the black community. Paul Breaux and his wife came to Lafayette in 1887 to teach classes at one local church and then another, this one the Good Hope Baptist Church, and Breaux later opened the four-room Washington Street School for the community's black children.

2. The first historically white four-year public institution of higher education in the former Confederacy to admit an African American undergraduate in the twentieth century was Virginia Polytechnic Institute, which admitted Irving L. Peddrew in 1953. See the essay by Peter Wallenstein in this volume.

3. Barbara Ann Worthy, "The Travail and Triumph of a Southern Black Civil Rights Lawyer: The Legal Career of Alexander Pierre Tureaud, 1899–1972" (Ph.D. diss., Tulane University, 1984), 93–118. Detailed later in this essay are desegregation suits against McNeese State College and Southeastern Louisiana College. A similar action against Northwestern State College in 1955, *Hamp Williams et al. v. Northwestern State College*, faltered when only three of the nineteen plaintiffs proved willing to press the suit to a conclusion. Ten years later, a desegregation order resulted from *Pearl Jones Burton et al. v. Northwestern State College*. In 1965, A. P. Tureaud represented white civil rights activist Mary E. Jamieson when Grambling denied her application for admission, a scenario undoubtedly encouraged by legendary Grambling president Ralph Waldo Emerson Jones. Judge E. Gordon West, who had ordered Louisiana Tech to admit blacks two months earlier, also ruled in favor of Jamieson.

4. Richard Kluger, *Simple Justice: The History of* Brown v. Board of Education *and Black America's Struggle for Equality* (New York: Random House, 1975), 155–58, 187–95; Worthy, "Travail and Triumph," 60–61, 71. See also Edward J. Kuebler, "The Desegregation of the University of Maryland," *Maryland Historical Magazine* 71 (Spring 1976): 37–49. For the origins of college segregation, see John Hope Franklin, "Jim Crow Goes to College: The Genesis of Legal Segregation in the Southern Schools," *South Atlantic Quarterly* 58 (1959): 225–35.

5. Worthy, "Travail and Triumph," 71–75.

6. David R. Goldfield, *Black, White, and Southern: Race Relations and Southern Culture, 1940 to the Present* (Baton Rouge: Louisiana State University Press, 1990), 58–59; Kluger, *Simple Justice*, 266–84; Worthy, "Travail and Triumph," 75–76. See also John T. Hubbell, "The Desegregation of the University of Oklahoma, 1946–1950," *Journal of Negro History* 57 (October 1972): 370–84; John T. Hubbell, "Some Reactions to the Desegregation of the University of Oklahoma, 1946–1950," *Phylon* 34 (June 1973): 187–96; Michael L. Gillette, "Blacks Challenge the White University," *Southwestern Historical Quarterly* 86 (October 1982): 321–44; and Alton Hornsby Jr., "The 'Colored Branch University' Issue in Texas—Prelude to *Sweatt v. Painter*," *Journal of Negro History* 64 (Fall 1979): 316–41.

7. Kluger, *Simple Justice*, 287–88, 291–94; Worthy, "Travail and Triumph," 76–81.

8. Kluger, *Simple Justice*, 289–90.

9. Worthy, "Triumph and Travail," 83–85. The term "broad-based" is used here to distinguish the SLI story, which was truly exceptional, from the admittance of a black undergraduate to study engineering at Virginia Polytechnic Institute in 1953 followed by three more black students in 1954 (see note 2). Those admissions fell under the "graduate and professional" category related to the litigation that extended from the 1930s into the 1950s.

10. Velma Hollier, interview, n.d., Lafayette, La., in the J. Carlton James Oral History Project, Southwestern Archives and Manuscripts Collection (SAMC), Dupre Library, University of Louisiana at Lafayette (ULL); George T. Madison to A. P. Tureaud, January 11, 1954, A. P. Tureaud Papers, Box 65, File 21, Amistad Research Center (hereafter cited as ARC), Howard-Tilton Memorial Library, Tulane University, New Orleans; Daniel Byrd to A. P. Tureaud, September 17, 1953, Tureaud Papers, Box 65, File 21, ARC; *Constantine et al. v. Southwestern Louisiana Institute et al.*, U.S. District Court, Western District of Louisiana, 102 F.Supp. 417 (1954) (hereafter cited as *Constantine v. SLI*); "4 Negroes Seek Entrance to SLI," *Lafayette Daily Advertiser*, January 5, 1954. Byrd, an NAACP field secretary present when the four were denied admission by SLI's registrar, had requested that Tureaud file the appeal. Byrd noted that Registrar J. Stuart Bonnet was "very courteous and nice" about the matter. He was also amazed to learned that SLI's fees were apparently much cheaper than those at Southern and Grambling. In the suit, Byrd wanted to ask the court to enjoin the State Board of Education from denying black students admission to any of the state colleges.

11. U. Simpson Tate to Robert L. Carter, December 30, 1953, Tureaud Papers, Box 65, File 21, ARC; *Dictionary of Louisiana Biography*, vol. 2, s.v. "Tureaud, Alexander Pierre," by Joseph Logsdon; *Constantine v. SLI*.

12. The plaintiffs contended that because the Louisiana legislature had acted to create LSU for whites and Southern for blacks, "and over and above that to distribute six State-supported colleges strategically in the several sections of the State for the convenience of its majority white citizens and has failed to provide similar facilities in the same sections for its minority Negro race, its legal obligation to its citizens is the same, as though it had set up college districts." *Constantine v. SLI*, Complaint, 8; *Constantine v. SLI*, Plaintiff's Memorandum of Law, March 17, 1954, 11.

13. Tureaud requested these statements from the plaintiffs; beyond that, to avoid potentially embarrassing publicity, he wanted them to maintain a discreet silence, so he advised them to refer all requests for public statements on the case to him. Martha Jane Conway to A. P. Tureaud, January 10, 1954; Shirley Taylor to Tureaud, January 12, 1954; Clara Dell Constantine to Tureaud, January 13, 1954; Charles Vincent Singleton to Tureaud, January 9, 1954; Taylor to Tureaud, January 10, 1954; and A. P. Tureaud to Clara Dell Constantine, Martha Jane Conway, Shirley Taylor, and Charles V. Singleton, January 2, 1954, all in Tureaud Papers, Box 65, File 21, ARC.

14. J. W. Peltason, *Fifty-eight Lonely Men: Southern Federal Judges and School Desegregation* (New York: Harcourt, Brace and World, 1961), 133, 227; *Biographical Dictionary of the Federal Judiciary*, 26; Worthy, "Travail and Triumph," 153. Judge Dawkins—described by Peltason (133) as "one of the more ardent segregationists serving on the

federal bench"—was appointed in 1953 to succeed his father, who had held the position since 1924. Judge Borah, a Truman appointee to the Fifth Circuit Court of Appeals, was a Republican well connected in New Orleans social circles; educated at Phillips Exeter, Washington and Lee, the University of Virginia, and LSU, he was in his thirtieth year on the bench when he heard the *Constantine* case.

15. Robert L. Carter to A. P. Tureaud, February 5, 1954, Tureaud Papers, Box 65, File 22, ARC; Order of Hon. Joseph C. Hutcheson Jr., Chief Judge, Fifth Circuit, January 7, 1954, Civil Action No. 4401, U.S. District Court for the Western District of Louisiana; *Constantine v. SLI*, Memorandum of Law, March 17, 1954, 6–7; *Constantine v. SLI*, Opinion of Judge Edwin F. Hunter Jr., April 23, 1954, 1; U. Simpson Tate to A. P. Tureaud, December 3, 1953, and A. P. Tureaud to Robert L. Carter, Assistant Council, NAACP, January 19, 1954, Tureaud Papers, Box 65, File 21, ARC.

16. U. Simpson Tate to Edwin F. Hunter Jr., February 10, 1954, and A. P. Tureaud to U. Simpson Tate, February 22, 1954, both in Tureaud Papers, Box 65, File 22, ARC; James J. Davidson Jr. to Joel L. Fletcher, January 28, 30, 1954, Joel L. Fletcher Papers, SAMC; *Constantine v. SLI*, Docket.

17. *Constantine v. SLI*, 419. Hunter said the issues in the Louisiana case were almost identical to those in a Texas case from the previous year, *Wichita Falls Junior College District v. Battle*, 204 F.2d 632 (1953), except that the commuting distances in that matter were 367 or 411 miles; see also U.S. Commission on Civil Rights, *Equal Protection of the Laws in Public Higher Education 1960* (Washington, D.C.: Government Printing Office, 1960; reprint, New York: Greenwood Press, 1968), 39.

18. *Constantine v. SLI*, 421 (as one precedent for this interpretation, Hunter cited *Westminster School District of Orange County v. Mendez*, 161 F.2d 774 [1947]); "Federal Judges Order SLI to Admit Negro Students," *Lafayette Daily Advertiser*, April 23, 1954.

19. In *Frasier v. Board of Trustees*, 134 F.Supp. 589 (1955), a federal court applied the *Brown* decision to the University of North Carolina, and the U.S. Supreme Court in 1956 upheld the lower court. See appendix 8; Peter Wallenstein, "Higher Education and the Civil Rights Movement: Desegregating the University of North Carolina," in *Warm Ashes: Issues in Southern History at the Dawn of the Twenty-first Century*, ed. Winfred B. Moore Jr., Kyle S. Sinisi, and David H. White Jr. (Columbia: University of South Carolina Press, 2003), 280–300. Not an admirer of Governor Kennon, Fletcher later said: "The integration of Southwestern has not been an easy cross to carry, but I determined that I would not let the shenanigans of Robert Kennon or anyone else injure this university; and so, for eight years, we have been successful, through the cooperation of businessmen, student leaders, and faculty to make academic progress in spite of this burden." Autobiographical materials, Fletcher Papers, Collection 12, Box 28, Folder 4, SAMC.

20. *Constantine v. SLI*, Judgment, July 16, 1954; *Equal Protection of the Laws in Public Higher Education 1960*, 70; W. C. Perrault to Shelby M. Jackson, July 26, 1954, USL Papers, Presidential Series, Box 205–m, SAMC. The commission's report states that five black students were enrolled for summer school in 1954.

21. For glimpses of the history of Lafayette or SLI, see Mario Mamalakis, "Alexandre

Mouton Donates Land for a Jewish Temple," *Advertiser Centennial*, 83; Amos E. Simpson, ed., *Southwestern Louisiana Institute: A Self Study* (Lafayette, La: Southwestern Louisiana Institute, 1960), in SAMC, on the school's various names; Michael G. Wade, "Farm Dorm Boys: The Origins of the NYA Resident Training Program," *Louisiana History* 37 (Spring 1986): 117–33, on New Deal programs at SLI; and Andrew Michael Garber, "The Miracle Mile: The Heymann Oil Center and the Oil Economy of Lafayette, Louisiana, 1953–1998" (Master's thesis, Appalachian State University, 1998). A useful reference, if treated judiciously, is J. Philip Dismukes, *The Center: A History of the Development of Lafayette, Louisiana* (Lafayette, La.: City of Lafayette, 1972); Dismukes asserts that Lafayette's development has been guided by a traditionally strong middle class. A considerable scholarly literature on Cajun history and culture has emerged. On cultural considerations, a good beginning point is James H. Dormon, *The People Called Cajuns: An Introduction to an Ethnohistory* (Lafayette, La.: Center for Louisiana Studies, 1983). On the Acadian diaspora, Acadian descendant Carl Brasseaux's *The Founding of New Acadia: The Beginnings of Acadian Life in Louisiana, 1765–1803* (Baton Rouge: Louisiana State University Press, 1987) has supplanted earlier works. On the African cultural contribution to south Louisiana, see Gwendolyn Midlo Hall, *Africans in Colonial Louisiana: The Development of Afro-Creole Culture in the Eighteenth Century* (Baton Rouge: Louisiana State University Press, 1992); and James H. Dormon, ed., *Creoles of Color of the Gulf South* (Knoxville: University of Tennessee Press, 1996).

22. Sources on the Academy of the Sacred Heart are an interview with Headmistress Mary Burns by Michael Wade, May 9, 2003, Grand Coteau, La.; and "Alumnae Meet at College of Sacred Heart," *Catholic Action of the South*, October 15, 1953, 7. Mother Lapeyre's explanation was that "a Catholic college is open to all properly qualified students." Pope Leo XIII's 1883 encyclical, *Rerum Novarum*, condemned racial discrimination as contrary to God's word. Church periodicals for south Louisiana readers, such as the *Southwest Louisiana Register* and *Catholic Action of the South*, are filled with evidence of the Church's position, and with actions taken to support it. These publications display a blend of racial liberalism and cultural conservatism, as they attack segregation while excoriating rock and roll; the common ground would seem to be that they regarded both phenomena as the work of the devil. As for Willie Francis, Arthur S. Miller's *Death by Installments: The Ordeal of Willie Francis* (New York: Greenwood Press, 1988) is competent, but not nearly as haunting as Mary Alice Fontenot's unpublished "Swing Low, Sweet Chariot: Willie Francis Rides Twice," Mary Alice Fontenot Papers, Collection 97, Box 7, Folder 15, SAMC.

23. Vaughan B. Baker, "Transcending Policy: Crossing Racial and Gender Boundaries in Spanish Louisiana" (paper presented at the annual meeting of the Southern Historical Association, Atlanta, November 2005).

24. "Negro Registers at SLI to Study in Engineering," *Lafayette Daily Advertiser*, July 22, 1954; "Negro Woman Applies for SLI Summer Session," *Lafayette Daily Advertiser*, June 7, 1954; "Registration Hits 3,251," *Vermilion*, September 24, 1954; "List of Negro Students, Fall 1954–55," Registrar's Records, USL Papers, SAMC. Florent Hardy Jr., "A Brief History of the University of Southwestern Louisiana 1900 to 1960" (Master's

thesis, University of Southwestern Louisiana, 1969), 91, says that seventy-five black students registered that fall.

25. Glynn Abel, interview by Michael Wade, April 28, 2000, Lafayette, La.; Joseph A. Riehl to Paul Wooton, July 27, 1954, Joseph A. Riehl Papers, Collection 15, Box 1, Folder 6, SAMC.

26. Julius Gassner, "Integration in Acadia," *Interracial Review* (February 1959): 28–29; Julius Gassner to Leon O. Beasley, December 30, 1982, copy in author's possession (Gassner taught at SLI from 1952 to 1957); Mrs. J. Wallace Lovell to Joel L. Fletcher, August 7, 1954, Fletcher Papers, SAMC; "Upholds Negroes' Right to Education at SLI," *Lafayette Daily Advertiser* clipping, n.d., SAMC.

27. "Upholds Negroes' Right to Education at SLI."

28. F. James Davis, *Who Is Black? One Nation's Definition* (University Park: Pennsylvania State University Press, 1991), 8–11; see also Grace Elizabeth Hale, *Making Whiteness: The Culture of Segregation in the South, 1890–1940* (New York: Pantheon Books, 1998).

29. Marcus B. Christian, "Color Confusion in Louisiana Causes Citizens Council to Err," *Louisiana Weekly*, March 31, 1956, 1.

30. Joseph A. Riehl to Colonel James A. Cowan, October 6, 1954, and Joseph A. Riehl to Captain H. F. Taggart, September 3, 1954, both in Riehl Papers, Collection 15, Box 1, Folder 6, SAMC; Gassner, "Integration in Acadia," 28–29; Gassner to Beasley, December 30, 1982; Fr. Alexander Sigur, interview by Patricia Rickels and Barry Ancelet, n.d., Lafayette, La., USL Oral History Collection. See also "Second Thought" and "SLI Newman Club Named Nation's Best," both in *Southwest Louisiana Register*, September 7, 1956, 1, Diocese of Lafayette Archives, Lafayette, La.; Thurston N. Davis, "Spanish Moss and Segregation," *America* 99, no. 8 (May 24, 1958), 249. Fr. Davis, S.J., was editor in chief of *America*, and the article is an account of his recent trip to the Catholic Student Center at SLI and to LSU. In it, he wrote: "In Lafayette, Msgr. Alexander Sigur and Father Jude Speyrer are understandably proud of the vigorous liturgical life that crowns all the informal and friendly activity of their teeming on-campus center. There isn't much talk about integration in the SLI center; they just go quietly about making it work. Studious young Negroes sit side by side with white students in the center's reading rooms and lecture hall. They know they are welcome; and there's no fuss about it." Later, calling a much-expanded Newman Center at LSU "a splendid complex," he mused: "how happy the Negro is about such things as the 'colored-only' drinking fountains on the LSU campus is another story."

31. Except that he did not reside in any dormitory, what the young man from Lake Charles did is uncertain. Bonnet said only that the father thanked him, saying that he would act on the advice. J. Stewart Bonnet, interview by Michael Foret, February 1981, and James W. Oliver, interview by Michael Foret, n.d., both in USL Oral History Collection; Calvin Trillin, *An Education in Georgia: Charlayne Hunter, Hamilton Holmes, and the Integration of the University of Georgia* (1964; reprint, Athens: University of Georgia Press, 1991), 100. For Hunter's recollections of her experience at the University of Georgia, see Charlayne Hunter-Gault, *In My Place* (New York: Farrar Straus Giroux,

1992); for a historian's account, see Robert A. Pratt, *We Shall Not Be Moved: The Desegregation of the University of Georgia* (Athens: University of Georgia Press, 2002).

32. Robert Crisler, interview by Michael Foret, n.d., USL Oral History Collection; Joseph A. Riehl, interview by Michael Foret, March 16, 1981, Lafayette, La. According to Riehl, Fletcher and the faculty "took the position that any student who came to Southwestern should be given a fair chance to succeed, regardless of color, or past, or anything else." Fletcher's stand came at personal cost to him, as is indicated by R. Vernon Guthrie to Joel L. Fletcher, June 13, 1954, Fletcher Papers, Box 23, File 16, SAMC, wherein Guthrie returns Fletcher's letter of resignation from the First Presbyterian Church of Lafayette.

33. Congressman Edwin E. Willis to Joseph A. Riehl, July 8, 1955, Riehl Papers, Box 1, Folder 7, SAMC; Biographical Form, Riehl Papers, Box 1, Folder 10, SAMC. Wade, "Farm Dorm Boys," details Fletcher's role in attracting significant New Deal programs to Southwestern. Fletcher's sincerity of commitment to all students was clear, but he actively sought enough applicants to charter a local chapter of the Sons of Confederate Veterans, although whether this represented a deeply held feeling or an effort to bolster his standing with disaffected whites is unknown (Joel L. Fletcher to Joseph A. Riehl, August 11, 1955, Riehl Papers, Box 1, Folder 7, SAMC).

34. "Federal Judges Order SLI to Admit Negro Students," *Lafayette Daily Advertiser*, April 23, 1954; Joel L. Fletcher to Dr. V. L. Wharton, February 13, 1956, Vernon Lane Wharton Papers, Collection 34, Box 1, Folder 15, SAMC; Dr. Mary Dichmann, interview by Michael Foret, July 14, 1981, USL Oral History Collection; Dr. James Oliver, interview by Patricia Rickels and Barry Ancelet, n.d., Lafayette, La.; "Negro Students Enrolled at SLI," *New Orleans Times-Picayune*, September 9, 1954; "Negro Students Attending SLI Without Incident," *Louisiana Weekly*, September 18, 1954, 1; Bonnet, interview. Wharton, in addition to being a fine administrator, was a significant figure among post–World War II historians of the South, author of *The Negro in Mississippi, 1865–1890* (Chapel Hill: University of North Carolina Press, 1947).

35. Crisler, interview; Shane K. Bernard, *The Cajuns: Americanization of a People* (Jackson: University Press of Mississippi, 2003), 18–19, 33–34. See also James G. Dauphine, *A Question of Inheritance: Religion, Education and Louisiana's Cultural Boundary, 1880–1940* (Lafayette, La.: Center for Louisiana Studies, 1993).

36. Milton Rickels (SLI English professor), interviewer unknown, n.d.; Roland J. Cambre (retired professor and head, Freshman Engineering), interview by Michael Foret, n.d.; Bonnet, interview; Vesta Bourgeois (retired professor and head, Department of Women's Physical Education), interview by Michael Foret, February 1981, all in USL Oral History Collection; C. S. Trotter to A. P. Tureaud, September 9, 1955, and A. P. Tureaud to Joel L. Fletcher, September 14, 1955, both in Tureaud Papers, Box 65, File 22, ARC. Cambre recalled one of the first black engineering students arriving with his father, who said to Cambre: "I want this boy to behave himself. I want him to get an education and if he don't behave, I want somebody to beat the hell out of him."

37. *Hilda V. Combre et al. v. John McNeese State College et al.*, Tureaud Papers, Box 65, Folder 4, ARC; Joe Gray Taylor, *McNeese State University, 1939–1987: A Chronicle*, ed. Cheryl Ware and Thomas Fox (Lake Charles, La.: McNeese State University, n.d.),

82–85; *Thomas C. Wells et al. v. Luther H. Dyson, President of Southeastern Louisiana College et al.*, Tureaud Papers, Box 72, Folder 2, ARC; LeRoy Ancelet, "A History of Southeastern Louisiana College" (Ph.D. diss., Louisiana State University, 1971), 99–100. Taylor emphasized his figures' inexactitude, as McNeese did not specify race on applications, and information on African American enrollments was based on yearbooks; not all students were photographed and, Taylor noted, "sometimes it is impossible to tell a black person or a white person."

38. *Hamp Williams et al. v. Northwestern State College et al.*, Tureaud Papers, Box 72, ARC; Otis R. Crew, Registrar, to John S. Kyser, May 13, 1955, John S. Kyser Collection, Correspondence, Box L, Folder 52, Cammie G. Henry Research Center, Eugene P. Watson Library, Northwestern State University, Natchitoches, La. Crew said that the plaintiffs did not see him on January 29, 1955, when they were purportedly denied admission. See also "Northwestern Asks Dismissal of Suit Brought by Negroes Seeking Admission," *Natchitoches Times*, June 8, 1955; and "Negroes Amend Suit Asking Admission to NSC," *Natchitoches Times*, March 9, 1956. John Kyser replaced H. Lee Prather as president of Northwestern prior to the April 21, 1955, filing of the case, which listed Prather as a defendant. On the growing opposition, see "Citizens Council to Be Organized Here," *Natchitoches Times*, April 13, 1956; and "Sen. Rainach Says NAACP Red-Led," *Natchitoches Times*, April 20, 1956. I am grateful to a good friend, Charles Pellegrin, assistant professor of history at Northwestern State, for the materials from the Cammie Henry Research Center and for the articles on Willie Rainach and the Citizens' Council.

39. Worthy, "Travail and Triumph," 105–11; "Nicholls State Enrolls First Negro Students Tuesday," *Lafourche Comet*, September 19, 1963; "U.S. Judge Orders Negroes Admitted to Nicholls St.," *Louisiana Weekly*, September 21, 1963, 1; "Negroes Register," *Nicholls Worth*, September 19, 1963, 1.

40. "Distribution of Students by Race within the Several Academic Areas," USL Papers, Presidential Series, Box 236–f, SAMC; "SLI Newman Club Named Nation's Best," *Southwest Louisiana Register*, September 7, 1956, 1; Gassner, "Integration in Acadia," 29; "Gulf State Newmanites to Convene April 6, 7, 8," *Catholic Action of the South*, 2a; "Old Times There Are Not Forgotten: USL's First Black Graduate Recalls Commencement 1956 with Mixed Emotions," *USL Alumni News* (Fall 1986), 12. Christiana Smith, the object of great admiration by the university's black students then and now, died in Dallas, Texas, in 2003.

41. On Rainach, see William McFerrin Stowe Jr., "Willie Rainach and the Defense of Segregation in Louisiana, 1954–1959" (Ph.D. diss., Texas Christian University, 1989). On the work of the legislature's segregationist junta, see Earlean M. McCarrick, "Louisiana's Official Resistance to Desegregation" (Ph.D. diss., Vanderbilt University, 1964); Joint Legislative Committee, *Biennial Report, 1954–1956*, May 14, 1956, in Louisiana State Library, Baton Rouge; and Adam Fairclough, *Race and Democracy: The Civil Rights Struggle in Louisiana, 1915–1972* (Athens: University of Georgia Press, 1995), 223–29.

42. Bertrand DeBlanc to Joel L. Fletcher, August 24, 1956, and "Backs Stand on Eligibility for Students," *Shreveport Times*, August 30, 1956, clipping, both in USL Pa-

pers, Presidential Series, Box 236–f, SAMC; *Equal Protection of the Laws in Public Higher Education 1960*, 72; Goldfield, *Black, White, and Southern*, 80. Goldfield's reading of the laws suggests that they were intended to delay the implementation of *Brown*. That they were. But they were also clearly designed to end the integration already accomplished at Southwestern Louisiana, McNeese State, and Southeastern Louisiana. Samuel L. Gandy, "Desegregation of Higher Education in Louisiana," *Journal of Negro Education* 27 (Summer 1958): 269, contains the text of both acts. Gandy, a Dillard University professor of philosophy, also notes that, while shared social life was almost nonexistent, cafeterias and lounges were open, and black students attended some athletic events at the Louisiana state colleges that had desegregated. Gandy rated interracial relations somewhat more friendly at McNeese than at Southwestern, and less favorable at Southeastern.

43. Various 1956 issues of *Catholic Action of the South*, published by the Archdiocese of New Orleans, especially M. F. Everett, "Despotic Police State Seen as Result of School Control Acts," *Catholic Action*, July 1, 1956, 1.

44. Worthy, "Triumph and Travail," 101–2; Clayton Arceneaux, interview by Michael Wade, May 3, 2003, Lafayette, La.; Gassner, "Integration in Acadia," 29; Joseph T. Taylor, "Desegregation in Louisiana—One Year After," *Journal of Negro Education* 24 (Summer 1955): 271. Taylor, a professor of sociology at Dillard University, noted that the governor had signed a bill providing for the establishment of a branch of Southern University in Lafayette, this after the legislature decided that it could not immediately carry out its plan of establishing a new black college in Lafayette Parish. Taylor observed that the black community was not enthusiastic about the idea. The following year, in "Desegregation in Louisiana—1956," *Journal of Negro Education* 25 (Summer 1956): 262–72, Taylor noted that although blacks had now been admitted to at least four historically white state colleges, there was rising opposition to the court decisions and "a conspicuous absence of constructive effort to meet the challenge provided by the demise of legal segregation." Nonetheless, a careful survey of *L'Acadien*, the SLI yearbook, for the mid-to-late 1950s indicates a significant number of African American students.

45. James Caillier and Jeri Caillier, interview by Michael Wade, April 29, 2000, Lafayette, La.

46. Thetis Simpson Cusimano, interview by Michael Wade, May 2, 2003, Lafayette, La.

47. *USL Basketball Guide*, 1966–67, 8, SAMC; Beryl C. Shipley, interview by Michael Wade, March 3, 2002, Lafayette, La.; Autobiographical Materials, Fletcher Papers, Collection 12, Box 28, Folder 8, SAMC.

48. "Shipley Years Marked by Success," in *Lafayette Remembered: The Centennial Album, 1884–1984* (Lafayette, La.: Lafayette Daily Advertiser, 1984), 177–78.

49. Dr. Robert R. Jones, interview by Michael Wade, May 4, 2003, Sunset, La. In addition to individual publications, Jones and Dormon were coauthors of *The Afro-American Experience: A Cultural History through Emancipation* (New York: John Wiley and Sons, 1974).

50. Michael G. Wade, "Johnny Rebel and the Cajun Roots of Right-Wing Rock"

(paper presented at a conference of the Louisiana Historical Association, March 2002, New Iberia, La.). See also Bernard, *Cajuns*, 63–64. Dr. Shane K. Bernard, archivist at the home of Tabasco Sauce, E. A. McIlhenny, on Avery Island, graciously provided me with copies of the music of Happy Fats and Son of Mississippi. Shane also introduced me to legendary Louisiana performer Johnny Allan, who kindly put me in touch with the singer who is Johnny Rebel.

51. A notable exception to this pattern of omission is Fairclough's *Race and Democracy*, 165, which briefly mentions the integration of SLI as well as the subsequent enrollments of black students at McNeese State College and Southeastern Louisiana College.

52. Dr. Mary Dichmann, interview by Michael Foret, July 14, 1981, USL Oral History Collection.

53. Constantine, interview.

54. Albert D. Kirwan, *The Revolt of the Rednecks: Mississippi Politics, 1876–1925* (Lexington: University of Kentucky Press, 1951; reprint, Gloucester, Mass.: Peter Smith, 1964); Peltason, *Fifty-eight Lonely Men*, xi. Peltason concluded that federal court decisions would have to be supplemented by executive and legislative action if they were to be enforced. While this was generally true elsewhere, SLI's integration was accomplished by local leadership in the face of executive and legislative inaction at the federal level and determined opposition at the state level. As for New Orleans, see Liva Baker, *The Second Battle of New Orleans: The Hundred-Year Struggle to Integrate the Schools* (New York: HarperCollins, 1996).

55. "Introduction: Reassessing the History of the Civil Rights Movement," in *New Directions in Civil Rights Studies*, ed. Armstead L. Robinson and Patricia Sullivan (Charlottesville: University of Virginia Press, 1991), 2, 6.

56. David K. Shipler, *A Country of Strangers: Blacks and Whites in America* (New York: Vintage Books, 1998), examines the continuance of racial divisions over thirty years after the civil rights advances of the 1960s. On why middle-class African Americans are often troubled by their very success, consult Ellis Cose's *The Rage of a Privileged Class* (New York: HarperCollins, 1993). Shelby Steele, *A Dream Deferred: The Second Betrayal of Black Freedom in America* (New York: HarperCollins, 1998), examines the limitations of a liberal-inspired, guilt-induced "culture of preference," which has not only proved unable to overcome racial, ethnic, and gender prejudices, but has perhaps reenergized them. For a more personal perspective, see Nathan McCall's unsparingly honest *What's Going On* (New York: Random House, 1997) and June Jordan's sometimes hopeful, often angry *Technical Difficulties: African-American Notes on the State of the Union* (New York: Pantheon, 1992). A burgeoning literature on the troubling nature of the human future includes Robert Kaplan's *The Coming Anarchy: Shattering the Dreams of the Post Cold War* (New York: Random House, 2000) and James Howard Kunstler's *Home from Nowhere: Remaking Our Everyday World for the 21st Century* (New York: Simon and Schuster, 1996).

3

The Long Journey from LaGrange to Atlanta

Horace Ward and the Desegregation of the University of Georgia

ROBERT A. PRATT

Into the 1950s, Georgia's public institutions of higher education maintained a rigid color line separating whites from blacks. Since the 1930s, the National Association for the Advancement of Colored People (NAACP), led by the tireless Charles Hamilton Houston, had challenged segregation in higher education. The NAACP's rationale in focusing first on segregation in colleges and universities was twofold: because there would be far fewer blacks in colleges than in the grade schools, the organization believed that white opposition would be less intense; and since many states did not have any postbaccalaureate training for blacks, they could hardly rely on the "separate but equal" argument. Denying blacks access to professional and graduate schools was more than segregation, but outright exclusion. In several significant cases, the Supreme Court ruled that states would have to enforce the "equal" as well as the "separate." In none, however, did it rule against segregation per se. *Plessy v. Ferguson* was still the law.[1]

Herman Talmadge's election as Georgia's governor in 1948 ushered in an era of virulent white supremacy and increased racial repression throughout the state. Talmadge was every bit the race-baiter that his father, Eugene Talmadge, had been, and he went to great lengths to make it clear that white supremacy was the cornerstone of his 1948 campaign, proclaiming, "My platform has one plank which overshadows all the rest ... my unalterable opposition to all forms of the 'civil rights program.'"[2]

Under Herman Talmadge, the dominant features of Georgia politics would remain states' rights and white supremacy. Preserving segregation in public education was a very high priority. Not all Georgians shared that priority, however, as Horace Ward made clear in his persistent dissent.

Horace Ward and the University of Georgia

On September 29, 1950, Horace Taliaferro Ward took the first step in cracking segregation at the University of Georgia. Born in 1927 in LaGrange, Georgia, Ward had earned a bachelor's degree from Morehouse College in Atlanta in 1949 and a master's degree from Atlanta University in 1950. His mentors, Morehouse president Benjamin E. Mays among them, encouraged Ward to pursue a career in law. Having no desire to go to law school out of state, Ward hoped to be able to attend the University of Georgia, located in Athens, seventy-five miles northeast of Atlanta. He was aware, however, that none of Georgia's white institutions had ever admitted a black student, so he knew immediately what he would be up against. One of Ward's professors, William Madison Boyd, who happened to be the president of the state NAACP, had been searching for a black student with solid academic credentials to apply to the University of Georgia. Ward agreed to apply.[3]

Ward sent his application to the university registrar, Walter N. Danner. Several days later, Ward received a reply from L. R. Seibert, executive secretary of the Board of Regents, to whom Ward's application had been forwarded. In an attempt to dissuade Ward from pursuing his application at Georgia, Seibert offered Ward financial assistance if he would attend an out-of-state law school. Ward wrote back to Seibert refusing the aid and insisting that his application be evaluated solely on its merits. On October 18, Seibert replied that a committee would review the matter.[4]

For three months, Seibert did not communicate with Ward. On January 5, 1951, Ward wrote to Seibert, asking for a status report on his application. Seibert wrote back, informing Ward that he hoped to complete the evaluation of the application "at an early date." Three more months passed, and still no official action on Ward's application. On April 26, Ward wrote Seibert yet another letter in which he stressed that he wanted to enter law school in the summer term, which was scheduled to begin on June 13. The decision finally came on June 7, 1951. In a letter from university registrar Walter Danner, Ward was informed: "Your application for admission to the University of Georgia has been considered and is hereby denied." The rejection letter had come just six days before the beginning of the summer term and more than nine months after Ward had filed his application.[5]

Still hoping to be admitted before the beginning of the summer term, Ward appealed immediately to university system chancellor Harmon Caldwell, who claimed that he had not been in communication with Danner and did not know the reason for Ward's rejection. Caldwell further claimed that he had no jurisdiction over the matter and that Ward should take up the issue with Danner. With the help of his attorney, Austin Thomas Walden—one of a few black lawyers in Georgia at the time—Ward continued his correspondence with University of Georgia officials throughout the summer. On July 5, Ward wrote to university president Omer Clyde Aderhold, protesting that he had been rejected solely on the basis of race. Aderhold responded by promising Ward that he would create a "special committee" to study the matter (a procedure that had never been adopted for a white applicant). To assist the committee in its deliberations, Ward was asked to supply detailed personal information, especially relating to his eligibility for military duty.[6]

Although believing it to be a meaningless gesture, Ward reluctantly agreed to meet with the special committee on September 8, 1951. The three-man committee consisted of law school dean J. Alton Hosch, law professor Robert L. McWhorter, and history professor E. Merton Coulter. Why President Aderhold chose these three faculty members to serve on the committee is unclear. What is known is that all three were committed to preserving segregation at the University of Georgia. As law school dean, Hosch toed the administration line on segregation, and his law school colleague McWhorter was a dependable ally. Coulter was well known for his racist views, which are clearly reflected in his writings, both professional and personal.[7]

One of the most surprising things about the meeting, Ward recalls, was that the committee asked him virtually nothing about his academic credentials, but rather chose to focus more on the personal aspects of his life. As Ward remembers, the interview began with questions about his fitness for military service. Ward had developed a hernia years earlier that he had never had surgically corrected. Because of the hernia (which the army considered a "medical disability"), Ward was classified as "4–F," meaning that he was physically unfit for military service. As Ward explains it, "the hernia had never bothered me, and I did not deem it a priority; hence, I had never bothered to have it corrected. I considered it totally irrelevant to my application to UGA, but it became a big deal for Dean Hosch."[8] Dean Hosch continued to press Ward about the hernia, implying that, because Ward was of service age (he was twenty-four at the time), it was unpatriotic of him not to have corrective surgery that would qualify him for military duty, especially in light of the fact that the United States was at war with Korea. Hosch reasoned that either Ward was shirking his military obligations or his priorities were confused. After Hosch had finished grilling Ward about military duty, McWhorter and Coulter tried to determine if Ward was really serious about attending law school or if, rather, he was a tool of the NAACP.[9]

A week after the meeting, Ward received a letter from President Aderhold informing him that the special committee had recommended denying Ward's application and that the president concurred with the decision. Again, Ward appealed to Chancellor Caldwell, but Caldwell, writing Ward on October 18, said he had no legitimate reason to overturn the decision. In the final step to exhaust all administrative remedies, Ward appealed to the Board of Regents.[10]

Shortly after receiving official notice of Ward's appeal, the Board of Regents decided that this was an ideal time to revamp the university's admission requirements and restructure the curriculum. In the past, the law school at the University of Georgia had admitted most candidates solely on the basis of their having completed a minimum of two years of course work at an accredited institution. Now, the board noted, the nation's better law schools had begun to administer entrance examinations to applicants. Therefore, to make sure that the university's academic reputation would not be diminished, the regents would now require "the faculty of the School of Law of The University of Georgia to confer with and cooperate with the officials of the Georgia Bar Association and members of the judiciary in this State [to] work out an adequate program of examinations for all who apply for admission." In order to achieve their ulterior motive—to keep Ward out—the regents voted unanimously that "all applications now pending at any stage . . . be considered . . . under the aforesaid resolutions."[11] The only application pending at the time was Horace Ward's.

On June 11, 1952, the Board of Regents unanimously adopted another resolution, which, the regents maintained, was designed "to further enhance the quality" of the law school:

(1) Any resident of Georgia applying for admission to an institution of the University System of Georgia shall be required to submit certificates from two citizens of Georgia, alumni of the institution that he desires to attend, on prescribed forms, which shall certify that each of such alumni is personally acquainted with the applicant, that he is of good moral character, bears a good reputation in the community in which he resides, and, in the opinion of such alumnus, is a fit and suitable person for admission to the institution. . . . (2) Every such applicant shall also submit a certificate from a judge of a court of record . . . [that applicant is] a person of good moral character and bears a good reputation in the community in which he resides. . . . The foregoing requirements shall apply to all applicants who have applied for admission . . . but have not been actually enrolled and admitted, and to all applicants who hereafter make application for admission to any such institution.[12]

The regents no doubt understood that it would be difficult, if not impossible, for any black applicant to produce such letters of reference from prominent white members of the state's legal establishment, even if—itself unlikely—two alumni supplied the requisite certificates.

Despite the legal maneuvering, administrative delays, and political posturing, there was never any doubt that university and state officials were determined to prevent any black enrollment at the University of Georgia. The overwhelming majority of white southerners opposed desegregation. University officials like President Aderhold had ample reason to believe that their support for segregation really did reflect white sentiment. Moreover, university officials could always claim that such issues were a matter of state policy and were, in effect, out of their hands. They were, as they stated on more than one occasion, merely complying with state law.

When Chancellor Caldwell first announced that Ward's application would be rejected, he claimed it was the only decision possible under state law, citing both the state constitution, which forbade integration in Georgia's public schools, and the recent actions of the state legislature, which in the 1951–52 session sought to eliminate the possibility that integration would occur in any of the state's seventeen public colleges. In a rider attached to the appropriations bill for that year—one that was attached *after* Ward's application to the University of Georgia—the legislature declared that if a black applicant were admitted to a white school, all state funds to that institution would be cut off.[13] Georgia's legal proscriptions against integration, like those in other southern states, were designed to preclude any breaching of the color line.

Convinced that the University of Georgia would never voluntarily admit Ward to its law school, Ward's attorneys filed suit in the federal district court in Atlanta on June 23, 1952, alleging that Ward's application to the university had been denied solely on the basis of "race and color," a fact that to them was patently obvious. The "new rules and regulations" for admission, Ward's attorneys alleged, constituted an insidious ploy designed with Ward's application in mind. Further, this lawsuit was to be considered a class action suit filed on behalf of all black citizens who had previously been denied admission to the University of Georgia on the basis of race and color.[14] A. T. Walden, who up to this point had been handling Ward's case alone, was now joined by nationally known NAACP attorneys Thurgood Marshall and Robert L. Carter, both of whom were seasoned litigators who were accustomed to legal maneuvers and courtroom shenanigans.

Using almost the entire eighty days given to them by Judge Frank Hooper to respond to the plaintiff's allegations, the state's attorneys asked that Ward's petition be denied on the grounds that he had not exhausted all administrative remedies, as the Board of Regents had not yet taken final action on Ward's application. Such final action by the regents was not necessary, Thurgood Marshall argued, pointing out that Ward had spent nearly two years seeking admission through the proper channels, only to be frustrated at every turn by repeated excuses and delays. Judge Hooper disagreed, believing that final action by the regents was necessary, which he demanded immediately. The regents met on January 14, 1953, and officially denied Ward's application, citing his refusal to take the necessary examinations and his failure to provide character references from university alumni. Even after the regents' ruling, the state's attorneys spent the next several months trying to delay the trial or have Ward's suit dismissed for one reason or another. Finally, Judge Hooper scheduled a pretrial hearing for September 2, and tentatively set the beginning of the trial for October 5, 1953, more than three years after Ward had applied to the University of Georgia.[15]

But on September 9, less than a month before the trial was scheduled to begin, Ward received a letter from the U.S. Department of Defense—his draft notice to report for induction into the U.S. Army. Ward had earlier received a "4–F" classification because of his hernia, but had since undergone corrective surgery, which resulted in his being reclassified as "1–A." As Ward prepared to take his place among the ranks of the nation's enlisted men, his case against the University of Georgia was consequently removed from the court docket.[16]

In a 1999 interview, Horace Ward explained the timing of his surgery and why he had elected to correct a hernia that he had once characterized as "not a priority." He remembers that at the time the hernia was not causing him any physical discomfort, though he realized he would have to have it corrected eventually, and then was as good a time as any. According to draft regulations, one had to notify the draft board if there was a change in one's medical condition that might result in reclassification. Ward notified the draft board of his surgery, and he was promptly reclassified. He also acknowledged that he was not aware that having the operation would necessarily result in reclassification, though he understood that it might. Ward is reluctant to admit it, but Dean Hosch's implication that Ward was trying to evade the draft may have prompted him—even if only indirectly—to have the surgery, which may well have been Hosch's intent. In a letter to Page Keeton, dean of the law school at the University of Texas at Austin, Hosch later wrote: "As you may know, there was an application by a Negro some time ago, but I understand that he had a hernia operation in order to get into the Army."[17]

Those who had fought to keep Ward out of the university could not have hoped for a more favorable turn of events. But some of his supporters were of the opinion that Ward's induction in the army was a bit more than mere happenstance, leading some to speculate about the possibility of political interference, although there is nothing in the written record to suggest anything more than that Ward was the victim of bad timing. Still, speculation about political impropriety lingers. But whether the untimely arrival of the draft notice was calculated or coincidental, university officials and the state's attorneys breathed a collective sigh of relief at the two-year stay they had been granted. Correspondence between university officials reveals that they were very satisfied with the outcome. "Yesterday I learned of Ward's induction in the Army and this will leave us free of his problem for a time anyway," Dean Hosch wrote Chancellor Caldwell, who replied that he was "very glad that Ward is out of the picture for the time being."[18]

White Georgians believed that much of the responsibility of maintaining segregation at the University of Georgia rested with Chancellor Caldwell, who was, after all, the highest-ranking official in the university system. From the very beginning, Ward's application to the law school had received national attention, prompting many interested observers to write to the chancellor to express their sentiments on the matter one way or the other. Most of the respondents praised Caldwell for standing firm in the face of such a grave crisis as the one now confronting the university. One woman from Indiana wrote:

> Keep up your honorable fight to keep the White race pure from negro contamination, and do not allow the *federal Missouri mule* [a reference to President Harry Truman] to succeed in his determination. . . . You Southerners have already more than amply provided splendid industrial institutions for the negro, which is all-sufficient for a *negro* to handle. The odious affair is just another dirty "Dred Scott" rotten political affair, and if you let Truman beat you on this . . . you're a gonner.

Caldwell received numerous other letters imploring him to preserve the sanctity of the white race; some of them were signed, while others came from individuals identifying themselves as members of the Ku Klux Klan or some other white supremacist group, but who usually signed their letters "anonymous."[19]

Not all of the letters written to the chancellor opposed Ward's admission. In fact, a few of them took the chancellor (along with the university and the state) to task for denying Ward his constitutional rights. One such letter, written by an alumnus of the university, chastised the chancellor and his cohorts:

> Are you an American? From what I have read and heard of your college, I don't think I'd want to meet a so called "American" like you. . . . I hope you aren't to blame for Horace Ward's being denied an education, but if you are, I don't ever want to meet you. If your college doesn't allow negroes or any other race to achieve goals and get an education, brother, I don't ever want to be able to say I went to the University of Georgia to learn a profession. I could say I went to learn *race segregation*, though.[20]

It is unlikely that Chancellor Caldwell replied to all of the letters he received about the Ward case, and nothing in the record indicates that he replied to this one. He did, however, respond to one letter, written by a woman from Savannah who criticized his role in the Ward affair. To her he explained: "For your information please allow me to say that Mr. Ward has not been deprived of the opportunity to secure a legal education. He has been offered scholarship aid that would enable him to attend some of the foremost law schools of the country at a cost no greater than that of attending the University of Georgia in Athens. His refusal of this offer leads one to ask whether his primary concern is the securing of a legal education."[21] But preventing Ward from attending the University of Georgia merely because he was black did in fact deprive him of his rights as a citizen. An offer of out-of-state tuition aid was hardly an act of beneficence.

Like most white Georgians of his day, Chancellor Caldwell held steadfast to the notion that the races should be kept apart, and that (as the above comment suggests) any black who was serious about an education should willingly accept segregation as the price for that privilege. But for an increasing number of blacks at mid-twentieth century, segregation was much more than an inconvenience—it deprived them of their rights as American citizens. Inspired by the success of earlier university desegregation cases, Ward's attorneys remained hopeful about their chances and continued to prepare for their ultimate showdown with the state's segregationists. As his adversaries schemed to come up with new ways to keep him out of the University of Georgia, Horace Ward was on his way to Korea to fight for his country.

Renewing the Fight for Admission

Within a few weeks after being discharged from the army, Ward wrote to university registrar Walter Danner on September 8, 1955, requesting that his application be renewed. Almost immediately, state attorney general Eugene Cook announced that the law school would be closed should Ward be admitted. Ward's attorneys, still awaiting word from the Board of Regents concerning Ward's renewed application, requested a pretrial hearing, which Judge Frank Hooper scheduled for January 9, 1956. The state asked for a postponement, however, because the attorney general had to attend the opening session of the General Assembly on that date. Judge Hooper granted the delay, and the hearing was rescheduled for February 20.[22]

For the next eleven months, the state's attorneys introduced one motion after another either to have the case dismissed or to have the proceedings delayed. At the February 20 hearing, the state argued that Ward should have to submit a new application since his original application had been interrupted by his military service. At a hearing on July 30, the state asked for a further postponement, this time arguing that six individuals who were members of the

Board of Regents when Ward first filed suit in 1952 were no longer members, and thus could not be held liable to litigation. The state also claimed that two other regents had previous commitments they could not be excused from, and that the son of one of the state's attorneys had to undergo surgery.[23]

At a hearing on September 10, Judge Hooper acceded to the state's insistence that Ward file a new application, saying that it was the only way he could determine whether the regents had acted in good faith. But Ward's attorneys objected that Ward's original application had been maintained since 1950, and that he should not be subjected to new regulations that went into effect after the fact. The state made one last attempt on November 2 to get the case thrown out on yet another technicality. Refusing to dismiss the case, Judge Hooper set the trial date for December 17, 1956. After six and a half years of legal maneuvers and delay tactics (including a suspiciously timed military draft notice), Horace Ward would finally have his day in court.

The case of *Horace T. Ward v. Regents of the University System of Georgia* began on December 17, 1956. Local civil rights attorney Donald Hollowell now headed up Ward's legal team, and assisting him were A. T. Walden and NAACP attorney Constance Baker Motley, one of the organization's brightest stars. Ward's attorneys set out to prove in court what had been evident to them from day one—that Ward's application to the law school had been denied for no other reason except the color of his skin, and that the state's political establishment, members of the Board of Regents, and high-ranking university officials had conspired to keep Ward out of the University of Georgia. Assistant Attorney General Freeman Leverett prepared the case for the state, and B. D. "Buck" Murphy, Governor Talmadge's personal attorney, handled the oral arguments. The state's position was that Ward was simply unqualified to enter the University of Georgia, and that race played no role in the university's decision not to admit him.[24]

At trial, University of Georgia officials took the witness stand and maintained a position that seems patently absurd to a rational mind: although they clearly wanted to preserve segregation in the university system's colleges and universities, they did not discriminate against Horace Ward in the efforts to do so. When Ward's attorneys raised the issue of the Appropriations Bill of 1951, which had authorized the state legislature to cut off funds to any white school that admitted a black student, attorneys for the state acknowledged the prosegregation laws, but insisted that those laws did not influence the university's decision to reject Ward's application. When Ward's attorneys charged that the regents' policy of offering out-of-state aid to black applicants was tantamount to exclusion, university officials claimed that the out-of-state aid program was a gesture of goodwill, and that it most certainly did not imply that blacks were ineligible for admission to the state's white universities. L. R. Seibert, executive secretary of the Board of Regents, testified that the program existed "because the colored people want it; they are delighted with it. You just ought to see some of the letters that they write me commending us and telling us what a great opportunity they have." When asked why such a program did not exist for white students, Seibert replied that white students had never requested it. Chancellor Caldwell went so far as to say that "in fact, the white students have charged we have been discriminating against them because we have been paying out over $275,000 a year for the Negro students."[25]

If Ward's attorneys were to establish that he was the victim of racial discrimination, they would have to prove racial motive as well as procedural irregularities. Proving the latter would not be that difficult. Under cross-examination, university registrar Walter Danner admitted that university officials handled applications from blacks differently than those from whites. The registrar's office processed applications from whites, but routinely forwarded applications from blacks to the regents. In Danner's words, applications "of that nature were sent to Mr. Seibert, that was the practice."[26] President Aderhold initially feigned ignorance about the application process, claiming that he did "not handle the admissions of the University," but minutes later contradicted himself by saying that "as far as I know, it [Ward's application] was handled differently."[27]

Next was the issue of Ward's qualifications. At the time, the major requirement for admission to the Georgia law school was two years of college; yet university officials deemed Ward unqualified, despite his being an honors student and having earned a bachelor's degree from Morehouse College and a master's degree from Atlanta University. The university's position was that while Ward had obviously been a good student, his academic record was tarnished by the fact that neither of the schools he had attended was a member of the Southern Association of Colleges and Secondary Schools (SACS), the regional accrediting association. Although both Morehouse College and Atlanta University had received "A" ratings from that same association, and were fully accredited using the same standards that were applied to white schools (a fact that Walter Danner himself acknowledged), black colleges and universities were not allowed to become members of SACS. Danner's own testimony had confirmed the existence of blatant racial discrimination within the university system. This exclusionary policy made it impossible for any black student in the state to be eligible for admission into any of the state's white universities. Still, attorneys for the university maintained the position (as did their witnesses, who testified under oath) that the University of Georgia did not have a policy in place that systematically excluded blacks.[28]

Aside from academic-related issues, the defendants argued that Ward, because of defects in his character, was unfit to enroll at the University of Georgia. The special committee that President Aderhold had appointed in 1951 to review Ward's application concluded that Ward's interview was unimpressive, and that he did not reflect the intellectual depth necessary for the study of law. As a convenient way of not having to acknowledge Ward's scholastic achievement, committee member and law school dean J. Alton Hosch testified that since Ward had already been rejected, committee members "gave most of our attention to Ward as a man," and that based on their observations, Ward's responses to their questions were "evasive," "inconsistent," and "contradictory." When asked to cite some specific examples of these inconsistencies, Hosch raised the issue of Ward's response to questions concerning his hernia. Hosch said, "I asked him why he didn't have an operation. He said he didn't have the money. Then I asked him did he have the money to go to school and complete three years . . . I thought that was inconsistent." These "inconsistencies," along with what the committee perceived to be a lack of genuine desire on Ward's part to pursue a legal career, led Hosch to conclude that Ward "didn't show that he had the qualifications that we thought necessary for . . . admission to Law School."[29]

That Ward was invited to an interview by this special committee was ample evidence that university officials never seriously considered Ward's application, and the creation of this committee was yet another attempt at subterfuge. The most compelling example of this duplicity, Ward's attorneys argued, was the unprecedented lengths university officials went to in order to keep one black student out. No other student's application had forced university officials to go so far as to modify admission requirements and to modify them in such a way as to exclude that one student, a fact that the university steadfastly denied. At trial, Charles Bloch, chairman of the state's Judiciary Council, claimed that these new requirements were not designed to keep Ward out, but to improve the caliber of Georgia's lawyers. Bloch's testimony revealed that he had engaged in ongoing correspondence with Chancellor Caldwell and the Board of Regents. Perhaps not coincidentally, Governor Talmadge appointed Bloch to the Board of Regents in January 1952, and the next month, on February 13, the regents adopted the resolution.[30]

Two major stories developed on the second day of the trial. The first resulted from the testimony of Chancellor Caldwell. A. T. Walden asked Caldwell, "Would you admit a qualified Negro to the University of Georgia?" Caldwell replied: "I have thought about that a lot . . . and the Regents are here, and they can fire me as soon as the meeting is over, but I'll tell you what I think about it. . . . If a case comes before me on appeal, and it appears on all facts . . . that the Negro is eligible for admission to an Institution, I will rule that he is eligible, and I'll take that decision to the Board of Regents."[31] The chancellor's sudden willingness to admit "a qualified Negro" to the University of Georgia came as something of a surprise to many courtroom observers, especially in light of his earlier testimony in which he admitted that "we do wish, in our institutions, [insofar] as possible, to preserve the segregation of the races."[32]

Sounding like a boldly progressive pronouncement, Caldwell's comments in effect underscored the university's contention that it had never erected any barriers to black applicants, so long as they were qualified. Neither Horace Ward nor his attorneys were convinced of Caldwell's sincerity. As Ward puts it: "Frankly, I considered the statement to be another ploy, because I thought of myself as being very well qualified. My experiences had taught me that they [university officials] could always find a way of 'disqualifying' any applicant."[33] Caldwell's statement quickly became a source of amusement in black legal circles. "Would you be willing to admit a qualified Negro?" became one of Constance Baker Motley's favorite questions in future desegregation cases.

The next major development of the trial came when Ward took the stand. Rather than focus on Ward's qualifications, Buck Murphy set out to discredit Ward by showing that he had no real interest in pursuing law school, but rather was merely a tool of the NAACP. During his relentless grilling, Murphy questioned Ward about his current residence, which led Ward to reveal that he was living in Chicago, and, to the astonishment of nearly everyone present had been enrolled in law school at Northwestern University since September. This sudden disclosure now changed the complexion of the case. Murphy recalled Danner to the stand, who testified that, since Ward had already matriculated at Northwestern, he could enter the University of Georgia only as a transfer student and would have to begin the application process all over again. As Murphy saw it, Ward had "voluntarily put himself in a position where he cannot be admitted on the basis of his 1950 application." But Ward's attorneys argued that regardless of his current status, Ward's application to the University of Georgia had been renewed continuously since 1950, and that these new developments did not change the merits of the case. Privately, however, they feared that this disclosure had essentially rendered their case moot, and the way in which it had been revealed would get them little sympathy from the judge.[34]

On February 12, 1957, Judge Hooper dismissed Ward's lawsuit against the University of Georgia on the grounds that Ward had refused to reapply to the law school under the new guidelines, and that Ward's enrollment at Northwestern had in effect rendered moot his application to the University of Georgia. In reading his decision, Judge Hooper concluded:

> It is now well established that the authorities in control of . . . any state supported law school in this country may not refuse admission to any person solely on account of race and color. . . . While [Ward's] application was filed in September, 1950 the case did not come on for trial until

December 17, 1956. During this interval of time, some six and one-half years, the plaintiff had consistently failed and refused to file any new application which would give to the Board of Regents sufficient information on which to base a decision as to his qualifications . . . and as a consequence there is no evidence in the record to indicate that defendants will refuse to admit plaintiff if he should in the future file an application as a transfer student. . . . Should the plaintiff file an application in the future and should it be denied, the plaintiff may again apply to the courts, but the Court should not now declare any discrimination even though it might have existed at or about September, 1950.[35]

While university officials and their attorneys breathed a collective sigh of relief, Judge Hooper's decision came as little surprise to those who had followed the trial. On its face, Judge Hooper's rationale appeared legally sound, but it was evident from the beginning—at least to Ward's supporters—that the judge's sympathies lay with the state. Not only did he allow the defense to engage in a line of questioning that often seemed irrelevant (much of which was intended to impugn Ward's character), but he also failed to acknowledge that the various administrative policy changes set up by university officials were designed for the sole purpose of excluding Ward from admission. Morehouse president Benjamin E. Mays later wrote that he was "shocked, stunned, and terribly disappointed when I heard top university officials swear in court that race had absolutely nothing to do with Ward's denial of admission. . . . I suppose these top officials had to lie, since [admitting] that Ward was kept out because of his race would have forced the university to admit him."[36]

Despite the testimony offered by the state's witnesses, it was clear that the resolutions that were passed with the stated purpose of improving the quality of the University of Georgia's law school were timed to derail Ward's application. Ward's attorney Donald Hollowell later summed it up: "I don't think the judge was ever inclined to support our position. It was almost as if he knew deep down that Ward should be admitted, but instead looked for any reason to avoid making that decision. But that was the kind of social and legal climate in which we operated in the 1950s."[37]

After Judge Hooper dismissed Ward's suit, Ward and his attorneys pondered whether they should file an appeal. The decision was Ward's, and as he remembers, it really was not that difficult. He thought that he had invested as much time in the case as he could and that it was time for him to move on with his life. His lawyers were disappointed, but they understood his reasons. Ward said that he had gotten tired of people "assailing my character and questioning my integrity," and he and his wife and son were eager to return to Chicago, which he thought of at the time as a place of refuge. He described that period in his life as "a real low point for me."[38]

Back in Chicago, Ward resumed his studies at Northwestern. As for his classroom experiences, Ward remembers them as being positive, though there was little in the way of racial diversity. He was one of only four black students in the entire law school, and there were no black faculty members. He studied diligently, not only out of a desire to succeed in his chosen profession but also because he felt the added burden of having to prove himself. University of Georgia officials had said that he was "not qualified" to enter their law school, that he did not possess the character to be a lawyer. Ward was determined to prove them wrong on all counts.

A Lawyer and the University That Rejected Him

While Ward was finishing his degree at Northwestern, two black Atlanta high school students, Hamilton Holmes and Charlayne Hunter, declared their intention to seek admission into the University of Georgia. Hamilton E. Holmes was a star athlete and valedictorian at Atlanta's Henry McNeal Turner High School, and his classmate, Charlayne A. Hunter, had finished third in her class, was the editor of the school newspaper, and had been voted Miss Turner High. They both considered Atlanta's white segregated Georgia State University, but Holmes, who wanted to study medicine, and Hunter, an aspiring journalist, were disappointed after reviewing Georgia State's course offerings. Both concluded that they wished to attend the University of Georgia.

On July 11, 1959, Holmes and Hunter made the front page of the *Atlanta Constitution*: "2 Negroes Try Doors at Athens." University of Georgia officials already had their strategy mapped out, and the registrar's response to Holmes's and Hunter's applications was to be the tack they would use for the next year and a half: "Registrar Walter N. Danner said the university is full up and already is turning down would-be freshmen. He said that because dormitories are full the only freshmen he can admit are those who are bona fide Athens residents." Since the University of Georgia required all freshmen to live in dormitories, the lack of dormitory space meant that Holmes and Hunter could not be admitted. Danner claimed that 500 other applications had been rejected for the same reason. With their plans to enter the University of Georgia temporarily on hold, Holmes enrolled at Morehouse for the fall semester, and Hunter enrolled at Wayne University (later Wayne State University) in Detroit. Both students, however, informed Danner that they wanted to be considered for admission in the winter quarter, 1960.[39]

Holmes and Hunter renewed their applications to the University of Georgia each quarter during the 1959–60 calendar year, and Danner replied each time that there was simply no space available. Holmes's and Hunter's attorneys were aware that a substantial number of transfer students were being admitted to Georgia every quarter. As fall 1960 approached, attorneys Donald Hollowell and Constance Baker Motley concluded that, since the University of Georgia seemed determined to keep up the shenanigans, a lawsuit was inevitable. After being rejected for admission in the fall quarter, Holmes and Hunter appealed to Chancellor Caldwell; when he refused to act, they appealed to the Board of Regents. While the regents stalled, Hollowell and Motley petitioned the U.S. District Court for the Middle District of Georgia for a preliminary injunction that would prohibit the university from denying admission to the plaintiffs solely on the basis of race.[40]

Meanwhile, Horace Ward, who had completed law school at Northwestern in January 1959, was getting ready to come home. Ward had always known that Chicago was a brief stopover for him, and he was delighted when Donald Hollowell invited him to join his Atlanta law firm. He was even more thrilled when Hollowell asked him to assist in this new desegregation suit against the University of Georgia. Ward returned to Georgia in August 1960, and promptly became associate counsel in the lawsuit.[41]

The trial of *Holmes v. Danner* began on December 13, 1960, with Judge William A. Bootle presiding. Lawyers for the plaintiffs tried to prove in this case what they had been unsuccessful in proving in Ward's case—that the University of Georgia did not admit blacks. When Chancellor Caldwell took the stand, he refused to admit that any form of legally sanctioned segregation existed at the university, despite the fact that he was forced to admit that he had written a note to President Aderhold acknowledging the university's subterfuge in using housing shortages to keep the black students out. (Ward and Vernon Jordan, a recent graduate of Howard University's law school who was also assisting with the case, had come across the note after inspecting the University of Georgia's application files.)[42] When Hollowell tried to point out to President Aderhold the remarkable similarities between this case and Horace Ward's, Aderhold said that both Ward and Holmes had been "evasive and inconsistent" in their interviews, and neither was qualified to enter the University of Georgia.[43]

Hollowell and Motley believed it only fitting to allow Horace Ward to conduct the questioning of Hamilton Holmes. Both Holmes and Hunter had been interviewed, which was now university policy. Under direct examination from Ward, Holmes testified that the interview committee had subjected him to an intense grilling on personal matters. All of the questions focused on his morals, and no one asked him anything about academics. The interviewers asked him if he was familiar with Athens's "red-light district" and if he had ever visited any house of prostitution. Ward wanted to prove to the court that Holmes had been questioned in a manner totally different from that which any white student encountered. On the final day of testimony, Constance Baker Motley asked Registrar Danner the question she referred to as "the old clincher": "Would you favor the admission of a qualified Negro to the university?" In echoing Chancellor Caldwell's declaration four years earlier, Danner's reply in the affirmative hardly surprised anyone.[44]

The long-awaited decision came down on Friday afternoon, January 6, 1961, roughly one month after the trial ended. Judge Bootle ruled that "although there is no written policy or rule excluding Negroes, including plaintiffs, from admission to the University on account of their race and color, there is a tacit policy to that effect" and that the plaintiffs "would already have been admitted had it not been for their race and color." Judge Bootle's decision did contain one surprise: the plaintiffs were to be admitted not by the following fall, as some had predicted, or for the spring quarter, beginning in March, but immediately. Holmes and Hunter began classes on January 11, 1961, and would graduate from the University of Georgia on June 1, 1963.[45]

Holmes and Hunter, along with their lawyers, were jubilant. No one was happier than Horace Ward. Although his case four years earlier had ended in defeat, Holmes and Hunter's had ended in victory, and he shared vicariously in their feeling of vindication. For Ward, everything he had gone through personally since September 29, 1950, had now been worth it, and he had no regrets about the decisions he had made. When Ward escorted Holmes and Hunter to campus to complete registration, an angry white man in the crowd shouted to Ward, "Hey you, nigger lawyer, get off this campus and don't ever come back."[46] More than thirty-five years passed before Horace Ward returned to the University of Georgia.

Becoming a Judge

Following the enrollment of the first black students at the University of Georgia, Ward continued to work in Donald Hollowell's law firm. In 1964, Ward decided to seek election in the thirty-ninth senatorial district in Fulton County. After winning the Democratic primary in the majority white district, he defeated his white Republican opponent in the general election, becoming the second African American to serve in Georgia's state senate in modern times. Ward won reelection four times, running unopposed in 1966, 1968, and 1970. In 1972, he defeated a black challenger in this district, which had become majority black in 1970.[47]

More than just a party stalwart, Ward was shrewd enough to forge the kinds of alliances necessary to get things done. One of Ward's closest allies in the state senate was Jimmy Carter, a native of Plains, Georgia, then in his second term. Carter befriended Ward early on and offered to assist the newcomer in any way that he could. The two legislators worked together on several important pieces of legislation and usually voted the same way. Their time together in the Georgia legislature was cut short, however, when Carter decided to run for governor. Jimmy Carter's subsequent election as Georgia's seventy-sixth governor in 1970 did not mark the end of his relationship with Horace Ward. As fate would have it, Ward's warm relationship with Carter soon netted him some handsome dividends.

During one of their conversations while serving together in the Georgia legislature, Ward had mentioned to Carter that he might prefer a judicial career over a legislative one. Carter did not forget the conversation, and on May 8, 1974, he appointed Ward to the Fulton County Civil Court, making him the first black trial court judge in Georgia's history. Three years later, on January 25, 1977, Governor George Busbee appointed Ward to the Fulton County Superior Court, where Ward served as one of eleven judges in the Atlanta Judicial Circuit.[48] Ward's friendship with Jimmy Carter had certainly helped facilitate his rapid ascent within the judiciary, and owing to a fortuitous set of historical circumstances, he was about to rise even higher.

Jimmy Carter's victory in the 1976 presidential election was due in no small measure to the overwhelming support he received from African Americans. And he knew it: during his four years in office he appointed more African Americans to government positions (including the federal judiciary) than any previous president. In the second year of his presidency, Carter was given the opportunity to fill a record number of newly created federal judgeships, which he saw as "a unique opportunity to begin to redress another disturbing feature of the Federal judiciary: the almost complete absence of women, or other members of minority groups." As he had done elsewhere, Carter urged Georgia's Judicial Nominating Commission to recommend a diversified slate of candidates, one that was representative of the state as a whole. Whatever the commission did, however, would be determined largely by the sentiments of Georgia's two U.S. senators: Sam Nunn and former segregationist governor Herman Talmadge.[49]

Horace Ward, at the time serving as a judge on the Fulton County Superior Court, was surprised and pleased to learn that the Judicial Nominating Commission had submitted his name for consideration. Senator Talmadge, who as governor of Georgia in 1950 had vowed to use every means at his disposal to keep Ward out of the University of Georgia law school, might have been expected to derail Ward's nomination. But the political landscape, especially in the South, had changed drastically since 1950, and apparently Senator Talmadge had become attuned to the new political realities. As Ward remembers it:

Both Nunn and Talmadge had apparently agreed to designate me for one of the openings. As I understood it, I was actually in Talmadge's area of influence, and he could have blocked my nomination on any number of grounds; in fact, he need not have given a reason. But he took the position that he was going to support me. There was some opposition to my candidacy. Some argued that I did not have the background; others said that I had not specialized in some sophisticated areas. Senator Talmadge called me and explained that there was some opposition, but he told me to hang in there, and assured me that he would support my nomination all the way. It's quite ironic, I guess. He now openly admits that he opposed my efforts to enroll at UGA, but be that as it may, he supported my nomination, and in all candor and fairness to the Senator, I would not have gotten the position had he not supported me.[50]

Despite some initial uncertainty, Ward's nomination eventually made it to the White House, and President Carter promptly nominated him for one of Georgia's district court judgeships. Following Senate confirmation, Ward was sworn in as a judge on the U.S. District Court for the Northern District of Georgia on December 27, 1979, becoming the first African American ever to serve on the federal bench in Georgia. Ward's Oath of Office Ceremony was held in the U.S. District Court in Atlanta—in the same courtroom where Ward's lawsuit against the University of Georgia had been argued twenty-three years earlier.

Ward's appointment to the federal bench was for him a dream come true. More than that, it was an indication of how far his state had come since his application to the University of Georgia's law school nearly thirty years earlier. Ward could now aptly say that he had witnessed the transformation of the South from the Old to the New—although he had been victimized by the former, he had lived long enough to become a beneficiary of the latter. The political worlds of Herman Talmadge and Jimmy Carter had converged at just the right moment, and now a black man of humble origins from LaGrange, Georgia, held a lifetime appointment as a district court judge.[51] Ward was fifty-two years old.

Horace Ward had risen to lofty heights since he first applied to law school at the University of Georgia in 1950, and it was perhaps because of the storybook-like ending to his career that he found it easier to forgive many of those who had allowed race prejudice and societal norms to lead them to make a mockery of justice. In fact, in his roles as lawmaker and judge, Ward had become better acquainted with many of those who had opposed his efforts to enter the University of Georgia, and was on good terms with most of them.

And while admitting that "UGA was never far from my mind," Ward confessed that he had not set foot on the campus since 1961. It was not any lingering resentment that had kept him away all these years, but rather the failure of university officials to acknowledge his role in the University of Georgia desegregation crisis. The red carpet had been rolled out for Hamilton Holmes and Charlayne Hunter-Gault in recent years, but Horace Ward—the one who was not admitted—had never been invited to return.[52] That was about to change.

Returning to the University

Horace T. Ward's struggle to desegregate the University of Georgia—as important as it is in the history of the civil rights movement—has not hitherto been well known. His efforts to break down racial barriers at Georgia's flagship university began in 1950 and continued until 1957, when his court case challenging the university's segregationist policies ended in defeat. Undaunted, Ward earned a law degree from Northwestern University and, in 1960, returned to Georgia, where he became associate counsel in the NAACP-sponsored lawsuit that eventually forced the University of Georgia, in January 1961, to admit its first black students, Hamilton Holmes and Charlayne Hunter, both of whom graduated in June 1963.

Breakthrough though the enrollment of Holmes and Hunter was, it initiated a drawn-out process of desegregation. Holmes, for example, would have liked to play football, but that was by no means permitted, and no black students represented the University of Georgia in intercollegiate athletics until years after Holmes had graduated. Total black enrollment at the University of Georgia, after beginning at two in January 1961, climbed to eight the next fall, and hovered at 6 percent in the 1990s.[53] By then, the university was prepared to celebrate what it had once resisted. Since observing its bicentennial in 1985, the university has seized several opportunities to honor Hamilton Holmes and Charlayne Hunter, as it did in 2001 when it commemorated the fortieth anniversary of its desegregation.

Horace Ward, however, remained largely forgotten into the 1990s. In the fall of 1995, a small group of University of Georgia faculty members planned a conference for the spring of 1996. The event was titled "Civil Rights in Small Places," and the objective was to highlight some of the local civil rights struggles since the 1950s that had not received much public attention. Since one of the planned sessions was to focus on the desegregation of the University of Georgia, the committee hoped that Judge Ward would agree to participate. Through a series of committee meetings, it was discovered that Ward had not been on the University of Georgia's campus since 1961, and that while he might respond favorably to such an invitation even without, an official letter of welcome from the university president was certainly in order. At the committee's request, President Charles B. Knapp wrote a letter to Ward requesting his participation in the conference and officially welcoming him to the University of Georgia.[54]

On April 15, 1996, more than thirty-five years after being ordered off the campus with a racial slur, the Honorable Horace T. Ward returned to the University of Georgia. President Knapp officially welcomed and introduced Judge Ward, paying tribute to the civil rights pioneer:

> We wish to recognize the path that Horace Ward blazed in his efforts to attend the University of Georgia. It is very likely that the later events of 1961 would not have occurred at the time they occurred had it not been for Judge Ward's efforts. As I recently learned, this is his first visit back to the University of Georgia in the ensuing thirty-five years. Judge, I know that at that time you did not get a hospitable welcome. But I want to make sure this afternoon that you know how welcome you are, and we hope it will not be another thirty-five years before you come back again.[55]

Following President Knapp's introduction, Judge Ward took center stage and began to recount his struggle to gain admission into the University of Georgia's law school forty-six years earlier. Some in the audience were familiar with his story, but others had not even heard of him, and in his characteristic soft-spoken tone, Ward explained to a younger generation that the University of Georgia in 1996 bore little resemblance to the University of Georgia he had tried to enter in 1950. "I should be one of the best-trained lawyers in the state," Ward said at one point. "I spent nearly seven years trying to get into one law school, and three years trying to get out of another." Later, when explaining the university's reasons for denying him admission, Ward said, jokingly, "The screening committee said that my statements during the interview were evasive and inconclusive. Now, some would say that those are good qualifications for being a lawyer."[56]

Throughout his entire informal presentation, Ward appeared relaxed, often smiling, joking, and reminiscing, clearly enjoying the moment. Horace Ward's triumphant return to the place where his remarkable story had begun finally closed the chapter on that part of his life. "All of the negative feelings left me," Ward said later. "The bitterness was gone. I put the past behind me, and looked to the future. I guess that's the way it should be."[57]

On June 29, 2001—fifty-one years after inaugurating his attempt to gain admission to the University of Georgia law school—Horace Ward turned seventy-four. For some years, Judge Ward had been preparing himself for retirement from the bench, having taken senior status in 1994.[58] But because he still enjoyed living the life of a federal judge, and because his health remained good, he continued to put off calling it quits. He had managed to rise to the top of his chosen profession, and he often referred to his "long journey from LaGrange to Atlanta," ever mindful of those who helped him along the way. Looking back, he could see the roles he had played, and he appreciated the interest people had come to show in them, but he tended to play them down. "I do not believe that there will ever be another Justice Thurgood Marshall. There might not be another Donald Hollowell. There certainly can be replacements for Horace Ward. I stand ready to pass the torch to a new generation of lawyers and judges committed to the task of fulfilling the ideal of equal justice for all."[59]

Notes

Material in this essay is drawn from Robert A. Pratt, *We Shall Not Be Moved: The Desegregation of the University of Georgia* (Athens: University of Georgia Press, 2002), and is used with the permission of the University of Georgia Press.

1. The U.S. Supreme Court's ruling in *Plessy v. Ferguson* (163 U.S. 537 [1896]) established "separate but equal" as the guiding principle for contact between the races, especially in the South. For a detailed discussion of the cases between the 1930s and midcentury challenging black exclusion from institutions of higher education, see Mark V. Tushnet, *Making Civil Rights Law: Thurgood Marshall and the Supreme Court, 1936–1961* (New York: Oxford University Press, 1994).

2. Herman Talmadge, quoted in Robert Sherrill, *Gothic Politics in the Deep South* (New York: Grossman, 1968), 48.

3. Horace T. Ward, interview by author, June 29, 1999, Atlanta.

4. The correspondence between Ward and Seibert is detailed in the records of Ward's suit against the university. See *Horace T. Ward v. Regents of the University System of Georgia*, Federal Records Center, East Point, Ga., December 1956, 212–16. For a more detailed account of Ward's efforts, as well as the eventual desegregation of the University of Georgia, see Robert A. Pratt, *We Shall Not Be Moved: The Desegregation of the University of Georgia* (Athens: University of Georgia Press, 2002). See also Maurice C. Daniels, *Horace T. Ward: Desegregation of the University of Georgia, Civil Rights Advocacy, and Jurisprudence* (Atlanta: Clark Atlanta University Press, 2001).

5. Peter H. Silverman, *"Horace T. Ward v. Board of Regents of the University System of Georgia*: A Study in Segregation and Desegregation" (Master's thesis, Emory University, 1970), 9. See also the University of Georgia's student newspaper, the *Red and Black*, June 21, 29, 1951.

6. Ward, interview.

7. For an example of Coulter's racist scholarship, see E. Merton Coulter, *A Short History of Georgia* (Chapel Hill: University of North Carolina Press, 1933), especially his discussion of Reconstruction, 328–79; see also Fred Arthur Bailey, "E. Merton Coulter and the Political Culture of Southern Historiography," in *Reading Southern History:*

Essays on Interpreters and Interpretations, ed. Glenn Feldman (Tuscaloosa: University of Alabama Press, 2001), 32–48. After a trip to Washington, D.C., in 1965, Coulter wrote one of his friends: "Washington is fast becoming an African city—as you know more than half of the population are Negroes. . . . The government service is almost completely overrun by them, from top to bottom; and Congress is now about to hand over to them the government of the city. . . . As lamentable as it is, it will be interesting to watch what happens to the national capital." Ellis Merton Coulter Papers, MSS# 1710, Box 49, Folder 1, Hargrett Library, University of Georgia, Athens.

8. Ward, interview.

9. Ibid.

10. Caldwell to Ward, October 18, 1951, *Ward v. Regents*, 266.

11. Regents Minutes (University of Georgia System), February 13, 1952, 15, Hargrett Library, University of Georgia.

12. Ibid., June 11, 1952, 2.

13. *Atlanta Constitution*, March 14, 1954.

14. *Ward v. Regents*, 7.

15. *Atlanta Journal*, January 15, 1953; Ward, interview.

16. Ward, interview.

17. Ibid. Ward refuses to speculate on what his decision concerning the surgery would have been had he known the consequences. Hosch's letter to Keeton (September 30, 1954) is located in the Aderhold Papers, MSS# 2127, Box 10, Folder "School of Law," Hargrett Library, University of Georgia.

18. Thomas G. Dyer, *The University of Georgia: A Bicentennial History, 1785–1985* (Athens: University of Georgia Press, 1985), 309.

19. D.D. to Harmon Caldwell, June 13, 1951, Chancellor's Papers, MSS# 2909, Box 24, Personal Files, Hargrett Library, University of Georgia. Because private citizens (as opposed to public figures) who wrote to Chancellor Caldwell to express their views on segregation perhaps expected that their correspondence would be kept confidential, it would be inappropriate for me to divulge their identities here. Therefore, I have chosen not to include their names in the text, and will refer to them in the notes by their initials only.

20. R.H. to Chancellor Caldwell, June 14, 1951, ibid.

21. Caldwell to E.P., June 22, 1951, ibid.

22. *Atlanta Journal*, September 14, 1955, January 4, 10, 1956.

23. Ibid., February 20, April 7, July 6, 9–10, 1956.

24. *Ward v. Regents*.

25. Ibid., 99–101, 115–20, 196.

26. Ibid., 26–28.

27. Ibid., 109–11.

28. Ibid., 30–33, 454–60.

29. Ibid., 147–50.

30. Regents Minutes, February 13, 1952, 15.

31. *Ward v. Regents*, 205–8.

32. Ibid., 198.

33. Ward, interview.

34. *Ward v. Regents*, 270; Plaintiff's Amendment to Complaint, January 3, 1957.

35. *Ward v. Regents*, 191 F.Supp. 419 (1957), 492, 494–95.

36. Benjamin E. Mays, *Born to Rebel: An Autobiography* (Athens: University of Georgia Press, 1971), 207.

37. Donald Hollowell, interview by author, March 2, 2000, Atlanta.

38. Ward, interview.

39. *Atlanta Constitution*, July 11, 1959; *Atlanta Journal*, July 25, 1959.

40. Plaintiffs' Brief, *Holmes v. Danner*, 191 F.Supp. 394 (M.D. Ga. 1960).

41. Ward, interview.

42. Charlayne Hunter-Gault, *In My Place* (New York: Farrar Strauss Giroux, 1992), 162–63; Ward, interview. Judge Bootle had granted permission for Holmes's and Hunter's attorneys to inspect the registrar's files. Horace Ward and Vernon Jordan did most of the research, and during their search they stumbled onto several pieces of incriminating evidence. During the time that the University of Georgia was reportedly facing a housing crisis, the dean of the agriculture department had gone to upstate New York to recruit students for the university's food-technology program. Ward and Jordan also discovered that a white female student, whose situation was almost identical to Hunter's, had been allowed to transfer to the University of Georgia. A letter had been written to Chancellor Caldwell asking him to use his influence to get the student admitted; attached to the letter was a handwritten note from Caldwell to President Aderhold, which read: "I have written Howard [Howard Callaway, a member of the Board of Regents] that it is my understanding that all of the dormitories for women are filled for the coming year. I have also indicated that you relied on this fact to bar the admission of a Negro girl from Atlanta."

43. In accordance with the University of Georgia's new admission procedures adopted in the wake of the Horace Ward affair, all students who applied to the university had to be interviewed. Ward and Jordan discovered that some of the white students were actually interviewed *after* they had already been admitted, and that some of them were hardly interviewed at all.

44. Calvin Trillin, *An Education in Georgia: Charlayne Hunter, Hamilton Holmes, and the Integration of the University of Georgia* (1963; reprint, Athens: University of Georgia Press, 1991), 41; Hunter-Gault, *In My Place*, 162.

45. *Holmes v. Danner*, 191 F.Supp. 394 (M.D. Ga. 1961), 402–10.

46. Ward, interview.

47. Ibid.

48. The superior court is the main trial court in Georgia and is a court of general jurisdiction that covers all areas of state cases. A superior court judge is called upon to try felony criminal cases, all types of civil cases (including tort actions, domestic relations, and equity cases), and many other special or extraordinary claims for relief, such as injunctions and appeals from lower courts and state agencies.

49. Jonathan Neal Merrill, "Jimmy Carter, Race Relations and the Judicial Selection Process" (Master's thesis, University of Georgia, 1992), 41. In October 1978, Congress passed the Omnibus Judgeship Act, which created 152 new federal judgeships—35 in

the circuit courts and 117 in the district courts. This act, representing the single largest increase ever in the size of the federal judiciary, was designed to relieve the massive backlog of federal court cases.

50. Ward, interview.

51. Of the ten new federal judges appointed in Georgia, seven were white men, two were white women, and one—Ward—was a black man. Not only did President Carter have a respectable record in appointing blacks to the federal bench, but his appointees in general (black and white) tended to be more sympathetic to black plaintiffs in civil rights cases. Carter's willingness to appoint black activist judges like Nathaniel Jones and A. Leon Higginbotham Jr. was yet another distinguishing feature of his nominations. For a variety of reasons, no blacks were appointed to the First, Fourth, Seventh, or Tenth circuits, and only in two circuits, the Second and the Ninth, did Carter appoint more than one black judge. But Carter was not to blame. His goal of achieving greater diversity on the federal bench was sometimes frustrated by unreconstructed U.S. senators, such as the successful attempt by Senator Harry F. Byrd Jr. of Virginia to block the appointment of James E. Sheffield.

52. Ward, interview.

53. For glimpses of developments on the racial front at the University of Georgia in the decade after January 1961, see Pratt, *We Shall Not Be Moved*, 111–28; Daniels, *Horace T. Ward*, 153–58; and the essay in this volume by Charles H. Martin.

54. The conference grew out of a discussion between William McFeely, John Inscoe, and Robert Pratt, all members of the University of Georgia's history faculty. Several others, including Robert Cohen of the School of Education, eventually joined the committee. Cohen drafted the letter to President Knapp asking him to extend the personal invitation to Judge Ward.

55. Comments by Charles B. Knapp, "Civil Rights in Small Places," conference held at the Georgia Center for Continuing Education, University of Georgia, April 15–16, 1996. The entire conference was videotaped, and copies of all tapes are in the author's possession. The videotapes were made available courtesy of John Inscoe.

56. Comments by Horace T. Ward, "Civil Rights in Small Places."

57. Ward, interview.

58. In order to become a senior judge, one must be at least sixty-five years old with at least fifteen years of service (if one is at least sixty-six, he or she needs only fourteen years of service, etc.). In some instances, the designation does not mean very much, other than that the president can appoint a successor. A senior judge can work at whatever pace he or she wishes and has the luxury of being able to decline certain cases, though he or she cannot select them.

59. Ward, interview. Ward's professional life had been rewarding, but his wife, Ruth, was murdered in their home by a neighbor in 1976, just four months shy of their twentieth anniversary.

4

Black Colleges and Civil Rights

Organizing and Mobilizing in Jackson, Mississippi

JOY ANN WILLIAMSON

The civil rights movement of the 1950s and 1960s was made possible by what sociologist Aldon Morris calls movement centers: "a social organization within the community of a subordinate group, which mobilizes, organizes, and coordinates collective action aimed at attaining the common ends" of that group.[1] The National Association for the Advancement of Colored People (NAACP), Student Nonviolent Coordinating Committee (SNCC), Southern Christian Leadership Conference (SCLC), and other regional and local organizations performed this role. The groups provided activists with funding, communication networks, social resources, and experienced leaders. Though the organizations sometimes supported different tactics, the ends were similar: dismantling white supremacy and providing first-class citizenship rights for all Americans. Activists used the movement centers in a two-pronged attack on racial domination. First, they employed them to organize communities and develop long-term strategies to plead their grievances. Second, they activated the movement center network to mobilize communities and initiate large-scale, short-term, public events. The organizing phase sustained the movement while the mobilizing phase disrupted normal daily life and forced white southern communities to respond to black concerns.

Historically black colleges and universities (HBCUs) were not social organizations explicitly working toward amelioration of racism, discrimination, and second-class citizenship. But they became important movement centers in the black liberation struggle and equipped students with tools easily co-opted for movement ends. Scholars typically relegate their importance to the mobilizing phase of the movement, when students at black colleges became the foot soldiers of the struggle beginning in 1960. Yet the campuses also provided a unique opportunity for youths to organize indigenous resources into power resources and attack the southern racial order.[2] Students obtained leadership training in student organizations and learned in the classroom about democracy, freedom, and constitutional rights. The campuses drew them into an environment where they learned, lived, and socialized together. Private spaces provided activists with a place to plan, pool social and financial resources, and bolster collective enthusiasm. Some students translated their education, academic and otherwise, into civil rights activism. Not all students became activists, but activist students used the shelter of the black college campus as a movement center to organize and mobilize for change.

This essay examines the roles of two black colleges in the early 1960s in the civil rights struggle in Jackson, Mississippi. Only six miles apart, Jackson State College, a public school, and Tougaloo College, a private school, played a part in the movement in Jackson. Examining the campuses together is instructive; the institutions reconciled their relationship to the movement in different ways. Tougaloo's private status shielded it from overt government interference. Key campus administrators supported the movement, and activist students used the liberal campus climate to attack racism and discrimination. Jackson State relied on appropriations and goodwill from a state legislature determined to protect the southern racial order, conditions that severely constrained overt participation in the movement.

Organizing and mobilizing necessarily looked different at each campus. But an important distinction lies between institutional support for the movement and students using the institution for that purpose. Activist students drew HBCUs, whether public or private, into the movement with or without institutional consent. Placing public and private HBCUs in separate categories obscures both the movement center role of the institutions and the organizing phase of the struggle. It also ignores both the fact that Jackson State constituents struck major and public blows against racial domination despite constant state and administrative pressure, and the fact that Tougaloo's private status did not completely immunize it from external interference. The battle between students, administrators, boards of trustees, and state officials over HBCUs' involvement in the civil rights movement reveals the important role of the colleges in the struggle and a glimpse into negotiations over the role of colleges in American society and social reformation.

The Colleges and the Presidents

In 1869, the American Missionary Association (AMA), in cooperation with the Freedmen's Bureau, purchased a 500–acre plantation on the northern outskirts of Jackson, Mississippi, to build a school for African Americans. Two years later, the state of Mississippi granted Tougaloo its charter and incorporated its board of trustees. The AMA moved quickly to craft the school into an institution imbued with a liberal and egalitarian spirit. The new college, which was "accessible to all, irrespective of their religious tenets, and conducted on the most liberal principles for the benefit of our citizens in general," focused on training teachers for Mississippi's black primary and secondary schools.[3] The student body was exclusively African American despite Tougaloo's open attendance policy, but the faculty, administrative staff, and board of trustees were racially mixed.[4] Over the years, a combination of tuition, AMA contributions, individual church donations, and philanthropic foundation funds supported the new college. Tougaloo's reputation grew when, in 1948, it became the first black college in Mississippi to be accredited as a four-year liberal arts college and gain an "A" rating from the Southern Association of Colleges and Secondary Schools. Tougaloo's status made it the most prestigious black college in the state.

Jackson State College opened in 1877 as a Baptist-supported institution for training black ministers. Its racially integrated board of trustees worked closely with the American Baptist Home Mission Society in New York to run the new institution. Baptists struggled to support the college, and in 1940 the state of Mississippi and its State Board of Trustees of Institutions of Higher Learning (State Board) took responsibility for the institution and transformed it into a teacher training school with a predominantly vocational curriculum. Legislators and the State Board only minimally supported the newest black public college in the state. Alcorn A&M College, Mississippi's black land-grant institution, received most of the limited federal and state funding earmarked for black higher education, and in some years Jackson State received more money from private sources—the Julius Rosenwald Fund and the General Education Board—than from the state. State financial support for black higher education grew at midcentury as the Mississippi legislature attempted to forestall the desegregation of public schools. As a preemptive measure, the State Board took steps toward accreditation of public black colleges by reconstituting them in 1951. Alcorn A&M and Mississippi Vocational College, Mississippi's only other public four-year HBCUs, continued to integrate teacher training with vocational training, while Jackson State became a liberal arts college. Jackson State's new status meant more financial support and legislative commitment to bolstering the faculty, facilities, and curriculum. Though the institution was not accredited until 1962, the changes made Jackson State the most prestigious public black college in Mississippi.[5]

In 1940, the State Board chose Jacob L. Reddix as the first president to run the institution under state control. Born in North Carolina and raised in Alabama and Mississippi, Reddix spent two years in the army, received a bachelor's degree from the Illinois Institute of Technology, taught high school, spent one semester of graduate study at the University of Chicago, and worked briefly with the Farm Security Administration of the U.S. Department of Agriculture prior to coming to Jackson State. His lack of administrative experience or an advanced degree was irrelevant since neither the legislature nor the State Board was committed to creating a strong black institution of higher education.⁶ Instead, Reddix held the requisite ideas on racial relationships in Mississippi and counseled patience in the fight for racial equality. He ruled the student body with an iron hand to ensure that students remained aloof from the societal issues of the time and warned that a violation of campus policies would result in suspension or expulsion.⁷ Reddix similarly ruled the faculty, all of whom were African American, as segregation laws required. Tenure did not exist at Jackson State, and the president could fire members of the faculty without due process. Those who criticized the Mississippi way of life or the campus incurred the wrath of Reddix and the board of trustees. Campus constituents treaded softly.

Reddix, like other conservative African Americans, was most likely not opposed to the concept of equal rights but disagreed with the pace and tactics employed by activists in the burgeoning civil rights movement. Particularly averse to the use of direct action tactics like boycotts, sit-ins, and marches, he favored legal maneuvers and less disruptive measures. Reddix vowed to keep the college open, and campus involvement in the civil rights movement threatened his mission.⁸ Also, Reddix was under immense pressure from the State Board. The board reserved the right to fire any campus constituent, including the president, at any time. Reddix acted out of support for the college but also out of self-interest. In 1957, the board demonstrated it would take drastic measures to curtail activism when it expelled the entire student body of Alcorn A&M College for a peaceful boycott of classes and fired Jesse Otis, the president, for his support of student efforts.⁹ Like other public college presidents at institutions across the South, Reddix was beholden to a governing body invested in maintaining a racial hierarchy. Until his retirement in 1967, he understood his role and functioned within the confines of the southern racial system.

In the selection of a college president, the trustees of Tougaloo also revealed their position on racial equality. Tougaloo's board of trustees appointed Adam D. Beittel as president in 1960. Beittel, a white man born to Quaker parents, nurtured liberal leanings at progressive institutions like Oberlin, where he received a master's degree, and the University of Chicago, where he earned his doctorate. Prior to assuming his position at Tougaloo, Beittel's administrative experience included the presidency of Talladega College (Alabama), which was also under the AMA, from 1945 to 1952. Beittel acted on his liberal ideals at Talladega by hosting an interracial conference on desegregation and voting rights, writing articles equating segregation with a violation of Christian principles and democratic ideals, and sending letters to the governor expressing his opposition to Alabama laws and customs. His actions drew heavy fire from white Alabamians as well as conservative faculty (both black and white) who worried that his actions focused unnecessary attention on the school. In the face of mounting pressure from a disgruntled faculty, Talladega's board of trustees reluctantly fired Beittel, but this did not dissuade Tougaloo's board of trustees from hiring him. The AMA's paternalistic attitude toward its colleges made the appointment of a white president at Tougaloo highly likely, and Beittel's familiarity with AMA schools and his qualifications made him competitive for the position. His experience with southern whites' attitudes and sensibilities, and his demonstrated loyalty to the Talladega board of trustees, solidified the Tougaloo board's decision.[10]

Campus constituents laid the groundwork for Tougaloo's prominent role in the Jackson movement prior to Beittel's arrival, but his appointment coincided with increasing civil rights activity. During his tenure, Tougaloo hosted a variety of activities, from Freedom Riders in need of a safe haven while in Mississippi to staging grounds for various marches into downtown Jackson. He also demonstrated his commitment to the movement through his own actions by voicing desegregationist sentiments on a local television show, joining civil rights organizations, and refusing to expel students for participating in demonstrations and protests. Yet the campus attitude toward the movement was not unanimous. Some of Tougaloo's faculty and staff worried about institutional integrity in the face of growing student activism, and one professor worked secretly with Mississippi officials to curtail civil rights activities on campus.[11] By and large, however, Beittel and other liberal administrators supported student activism and set the tone for campus involvement in the movement. Tougaloo's primary purpose remained a high-quality liberal arts education, but according to Tougaloo chaplain Ed King, Beittel "saw no contradiction between the college being an oasis of freedom" and an academic enterprise.[12]

Beittel and Reddix held different ideas on how to attain racial equality, but they should not be juxtaposed as a "white liberal" versus a black "Uncle Tom." The story of campus involvement in the civil rights movement is more nuanced than that. Both men were under intense pressure to conform to Mississippi mores. Beittel's employment at a private institution allowed him to support student efforts and the use of campus facilities for movement efforts. But Tougaloo's board of trustees worried about the school's prominent role in the movement and eventually penalized Beittel for allowing the campus to become a movement center. Reddix was a public employee with no tenure or occupational autonomy. The governor, board of trustees, and legislature expected full compliance and promised to fire him if he allowed students to use Jackson State to launch movement projects. Presidential attitudes on racial advancement were contributory, but they alone did not dictate campus involvement in the movement.

Instead, the attitudes of the governing boards were more powerful than the discrete ideas of the presidents. The governing boards appointed Reddix and Beittel twenty years apart, but both boards handpicked them to run the institutions according to the trustees' vision. Tougaloo's board may have been more liberal, but it terminated its support for President Beittel when it thought Tougaloo's role in the movement had become too costly. Similarly, President Reddix's conservative attitudes were less meaningful than those of Mississippi officials controlling the purse strings and the fate of Jackson State in general. When conjuring a picture of campus involvement in the civil rights movement, the story of student organizing and mobilizing must be paired with presidential attitudes toward student efforts, the response of the governing boards, and pressure from state officials.

The Civil Rights Movement in Mississippi

African Americans experienced a renewed democratic spirit after World War II and became more aggressive in their demands for full citizenship. Even during the war, black Mississippians began to organize their forces for an attack on the southern racial hierarchy. At Jackson State, this sentiment found vision in the Youth Council. The organization explained its mission in the November 1942 edition of the student newspaper, the *Blue and White Flash*: Members will use "psychological and constitutional procedures to help Negroes in their struggle for full emancipation and to secure this ideal." It implored students to join and "help solve the problem of segregation and racial discrimination." The campus also celebrated Negro History Week as an annual event. In 1944, a speaker at the Negro History Week events lectured on the Emancipation Proclamation, crimes under the banner of states' rights, and the value of the ballot.[13] This type of public display remained an anomaly since Mississippi government agencies clamped down on growing agitation in the black community. Many campus constituents no doubt held radical notions of racial equality, but rarely did such sentiments become part of a public forum on campus. Vocal individuals bore the brunt of administrative or state punishment for their actions.

At Tougaloo, the Reverend William Albert Bender, the school's sixty-year-old black chaplain, an NAACP member, attempted to vote in the 1946 Democratic primary. The registrar refused to allow him to do so, and Bender filed a complaint with the state attorney general. In retaliation, hostile whites burned a cross on the Tougaloo campus. Beginning in the early 1950s, Ernst Borinski, a German Jew who was head of the Department of Sociology and chairman of the Division of Social Science, sponsored the Social Science Forum and invited speakers to discuss politics, race, popular culture, and government. The forum drew an interracial audience since students and faculty from Millsaps College, a private white institution, sometimes patronized the series. At the same time, the Reverend John Mangram, an African American and the school's new chaplain, also participated in the NAACP. Bringing further unwanted attention to Tougaloo, Mangram helped organize the Fourth Annual Southeast Regional NAACP Conference in 1956 and the Tougaloo youth branch of the NAACP in 1960. These individual acts of resistance primed Tougaloo for the role it played in the Jackson phase of the civil rights movement.[14]

After the 1954 decision in *Brown v. Board of Education*, whites, too, organized their forces. State legislators, bankers, real estate agents, and other white-collar professionals created the White Citizens' Council less than six months after *Brown*. The Citizens' Council declared itself "dedicated to the maintenance of peace, good order and domestic tranquility in our Community and in our State and to the preservation of our States' Rights."[15] The Mississippi Sovereignty Commission grew out of the same antidesegregation spirit, and the two groups worked in tandem to defeat desegregation efforts in general and school desegregation in particular. Created by an act of the Mississippi legislature on March 29, 1956, the commission conducted investigations, created a Speakers Bureau to present Mississippi's case to the nation, and donated money to groups and individuals (including African Americans) who supported segregation.[16] With the assistance of the Citizens' Council and the Sovereignty Commission, white Mississippians terrorized civil rights activists and successfully blocked efforts to alter the racial hierarchy well into the 1960s.

Conditions in Mississippi stalled direct action there, but the civil rights movement grew strong in other southern locales. In February 1960, four students at North Carolina A&T inaugurated the direct action phase of the civil rights movement with a sit-in at a local Woolworth's lunch counter. Black college students in other southern states followed their lead and conducted sit-ins to desegregate a variety of facilities. Activists soon organized their efforts under the umbrella of a new organization, SNCC. As facilities dropped their racially exclusive service policies, the organization turned its attention to voter registration. Mississippi proved to be the most resistant state to reform, whether in desegregating facilities or in voter registration, and SNCC members decided to focus their efforts on the state. In 1961, SNCC sent a small team of activists to Mississippi to canvass for local activists and movement centers it could tap for support. Mississippi activists incorporated SNCC members into the fold and introduced them to established leaders, social networks, and various resources on which they could capitalize in order to organize and mobilize for change.[17]

SNCC's focus on Mississippi and the dominant role of students in the movement made Mississippi HBCUs and their constituents invaluable for movement ends. The location of Jackson State and Tougaloo made them attractive for movement purposes. Mississippi officials considered the sit-ins, marches, and boycotts in Jackson a particular insult since Jackson was Mississippi's capital city and urban center, home of the Sovereignty Commission, the State Board, and the Citizens' Council. The close proximity of the campuses, and their nearness to Mississippi NAACP field secretary Medgar Evers's office, facilitated student participation in a variety of civil rights campaigns. Also, studies on HBCU student participation in the civil rights movement found that those at the most prestigious institutions participated at a higher rate than those as less reputable colleges.[18] Tougaloo and Jackson State were hardly prestigious in the grand scheme of higher education, but they were more prestigious than the three other private black colleges and the two other public black colleges in Mississippi. There was unanimity on neither campus on how to attain first-class citizenship. Some campus constituents accused activists of hijacking education and transforming institutions of higher education into centers for political activity. But each campus had a cadre of dedicated activists who attempted to use their campus as a movement center.

Organizing and Mobilizing

Tougaloo was small, with about 500 students in 1960, but activist students took advantage of the relatively liberal campus climate and used their campus to organize and mobilize against white supremacy. The first organization to focus on civil rights was the campus branch of the NAACP, which was parallel to the Jackson NAACP Youth Councils. The groups functioned with the support of Medgar Evers, worked together on various projects, and shared membership. Participation in the youth chapters remained small in the beginning but grew along with the civil rights movement in Jackson. Colia Liddell, a Tougaloo student and president of the North Jackson NAACP Youth Council, approached a new Tougaloo professor, John Salter Jr., in 1961 about becoming involved, as she considered the campus chapter too small and ineffective, and Salter wholeheartedly accepted her invitation to become chapter adviser of the North Jackson Youth Council. Within a year, the organization claimed roughly 500 members, including Tougaloo students, a few Jackson State students, and students from the local black high schools: Lanier, Jim Hill, and Brinkley. Tougaloo students also rejuvenated the campus chapter with Salter's wife, Eldri, as their adviser.[19]

Nine Tougaloo members of the NAACP inaugurated massive and sustained direct action in Mississippi with a sit-in at the whites-only Jackson Municipal Library on March 27, 1961. According to Sam Bradford, a participant, the sit-in "was by no means something that was hazardly blown together. As a matter of fact, we planned it. It emanated from the youth chapter of the NAACP." Police arrived soon after the sit-in began and asked the students to disperse. The students refused to leave the library until police arrested them. After being charged with intent to provoke a breach of the peace, the Tougaloo Nine, as they were called, spent the night in jail before being released. The charges carried possible penalties of a $500 fine and six months in jail. Tougaloo administrators, who disavowed prior knowledge of the sit-in, refused to punish the students for their involvement. Away at a conference in Atlanta, President Beittel hurried home, visited the Tougaloo Nine in jail, and assured them they could make up their midterm exams. Interviewed on a local television show, Beittel expressed his support for the students: "There is a difference between going to jail for stealing something and going to jail for a conviction. I should respect them for being willing to pay the price for what they believe to be right."[20]

State control of Jackson State prevented its 1,300 students from forming a campus chapter of the NAACP, but students co-opted existing organizations to organize and mobilize. The Student Government Association (SGA) became the organization through which activists learned of, discussed, and implemented civil rights activities. Members of the SGA often were among the most politically active students on campus. Jackson State students also helped created the Mississippi Improvement Association of Students (MIAS), a clandestine off-campus organization, in early 1961. The MIAS platform mirrored that of other organizations: "The immediate and effective action is to unify ourselves against powerful opposition here in Mississippi [which is evidenced] by biased attitudes, unequal job opportunities, unequal public facilities, disrespect to Negro ladies, unequal educational opportunities, and financial aid to organizations which stimulate such acts." Jackson State students dominated its membership, which was in large part why the members remained anonymous. According to James Meredith, a member: "Loyalty was irrevocable. It was literally impossible for an oath member to betray the organization or any of its members. Only security such as this would encourage a Negro in Mississippi to venture into the forbidden realm of 'White Supremacy.'"[21] Tougaloo students supported MIAS by printing its literature on Tougaloo's campus—action that would have been impossible at Jackson State.

With the help of these organizations, Jackson State students mobilized in support of the nine Tougaloo students jailed after the library sit-in. Their inability to use college-approved media to spread the word did not hinder their efforts. The evening of the sit-in, 700 to 800 youth, many of them Jackson State students, congregated on campus near the college library. According to Meredith, MIAS spearheaded the demonstration. President Reddix, unnerved by the protest, attempted but failed to disperse the crowd. Reddix became so frustrated, recounted Meredith, that he began "snatching students at random and shoving them toward a [campus] policeman or dean with orders to expel them." To make matters worse, rumors spread that Reddix slapped a female student. Meredith doubted the rumor, but word of mouth carried the news on campus. "This incident introduced another factor into the demonstration," he later wrote, "because it reminded the students of their many long-standing grievances against the administration."[22] The demonstration dispersed when word came that city police were on the way.

Protests continued the following day with a twofold focus: support for the Tougaloo Nine and grievances against the Jackson State administration. Governor Ross Barnett threatened to close the campus, and President Reddix threatened those involved with expulsion. Students disregarded the threats, boycotted classes, and planned a march to the city jail. The SGA spearheaded the carefully orchestrated demonstration. Fifty students volunteered to march while other students attended a rally on campus to draw attention away from the marchers. The rally participants sang songs and prayed as the marchers moved in a single-file line on each side of the street to avoid arrest for blocking traffic. Police swiftly and violently reacted to the march with blockades, tear gas, billy clubs, and (for the first time in Mississippi history) attack dogs. The entire fiasco coincided with the centennial celebration of Mississippi's secession from the Union. The same day Jackson police released the Tougaloo students from jail and unleashed attack dogs on Jackson State students, white Mississippians celebrated white supremacy with a parade, balls, a pageant, and a secession reenactment in front of the Old Capitol.[23]

The Jackson State administration clamped down on students after the demonstration. First, it created and enforced stiff rules and penalties regarding student conduct. Clubs, classes, and groups could meet only with the consent of the dean of students and the physical presence of a faculty sponsor. The president himself cleared requests for meeting space. The new campus regulations even barred off-campus meetings without the dean's consent. A coded reference to the civil rights movement warned: "No student or student organization shall participate in any controversial activities or issues on or off the campus unless he has been duly authorized by the college administration." Students in violation of the college's rules and regulations could find themselves suspended or expelled. Second, President Reddix accused the SGA of "embarrassing" the school and dissolved the organization. Third, Reddix expelled Walter Williams, the SGA president. Students petitioned to protect

Williams and reinstate the student government, but Reddix was not swayed. He and the board of trustees understood the power of the SGA as an organizing tool. Student organizations lost their freedom as the administration curbed civil rights activity on and off campus.[24]

Members of MIAS sympathized with Reddix's delicate situation but used their anonymity to chastise Reddix for his role in quashing activism on campus:

> MIAS does not look upon the administration and staff of Jackson State College as foes, but as allies, and we seek their support in accomplishing our goal. However, we realize that it is literally against the law for Negroes to actively seek to change the social and political structure for their betterment in the state of Mississippi. Jackson State College is a state supported and controlled institution; and if the administration of any State supported school follows the politics as handed down by the state officials, it will naturally conflict with the aims of MIAS.[25]

Jackson State students resented Reddix's interference in their quest for racial equality.

At the time of the Tougaloo sit-in and the Jackson State demonstration, James Meredith's application to transfer from Jackson State to the University of Mississippi was pending. The absence of a campus NAACP chapter and the dissolution of the SGA meant little formal organizing support on campus. Instead, Meredith relied on Medgar Evers and the NAACP, located only blocks from the campus. He also turned to informal friendship groups. Meredith was not alone on campus in his desire to dismantle segregation, and he found like-minded students whom he called the In Group. These students worked together without official university status to plan activities and discuss issues relating to civil rights. According to Meredith, they also bolstered his resolve: "There is little reason for me to doubt that this group kept me thinking of definite action. I imagine that at some time in the month preceding the decision to apply every possible course of action had been explored by the group." One hundred twenty-eight Jackson State students signed a letter of support for his application to Ole Miss after it became public. Self-identification was risky, and their signatures demonstrated their dedication to the cause. Formal civil rights organizations could not exist on campus, but friendship groups and other personal relationships served the same purpose.

Meredith's story sheds light on President Reddix's attitudes toward racial advancement and his own place in it. Meredith's application infuriated Mississippi officials. Governor Ross Barnett declared, "No school will be integrated in Mississippi while I am your governor." He prepared to close the University of Mississippi rather than desegregate the institution, and vowed to go to jail in defiance of the federal court order to admit Meredith. The Sovereignty Commission sought evidence to bar Meredith's enrollment on voting irregularities and moral grounds. And the board of trustees attempted to use Jackson State's lack of accreditation as a barrier. The state also pressured President Reddix to find some grounds on which to nullify Meredith's ability to transfer. According to Meredith, the board of trustees "used pressure including the threat of firing him to force him to expel me from Jackson College after I applied to the University of Mississippi in order to disqualify me as a transfer student. He was very proud of the fact that he had successfully resisted the Mississippi College Board."[27] In 1962, with a federal court order, Meredith enrolled at the University of Mississippi. Reddix's actions did not, by themselves, allow Meredith to enroll at Ole Miss. National media attention and federal involvement left the board of trustees little choice. But Reddix could have sabotaged the process and blocked Meredith's application. His resistance to external pressures facilitated Meredith's enrollment and struck a major blow against white supremacy in Mississippi.

Reddix was no closet radical, however. He fully believed that Jackson State should educate the black leaders of the future, but he held conservative attitudes toward black advancement—attitudes that clashed with student ideas on civil rights. Despite his objections to overt student activism, Reddix believed his contributions to the movement were valuable, as he stated in his 1974 memoir:

> I have never personally participated in an organized protest. Undoubtedly, I have been criticized for not doing so. For more than fifty years, I have devoted my life to the education and enlightenment of young people. By using whatever means I have had at my disposal, I believe that I have contributed to the training of young people for full participation as responsible citizens in a democracy. During my twenty-seven-year tenure as president of Jackson State College, the institution has granted upward of 5,000 degrees to its students. I believe this contribution is as important as participating in organized protest.[28]

Reddix did not condone the way the students did, in fact, use the campus. His conservative attitude toward active protest, and his role as president of a public HBCU, left him in a precarious position. He believed his actions protected Jackson State, and therefore, contributed to the elevation of black Mississippians, but Jackson State students resented his passive support of their actions.

Students at Tougaloo, for their part, did not create clandestine organizations. President Beittel supported their efforts as long as students did not ignore their academic pursuits. The NAACP attracted a number of Tougaloo students interested in direct action tactics. One of the organization's successful campaigns was a boycott of the segregated county fair in October 1962. College and high school NAACP members distributed handbills (secretly, of course, since it was illegal) and created telephone chains to spread the word. Few African Americans attended the fair, and the NAACP celebrated its victory. A second boycott occurred in November, this time of white Jackson businesses. Again, college constituents played a central role in the planning and execution of the boycott. Campbell College, a black junior college in Jackson, became boycott headquarters, and Tougaloo's printing press duplicated all the necessary literature. Several Tougaloo students remained on campus during the Christmas holiday to sustain the boycott's momentum. The Jackson NAACP Youth Councils, the Tougaloo NAACP chapter, and interested individuals worked together and crippled the white Jackson business community with a boycott that lasted through the Christmas season.[29] Organizers relished their economic impact on the local businesses and turned their attention to other targets in Jackson.

Tougaloo and SNCC also maintained a close relationship. Several Tougaloo students wrote news articles for SNCC publications, created a campus affiliate, and worked in SNCC projects in Mississippi during their summer vacations. SNCC even had a representative on campus: Joan Trumpauer, a white transfer student and former Freedom Rider. Tougaloo administrators and SNCC officials initiated a work-study program through which SNCC members earned college credit for their work in the movement. As was stated at the time:

> SNCC has found that there are many students who want to work in the civil rights movement but are afraid to take time out from school for fear that they will never return. SNCC is also faced with the problems of its present staff not completing their college educations.... SNCC and Tougaloo College, which is interested in both the civil rights movement and preparing people for good jobs and graduate school, have initiated the Work-Study Project in the hope that it will help to solve these problems.

Project participants alternately worked in SNCC voter registration efforts across Mississippi and participated in lectures, discussions, and classes on black history and the U.S. government.[30] The project sought to develop the indigenous leadership potential of students and of the black Mississippi residents with whom they came in contact. Tougaloo's support of the program facilitated student involvement in the movement in a way unmatched at most HBCUs during the civil rights era.

Tougaloo students hammered away at segregation through campus-based organizations as well. The SGA did not play a prominent role as an organizing tool, though movement activists dominated the organization for several years.

Instead, activists created organizations for the specific purpose of dismantling white supremacy. In 1963, Tougaloo's Cultural and Artistic Committee coordinated attacks on segregated entertainment in Jackson and scored major successes. One of the biggest blows came when the "Original Hootenanny U.S.A." canceled its appearance in Jackson. Tougaloo students Austin Moore, Calvin Brown, and Steven Rutledge (the white president of the student body) met the artists at the Jackson airport and convinced them not to play in the segregated city auditorium. Instead, Tougaloo's chapel hosted a free and integrated concert while original ticket holders stood in line for refunds. In early 1964, the stars of the popular television show *Bonanza* canceled their appearance in Jackson. A formal statement read: "We have been advised that the state coliseum . . . will be in fact segregated. Unless you can demonstrate to us without equivocation that our information is incorrect, this will constitute our notice of withdrawal." The white Jackson community, including the mayor, vowed never to watch *Bonanza* again.[31]

Jackson State students were not uninterested in civil rights activism in 1962 and 1963. The proximity of Jackson State to other movement centers made continued involvement in the struggle a possibility, but conditions on campus made organizing and mobilizing difficult. Also, the state stepped up its harassment of campus constituents. The Sovereignty Commission took an active role in quelling dissent by attempting to sway student sentiment on the civil rights movement. In fall 1963, the commission sought speakers who associated the movement with a Communist conspiracy, a popular tactic to discredit the movement. The commission contacted the presidents of the three public black colleges in the state and demanded they invite the Reverend Uriah Fields, an African American, to each campus. Fields had served as secretary of the Montgomery Improvement Association, the organization that spearheaded the 1955 Montgomery bus boycott, but left the association after accusing it of entertaining financial contributions from suspected Communists. His message coincided with what the commission wanted black students to hear: "He'll speak in defense of America, of *American* not socialist or Communist solutions for American problems. In doing so, he stands firmly for the purpose of 'less government, more responsibility and a better world.'"[32] Rather than issue the invitation itself, the commission's director told the presidents, "the invitation should originate with the schools without any connection with the Sovereignty Commission."[33] This way the colleges appeared to condone Fields's interpretation of the movement and discourage student participation in it.

Similarly, the State Board passed a Speaker Ban in August 1964, in part as a response to the SNCC Freedom Summer campaign. All of Mississippi's public colleges, including Jackson State, were affected. The Speaker Ban blended the themes of anti-integration, states' rights, and the threat of Communism. It specifically referenced an "invasion" of Mississippi by hostile outsiders looking to overthrow local government. The State Board passed the resolution to "protect student life from undue pressure by those engaged in activities contrary to the laws of the State of Mississippi and to the image of the citizenship of the state; and [to ensure] that all things be had and done which may be considered proper to eliminate development of socialistic and communistic trends among the college or university youth."[34] The State Board refused to acknowledge that the activism in the state came not from outsiders but from Mississippi residents, some of whom used their own public college campuses to organize and mobilize against the state.

The state monitored events on the Tougaloo campus and the movements of Tougaloo constituents as the college's role in the movement increased. Tougaloo's private status buffered it but did not completely protect it against external pressures. A bill to revoke the school's ninety-four-year-old charter in the name of "public interest" reached the floor of the state senate in February 1964. The argument was twofold. First, Tougaloo's original charter restricted the campus to $500,000 worth of assets, a figure Tougaloo had surpassed years earlier with no repercussions. Second, and more to the heart of the matter, Lieutenant Governor Carroll Gartin accused Tougaloo of neglecting its charter altogether: "The big question to be decided is whether the school has substituted civil disobedience instruction for the curriculum it was authorized to have under its charter." The legislature also approved a bill that invested the state's Commission on College Accreditation with discretionary powers.[35] Passage of the bill revoked reciprocal accreditation from the Southern Association of Colleges and Secondary Schools and the state. The loss of state accreditation prevented education students from receiving state teacher's licenses. The state hoped the loss of accreditation would tarnish Tougaloo's reputation, limit attendance, and force those teachers who received their degrees from Tougaloo to leave the state.

Legislators introduced both bills to punish Tougaloo for its support of civil rights activism, and they never pretended otherwise. Tougaloo mounted an aggressive publicity campaign to call attention to the situation and embarrass Governor Paul Johnson into either vetoing or limiting the influence of each bill. President Beittel enlisted the assistance of the American Association of University Professors, the Southern Association of Colleges and Secondary Schools, the United Church of Christ, Tougaloo's fellow institutions under the AMA, and other institutions and organizations with a vested interest in protecting higher educational autonomy.[36] Tougaloo's efforts were successful. The bill to revoke Tougaloo's charter died in the Judiciary Committee, and though passed, the act separating accreditation proved ineffective. Tougaloo won this battle, but the war was far from over. The entire episode demonstrated the level of hostility toward Tougaloo and thus the college's importance to the civil rights movement.

Beittel's forced resignation in April 1964 offers another example of Tougaloo's vulnerability to external pressures. Tougaloo's board of trustees adamantly denied that Beittel's support for civil rights had contributed to the decision to request his resignation, but a connection existed. The board grew weary of constant harassment by the state. Beyond the two legislative bills, the Sovereignty Commission actively courted possible informants on campus, fostered false rumors of links between Tougaloo's faculty and staff and a Communist conspiracy, and sponsored court injunctions against the board and other campus constituents. It even enlisted the assistance of the Citizens' Council, which initiated its own investigation. The board spent time and money, needed for improving the underfunded college, on defending it. Eager to expand their financial base, the trustees entertained a partnership with Brown University to be funded by the Ford Foundation. Brown University president Barnaby Keeney warned the trustees that Beittel's firing was imperative: Ford "will not do much, if anything, until they have this assurance." Beittel's civil rights stance and Tougaloo's role in the civil rights movement became stumbling blocks, and Ford money became conditional. The combination of state pressure and financial needs was a powerful mix. So in 1964, the board relieved Beittel of his duties.[37]

Another twist on the story of the liberal or conservative nature of public and private institutions occurred in the later 1960s, during the Black Power era, when students turned their focus inward and demanded change on campus. The appointment of Beittel's successor became a flashpoint at Tougaloo. The institution, in its almost 100–year history, had never had a black president—the AMA's liberal attitudes toward racial uplift at its institutions rarely translated into confidence in black control of those same institutions.[38] George Owens, a black man and Tougaloo's business manager, served as interim president while the board of trustees searched for an appropriate candidate. Viewing the appointment of another white president a campus-based reminder of white supremacy and black second-class status, students demanded that a black man be appointed, and they named several possibilities. After an unsuccessful search, Tougaloo trustees appointed Owens as president in 1966. Some Tougaloo constituents welcomed Owens, while others worried he would be a puppet president. Critics maintained that his background did not fit him for the position, that he was chosen to appease students rather than lead the college, and that his relatively conservative attitude toward student/campus involvement in the black liberation struggle undermined Tougaloo's prominent role in the Jackson movement.[39]

HBCUs as Movement Centers

Scholars rightly locate HBCU students at the center of the civil rights movement. Students did not work alone, but they took the reins of the movement and determined its path in the 1960s. Yet HBCUs themselves played an important part in the struggle. Focusing on student off-campus mobilization efforts obscures the role of the campus space as an organizing center. HBCUs attracted intelligent and motivated black youth and molded them into leaders. The physical environment brought these youth into close contact. The campus ethos encouraged intellectual curiosity, excellence, and racial responsibility. Activist students used these factors as a springboard to organize against the racial hierarchy with or without administration consent. Indigenous movement centers, including HBCU campuses, provided activists with a space in which to create long-term strategies to sustain the movement.

Private and public HBCUs differed in their relationship to the civil rights movement. Tougaloo was a movement center in the fullest sense. Key administrators, including the president, supported student participation in the movement and allowed students the opportunity to pool resources to attack white domination in Mississippi. Tougaloo's private status, however, did not immunize it from external pressure. Financial conditions and the high-profile role of Tougaloo students and staff in the black liberation struggle worried Tougaloo's board of trustees. President Beittel's forced resignation and his replacement with President Owens offer examples of how even private institutions made decisions that curtailed the movement center role of their campuses. Jackson State's dependence on the State Board and the Mississippi legislature kept the college from becoming as much of a movement center as Tougaloo was. But Jackson State students were far from unorganized or content with second-class citizenship. Some participated in off-campus groups like the NAACP, created clandestine organizations like MIAS, co-opted organizations like SGA for movement aims, or used informal networks to plan and mobilize. They participated in the movement at a lower rate than their counterparts at Tougaloo, but together, black students at Jackson State and Tougaloo inaugurated the direct action phase of the civil rights movement in Jackson, Mississippi.

Notes

1. Aldon Morris, *The Origins of the Civil Rights Movement: Black Communities Organizing for Change* (New York: Free Press, 1984), 40.

2. In *Origins of the Civil Rights Movement*, Morris discusses this as the primary role of movement centers.

3. "An Act to Incorporate the Trustees of Tougaloo University," May 1871, American Missionary Association Archives, Box 112, Folder 11, Addendum (1869–1991), Series

A, Subseries Tougaloo Correspondence, Amistad Research Center, Tulane University, New Orleans.

4. Tougaloo did have one white student prior to the 1960s. In 1879, the first normal school graduating class included Luella Miner, daughter of Tougaloo's treasurer (Clarice Campbell and Oscar Allan Rogers Jr., *Mississippi: The View from Tougaloo* [Jackson: University Press of Mississippi, 1979], 14).

5. Leila Gaston Rhodes, *Jackson State University: The First Hundred Years, 1877–1977* (Jackson: University Press of Mississippi, 1979), 97–103, 116–20; Jacob L. Reddix, *A Voice Crying in the Wilderness* (Jackson: University Press of Mississippi, 1974), 132–33; Board of Trustees Minutes, January 18, 1951, Board of Trustees Biennial Report 1949–51, 7, cited in Sammy Jay Tinsley, "A History of Mississippi Valley State College" (Ph.D. diss., University of Mississippi, 1972), 63–64. In 1940, the institution was named the Mississippi Negro Training School and became a two-year institution. In 1944, it became Jackson College for Negro Teachers and transitioned to a four-year institution. In 1956, it became Jackson State College.

6. Reddix makes no mention of his ideas on racial advancement but does hint that his lack of administrative experience was irrelevant for the position. According to him (*Voice*, 126), State Board chairman Jeptha Barbour stated: "The members felt that anybody who was born in the poorest county in Mississippi, under the conditions of the schools at that time, but who could get a good education and achieve what you have in spite of these handicaps, should be the president of the new college." Reddix was born in North Carolina, not Mississippi.

7. For example, see Jacob Reddix to Albert Jones, April 26, 1961, Sovereignty Commission File 2–138–0–9–1–1–1, Mississippi Department of Archives and History, Jackson (hereafter cited as MDAH; all Sovereignty Commission Files are located at MDAH).

8. Walter Williams, a former Jackson State student, and John A. Peoples, a former Jackson State president, both remembered that Reddix maintained a lifetime membership in the NAACP (Walter Williams, interview by author, December 9, 2004, Chicago; and John A. Peoples, interview by author, August 28, 2003, Jackson, Miss.). I have been unable find evidence to support this claim, but, if true, his involvement in the NAACP signals an interest in civil rights. His leanings toward legalistic strategies fit with the NAACP national office mandate, though it conflicted with the much more aggressive tactics of local Mississippi NAACP chapters.

9. Board of Trustees of Institutions of Higher Learning, Minutes of Special Meeting, March 9, 1957, MDAH.

10. "Talladega College Scene of Bi-Racial Conference on 'Civil Rights' This Weekend," *Talladega Daily Hornet*, April 10, 1948, Administrative Files, Record Group 4–13–1, Box A. D. Beittel, Folder A. D. Beittel, Talladega College Archives, Talladega, Ala.; A. D. Beittel to Merl Eppse, February 5, 1949, Administrative Files, Record Group 4–13–2, Box A. D. Beittel, Folder 1–1, Talladega College Archives; A. D. Beittel, "Some Effects of the 'Separate but Equal' Doctrine of Education," *Journal of Negro Education* 20, no. 2 (Spring 1951): 140–47; Henry N. Drewry and Humphrey Doermann, *Stand and Prosper: Private Black Colleges and Their Students* (Princeton, N.J.: Princeton Uni-

versity Press, 2001), 148–52; A. D. Beittel, interview by George Henderson, June 2, 1965, John Quincy Adams Manuscript Papers, Box 6, Folder A. D. Beittel, Oral History Project, Millsaps College Archives, Jackson, Miss.

11. Beittel, interview; Ed King, interview by author, August 28, 2003, Jackson, Miss.; Anne Moody, *Coming of Age in Mississippi* (New York: Laurel, 1976); Campbell and Rogers, *Mississippi*; John Salter Jr., *Jackson, Mississippi: An American Chronicle of Struggle and Schism* (Malabar, Fla.: Robert E. Krieger, 1979); Constance Slaughter Harvey, interview by author, August 26, 2003, Jackson, Miss.; Erle Johnston to File, April 13, 1964, 1, 2, Sovereignty Commission File 3–74–2–17–1–1–1, and Mr. Zero to Sovereignty Commission, May 5, 1964, Sovereignty Commission File 3–74–2–19–1–1–1 through 2–1–1. John Held, chairman of Tougaloo's Department of Philosophy and Religion, became an informant for the Sovereignty Commission and adopted the pseudonym Mr. Zero.

12. King, interview.

13. Susie Baughns, "Join the Youth Council!" *Blue and White Flash* 3, no. 1 (November 1942), 2, and *Blue and White Flash* 4, no. 2 (March 1944), in *Blue and White Flash* (Student Publication) March 1942–May 1967, Record Group 7, Box 1, Jackson State University Archives, Jackson, Miss. (hereafter cited as JSUA). This was not an NAACP Youth Council; Jackson State did not have an NAACP chapter until 1968.

14. John Dittmer, *Local People: The Struggle for Civil Rights in Mississippi* (Urbana: University of Illinois Press, 1994), 3; Gabrielle Simon Edgecomb, "Ernst Borinski: Positive Marginality: 'I Decided to Engage in Stigma Management,'" in *From Swastika to Jim Crow: Refugee Scholars at Black Colleges* (Malabar, Fla.: Krieger, 1993), 117–28; Ruby Hurley to John Mangram, March 28, 1956, and John Mangram to Ruby Hurley, January 25, 1960, Box John D. Mangram, (no folder), Tougaloo College Archives (hereafter cited as TCA).

15. *The Citizens' Council* 2, no. 2 (November 1956), 1, Citizens' Council Newspapers, 1956–57, Accession Number 90.25, (no box or folder), TCA.

16. Erle Johnston to Federation of Constitutional Government, May 4, 1964, Erle Johnston, "Canton Lions Club Speech," May 13, 1964, Erle Johnston to Herman Glazier, March 16, 1965, and Erle Johnston to Paul Johnson, March 29, 1965, cited in "Sovereignty Commission Agency History," 3, summary report included in Sovereignty Commission File; Yasuhiro Katagiri, *The Mississippi State Sovereignty Commission: Civil Rights and States' Rights* (Jackson: University Press of Mississippi, 2001).

17. Clayborne Carson, *In Struggle: SNCC and the Black Awakening of the 1960s* (Cambridge, Mass.: Harvard University Press, 1981); Charles Payne, *I've Got the Light of Freedom: The Organizing Tradition and the Mississippi Freedom Struggle* (Berkeley: University of California Press, 1995).

18. Donald R. Mathews and James W. Prothro, *Negroes and the New Southern Politics* (New York: Harcourt, Brace, and World, 1966), 425–29; John Orbell, "Protest Participation among Southern Negro College Students," *American Political Science Review* 61 (June 1967): 446–56. These and other studies often juxtaposed public (less reputable) against private institutions (more reputable).

19. Salter, *Jackson, Mississippi*, 4, 19, 56.

20. James "Sam" Bradford, interview by Robert Walker, cited in "Tougaloo Nine:

Demonstration Comes to Mississippi," May 1, 1979, 5, Vertical File, Box Tougaloo College, Folder Tougaloo Nine, TCA; Cal Turner, "Tougaloo Group Ignore Officers," *State Times*, March 27, 1961, Box Tougaloo College, Folder Tougaloo Nine, 1960–67 clippings, TCA; W. C. Shoemaker, "President Quells Student Disorder," *Jackson Daily News*, March 28, 1961; A. D. Beittel, interview with WLBT, September 1961, cited in Campbell and Rogers, *Mississippi*, 198–99 (the original WLBT transcript and tape no longer exist).

21. Williams, interview; Mississippi Improvement Association of Students, General Boycott Order #1, March 23, 1961, Sovereignty Commission File 2–138–0–6–1–1–1; James Meredith, *Three Years in Mississippi* (Bloomington: University of Indiana Press, 1966), 94.

22. Meredith, *Three Years*, 95 (both quotes). John Dittmer (*Local People*, 88) credits Medgar Evers and Jackson State students Dorie Ladner and Joyce Ladner with organizing the demonstration. Either interpretation supports the idea that black college students spearheaded it.

23. Meredith, *Three Years*, 93–98; Wallace Dabbs, "Jackson State College Students Stage Protest," *Jackson Clarion-Ledger*, March 28, 1961; Edmund Noel, "Nine Jailed in 'Study-In,'" *Jackson Clarion-Ledger*, March 28, 1961; "Negroes Try Jail March in Jackson," *Jackson Clarion-Ledger*, March 29, 1961.

24. Jackson State College Student Handbook, September 1961, 40, JSUA; John A. Peoples, *To Survive and Thrive: The Quest for a True University* (Jackson, Miss.: Town Square Books, 1995), 58; "Report Classes Boycotted at Jackson State," *Jackson Daily News*, October 7, 1961, Sovereignty Commission File 10–105–0–4–1–1–1; Williams, interview. Williams, reflecting on his expulsion, believes that Reddix probably suspended him because of pressure from Mississippi officials.

25. Mississippi Improvement Association of Students, Policy Letter #3, April 20, 1961, James Meredith Collection, Box 1, Folder 19, University of Mississippi Archives, Oxford, Miss.

26. Meredith, *Three Years*, 51, 87.

27. William Peart, "Ross Risks Jail to Halt Mixing," *Jackson Daily News*, September 14, 1962, James Meredith Collection, (no box), Folder Newspaper Clippings 1962, JSUA; David Sansing, *Making Haste Slowly: The Troubled History of Higher Education in Mississippi* (Jackson: University Press of Mississippi, 1990); James Meredith, "Behind the Scenes at Jackson State University," *Outlook* 9, no. 2 (September 1983): 1, James Meredith Collection, (no box), Folder Weekly Communicator, JSUA; James Meredith, interview by author, August 23, 2003, Jackson, Miss.

28. Reddix, *Voice*, 222.

29. Salter, *Jackson, Mississippi*, 49–86.

30. "Tougaloo Work-Study Project" Memorandum in Dona [Moses?] to Mississippi Field Staff, [1964], Ed King Collection, Box 2, Folder 84, TCA.

31. Ibid.; "Hootenanny Group Cancels Jackson Performance," *Student Voice*, November 21, 1963; "Nobody's Coming," *Free Press*, February 1, 1963, in Ed King Collection, Box 9, Folder 450, TCA; Ed King, unpublished manuscript, Chapter "63–64 Concerts," 1–9, Clarice Rogers and Oscar Rogers Papers, Box 2, Folder 2–34, TCA.

32. American Opinion Speakers Bureau information sheet on Reverend Uriah J. Fields, [n.d.], Sovereignty Commission File 10–105–0–15–1–1–1.

33. Erle Johnston Jr., "Rev. Uriah J. Fields, Negro Clergyman, Evangelist, Author, and Lecturer of Montgomery, Alabama," September 23, 1963, Sovereignty Commission File 10–105–0–13–1–1–1.

34. Board of Trustees of Institutions of Higher Learning Minutes, August 20, 1964, 5, MDAH.

35. Senate Bills Nos. 1672 and 1794 of the Mississippi Legislature, Regular Session, 1964; "Action on Tougaloo Is Due for Delay," *Jackson Clarion-Ledger*, March 6, 1964; A. D. Beittel to William Fidler, June 6, 1964; A. D. Beittel to Hollis Price, May 27, 1964; and A. D. Beittel to Gordon Sweet, June 6, 1964, all in Box Tougaloo College History, Folder Accreditation Revocation (state), TCA; "Tougaloo Bill Appears Dead," *Jackson Clarion-Ledger*, April 14, 1964, Subject Files Tougaloo College, 1960–1969, MDAH.

36. Beittel to Fidler, June 6, 1964; Beittel to Price, May 27, 1964; Beittel to Sweet, June 6, 1964.

37. Erle Johnston to File, April 13, 1964, Sovereignty Commission File 3–74–2–17–1–1–1; Shelby Rogers to Earle [sic] Johnston, [May 1964], Sovereignty Commission File 3–74–2–13–1–1–1; Writ of Temporary Injunction, Chancery Court of the First Judicial District of Hinds County, Miss., June 6, 1963, Ed King Papers, Box 8, Folder 374, TCA; A. L. Hopkins, "Meeting with Committee of Citizens' Council," November 13, 1962, Sovereignty Commission File 1–3–0–11–1–1–1; Barnaby Keeney to Lawrence Durgin, March 9, 1964, Barnaby Keeney Office File Register, Tougaloo College, 1964–65, Miscellaneous Correspondence, Brown University Archives, Providence, R.I.; Joy Ann Williamson, "'This Has Been Quite a Year for Heads Falling': Institutional Autonomy in the Civil Rights Era," *History of Education Quarterly* 44 (Winter 2004): 489–511.

38. James D. Anderson, *The Education of Blacks in the South, 1865–1935* (Chapel Hill: University of North Carolina Press, 1988).

39. Owens's background included a bachelor's degree from Tougaloo, graduate work at Columbia University, and work experience as a junior corporate executive and as business manager at Talladega College and Tougaloo College (Campbell and Rogers, *Mississippi*, 219). The Sovereignty Commission monitored Owens for signs of support for the civil rights movement. The commission found that Owens was more conservative than Beittel in that he did not speak out or participate in any overt organizing, but Owens allowed Tougaloo's campus to house voter registration workers (Erle Johnston to File, "Inauguration of President of Tougaloo College, March 24, 1966, Sovereignty Commission File 3–74–2–51–1–1–1; Erle Johnston to File, "Tougaloo College," [November 1964?], Sovereignty Commission File 3–74–2–36–1–1–1; and Mr. Zero to Bert Buchanan, October 28, 1964, Sovereignty Commission File 9–330–5–1–1–1).

5

Prying the Door Farther Open

A Memoir of Black Student Protest at the University of Maryland at College Park, 1966–1970

HAYWARD "WOODY" FARRAR

Desegregation came slowly and grudgingly to the University of Maryland at College Park. The university's longtime president H. C. Byrd best expressed the school's attitude toward blacks when, in 1935, he said, "If we don't do something about Princess Anne [site of Maryland State College for Negroes] we're going to have to educate them at College Park where our girls are." The National Association for the Advancement of Colored People (NAACP) opened the university's law school, in Baltimore, to token black enrollment in 1935 with its *Murray v. Maryland* lawsuit. In the early 1950s, lawsuits led to further black enrollment in Baltimore as well as to the initial black enrollment at College Park. In 1950, Esther McCready entered the nursing school in Baltimore. In 1951, future member of Congress Parren Mitchell enrolled in the sociology graduate program at College Park, and Hiram Whittle, admitted into the engineering program, became the first black undergraduate student at College Park.[1]

The University of Maryland grudgingly accepted the *Brown v. Board of Education* decision in 1954 by opening its College Park undergraduate campus to in-state blacks only. For the next twelve years, black students were an insignificant and unwelcome presence on campus. The level of the university's racism can be seen by its refusing to allow the Congress of Racial Equality (CORE) to have a chapter on campus, and its refusing to allow Martin Luther King Jr. and other civil rights leaders to speak on campus while welcoming George Wallace as a speaker. The university also refused to allow its campus chaplains to participate in civil rights protests.[2]

As late as 1966, the University of Maryland was still overwhelmingly white. Only a handful of blacks attended the university's law and medical schools in Baltimore and its newly opened Baltimore County campus. Maryland State College, on the Eastern Shore of Maryland, though under the University of Maryland Board of Regents, was the "Negro" segment of the University of

Maryland, and a badly neglected one at that. As for the school's main campus at College Park, blacks were around 1 percent of the undergraduate and graduate student body of 28,000. The fewer than 300 black students were quite invisible in such a large student population. As for black faculty and staff, they were virtually nonexistent at College Park in 1966—the year I entered the university.[3]

Glacial Change

The winds of change swept through American higher education during the 1960s. College students, black and white, called attention to any number of social problems. Among the social disorders generating student protest were the denial of civil and voting rights to southern blacks, America's involvement in Vietnam, and the impersonality, soullessness, and materialism affecting American higher education and life during the 1960s. More numerous than ever before, America's college students viewed themselves as citizens of a new, idealistic, and freer "counterculture." They had great expectations and the numbers and economic muscle to pursue these expectations.

Black college students generated much of the social turmoil of the 1960s. Students at historically black colleges and universities (HBCUs) such as Fisk, Spelman, North Carolina A&T, and Howard were the shock troops of the civil rights movement, making up the backbone of the Student Nonviolent Coordinating Committee (SNCC) and other such groups. At predominantly white colleges, black students, influenced by Black Power ideology, were organizing and agitating to make these schools acknowledge their presence and needs as well as those of the black community they came from.[4]

However, the wave of radical protest against racism, economic injustice, and the Vietnam War seemed to have passed by the University of Maryland at College Park in 1966 and 1967. To be sure, there was a chapter of Students for a Democratic Society (SDS) at College Park, but it was a rudimentary organization shunned and despised by the mainstream student body. There was also an interracial group called CORE, which, though not connected with the national organization with the same name, sought racial desegregation at the university and its surrounding town of College Park. Headed by Earl Wynn, Andrew Chisholm, and Bob McLeod, and advised by Arthur Adkins, a liberal white professor, CORE struggled mightily in 1966 and early 1967 against black apathy and white indifference concerning race relations at the University of Maryland. However, Wynn, Chisholm, McLeod, and Adkins all helped create the foundation for the progress that came later.[5]

The fall of 1967 saw the beginning of the end of the University of Maryland's racial apathy. The number of black students at College Park increased somewhat, and these new students were more interested in forming a black community there than previous generations. The winds of Black Power were beginning to blow at College Park. CORE grew in membership and actually began various social programs to improve the lot of black students at the university. Among these programs were an academic tutoring program, supplying volunteers to the University of Maryland's Upward Bound program, and sponsoring various dances, parties, and social functions to enable black students to feel less isolated from each other and the school. CORE also brought to the campus speakers like Nathan Hare to inform the students of current trends in the black movement. While all of these programs were a vast improvement over what had gone on before, none of them challenged the university's refusal to do anything to recruit or retain black students and faculty.

None of the school's Greek-letter fraternities or sororities had black pledges or members. Most of them were housed in a horseshoe-shaped complex of houses across U.S. Route 1 from the campus. This complex, called "fraternity row," was a constant reminder to black students of their exclusion from one of the mainstays of college life. Adding insult to injury was the prominent display by one of these fraternity houses, Kappa Alpha, of the Confederate flag on its porch. Blacks were poorly represented in the university's clubs, honorary societies, Student Government Association (SGA), class offices, and athletic teams. The only black to hold a significant SGA office was Jonathan L. Prater, who was sophomore class president in 1967. Black athletes were few and far between—no more than three on the football team and just two on the basketball team. (Darryl Hill, the first black member of the University of Maryland's football team, played from 1964 to 1966; Ken Dutton, Kene Halliday, and Leonard Spicer were on the football team from 1966 to 1970; Billy Jones and Junious "Pete" Johnson were the first—and from 1966 to 1970 the only—two blacks on the basketball team.) More injurious to the morale of black students at College Park was the almost total absence of black faculty and staff. The university administration's refusal to acknowledge the presence of black students or their concerns was demoralizing if not openly discriminatory. This indifference not only encouraged white students to despise and ignore black students but also fostered feelings of self-hate and apathy among black students.[6]

Because of the university's indifference toward black students and the school's reputation as a racially segregated institution, black students did not often consider the University of Maryland when choosing colleges. College-bound black high school graduates in Baltimore, for example, were more likely to attend one of the public historically black colleges—Morgan State College, Coppin State College, Bowie State College, or Maryland State College—than the state university. The University of Maryland did not draw well from the large black community in Washington, D.C., either, though the College Park campus was just eight miles from the D.C. line. As 1967 turned into 1968, Maryland's higher education system—save for the few hundred black students at the University of Maryland and a smattering at Towson State and Frostburg State—was as racially segregated as it had been before the 1954 *Brown v. Board of Education* decision.[7]

A Black Student Union

The assassination of Martin Luther King Jr. on April 4, 1968, touched off a series of riots and other disorders in black communities throughout the United States, as black folk—and not a few whites—expressed their grief and anger. The University of Maryland was not spared from the turmoil. On the day after the King murder, a spontaneous demonstration of black and white students prompted the university to cancel classes for that day. King's assassination roused the University of Maryland's black students out of their apathy. CORE, the group most directly concerned with black student problems, decided to do something drastic to make its presence known at College Park.

Two weeks after King's assassination, CORE members interrupted the annual convocation speech given by University of Maryland president Wilson H. Elkins. A small group of black students walked out onto the floor of Cole Field House, approached the podium where Elkins was making his presentation, and read out ten demands. Among these demands were the establishment of a black studies program, increased recruiting of black students, hiring of black faculty and staff, and more courteous treatment by the campus police. Before all ten demands were read, the group was mobbed by state troopers assigned to guard Elkins and quickly hustled out. The morale of the black student population rose greatly as a result of CORE's show of defiance. Attendance increased at CORE meetings, and hitherto silent black students clamored for more militant action by the organization.

That action took place in early May 1968 as CORE voted to change its name to the Black Student Union (BSU) and invite those few white students in the organization to leave it. The name change met no opposition, but the move to oust whites from the organization did. Some black students thought it odd that a group dedicated to ending racial exclusion at the University of Maryland should practice racial exclusion itself. As a result, the BSU never explicitly prohibited white membership, though its future activities left no room for white student participation. Oddly, Arthur Adkins, the white faculty adviser to CORE, was retained as the faculty adviser to the BSU. With the conversion of CORE into the BSU accomplished, its president, Earl Wynn, who had provided dogged and effective leadership for the school's black students, graduated from the university in June 1968. That month, the University of Maryland's black students, now heavily influenced by the riots and anarchy that marked 1968, went back to their homes anticipating a further hot summer of urban ghetto riots. However, the long-awaited, apocalyptic, ultimate ghetto super riot never occurred. The riots sparked by the assassination of Martin Luther King in 1968 were the last major urban ghetto disturbances until the 1980 riot in Miami, Florida. Deprived of the chance to fight the "system" in the streets of Baltimore, Washington, Philadelphia, and elsewhere, many black students looked forward to fighting it on the campuses of their colleges. The University of Maryland was no exception to this rule.[8]

In October 1968, the BSU held its fall elections. Bob McLeod was elected president, I was elected vice president, and Wayne Stovall was chosen to be the steering committee and social committee chairman. The black student population increased again that year. A new breed of militant black students accounted for most of this increase. Leading these committed black freshmen was Terence Cooper, who quickly became a power within the BSU.[9]

The organization was soon confronting the University of Maryland on a number of issues. One was the alleged rejection of a black applicant for a research project conducted by the School of Home Economics. A black student applied to be a human guinea pig for a nutrition experiment and was turned down because of "differences between black and white metabolisms." The BSU took this as an insult to blacks and staged a demonstration in front of the university's Home Economics building. This demonstration brought out around 200 students, mostly black, who either sat or stood on the steps of the building waving signs, posters, or flags and singing civil rights anthems. The vice president for student affairs, J. Winston Martin, hurried over to the demonstration to confer with BSU officials and address the students. Martin and BSU president McLeod agreed to end the demonstration with a "walk-through" of the Home Economics building. That defused the tensions. Later, the School of Home Economics, thanks to some friendly persuasion from Martin, recanted its stand and admitted the black student to the experiment. This successful confrontation helped to establish the BSU's credibility on campus.

The resolution of the Home Economics dispute was the only success the BSU had during the fall of 1968. Most of the semester was spent in internal bickering. This dissension centered over the relationship between President Bob McLeod and the steering committee. McLeod, a vigorous and assertive leader, thought he knew what was best for the organization and wanted to run it with an iron hand. The steering committee, reflecting the diversity of the black student population at College Park, had no clear idea of where they wanted the BSU to go. At that time, the black students at College Park were divided among black nationalists, racial assimilationists, supporters of the

Black Panther Party, Black Muslims, Pan-Africanists, violent revolutionaries, nonviolent reformers, "hippies," conservatives, and feminists.

Black students were divided by more than ideology, however. They were also divided between resident students and commuters; between those from Baltimore and those from Washington, D.C., and its suburbs; between affluent and poor; and by skin color. Overcoming such divisions to create a black community strong enough to neutralize racism at College Park was the BSU's major challenge.[10]

All that kept black students together was a shared disgust at their second-class status at the university. As the BSU vice president, I was caught between McLeod and the steering committee. At that time, my major concern was keeping the organization from flying apart. I instinctively saw the fissures within College Park's black population and believed that the only way to deal with these fissures was to make the BSU a democratic, nonpartisan, nonideological service organization for black students, one that could accommodate all points of view. I believed strongly that consensus could slowly be formed and true unity achieved for blacks at College Park. In pursuit of that goal, I served as a mediator between McLeod and the steering committee.

The turmoil within the BSU climaxed in February 1969. Because of its internal problems, the organization could not deal effectively with issues concerning black students. These issues included the absence of a black studies program (a demand of black students everywhere), the lack of black faculty and staff, the small number of black students at College Park, and their exclusion from many student organizations and functions. But as long as the impasse between McLeod and the steering committee continued, nothing could be done about these issues.

This impasse was broken in early February 1969. McLeod announced that he was dropping out of the University of Maryland, thereby removing himself from the presidency of the organization. I became the new president. Wayne Stovall, the publicity and social chairman, became the vice president, and Terence Cooper was chosen to chair the steering committee.

New Black Student Leadership

On the surface, I was an odd choice to lead a militant black student organization. A nineteen-year-old junior from Baltimore, I was a newcomer to the College Park black community. As a freshman and sophomore, I spent most of my time on my studies, amassing a grade point average high enough to become the first black member of the University of Maryland's General Honors Program. During those first two years, most of my friends and acquaintances were white, and in many ways my cultural leanings were far more white than black. Yet I was well aware of the second-class status of black students at the University of Maryland and resolved to be part of the process to improve that status. During my sophomore year, 1967–68, I joined CORE and participated in the disruption of President Elkins's convocation speech. That summer I immersed myself in books pertaining to the black experience, especially *Black Power: The Politics of Liberation* by Stokely Carmichael and Charles Hamilton. I returned to campus in the fall of 1968 more militant than ever. (I did not, however, completely accept Black Power separatist ideology, believing then that black separatism was just a temporary transition to full integration in American society; others thought Black Power should lead to permanent separation from the system.) That fall, eager to take a leadership role in the newly formed BSU, I was elected vice president—after giving a rousing campaign speech proclaiming the superiority of all things black. Then, due to the events described earlier, I became president of the organization.

Though I was now president of the BSU, and as such the titular leader of the black student community at the University of Maryland, I kept my white friends and contacts at the school. Unlike black student leaders described in George Napper's *Blacker than Thou*, I never really went through the conversion process to "blackness."[11] Consequently, I did not fit the pattern or stereotype of black student militants of the era. Not caring about being "black," I had nothing personally to prove. Therefore, I was extremely flexible, even opportunistic, in leading the BSU, serving as a spokesperson for the black student community and as a liaison between the BSU and the University of Maryland. In that last role, I was particularly effective, since my reputation as an outstanding student plus my mild-mannered, professorial bearing gave me access to, and credibility with, the university's administration that a more militant-seeming student leader would not have had.

As president of the BSU, my leadership was characterized by shiftiness and double-talking. No one really knew where I stood, since I seemed to stand for whatever those around me stood for at any particular time. My way of dealing with conflicting points of view or conflicting people was to agree with everything and everyone. I talked out of all sides of my mouth, misrepresented my positions, and even lied about where I stood, all to keep the BSU together. I was whatever the occasion called for. When the situation called for tough talk, I talked tough. When I had to be conciliatory with blacks or whites, I was that—anything to advance the BSU, the black student community at the University of Maryland, and myself. I not only had a burning desire to see black students acknowledged and respected at the university, I had an equally burning ambition to retain my position and status within the black and white communities. I reveled in the spotlight, first as BSU vice president, then as president, and I believed that a powerful black student community respected by all would further my personal desire for status and respect.

Knowing that taking a single strong ideological stand and imposing it on the BSU could destroy the organization, and leave me open to opposition that could unseat me, thereby depriving me of the status and the spotlight being president gave me, I took all the ideological stands present at College Park and, as a result, stood for no ideology at all. I got away with this due to the scattering of the University of Maryland's small black population throughout its huge College Park campus, the kaleidoscopic diversity of that population, and my ability to play off all sides against the middle. In that sense, my leadership was more that of an urban political boss, or labor union leader, than of a principled, charismatic leader such as Malcolm X or Martin Luther King, my nominal heroes. Nevertheless, I was occasionally criticized by the some of the membership for being "wishy-washy" and not "ruthless" as the BSU president. They were right about my leadership style, but I believed at the time that a more assertive form of leadership would tear the organization apart. It must have worked, for I served out a full term as BSU president, and the organization stayed together to pressure the university into granting our wishes with a minimum of disruption.

I was not alone in pursuing this leadership style. The BSU vice president, Wayne Stovall, was even more opportunistic and pragmatic than I and was able to do things that I was too uptight or respectable to do. Consequently, Stovall complemented me perfectly. I served as the spokesperson and figurehead, a role I enjoyed, while Stovall did much of the behind the scenes wheeling and dealing with black students, white students, and the administration that the BSU needed in order to preserve and promote itself. Popular with all at College Park, Stovall attracted much black student support for the BSU through his extensive social contacts. Knowing where the bodies were buried at College Park made Stovall even more effective in garnering financial and administrative support for the BSU. As such, he was invaluable to the organization and in some ways more important and powerful than I.

Of course, the BSU had to have some idealism in its leadership. It could not have accomplished as much as it did if *all* of its leaders were hustlers. Providing the idealism was steering committee chairman Terence Cooper, the only member of the BSU's top echelon with a consistent ideology. A staunch black nationalist, Cooper carried himself with a dignity and bearing that generated respect and admiration from all who knew him and worked with him. He also radiated a charisma and an authority that I and the glad-handing Wayne Stovall lacked. As such, he was the spiritual leader of the BSU and gave it the integrity, respect, and credibility it had to have to gain the support of the University of

Maryland's black students and to inspire fear, if not respect, in the hearts of the school's white students, faculty, and administration.

Despite very different personalities and outlooks, Wayne Stovall, Terence Cooper, and I worked extremely well together. All three of us were Baltimoreans and graduates of the Baltimore City College High School. We saw in each other qualities that each of us, as individuals, lacked, and each respected the others for that. We subordinated our personal egos to promote a strong and effective BSU and, despite at times having strong differences of opinion, respected each other and those differences. As president, I considered myself first among equals and, though status and power hungry, respected the abilities of Stovall and Cooper enough to defer to either or both of them when necessary to promote the organization. Though I was not socially close to either Stovall or Cooper, I did have an enormous amount of respect and admiration for them, something reciprocated by both toward me and toward each other. We all realized how important unity was at the top of the BSU, for without it there could be little unity among the rank and file.

Of course, the BSU was hardly a three-man organization. The BSU's steering committee was composed of representatives from the various dormitory complexes on campus—the Hill, the Cambridge Dorm complex, the Ellicott Dorm complex, the Elkton Dorm complex, and the trailer dorms—and the commuters. The BSU also had officials appointed by the steering committee to handle the treasury, publicity, social activities, and academic and political education. I made all executive decisions with the advice and consent of Wayne Stovall and Terence Cooper. They were then ratified by the steering committee. Then the general body at weekly plenary meetings would ratify those decisions as well as make proposals to the steering committee. All this was extremely democratic, which is how I wanted it. I believed that the BSU could take the risks it had to only with the unwavering support of the black students who made up its membership. Without such support, the leadership would have to crawl out on a limb, a place I did not want to be. My attitude was "see where the crowd goes, then lead them."

Among those making up the steering committee and running various BSU functions were Carolyn Austin, whose calm, poise, and common sense provided much-needed stability to the BSU; Valerie McNeal, one of the first black feminists at the University of Maryland; Darryl Bryant, who was the treasurer and, as such, kept an eye on the BSU's meager finances; Chris Young, whose realistic assessments of the University of Maryland's social and racial order were invaluable to the organization; and Karl Wyatt, the organization's theoretician, who founded the BSU's newspaper, the *Black Explosion*.

Others who gave their time and services to the organization were Walter

Thomas, Cheryl Edwards, Tommy Davis, Charles Onley, Erastus Johnson, Gerri Major, Janice Stewart, Michael McNair, and Robert Blandford. In fact, the BSU never had more than fifteen to twenty working members—something kept well hidden from the world. The leadership of the College Park BSU was predominantly male, which was true for most black student unions of the era. Unlike today, when black female students outnumber black male students in higher education, back then the male-female ratio was just about even or favored men. Second-wave feminism had not yet begun to any great extent in the black community, and young black women of the era believed that they should promote black male leadership. This was true at College Park as elsewhere. Today at schools like Virginia Tech, most of the black activist student leadership is female. As the faculty adviser of the Virginia Tech NAACP chapter for thirteen years, I know whereof I speak.[12]

Vital to the success of the organization was promoting the idea that the group had the fanatical support of *all* the black students at College Park, roughly 750 in number by 1969. In pursuit of this end, reporters from the school newspaper, the *Diamondback*, were barred from BSU meetings, and BSU officials did not give interviews or otherwise talk to the campus press, or for that matter any press. This secrecy, which aggravated the ever-increasing paranoia white students and administrators had at College Park concerning black students in 1969, prompted them to grossly exaggerate the power—actual and potential—of the BSU.

Even so, the organization could depend on the vast majority of College Park's black students to show up at its demonstrations and other social functions. Every black student was a member and was considered a part of the BSU even if he or she never attended a meeting. While I was president, the organization never played "blacker than thou" games with its membership. In other words, it did not try to define a single standard of "blackness" and impose it on black students the way black student organizations on many other campuses did. My personal tastes and outlook were still predominantly "white," and I would not tolerate others telling me what to be and refused to do likewise. I wanted an organization where all black students, regardless of their inclinations, would feel at home, and though I was not the most imposing of leaders, I was able to impress that idea on the BSU. Therefore, the organization, while lacking ideological coherence, had a higher degree of operational unity, and more support from its black student constituency, than did black student organizations that hewed to a single standard of "blackness."[13]

As for white students who were interested in the organization's goals, they were subtly discouraged from membership. Actually, I favored having white students as members—something few other black student union leaders in that era advocated. I would not have minded my numerous white friends and cronies sharing my work in the organization. Furthermore, I was an integrationist along the lines of Martin Luther King and wanted a truly interracial society at College Park. A black student union that openly barred whites would not in the long run promote that goal. True, however, to my refusal to press issues in the BSU that would jeopardize the unity of the organization or my position in it, I did not openly call for the admission of whites to the organization. I kept my opinions about this issue secret from my fellow black students, hoping that the issue would go away. My white friends knew and understood my dilemma and did not press the point with me. I soothed my guilty conscience by reminding myself that the B'nai B'rith did not have Gentile members, nor did the Holy Name Society or the Jesuits have Protestants.

The BSU was not alone in its desires for progressive racial and social change at the University of Maryland. By 1969, the overall student body was dropping its 1950s social attitudes and joining the rest of America's student population in radical protest for social justice and against the Vietnam War. The school's SGA became quite sympathetic to the BSU's struggle for racial justice, especially after the Third Party, a group of radical whites, took control of the SGA. Members of the Third Party, such as Mike Gold and Mark Erich, were either my cronies or Wayne Stovall's and as such could be expected to provide support for the BSU's aims. In order to appease the black revolutionary nationalist segment of the university's black community, the BSU could not openly support the Third Party, but my and Stovall's under-the-table backing of this group would have important implications for the BSU's future.

As for the administration, the University of Maryland was blessed with administrators as pragmatic, opportunistic, and idealistic as the top echelon of the BSU. Wilson H. Elkins, the president of the university, was not known for his strong stands on racial issues, or any thing else for that matter. This made him the target of an unusual amount of criticism, even hatred, from black and radical white students. However, in retrospect, he was far more progressive than he seemed at the time, for he either quietly encouraged or at least did not interfere with those administrators—especially J. Winston Martin, the vice president for student affairs, Francis C. Haber, who chaired the history department, and William Sedlacek, of the Academic Counseling Center—who wanted progressive racial change at the university. These men reached out to the BSU and established excellent, though undercover, working relationships with Stovall and me. Terence Cooper, black nationalist as he was, was not as close to these administrators as Stovall and I were, but he had sense enough not to interfere with negotiations that we carried on with them.

As for black faculty and staff at College Park, they were few and far between, but all of them gave of themselves to the BSU, and they deserve much of the credit for the peaceful racial change that took place there. Among these unsung helpers was Julia Davidson, who ran the Intensive Educational Development Program, and as such was the virtual spiritual mother to all of the black students at the University of Maryland, whether they were members of her program or not. Graduate student Glen Brooks, along with Davidson, provided the wisdom and maturity so needed by the leadership of the BSU, who were, after all, just eighteen, nineteen, twenty, and twenty-one years old. Mary Frances Berry and John Blassingame—later on distinguished historians but in 1969 just beginning their careers as members of the University of Maryland history department—lent their scholarly expertise to the BSU, especially when it came time to set up the school's Afro-American studies program. The fact that I was an honors history major helped solidify their relationship to me and to the BSU. Fortunately, the BSU's leadership and rank and file had brains enough to listen to the handful of black faculty and staff and take strength from their wise advice, counsel, and support.[14]

Now that the BSU had a leadership team that had the support of the black student body, it searched for ways to call attention to black students' concerns and needs. In early March 1969, the BSU and the University of Maryland—in quite different ways—were jolted by charges by the U.S. Department of Health, Education, and Welfare (HEW) that the state of Maryland was maintaining a racially segregated higher education system. HEW specifically pointed to the 98 percent white student body composition at the University of Maryland at College Park as an example of this unlawful situation. With its contentions concerning the university's lack of interest in black students now vindicated and supported by the federal government, the BSU had an issue with which it could challenge the university.[15]

Giving the BSU added hope were rumors from the administration that a black or Afro-American studies program/department was about to be established. This, of course, had been a demand of black student groups all over the country and had been an issue that on some campuses generated much violence, chaos, and anarchy. In late February 1969, possibly in anticipation of such a demand coming from black students, President Elkins wrote Francis C. Haber, chair of the university's history department, asking him to establish a committee to investigate the possibility of establishing an Afro-American studies program. Elkins was not the only prescient college president. In May 1968, for example, University of Illinois chancellor Jack Peltason wrote Robert Rogers, dean of the College of Liberal Arts and Sciences there, asking him to develop black studies courses.[16]

Elkins's action was welcomed by the BSU. At the time, I especially feared violent confrontations since I wanted to see neither myself nor the black students I represented suspended, expelled, arrested, injured, or killed attempting to attain the group's goals. Though I would not run from potentially violent confrontations, and was willing to take risks when needed, when possible I preferred negotiation and deal making to soul-satisfying but ultimately futile violent protests. If the university wanted to talk things over, well that was fine with me. I thought that was the grown-up thing to do anyway. Fortunately, most of the black students at College Park, many of whom were first-generation college students, as I was, agreed with me. Though there were those within the BSU who preferred martyrdom or "revolutionary suicide," I weathered their constant attacks on my "blackness" and my manhood.

Touching Off Change

Still, I made threats if that is what it took to get the school to the negotiating table. This is what happened in late March 1969, as I warned the University of Maryland's Board of Regents of the dire consequences of their ignoring HEW's charges of racial segregation at College Park. My appearance before the board was totally unplanned. While on my way to class, I was asked by an SGA representative if I wanted to accompany SGA members to Baltimore to meet with the board. I did not feel like going to class that day, so I decided to go with them. After Mike Gold, the SGA president, made his presentation to the board, he turned to me and asked me if I had anything to say. On the spur of the moment, I told the board that the university had so far "avoided the violence that had characterized race relations at schools such as San Francisco State University." But, I continued, "this happy condition" would not last long if the board did not truly desegregate the school as per HEW orders. I murmured that "the time has come today for the board to do what they should have done in 1954 and completely desegregate the school." Having said this, I slumped back in my chair wondering why bright lights had been shining in my face and where the whirring sound had come from while I spoke. The board was pleasant but defensive in responding to my off-the-cuff but well-spoken comments, claiming that it was not sure what HEW wanted and extolling Wilson Elkins's leadership in race relations.

On my return to College Park that Friday evening, I had no idea of the impact my spontaneous remarks to the board had made. As it turned out, the bright lights and the whirring sounds came from my being taped for viewing on the evening news. My remarks also appeared in the *Baltimore Evening Sun* that same day and the *Baltimore Sun* the next morning.[17]

My somewhat mild threats made a great impression on the College Park community. Now the BSU could not be ignored, and many fearfully anticipated black student–led chaos and anarchy. To follow up on the momentum caused by my remarks, the BSU drew up a set of remarks they wanted President Elkins to make at his annual spring convocation speech. These remarks, had he made them, would have put him on record as favoring progressive racial change at College Park.

This, President Elkins would not do. Not caring to make forthright public comments about anything, he preferred to work behind the scenes or through others to effect change, especially racial change at the University of Maryland. Oddly, this mirrored my leadership of the BSU, since I presided over the BSU in much the same way. In any event, Elkins refused to voice outright support of a black studies program or quickly desegregating the university. Instead, he chose to give a statement on race relations so innocuous as to be meaningless. The BSU, through my contacts with the SGA, received an advance copy of Elkins's convocation speech. Incensed by what they felt was a slap in the face to black student aspirations, the BSU steering committee met to determine what retaliation, if any, would take place.

The committee, divided as always, argued for hours over a course of action. Some wanted to start a riot at the convocation, some wanted to boycott it, and some wanted to forget the whole thing. I rarely, if ever, participated in steering committee disputes. I left maintaining order to Terence Cooper, who was better at strong-arming people. My tactic was to let the steering committee members argue themselves out, and then propose a solution to the dispute, usually one representing a consensus, as I defined it. In most cases, the committee would go along. In this instance, the committee split six to six between violently disrupting the convocation and nonviolently boycotting it. In this case, I had the deciding vote so, true to my style, I called for a consensus solution. The BSU would not boycott the convocation, but it would not violently disrupt it either.

The plan was for the black students there to get up silently and walk out while President Elkins made his watery comments on race relations. This proposal satisfied all sides since it called for a more active protest of Elkins's mealymouthedness on race relations than a boycott would but would also be nonviolent and dignified. In that way, the BSU maintained the support of the militant and not so militant factions within the University of Maryland black community. BSU unity was paramount in my mind, and this compromise solution, while not appealing to the fire-breathers within the organization, would keep the most people happy. Besides, I suspected that those who talked the toughest would be somewhere else when the going got tough.

Wednesday, March 26, 1969, was the day of the convocation. According to plan, when President Elkins launched into his remarks concerning "Negroes" (as blacks were called in 1969 Maryland), approximately 200 black students, led by me, Wayne Stovall, and the steering committee, silently stood up and filed out of Cole Field House, site of the speech.[18]

Once the crowd was outside, both Stovall and I were at a loss as to what to do next. We could have led the students on a rampage, taken over a building, or done any one of many anarchical acts, much beloved by radical students of the 1960s. Stovall and I did none of those things. Groggy from staying up the previous night worrying about the convocation walkout, I decided to go to the BSU office located in the basement of the Student Union building to decompress. Stovall and other BSU members joined me. The crowd decided to go to lunch rather than to war. While on the way to the office, I ran into President Elkins, flanked by reporters and state troopers. Though dead on my feet from sleeplessness, I had the presence of mind to invite President Elkins to a BSU meeting. Surrounded by reporters, state and campus police, and curious black and white students, I, though short and stocky, towered over the even shorter though not so stocky Wilson Elkins as I invited him to a meeting. Despite newspaper accounts of strained words between President Elkins and me, we both used our best Uriah Heap mannerisms as I tendered the invitation and Elkins accepted it. Again, the odd congruence in style shown by the president of the BSU and the president of the University of Maryland manifested itself.[19]

The black student walkout on President Elkins caused the administrators and white students to wonder what the blacks were going to do next. The spring of 1969 was marked by black and radical white student disruptions of college campuses. Perhaps the most notorious was the takeover of the Cornell University administration building by armed black students. That, plus the years-long war between black students and administrators at San Francisco State (alluded to in my comments to the board), a black student strike at the University of California at Berkeley campus, and other such disturbances—over 115 in all that spring—caused the powers that be at the University of Maryland to be quite attentive to black concerns in the hope of avoiding similar chaos.[20]

One example of this was Wilson Elkins's keeping his date with the BSU. On April 23, 1969, he met with not only black students from College Park, but also with the leaders of black student organizations from the University of Maryland Baltimore County (UMBC) and Maryland State College. The chance for black students to confer with the head of all the campuses of the University of Maryland system was too good for the black students at the non–College Park campuses to pass up. At the same time, the leaders of the black student organizations on these campuses, by some incredible coincidence, either knew each other or lived in the same neighborhood in Baltimore. Carlton Blue, the head of the Maryland State College Student Government Association, was the son of an old friend of my family. George Favor of UMBC lived down the street from me in Baltimore. William H. Murphy Jr., of the Black American Law Student Association at the University of Maryland law school, lived across the alley from Favor. Naturally, it was easy for these leaders to get together to draw up a common strategy to face Elkins when he met with the BSU and them.

Drawing the largest crowd ever to attend a BSU meeting, the gathering had to take place in a campus auditorium, not the room where the BSU normally met. The audience watched in polite wonderment as the representatives from the various campus black student organizations grilled President Elkins on his racial policies. Terence Cooper, BSU steering committee chairman, moderated the meeting, while Wayne Stovall, the vice president, represented the organization on the panel. I, graciously giving up the spotlight to my two top assistants, sat to one side of the panel table, where I occasionally interjected questions and comments as the meeting went on. This was just one example of the collective leadership of College Park's BSU. Representing UMBC were Eric Smothers and George Favor, while Carlton Blue represented the students at the predominantly black Maryland State. William Murphy Jr. of the University of Maryland law school, who had intensively prepared the other black student leaders for this meeting, could not himself attend. President Elkins was accompanied by some of his top assistants.

Although some of the comments and questions directed toward Elkins were heated, the overall tone of the meeting was cordial. Elkins discussed the committees formed to establish an Afro-American studies program and to write an affirmative action plan. After intense questioning by Carlton Blue of Maryland State, he also expressed the desire to make that school an integral part of the University of Maryland system, something long desired by students, staff, and faculty there. Consequently, he announced that a committee to investigate that possibility would be formed.

If anything, that was the major result of the meeting, for within the next year Maryland State College became the Eastern Shore campus of the University of Maryland. Another major result of the meeting was a considerable lessening of racial tension at College Park. Wilson Elkins's meeting with the College Park BSU and other black student representatives showed his interest in improving race relations at the University of Maryland. Though he was not too eloquent in showing that interest at the meeting, the very fact that he met black students at a meeting of their organization spoke for itself. Also defusing tensions was his appointment of Glen Brooks and me to the committees setting up the Afro-American studies program and the affirmative action plan.[21]

The establishment of these committees was a major goal of the BSU and, through its president and Glen Brooks, its unofficial faculty adviser, it was sure to have a major input into their deliberations. As a result, the threat of black student disruption and violence at College Park evaporated, at least for the rest of the spring of 1969.

A Black Studies Program

The BSU paid the most attention to the Afro-American studies committee. Serving on that committee along with Glen Brooks and me of the BSU were Francis C. Haber, the chairman of the University of Maryland Department of History; Dan Carter and John Blassingame, also of the history department; Morris Freedman from English; Robert Hirzel from sociology; and Don Piper of the Department of Government and Politics. The proceedings were quite cordial, since all the committee members were on the same page. John Blassingame, later a distinguished historian but then a research assistant on the Booker T. Washington Papers project, soon dominated the committee meetings, and the Afro-American studies program that resulted bore much of his influence. An honors history major myself, I agreed with Blassingame and the others that the program should have intellectual coherence and rigor, and generally gave my stamp of approval to the committee's deliberations.

The final program, though not as extensive or community based as some other black studies programs, was still a good start for the University of Maryland and formed a solid base for future expansion. It involved the creation of an Afro-American studies committee, composed of the director of the program, representatives of disciplines supplying courses and faculty to it, and substantial student representation. The program would also have office space, clerical staff, and a budget. It would provide scholarships and fellowships to outstanding students pursuing Afro-American studies, and released time for faculty teaching in the program. Finally, it would sponsor conferences, symposiums, and institutes for dealing with the study of black culture. The courses offered by the program included Afro-American history, sociology of race relations, Afro-American literature, and Afro-American folklore.[22]

Choosing a director for the program proved to be unexpectedly smooth. The only real candidate was Mary Frances Berry, who had joined the history department in the spring of 1969 after earning a Ph.D. and a J.D. from the University of Michigan. Already distinguished in her field, she was highly thought of by Francis Haber, the chairman of the Afro-American studies proposal committee. While not officially a member of the committee, Berry sat in on some of its deliberations. She so impressed me that I nominated her to be the director. Her qualifications for the position were so obvious that if I had not nominated her, someone else would have, and she probably would have gotten the job regardless of what the BSU thought or wanted. Still, her having my support and, by extension, that of the BSU could not have hurt her chances, so she was proposed by the committee to be the first director—something that was quickly approved. The BSU and I approved the final report, though with the proviso that it be viewed as only a first step forward, not a foreclosure of future planning and implementation of black studies programs, and that future planning involve more community-oriented programs for Afro-American studies. This was accepted by the administration in late May 1969, and the program itself started operations in the fall of that year.

I also contributed to the committee to write the affirmative action plan to satisfy HEW. The plan, the first of many written at College Park, called for the creation of a cultural study center to examine the academic and social needs of minority students; increased recruiting of black students, especially from predominantly black high schools in Baltimore and Washington, D.C., most notably Douglass High School in Baltimore and the Dunbar high schools in Baltimore and D.C.; increased recruiting of black faculty and staff; increased financial aid to minority students, especially those from nearby majority black Washington, D.C., who had to pay out-of-state fees; increased counseling and other academic support services ensuring that all organizations at the university provide equal opportunity for all students to be members; and the establishment of urban studies and Afro-American studies programs. This plan answered many of the demands of the BSU, and was also approved in late May 1969.[23]

The BSU could be proud of the fact that it had attained an Afro-American studies program and a comprehensive affirmative action plan—and without resorting to the disruption and violence that had characterized black student confrontations at other campuses. My participation in the drawing up of both programs was perhaps my most important contribution to the BSU and one that I, due to my inclinations and temperament, was most qualified to give.

A Firm Financial Base

Still, the BSU was not home free. Now that it had gotten the University of Maryland to acknowledge the presence of black students and to bring blacks into the mainstream of life at College Park, it had to solidify itself as a permanent campus organization. For this, it needed money, preferably a regular annual appropriation from the SGA, which doled out funds each year to various student organizations.

Attaining a firm financial base was at the top of the agenda for the BSU as the 1969–70 school year opened. That fall, I returned to serve out my last two months as president. The organization was to hold elections in November 1969. Since I was a senior, I was ineligible to run again. Terence Cooper also returned, now as the number-two man and heir apparent to the BSU throne, since Wayne Stovall, the vice president, did not return to the university. Stovall's functions as facilitator, deal-maker, and fixer were now assumed by Darryl Bryant, the treasurer; Foster Hull, a freshman member of the steering committee; and Daniel Kit, also a freshman steering committee member. Karl Wyatt, the group's theoretician, also gained in power. With this infusion of fresh administrative blood, the BSU was stronger than ever.

But to maintain that strength, it had to get guaranteed appropriations. In late September 1969, the BSU made a budget request to the SGA for $5,000. This would pay off past debts and provide for a mimeograph machine, clerical help, telephone service, and funding for speakers and concerts. There was opposition to this request within the SGA due to the BSU's alleged barring of white students. Consequently, the SGA appropriated only $1,000 to pay off past debts.

Few things upset me, but this action did, and it incensed the rest of the top echelon of the BSU as well. Deal-maker that I was, I believed that the SGA, still controlled by the Third Party, owed me and the BSU financial support for our covert and risky support of the party that previous spring. Nothing irritated me more than to be done out of a deal, and I vowed revenge. I got together with Darryl Bryant and Terence Cooper and drew up a new budget to be resubmitted to the SGA. Rather than ask for the $5,000 that the group actually needed, I proposed a request for $10,000. The rationale for such an inflated request was that the SGA would probably cut the request again, but now down to a figure that the BSU could live with. My associates and I also planned forceful, even violent, countermeasures in case the SGA turned us down again.

This was a confrontation the BSU could not afford to lose. It had to provide services to the University of Maryland's black students or it would not survive as an organization to watch over their interests. Such services included a newsletter or newspaper, bringing speakers to campus, sponsoring concerts and dances, and providing tutoring services. Without such activities, the BSU would wither and die, and the newly formed Afro-American studies program and Affirmative Action office would be left without an organized black student group to support them. An SGA appropriation was vital for financing these activities. Furthermore, black students paid a student activities fee, which financed the SGA, so, why could they not get some of that money back through SGA's financing the organization devoted to their interests? Other groups such as the Agriculture Club, Chamber Music Society, and Fire Prevention Association received annual appropriations. Why not the BSU?

These were the arguments I used to rouse black student support for the BSU's budget request, and on October 2, 1969, Terence Cooper, Darryl Bryant, and roughly thirty other black students and I personally presented the budget to the SGA. This time, force was to be used if the SGA refused the request. At the meeting, SGA vice president Stuart Robinson recommended that the BSU receive only $1,400, while the Campus Coalition Against Racism (CCAR) receive $4,000. The CCAR was a predominantly white group formed with BSU support to provide an outlet for white interest in black concerns. This organization was advised by William Sedlacek, who, among all white members of the faculty, was perhaps the most supportive of black concerns. Mike Gold—SGA president, a Third Party member, and a good friend of mine—proposed that the BSU be given $5,200. Any more would violate state law since some of the $10,000 asked for was to be used for political education and off-campus projects. Gold's suggestion was voted down, and Robinson's budget recommendation passed.[24]

Robinson's recommendation was not acceptable to the BSU. When the SGA adjourned its meeting, the other black students and I locked the doors of the meeting room and threatened to keep the SGA officials hostage until they reconsidered the budget request. The campus police came to open the doors to the meeting room, and about twenty hostages were released. However, Mike Gold and I, seeing that things were getting out of hand, told the police to leave the remaining students to settle things for ourselves. The police left. The SGA then reconsidered the budget and voted, with only one dissenting vote, to appropriate $6,040 to the BSU. That satisfied the black students, and they left the room. I stayed behind with Gold to cement the deal they had struck in the heat of the confrontation—that the BSU budget would be reconsidered yet again, after the SGA dealt with other matters and the black students had left. Gold assured me that he had enough votes to pass it in the legislature and that it would allow the SGA to save face. At the same time, we worked out a deal that involved the CCAR receiving $4,000, which they would then spend at the "direction" of the BSU. That would essentially give the BSU the $10,000 it had asked for.[25]

The BSU and CCAR budgets were reconsidered, and both passed twelve to nine, the BSU receiving $6,000 and the CCAR $4,000. Again a deal was struck where the CCAR would have unrestricted use of $1,000 of their appropriation, while the BSU would control the rest, giving that group $9,000 out of the $10,000 it had asked for. Since the BSU really needed $5,000 for its survival, the extra money would strengthen it even further. The BSU's winning of its SGA budget fight meant permanent financial security; the BSU received $18,000 in the 1970–71 school year without a struggle and routinely received even higher amounts in all the years following.

This confrontation over the budget was a major victory for the BSU and its constituency. It did not come without criticism, however. Quite a few whites were perturbed over the SGA's appropriating funds, under duress, to a campus group that barred them from membership, and about twenty shortly thereafter appeared at the BSU office to apply for membership. Had I had my way, the whites would have been admitted, for it was always my secret desire to have an interracial BSU. But I realized that no one else in the organization felt that way, and true to my leadership style, I finessed the issue. First, I claimed that the BSU already had a white member and that anyone who agreed with the goals of the organization as stated in its constitution could be a member. I persuaded the steering committee to agree to accept the applications of prospective white members with the secret provision that the committee would sit on the applications until the applicants lost interest. This ploy worked, and the issue of whites in the BSU faded away. Besides, the organization worked so closely with the interracial CCAR, both groups having black members in common, that the matter of an all-black BSU seemed irrelevant.

I continued to be a symbol of interracial cooperation at College Park. Although the *Diamondback*, the school newspaper, called me the "leader of a chain wielding gang of racists," nobody who knew me well gave credence to the charge. I did allow—even planned for—the holding of SGA hostages the night of October 2, but besides the school newspaper, no one associated me with that disruption.[26]

The University of Maryland administration, perhaps happy to see student groups at each other's throats, stood clear of the BSU/SGA confrontation. Furthermore, since the administration had essentially given the BSU what it wanted that preceding spring, the organization had no further dispute with President Elkins and his staff, who were now preoccupied with dealing with radical white student protest. Finally, the disruption that took place on October 2 was mild in comparison to black or white student unrest elsewhere or to radical white student protest to come at College Park. For it was radical whites at the University of Maryland who, for the remainder of the 1969–70 school year—especially in May, after the widening of the Vietnam War to Cambodia and the shooting deaths at Kent State University in Ohio and Jackson State College in Mississippi—took over buildings, disrupted classes, blocked traffic, and generally added the University of Maryland to the list of campuses wracked by student violence. The black students at College Park—enjoying the benefits of an Afro-American studies program, increased attention paid to their academic and social progress, increased numbers due to intensive recruiting, and a financially secure BSU—stayed well clear of these confrontations.

Most black students avoided these confrontations because the vast majority of black students at College Park—many of them the first of their families to attend college, others representatives of the black elite of Maryland or Washington, D.C.—were not as radical as their white counterparts came to be in 1970, and they did not want to jeopardize their hard-won status at the school by participating in what they believed were white folks' squabbles. They thought that black issues were all that counted, and protests against the Vietnam War were irrelevant to their interests. That attitude was odd in light of the war's impact on the black community. Still, by the 1970s the black community in Maryland was turning inward to concentrate on black separatism and nationalism. This tended to be true elsewhere as well. For example, according to Joy Ann Williamson, at the University of Illinois:

> White activists set their sights on broad and international issues, such as free speech and ending the war in Vietnam, while Black Students focused on domestic and immediate concerns, such as adjusting to an overwhelmingly white university and eradicating racism and discrimination. Black students viewed white student protest issues as ephemeral and abstract and instead focused on creating healthier conditions for themselves in their immediate environment—the University of Illinois campus.[27]

With the Afro-American studies program in gear, the affirmative action plan seemingly working, and the BSU now financially stable, I could retire with honor as head of the BSU. This I did in November 1969, as my handpicked successor, Terence Cooper, was overwhelmingly elected to succeed me as the BSU president. Cooper provided firm, stable, and effective leadership during his time in office.[28]

Recruitment of Black Students and Black Faculty

Thanks to the pressure the BSU brought on the school, the University of Maryland at College Park began to actively recruit black students. Consequently, in fall 1970 the number of black undergraduate and graduate students increased to 1,285—a 79 percent increase over fall 1969, when there were 718 students at College Park. Due in no small part to the efforts of the BSU, the black enrollment at the University of Maryland had increased from less than 1 percent of total enrollment to around 4 percent. Nevertheless, that number was still way too low. Clearly the University of Maryland at College Park had a long way to go before it was truly desegregated. Thanks to the BSU, however, it got started on its way—a journey that continues today.[29]

The black student protest at the University of Maryland from 1966 to 1970 laid the foundation for a firm and obvious black presence at the University of Maryland at College Park. That the institution established an Afro-American studies program, added more black faculty and staff, and almost exponentially increased its black student enrollment—with hardly any of the disruption and violence other institutions such as Cornell or San Francisco State or Columbia or Berkeley experienced in meeting the demands of black students—can be attributed to the following factors.

First, the University of Maryland administration was willing to talk to black students through their organization once they made their concerns known. Administrators and faculty such as J. Winston Martin, Francis Haber, and William Sedlacek were sincerely committed to a desegregated University of Maryland. Even more important was the willingness of the black students at College Park, through their organization, the BSU, to attain their goals through negotiation, not confrontation. Although the organization was disruptive on occasion and their leader a fire-breather when he had to be, these disruptions were minor compared to the building takeovers, student strikes, arson, and even deaths that marked black and white student confrontations with administrators elsewhere. Furthermore, the BSU, through me, its president, was as willing to sit down and talk as was the administration. I believed that everything was negotiable. The other leaders of the BSU and I did not want violence, and we all could be quite proud of the fact that during our time running the organization, not one black student was suspended, expelled, arrested, or injured through any activity of the BSU. This record was matched by few other black student unions.[30]

In the years since 1970, the black presence at the University of Maryland at College Park has grown tremendously, and the institution is annually in the top ten of all historically nonblack colleges and universities in the numbers of black students enrolled and graduated. It also has among the highest numbers of black faculty and staff of any nonblack state land-grant university. It has any number of distinguished black faculty, among them political scientists Ronald Walters and Linda Faye Williams and historians Alfred A. Moss Jr., Sharon Harley, and Elsa Barkley Brown. During the 1980s, a black scientist, John Slaughter, presided over the College Park campus, and some of the colleges have had black deans. The NYAMBURU cultural center, established by J. Otis Williams in 1970 in a temporary wooden building on campus, now is in a beautifully and Afro-centrically renovated three-story structure adjacent to the student union building. The BSU, now one of many black student organizations, still exists and flourishes, as does the *Black Explosion*.

Nevertheless, racism has not gone completely away at College Park, nor has resistance to racial change. Affirmative action programs such as the Banneker scholarship program, designed to recruit black students and improve the university's poor image in the black community, underwent legal challenges in the 1990s. In the case of the Banneker program, the legal challenge was successful. This slowed diversity initiatives considerably. In the wake of the recent Supreme Court decisions upholding but narrowing affirmative action, there are fears that the university will take the most restrictive interpretation possible, thereby further slowing diversity efforts. Black students still feel a chilly racial climate. Racist attitudes die hard, as indicated by the death threats the BSU president received in 1999, but the racial climate had improved to the point where the university president, C. D. Mote, called in the Federal Bureau of Investigation and offered the public a $5,000 reward for the apprehension of the perpetrators.[31]

Despite numerous and frustrating setbacks to racial justice at the University of Maryland at College Park, the momentum desegregation gained as a result of its black students in the late 1960s has never stopped. Black students, faculty, and staff have a presence and power on campus only dreamed about by their predecessors during the 1950s and 1960s. The risks taken and sacrifices made by the members of the BSU in the late 1960s were not made in vain, and their dreams of a visible, viable, and significant black presence at College Park have come true. Blacks will never again be as insignificant at the University of Maryland at College Park as they were before the coming of the BSU.

A Note on Sources and the Significance of Memory

The above essay is essentially an account of my role in the struggle to desegregate the University of Maryland at College Park from 1967 to 1970. As far as I know, there are few if any published first-hand accounts of black student unions of that era, and I decided to focus almost exclusively on the black student union that I led. Quite a few of the black student activists of the time burned out early and can't or won't discuss that era. It took some toll on me, but few came through that period as well as I did. I have long felt that someone needed to tell the story of the BSU at College Park in that era, and the events that I participated in remain vivid in my mind. In fact, all that I have become today comes out of my years with the BSU. The survivors of that era are in their mid to late fifties or early sixties, and some are beginning to prematurely pass from the scene. Our memories are real and need to be shared, studied, and analyzed.

Over the years, I have tried to contact those who participated in this struggle with me. I have had little success in this effort. Tragically, we were scattered to the four winds during the 1970s and lost touch with each other. I have kept up with Terence Cooper, Thomas Davis, Michael McNair, William Sedlacek, and a few others. To my eternal regret, I have not yet been able to contact Wayne Stovall, whom I last saw in Boston in 1972, or Bob McLeod. I do not yet know what they are doing now. Still, I am continuing to try to track them down for a future book-length study of black students at the University of Maryland at College Park. In that work, I will gather the memories of as many of those whom I worked with in the BSU as possible so their voices can be heard. I will also compare the BSU and its participants at College Park with other black student unions around the country.

Of those people I have kept contact with, generally, their thoughts are that not enough progress was made during the time we were there, and their memories are not very positive. One must understand that our expectations in the 1960s—like all young activists black and white—were extremely high. When things did not change as fast we liked, many of us became disappointed and disillusioned.

Such disappointment has continued down to the present, especially concerning the attitudes and activism of present-day black students who enjoy the existence of Africana studies programs, black cultural centers, black faculty and staff, and other improvements that did not exist when we were students. Jimmy Garrett—who, at San Francisco State College in 1966, helped establish the first ever black student union—declared in a 2006 issue of *Diverse Issues in Higher Education* that black student unions' struggles during the 1960s created the support structures that exist today for students of color. Black studies programs, cultural centers, and so on, he said, are "a direct result of our struggle." People of color in academia, he went on, "owe us a tremendous amount. They don't pay it, but they owe a tremendous amount to the sacrifices of people who lost their hands, their fingers, their eyes; people who spent time in prison—students. That's the last generation of [black] leadership."[32]

The views expressed by Garrett—who is now Dr. James Garrett, dean of instruction at Vista Community College, Berkeley, California—may not be unusual. I venture a guess that many activists in the struggle against campus racism of the era feel the same way. I know I do. William Sedlacek, one of the most important antiracism activists at the University of Maryland at College Park—in my opinion the most important, since he has fought racism there for forty years—said in 2005 in the school newspaper that he isn't satisfied with the university's current policies. Wishing that the university would once again be on the cutting edge of diversity in higher education, he called the current policy "lawyers playing it safe. The lawyers want to know, 'How can we play it safe,' but in essence, what the university has done over the years is not play it safe."[33]

Dr. Sedlacek was instrumental in the great progress the University of Maryland at College Park had made over the years in becoming desegregated, but was concerned that the university would backslide in the wake of the U.S. Supreme Court's 2003 decision in *Grutter v. Bollinger*, which narrowed the ability of universities to make use of affirmative action. I have kept in contact with Dr. Sedlacek, and he was very helpful in the composing of this essay, sharing the extensive documentation concerning race relations at College Park he has amassed. We have talked about coauthoring a study of racism at the University of Maryland. He is the best possible personal source concerning the events over the years, going back to the time of those described in this essay.

What about the other administrators and staff mentioned in this study?

Wilson Elkins, J. Winston Martin, John Blassingame, and Francis Haber unfortunately all passed away before I could contact them. I am sure they would have been pleased with my descriptions of them—especially Wilson Elkins, who in my opinion was hardly the reactionary racist we thought he was. Looking at him now, I believe that his leadership style was just what was needed at College Park. He has never received proper credit for the positive racial changes that took place there from 1967 through the early 1970s. I believe a reconsideration of Elkins and others like him is needed. I have kept sporadic contact with Mary Frances Berry, the first director of the Afro-American studies program at College Park. She has generously acknowledged my role in her appointment to that position, and once said I sounded like Jack Nicholson in my dialogues with the University of Maryland's high command.

Two secondary sources that were of particular help in my composing this essay were Joy Ann Williamson's *Black Power on Campus: The University of Illinois, 1965–75* and Nadine Cohodas's *And the Band Played Dixie: Race and the Liberal Conscience at Ole Miss*. Williamson's book is an exhaustive study of black students at the University of Illinois—a school that, though in the Midwest, was very similar to the University of Maryland at College Park. Not yet published when I first wrote this essay, Williamson's book was helpful in putting the College Park BSU and its development in a broader context.

My account of my activities with the BSU at the University of Maryland and my descriptions of those with whom I worked I hope will encourage those who participated with me in the struggle against racism at College Park to come out of the woodwork to tell their stories. This struggle was a collective one, and I hope this essay will be a first step in seeing to it that all our voices are heard.

Notes

An earlier version of this essay was presented as a paper, "Prying the Door Open: Black Student Protest at the University of Maryland, 1968–1970," at the annual meeting of the Association for the Study of Afro-American Life and History, Houston, Texas, October 1986.

1. *Baltimore Afro-American*, June 22, 1935, April 22, 29, October 14, November 25, 1950; *University of Maryland v. Donald Murray*, 169 Md. 478 (1936); *McCready v. Byrd, President et al.*, 195 Md. 131 (1950); *Baltimore Sun*, August 15, 1950; *Outlook* (University of Maryland at College Park faculty and staff weekly newspaper), February 7, 1994; the essay by Peter Wallenstein in this volume; George W. Callcott, *A History of the University of Maryland* (Baltimore: Maryland Historical Society, 1966), 351, 353.

2. Callcott, *History of the University of Maryland*, 394.

3. The University of Maryland did have the distinguished black historian John Hope Franklin as a visiting professor in the 1963–64 school year.

4. Joy Ann Williamson, *Black Power on Campus: The University of Illinois, 1965–75* (Urbana: University of Illinois Press, 2003), 24–27.

5. By 1966, the school was admitting out-of-state black students and had dropped its ban on student civil rights organizations; Bob McLeod, for example, was from Washington, D.C.; and a CORE chapter was in existence.

6. The alienation black students feel at traditionally white universities is still a major problem today. See Beverly Daniel Tatum, *"Why Are All the Black Kids Sitting Together in the Cafeteria?" and Other Conversations about Race* (New York: Basic Books, 1997); and Joe R. Feagin, Hernan Vera, and Nikitah Imani, *The Agony of Education: Black Students at White Colleges and Universities* (New York: Routledge, 1996).

7. The low numbers of black students at the University of Maryland at College Park were not unusual. At the University of Illinois at Urbana-Champaign, a flagship university never racially exclusive under state law, the number was only 223 in 1967 (Williamson, *Black Power on Campus*, 35).

8. The University of Illinois CORE went through a similar transition in the fall of 1967, changing its name to the Black Students Association (Williamson, *Black Power on Campus*, 47). At that time, black student unions/associations were forming all over the country, even at such unlikely places as the University of Mississippi (Nadine Cohodas, *The Band Played Dixie: Race and the Liberal Conscience at Ole Miss* [New York: Free Press, 1997], 134).

9. The black student enrollment in the fall of 1968 totaled 668 (554 undergraduates and 114 graduate students). Glenwood C. Brooks and William E. Sedlacek, "Characteristics of Black Undergraduate Students at the University of Maryland College Park, 1968–69," Research Report #1–69, Cultural Study Center, University of Maryland. The first official census of black students at the University of Maryland at College Park was taken in the 1968–69 school year. Before that year, the enrollment numbers are estimates.

10. For context, see William H. Grier and Price M. Cobbs, *Black Rage* (New York: Basic Books, 1980), 130–53; Jacqueline Fleming, *Blacks in College* (Washington, D.C.: Jossey Bass, 1984), 1–25; William E. Cross Jr., *Shades of Black* (Philadelphia: Temple University Press, 1992), 115–44; and Williamson, *Black Power on Campus*, 47–50.

11. George Napper, *Blacker than Thou: The Struggle for Campus Unity* (Grand Rapids, Mich.: Erdmans, 1973), 25–51; Cross, *Shades of Black*, 145–88.

12. Walter Thomas is now the pastor of the New Psalmist Baptist Church, one of the most influential black churches in Baltimore. Tommy Davis was the head of Drug and Alcohol Abuse Programs for the state of Maryland. Mike McNair—the only member of the 1960s BSU to have remained at College Park continuously from that era—is a high-ranking officer in the University of Maryland campus police.

13. Napper, *Blacker than Thou*, 25–51.

14. Julia Davidson and Glen Brooks joined the University of Maryland staff in 1968. Mary Frances Berry later became a provost at the University of Maryland, chancellor of the University of Colorado at Boulder, and assistant secretary of education for the federal government. She was chair of the U.S. Civil Rights Commission and the Geraldine Segal Professor of Social Thought at the University of Pennsylvania. The late John Blass-

ingame subsequently wrote *The Slave Community: Plantation Life in the Antebellum South* (New York: Oxford University Press, 1972), a landmark work in African American history, and was the longtime director of the Afro-American Studies Department at Yale University. In the fall of 1969, B. Marie Perinbam joined Mary Frances Berry as the second black member of the University of Maryland's history faculty. There are no available counts of black faculty and staff prior to 1971.

15. *Baltimore Evening Sun*, March 21, 1969; *Baltimore Sun*, March 22, 1969.

16. Letter from Wilson H. Elkins to Francis C. Haber, February 25, 1969, author's personal collection; Williamson, *Black Power on Campus*, 95.

17. *Baltimore Sun*, March 22, 1969.

18. *Baltimore Evening Sun*, March 26, 1969; *Baltimore Sun*, March 27, 1969; *Diamondback*, March 27, 1969.

19. *Baltimore Evening Sun*, March 26, 1969; *Baltimore Sun*, March 27, 1969; *Diamondback*, March 27, 1969.

20. Napper, *Blacker than Thou*, 54. During the 1968–69 academic year, black students, though no more than 6 percent of the nation's college population, were involved in at least half of all protests on predominantly white campuses (Williamson, *Black Power on Campus*, 26).

21. *Baltimore Sun*, April 24, 1969. Wilson Elkins did not originally plan to appoint Brooks or me to the Afro-American studies planning committee, but the confrontations between the BSU and the administration changed all that.

22. Report of the Special Committee on Afro-American Studies, May 1, 1969, author's personal collection.

23. "A Plan for the Desegregation of the College Park Campus of the University of Maryland," May 16, 1969, author's personal collection.

24. William Sedlacek over the years has become a distinguished researcher and writer in the fields of minority student achievement and race relations. Much of the racial progress made by the University of Maryland at College Park over the past forty years can be attributed to his research, writing, and leadership on racial issues. Currently, he is assistant director of the University's counseling center.

25. *Diamondback*, October 3, 1969; *Washington Post*, October 4, 1969.

26. *Diamondback*, October 3, 10, 1969; *Washington Post*, October 4, 1969. The "white" student in the BSU was Francisco Roman, a black Puerto Rican from New York City. There, Puerto Ricans, regardless of color, were designated "white" on their birth certificates.

27. Williamson, *Black Power on Campus*, 36.

28. Terence Cooper is now an official with the National Association of Housing and Rental Officers and runs the African American Literary Society, which is only fitting since he was a creative writing major at College Park. I spent the remainder of my time at the University of Maryland writing articles for the new BSU newspaper *Black Explosion*, maintaining my excellent academic performance and being elected to Phi Beta Kappa, dodging the draft, and gaining admittance to the University of Chicago's graduate program in history. To avoid the army, I joined the navy and became a naval officer during the first half of the 1970s. I spent the latter half of that decade obtaining a Ph.D.

from the University of Chicago, studying under John Hope Franklin. Then I spent from 1980 to 1992 teaching history at HBCUs Fisk, Spelman, and the University of Maryland at Eastern Shore. This fulfilled a goal I had set for myself while with the BSU. Currently, I am an associate professor on the history faculty at Virginia Tech.

29. Glenwood C. Brooks and William E. Sedlacek, "Black Student Enrollment at the University of Maryland College Park 1969–70, 1970–71," Research Report #4–71, Cultural Study Center.

30. The University of Illinois, in contrast, went through considerable turmoil in its adjustment to the needs of its black students with building takeovers, scores of arrests, and a black studies program initially marked by much staff turnover and instability (Williamson, *Black Power on Campus*, 17, 37–43, 81–94, 119–27, 140–41).

31. Hate crimes at College Park continue into this century. For example, thirty-nine such incidents, mostly against gays, were reported in the 2001–2 school year. This was a matter of great concern to the administration, however, and in subsequent years the frequency of these incidents seems to be diminishing. *Diamondback*, October 18, 2002, February 24, 28, 2005. While president of the BSU, I received death threats. Little was done about them, though. Back then, such threats were viewed as a badge of honor.

32. Ibram Rogers, "Celebrating 40 Years of Activism," *Diverse Issues in Higher Education* 23 (June 29, 2006): 18–22.

33. *Diamondback*, February 28, 2005.

6

Hold That (Color) Line!

Black Exclusion and Southeastern Conference Football

CHARLES H. MARTIN

On September 23, 1967, the University of Mississippi (Ole Miss) Rebels opened their Southeastern Conference (SEC) football schedule with a 26–13 win over the University of Kentucky Wildcats in Lexington. This expected victory by a traditional conference powerhouse over one of the weaker teams in the league would normally not have been historically significant. Making the game noteworthy was the presence of sophomore defensive halfback Nathaniel "Nat" Northington in the Wildcats' starting lineup. Although he played for only three minutes before a shoulder injury forced him to the sidelines, Northington became the first African American ever to compete in a varsity football game in the SEC.

The path-breaking decision by the University of Kentucky to field an integrated varsity football team that day—and thereby break the SEC's unofficial policy of racial exclusion—inaugurated a new era in a conference once described as "the final citadel of segregation."[1] By the fall of 1971, six more of the ten SEC members had also included black players on their varsity squads. Furthermore, two of the remaining schools—Louisiana State University (LSU) and the University of Georgia—had awarded football scholarships to African Americans who were currently playing on their freshman squads and would move up to the varsity team the following year. Only the University of Mississippi continued to field all-white teams. Finally, in the fall of 1972, Ole Miss added its first African American player to the Rebel squad, bringing the era of Jim Crow to an end in SEC football.

The story of major college sports in the South cannot be separated from the region's commitment to the ideology of white supremacy, the maintenance of public segregation, and the practice of racial exclusion in higher education. For the first six decades of the twentieth century, Jim Crow reigned as thoroughly on the playing fields of Dixie as it did in other areas of southern life. For whites, to compete against an African American, even for a few hours on the football field, would constitute racial equality and thus violate the natural order of white supremacy and black subordination. At the same time, white southerners displayed great passion for college football, and southern universities eagerly sought prestige and profits through intercollegiate competition, especially highly publicized intersectional contests against nationally ranked opponents from the North or West. However, embedded in the ideology of college sport was an emphasis on the egalitarian nature of competition among gentlemen ("may the best man win") and the exclusion of social divisions from beyond the sidelines. Southern whites resolved this seeming contradiction between their racial beliefs and their athletic values by defining sports competition as a social activity that was purely a private or personal matter. According to this view, southern universities were within their rights when they demanded that nonsouthern opponents bench any black members of their squads for intersectional contests, regardless of the game's location. In both the literal and symbolic sense, the football field represented "contested terrain" where competing racial ideologies fought for dominance in intercollegiate sports.

A study of the racial policies and practices of the member institutions of the Southeastern Conference, the most prestigious athletic conference in the South, will illuminate the process of racial change across the Old Confederacy. Such an examination can delineate the role played by institutions of higher education in this regional transformation and expose the internal dynamics of support for and resistance to change within individual universities. Since college football enjoyed an exalted position within southern culture, the abandonment of racial exclusion by the prestigious SEC signaled a major shift away from diehard resistance by southern whites and suggested a new, more positive view toward African American students. This essay will give special attention to the University of Kentucky, the first SEC member to field an integrated team, and the University of Mississippi, the last conference school to recruit black football players. By studying the contrasting experiences of these two universities, one can examine in microcosm the conflict between the determination to maintain white supremacy and the desire to win football games, as well as the process by which democracy finally triumphed over Jim Crow on southern football fields.

The Rise of the Southeastern Conference

In the late nineteenth and early twentieth centuries, male students at southern universities eagerly embraced the new sport of football, despite some initial opposition from religious leaders and cautious administrators. The University of North Carolina and Wake Forest University staged the first official football game in a former Confederate state in October 1888. By 1892, a number of southern colleges, including the University of Tennessee, the University of Georgia, the University of Alabama, and Auburn University, were sponsoring football teams. In order to standardize the rules and regulations governing competition, colleges in the region eventually formed athletic conferences. By the late 1920s, the largest of these was the Southern Conference, founded in 1921, which included over twenty teams from twelve states. In 1932, thirteen colleges withdrew from the sprawling league and formed the SEC. The founding members of the new conference were the Universities of Alabama, Florida, Georgia, Kentucky, Mississippi, and Tennessee, as well as Auburn University, the Georgia Institute of Technology, LSU, Mississippi State University, Tulane University, the University of the South (Sewanee), and Vanderbilt University. Following the departure of Sewanee in 1940, Georgia Tech in 1964, and Tulane in 1966, ten core members remained in the league.[2]

SEC schools continued the traditional southern policy of refusing to compete against integrated opponents in intersectional contests into the 1940s. Through the end of World War II, many northern universities accepted this "gentleman's agreement" to ban black players. But after the war they reversed course and defended democracy on the gridiron, forcing several SEC members to accept this new rule for competition, at least for games held outside Dixie. In 1947, for example, Vanderbilt defeated an integrated Northwestern squad in Evanston, Illinois, and the following year the Commodores visited Yale, whose squad included halfback Levi Jackson. The University of Georgia modified its racial policies in 1950 when the Bulldogs traveled to San Francisco to play a St. Mary's team featuring halfback John Henry Johnson. Such interracial contests reflected the triumph of athletic ambition over traditional racial restrictions. The fact that these transgressions of the color line took place outside the South constituted a less serious violation of Jim Crow principles and revealed that football enjoyed a partial dispensation from the rules of rigid segregation.[3]

The southern white reaction to the U.S. Supreme Court's 1954 ruling in *Brown v. Board of Education* disrupted the trend toward interracial competition by SEC teams. In a backlash against the *Brown* decision, southern politicians developed a "massive resistance" movement against court-ordered school desegregation. As part of this crusade, they demanded that college athletic programs join the fight against any form of integration. Georgia governor Marvin Griffin captured this aggressive mood in December 1955, when he declared: "We cannot make the slightest concession to the enemy in this dark and lamentable hour of struggle. There is no more difference in compromising the integrity of race on the playing field than in doing so in the classroom. One break in the dike and the relentless seas will rush in and destroy us." Griffin's comments came during a controversy over Georgia Tech's acceptance of an invitation to play an integrated University of Pittsburgh squad in the January

1, 1956, Sugar Bowl. In response to the Georgia Tech–Pittsburgh contest in New Orleans, the Louisiana legislature promptly passed legislation prohibiting interracial athletic events within the state. The Georgia assembly discussed a similar law in early 1956 and almost passed such a bill in February 1957. Because of more subtle political pressure, other SEC schools—especially Ole Miss and Mississippi State—continued to reject such contests. Nonetheless, administrators at other SEC universities cautiously resumed selected intersectional games, fearing that the absence of such popular contests would hurt their team's national profile and their athletic department's revenue. In October 1957, Georgia traveled northward to Ann Arbor to take on the University of Michigan before 85,000 fans in a major national contest.[4]

The slow advance of classroom integration eventually undercut threats from segregationist politicians. By the mid-1960s, every SEC team had scheduled integrated opponents on the road and was preparing to host such teams at home, if they had not already done so. As the last conference members finally yielded to federal pressure and admitted black undergraduates to classes, attention shifted to the possible desegregation of SEC football teams. Contrary to popular myth, most southern white coaches did not immediately rush to recruit African Americans. In fact, football remained a special, privileged white space for as much as a decade after the first black undergraduates set foot on campus. The eventual acceptance of African Americans into such a special area as the football field marked the beginning of the shift from limited desegregation of southern universities toward real integration and inclusion. It also meant that at least some whites had come to view black students, especially strong, fast male students, as an asset to be voluntarily sought out, rather than a liability forced upon the school by the federal government. The University of Kentucky provides an excellent starting point for examining the process of racial change in southern college sports and, more specifically, those social forces that delayed, tolerated, or encouraged the desegregation of athletic competition in the SEC.

The University of Kentucky Takes the Lead

The northernmost member of the SEC achieved the first major breakthrough concerning football integration. At first glance, it would seem that the University of Kentucky (UK) enjoyed several advantages vis-à-vis the rest of the conference. The school's location in a border state—a slave state that had remained in the Union in 1861—gave it a somewhat different historical tradition from every other SEC member. Kentuckians also maintained strong economic ties to their midwestern neighbors. Furthermore, Kentucky's relatively small African American population, 7 percent of the state's total population in 1950, did not represent a political threat to white rule. Finally, in the early 1960s students and administrators at UK tended to be less conservative than their counterparts on other SEC campuses. At the same time, however, Kentucky was a southern state in matters of race. Despite rejecting secession in 1861, the state of Kentucky continued to recognize slavery until the end of the Civil War, and many white men from its divided population served in the Confederate army. After the war, the legislature eventually reduced the freedmen's new legal rights and required total segregation in the state's public school system. In a sense, as some historians have quipped, Kentucky waited until Reconstruction to secede from the Union. Serious outbreaks of racial violence, including lynchings, were commonplace into the early twentieth century. Despite several mitigating factors, then, Kentucky's white residents continued to strongly embrace "southern" values on racial issues through the end of World War II.[5]

The University of Kentucky, founded in Lexington in 1865 as an agricultural and mechanical college for white students, acquired its modern name in 1916. Beginning in the 1930s, African Americans challenged educational segregation by applying for graduate and professional training at the university. They argued that the limited programs of study at all-black Kentucky State University were not equal to those available in Lexington. In 1948, Lyman T. Johnson, who held an M.A. from the University of Michigan, filed suit against UK after he was denied admission to the graduate school. In 1949, a federal judge ruled in Johnson's favor and ordered the university to admit qualified African Americans into the graduate school and the Colleges of Law, Pharmacy, and Engineering. Johnson and twenty-nine other black students subsequently enrolled in summer school. Despite the ruling, the university still automatically rejected black applicants for undergraduate study, except for one engineering major who benefited from the revised understanding of "separate but equal." After the *Brown* ruling in May 1954, UK officials accepted the inevitable, and in September some twenty black students registered without incident for undergraduate classes.[6]

The desegregation of Kentucky's public school system after 1954 progressed faster, or at least less slowly, than in most southern states, and with less violence. Rather than encouraging resistance to the Supreme Court ruling, Governor Lawrence Wetherby publicly declared: "Kentucky will do whatever is necessary to comply with the law." His successor, Albert B. "Happy" Chandler, actually responded to anti-integration disturbances in two communities by ordering law enforcement to keep the schools open. Louisville desegregated its first public schools in the fall of 1956, and integration slowly spread across the state, despite considerable "passive resistance" from local school boards. In the spring of 1957, teams from black high schools were allowed to compete for the first time in the historically white state basketball tournament. The absence of widespread overt resistance to public school integration, together with the acceptance of interracial competition in high school sports, fostered a far more supportive environment for changes in athletic policy at the University of Kentucky than could be found elsewhere in the SEC.[7]

After World War II, the University of Kentucky encountered resistance to its athletic tradition of refusing to compete against African Americans on the gridiron. In September 1946, the Kentucky squad ventured across the Ohio River to play the University of Cincinnati. At the request of university officials, Cincinnati coaches agreed to bench senior end Willard Stargel, a World War II veteran, for the match, which the Wildcats won 26–7. The following year, though, when Kentucky visited Michigan State, the host Spartans refused to honor the "gentleman's agreement," and sophomore halfback Horace Smith played in the first half against the Wildcats in UK's first integrated football game. On July 9, 1948, in a major break with tradition at home, Kentucky's football field and its basketball team both hosted their first competition involving an integrated team. The game matched two separate squads that collectively made up the U.S. Olympic basketball team. One unit was built around Coach Adolph Rupp's Wildcats, the 1948 National Collegiate Athletic Association (NCAA) champions. The other consisted of amateur players from industrial league teams, including former UCLA star Don Barksdale, the first African American to make the Olympic team. Some 14,000 fans watched Barksdale lead his team to a 56–50 victory in the precedent-shattering outdoor game at Stoll Stadium. Three years later, in December 1951, the Wildcat basketball team hosted another integrated contest, this time in Memorial Coliseum, against St. John's University, ranked number one in the Associated Press poll, and African American star guard Sol Walker. By scheduling these events in Lexington, UK stood alone in the SEC in its disloyalty to Jim Crow at home.[8]

In the early 1960s, the University of Kentucky became the first SEC member to propose the athletic integration of the conference. President Frank G. Dickey initially raised the issue in a December 1961 press conference, predicting that the desegregation of the conference would happen within "just a matter of years" and expressing the hope that UK would be "one of the leaders in bringing this about." But he also cautioned that such a major change would require "a joint movement among" five or six SEC members. During the ensuing months, Dickey privately received some support for his views from fellow administrators at Vanderbilt, Tennessee, Georgia Tech, and Tulane. But representatives of Ole Miss, Mississippi State, Alabama, and Auburn reacted with alarm to his proposal, warning that if sports integration began, "riots would take place and the conference would be reduced to only three or four institutions." Fearful of being isolated within the conference, University of Kentucky officials proceeded cautiously for the next two years.[9]

Dickey's proposals eventually received strong support on campus. The student newspaper, the *Kentucky Kernel*, endorsed an end to racial exclusion and campaigned throughout the decade on behalf of recruiting black athletes. In a March 1963 editorial, the newspaper boldly called upon the university to fulfill "its moral obligations" by taking the lead concerning athletic integration in the SEC. Later that month, the faculty of the College of Arts and Sciences adopted a resolution likewise urging President Dickey to support desegregation of all athletic teams. In April, the board of trustees agreed that the school's athletic association should address the issue. As the *Kentucky Kernel* continued its campaign against the color line, it received support from several newspapers, including the *Lexington Leader* and the *Louisville Courier-Journal*. An editorial in the *Courier-Journal* asserted that "southern prejudice and customs should no longer dictate" UK's policies and pointed out the potential benefits of sports integration to the SEC: "Think of what a rich recruiting field the South would offer if its own schools started seeking out good Negro athletes, instead of losing them by default to the rest of the country!"[10]

At the end of April 1963, the directors of the University of Kentucky Athletic Association endorsed "equal opportunity for all students" to participate on Wildcat teams. The board further recommended that sports integration take place "at the earliest possible time taking into account our conference obligations." Following talks with other SEC schools, the board officially announced on May 29 that henceforth Kentucky's athletic teams "will be open to any student regardless of race." The impact of the board's declaration was somewhat muted when the athletic department simultaneously announced that all football scholarships had been awarded for the upcoming year and that no African Americans were included on the list of high school recruits. Nonetheless, the board's action and earlier statements by President Dickey provoked speculation in the press over whether the integration issue, as well as internal disagreements over academic standards and other problems, might lead to the breakup of the SEC. Various rumors circulated that Kentucky, Georgia Tech, Tulane, Vanderbilt, and possibly Florida might pull out of the conference and leave the more conservative Deep South schools to play each other. Although Georgia Tech and Tulane did later withdraw for unrelated institutional reasons, their departure did not destabilize the SEC, and athletic integration proceeded at a snail's pace.[11]

The relative mediocrity of the Kentucky football program over the decades added a dose of pragmatic self-interest to the discussion of athletic integration. The Wildcats had traditionally been one of the least successful football teams in the SEC. The one exception to this dismal record had been the tenure of Paul "Bear" Bryant, who led the Wildcats to appearances in three major bowl games while head coach from 1946 through 1953. After his departure, Kentucky football fortunes soon regressed to their normal disappointing levels. The recruitment of African American players thus offered the University of Kentucky an opportunity to gain a competitive advantage over its SEC rivals. The desegregation of the state's white high school sports association in the late 1950s had made interracial competition familiar to if not necessarily popular with whites across the state. Unfortunately for the Wildcats, many of the area's top black high school players came from Louisville, the state's largest city. Located across the Ohio River from Indiana, Louisville was the least "southern" part of the state, and many northern universities had already established strong recruiting links to the city's top black players. Moreover, the University of Kentucky was located in Lexington in the blue grass section of the state, which emphasized its southern heritage. Nonetheless, Kentucky administrators were determined to upgrade the university's national image and viewed sports as one mechanism to achieve that goal.

In Lexington, the arrival of a new president, John W. Oswald, during the summer of 1963 reinforced the move toward integration, since Oswald supported Dickey's liberal policies on race. Football coach Charlie Bradshaw and his staff continued to evaluate black high school prospects as part of their scouting program. In the spring of 1964, Bradshaw announced Kentucky's new recruiting class for the fall, which did not include any African Americans. However, Bradshaw reaffirmed his commitment to signing players regardless of race and predicted that the first black Wildcat would come from within the state, "because we owe it to the taxpayers who support this institution." The following year, the Wildcat coach again reported that his staff had failed to sign any African American recruits, although the school had made a formal scholarship offer to at least one black prospect. The university's determination to locate the perfect candidate to break the color line, together with the attractive opportunities for black Kentuckians at nearby midwestern schools, apparently handicapped its recruitment efforts.[12]

The Kentucky football program finally succeeded in starting the integration of its varsity football team and the SEC in December 1965. During the fall, Wildcat coaches focused their recruiting efforts on several African American prospects, including halfback Nathaniel "Nat" Northington, an all-state football player and "A" student at Jefferson High School in Louisville. Governor Edward T. Breathitt Jr., who sat on the University of Kentucky's board of trustees, assisted the recruiting campaign and, along with President Oswald, personally escorted the young athlete around the Lexington campus on his official visit. On December 19, 1965, Northington signed a scholarship agreement with Kentucky, becoming the first African American to receive a football scholarship to an SEC school. Oswald, Breathitt, and Bradshaw all attended the ceremony, with Oswald telling reporters that the event represented "a great and historic day for Kentucky, for its athletic program, and for the Southeastern Conference." Later that week, Bradshaw announced the signing of a second black player, all-state end Greg Page of Middlesboro, Kentucky. Page's decision meant that he and Northington would be able to provide emotional support for each other during their first year on campus, thereby increasing their chances of surviving the special pressures awaiting them as racial pioneers.[13]

During the fall of 1966, both Nat Northington and Greg Page enjoyed successful seasons on the freshman team. First-year squads played only a limited schedule, however, and most southern sports fans did not consider the SEC to have been officially integrated, since the two athletes had not yet participated in varsity competition. In the following spring, Charlie Bradshaw signed three more African Americans, Wilbur Hackett and Albert Johnson of Louisville and Houston Hogg of Owensboro, offering further evidence that the Wildcat football program had abandoned all racial restrictions. When classes began in the fall of 1967, five African Americans were enrolled on football scholarships at Kentucky, as well as state sprint champion James Green on a track scholarship. This contrasted dramatically with the rest of the SEC's football teams, where only Tennessee had issued a scholarship to an African American player on its freshman squad. Racial exclusion clearly remained very much alive elsewhere in the conference.[14]

As the 1967 fall season approached, considerable attention focused on the anticipated appearance of either Page or Northington as the SEC's first African American varsity player. But during the preseason drills in August 1967, an unexpected tragedy cast a shadow over the Wildcat football program and endangered the integration experiment. Page and Northington both performed well in practice and were assigned to the second team on defense. The training sessions that they and the other Wildcats experienced were quite intense. Coach Charlie Bradshaw ran physically demanding practices that were considered unusually rough even by the standards of the day. During an August 22 session, Bradshaw instructed the varsity to execute a special pursuit drill in which the entire defensive team gang tackled and piled on top of an offensive ballcarrier. In one round of this brutal drill, Page hit the runner first, and then both of them were buried under an avalanche of their teammates. While the other players staggered back to their feet, Page lay motionless on the ground. When he failed to respond to treatment at the field, emergency personnel rushed him to the university medical center, where doctors determined that he had suffered a broken neck and was paralyzed from the shoulders down. While Page remained in critical condition, teammates, university officials, and SEC commissioner A. M. Coleman visited the injured player. Meanwhile, football practice continued amidst debate over the violent nature of football and the Wildcat practices. The three black freshman players and especially Northington, who was Page's roommate, were deeply concerned about their teammate. Although the players did not believe rumors that Page had been deliberately injured, these stories placed additional pressure on all of them.[15]

Nat Northington somehow managed to find the strength to continue practicing. In the season opener against Indiana University on September 23, he saw his first varsity action. Unfortunately for the young athlete, he dislocated his shoulder in the 12–10 loss to the Hoosiers, and the injury plagued him for the next month. Northington's spirits sank even lower the following week when on Friday, September 29, Greg Page finally died after lingering for thirty-eight days. The Wildcats were scheduled to host the Old Miss Rebels the next day in Lexington, and after consulting with Page's parents, the university went ahead with the game. Perhaps shaken by news of Page's death, the Wildcats lost to the Rebels 26–13. After the game, Bradshaw praised his players for displaying "a lot of character" under difficult circumstances. Despite considerable physical and emotional pain, Northington had started the game at defensive halfback. He played for only a little over three minutes against the Rebels before he once again dislocated his shoulder. Nonetheless, in that brief appearance Northington had become the first African American to play in a varsity football game between two SEC teams. The following day, about 500 people attended a memorial service for Page at the football stadium. On Monday, his funeral was held in his hometown of Middlesboro at the white First Baptist Church, the first time that a funeral for an African American had ever been conducted there. Local government officials, university administrators, and Governor Edward Breathitt, who served as a pallbearer, were among those who attended the service.[16]

Northington's shoulder injury prevented him from playing in the next three games, all of which the Wildcats lost, extending their losing streak to five games. Kentucky's football fortunes appeared to be collapsing, and the SEC's great integration breakthrough teetered on the brink of disaster. Physically battered and emotionally drained, Northington finally decided to quit the team and drop out of school, despite the pleas of his coaches. When tracked down by a reporter for the student newspaper, Northington explained that he was not leaving due to racial problems but because of all the personal difficulties he had faced on and off the gridiron. As the discouraged young man removed his possessions from his dormitory, he stopped by the room of Wilbur Hackett and Houston Hogg. Northington told them that he was departing, but at the same time he urged them "not to leave," in order to keep the integration experiment going. Away from home for the first time and in a new environment, the two worried freshmen discussed their future with teammate Albert Johnson and sprinter James Green. After meeting with their coaches, the four athletes decided that they could not quit just because times were tough and agreed to remain in school. With their decision, Kentucky's effort at athletic integration had survived, though the Wildcat football team finished the year with but two wins and eight losses.[17]

The 1968 season at Kentucky opened on a more optimistic note. Although Albert Johnson eventually left the team because of injuries, Hackett and Hogg returned with renewed dedication. Hackett impressed coaches with his ability and soon moved into a starting position as a linebacker. In late September, the two athletes became the first black Wildcats to venture into the Deep South when Kentucky traveled to Jackson, Mississippi (where Ole Miss annually staged one or two home games), for a September 28 contest against the Rebels. Both players were apprehensive about making their first trip to Mississippi. Because of concerns about their safety, the two universities agreed that several Mississippi highway patrolmen would provide additional security for the Wildcats at the stadium. When Hackett and Hogg arrived in Jackson, they were relieved to discover that local people responded to them just the same as they did to their white teammates. In the course of the eventual game against the Rebels, the two Wildcats again found that they were treated no differently from the other Kentucky players.

The behavior of several state highway patrolmen assigned to protect the Wildcat team was another matter, however. As they stood on the sidelines, these large, hefty law enforcement agents regularly shouted out lines from a racist football joke that was circulating within the state. According to the joke, two black football teams were playing, and late in the game the losing team gained an opportunity to score near their opponent's goal line. The coach yelled to his quarterback, "Give 'at ball to LeRoy." On the ensuing play, the quarterback instead handed off to a different runner, who was slammed hard to the ground at the line of scrimmage. "Give 'at ball to LeRoy," the coach shouted in a louder voice. Again the quarterback handed off to another player, and this ball-carrier was knocked down behind the line of scrimmage and had to be helped off the field. Screaming at the top of his lungs, the frustrated coach yelled one last time, "Give 'at ball to LeRoy!" This time the quarterback turned toward the sidelines and shouted back, "LeRoy say he don't want 'at ball!" Hackett and Hogg were not familiar with the joke, but they quickly grasped its antiblack message. As the patrolmen continued to yell out insulting references to "LeRoy," the two Wildcats became both alarmed and furious, narrowly avoiding confronting their alleged protectors.[18]

Hackett and Hogg experienced several other racial incidents during their careers at Kentucky, but nothing upset the duo as much as did the situation with the highway patrolmen in Jackson. In an interview with the student newspaper after his senior season, Hackett recalled hearing opponents occasionally utter racial slurs during games, more so at Hogg because the fullback attracted considerable attention as a ballcarrier. Hackett also encountered one unpleasant incident concerning meals when he and several teammates were denied service at a hamburger joint in Baton Rouge after a game. He added that there had been occasional small conflicts between blacks and whites on the Kentucky team. Nonetheless, his teammates elected him a cocaptain for both his junior and senior years, reflecting the respect that they held for him as a team leader. Despite Hackett's efforts, the Wildcats struggled on the field. After Kentucky finished with a 3–7 record in 1968, Charlie Bradshaw resigned as head coach. His replacement, John Ray, continued to recruit African Americans, but his teams never won more than three games in a season. Eventually he, too, lost his job, as Kentucky football remained mired in the conference cellar. Despite the university's bold action in breaking the SEC color line, Kentucky failed to gain any long-term advantage from recruiting African Americans, once conference rivals also integrated. Nonetheless, the University of Kentucky had taken a courageous stand in favor of democracy on the gridiron at a time when no other SEC school dared to act.[19]

Tennessee Follows Kentucky's Example

The University of Tennessee became the second SEC member to include African Americans on its varsity football team, just one year after Kentucky. The college's urban location in Knoxville, the modest size of Tennessee's black population, and the state's Upper South mentality created a less hostile atmosphere for racial change on campus than in the Lower South. However, many white residents and the state's political leadership had historically opposed any school integration. Consequently, university administrators refused to take any actions on desegregation that might upset white public opinion. The first African American graduate student, Gene Mitchell Gray, enrolled in January 1952, but, as with Lyman Johnson at the University of Kentucky, only after winning a lawsuit in federal district court. Unlike University of Kentucky officials, the University of Tennessee's board of trustees stubbornly refused to make any changes in undergraduate admissions following the *Brown* decision in 1954. Only in late 1960 did the trustees finally abandon their resistance, and three African Americans quietly registered for undergraduate classes in January 1961.[20]

The University of Tennessee maintained its traditional policy of refusing to compete against African Americans into the 1950s. By the middle of the decade, though, university officials had quietly allowed several of the school's athletic teams to ignore this policy for away games. However, the Tennessee Volunteers football squad retained its color line, demonstrating that for white southerners, the gridiron remained a special area of protected white space. Despite easing restrictions on out-of-state contests, the university still declined to permit integrated athletic events in Knoxville. For example, in April 1961, three months after the university's first black undergraduates had begun classes, Tennessee officials hastily canceled a dual track meet when the visiting squad unexpectedly arrived with two black runners (see appendix 9). The following year, the athletic department shifted course and scheduled a major intersectional football game against the University of California at Los Angeles (UCLA) for the fall of 1965. When that season arrived, the Volunteers actually hosted two integrated contests, one in Knoxville against the University of Houston and another in Memphis against UCLA. Shortly thereafter, in February 1966, the university announced that henceforth it would award athletic scholarships without regard to race.[21]

Several developments assisted the university in preparing for the enrollment of its first African American football player. The initial desegregation of the Knoxville public schools in 1963 and 1964 introduced interracial competition on the high school level, providing a precedent for similar action by the University of Tennessee. The hiring of Doug Dickey in 1964 as the Volunteers' new, young head coach also helped. While serving in the U.S. Army, Dickey had coached an integrated military football team, and he proved more flexible on racial policy than his predecessors. Nonetheless, Dickey failed to land any black recruits in 1964, 1965, or 1966, provoking some modest criticism from liberal students. Finally, in the spring of 1967 the Volunteers coach signed halfback Albert Davis, the top offensive prospect in the state, and halfback Lester McClain, an honor student at a predominantly white high school, to athletic scholarships. When Davis failed to qualify academically for admission, McClain became the first African American football player at the university. During his first season, McClain moved to the wide receiver position, where he led the freshman team in receptions. In the fall of 1968, he joined the varsity team, becoming the second African American to officially participate in SEC football competition. McClain proved to be a valuable performer for the Volunteers, finishing his career with seventy pass receptions, the fifth-highest total of any Tennessee player to that date. During his four-year career, McClain occasionally overheard teammates use racial slurs, and he endured similar comments from some opponents on the playing field. Although he was discouraged at times by the normal adjustments of college life, as well as the special pressures that came with being a racial pioneer, McClain refused to leave school. As he later recalled, "I just couldn't [drop out]. I knew the next day the headline would say: 'Lester McClain, first black athlete, quits UT.'" Tennessee continued to recruit African American prospects, and by McClain's senior year in 1970, six other black players had joined him on the varsity.[22]

Integration at Four Additional SEC Schools

The pioneering actions taken by the University of Kentucky and the University of Tennessee should have made it much easier for other SEC members to accept African American athletes. Nonetheless, they continued to delay taking action. During the fall season of 1969, no additional SEC school fielded an integrated football team, despite Kentucky's and Tennessee's examples. Then, in 1970, the gates at last began to swing open. That fall, four more conference members—Vanderbilt, Florida, Auburn, and Mississippi State—had black players on their varsity squads. The shift in policy by these four universities represented a crucial turning point for the SEC, with a majority of its members now sporting integrated teams.

Vanderbilt University enjoyed both advantages and disadvantages in the area of race relations when compared to other SEC members. Vanderbilt's status as a private college freed it from the heavy-handed political pressure to which other conference schools were subjected. Yet many members of its board of trustees held very conservative views on race, and they did not approve the elimination of all racial restrictions on undergraduate enrollment until 1962. Alexander Heard, who assumed the position of chancellor in 1963, worked diligently to improve the university's national status and liberalize its racial policies, including recruitment of African American athletes. In 1966, Vanderbilt hired as its new football coach Bill Pace, who was only thirty-four years old. Liberal students on campus, who hoped Pace would include recruitment of African Americans in his strategy for revitalizing Vanderbilt football, were initially disappointed with the lack of results. Pace's failure contrasted with the success of basketball coach Roy Skinner, who fielded the SEC's first integrated basketball team during the 1967–68 season. In the spring of 1969, Pace finally awarded the university's first football scholarship to an African American, Taylor Stokes of Clarksville, Tennessee. Stokes advanced to the Commodore varsity in the fall of 1970, but a preseason injury forced him to sit out the season. Meanwhile, a nonscholarship transfer student, James Hurley, joined the squad as a defensive end and played often enough as a substitute to earn a varsity letter. In 1971, Stokes returned to action and was joined by two additional African American teammates. Despite the integration of the team, the Commodores continued to finish near the bottom of the SEC standings throughout the 1970s, just as they had in the 1960s.[23]

The University of Florida followed a more contentious path to integrated athletic competition. The university's trustees and administrators, as well as the state courts, blatantly ignored the Supreme Court's 1950 *Sweatt v. Painter* ruling desegregating the University of Texas law school until 1958, when a federal judge ordered them to remove all racial restrictions on graduate and professional programs. Even then, school administrators refused to admit black undergraduates until September 1962, just weeks before James Meredith entered Ole Miss. The university's poor reputation with black Floridians, together with the difficult nature of the state's Senior Placement Examination, kept the number of black undergraduates low for most of the 1960s. Beginning in 1958, following the enrollment of the university's first black law student, university officials permitted the Gator football team to compete against integrated opponents on the road, and in 1966 the school hosted its first integrated home game.[24]

In 1968, the obvious absence of African Americans from the Gator roster provoked the local chapter of the National Association for the Advancement of Colored People (NAACP) and the University of Florida's Afro-American Student Association (AASA) to publicly criticize Coach Ray Graves and the university's athletic department. The NAACP complained that many black athletes across the state had received scholarships at other major universities, but not from Florida. Its conclusion was simple—Graves simply did not want to coach black players. For its part, the AASA denounced the athletic department for excluding black athletes from scholarships and condemned the Senior Placement Examination for being biased in favor of white middle-class students. Graves denied the accusations against him and blamed the entrance exam for eliminating most African American football prospects. In the fall of 1969, Graves's first two black recruits arrived on campus. Leonard George of Tampa, Florida, and Willie B. Jackson of Sarasota, Florida, spent their first year on the freshman team, and then both became three-year lettermen on the Gator varsity under new head coach Doug Dickey. At the end of their sophomore year, in April 1971, the two athletes remained in school when nearly half of the university's African American students withdrew from classes to protest the handling of minority demonstrations on campus. During the early 1970s, Dickey helped repair the athletic department's poor relationship with the black community and quickly expanded the number of African Americans on scholarship. Eventually, black Floridians started to support the Gators, but many retained bitter memories of this earlier hostile relationship.[25]

Auburn University was the third SEC member to drop the color line for football competition in 1970. During the 1950s and 1960s, the major efforts by African Americans and the federal government to desegregate Alabama's higher education system focused on the University of Alabama, rather than Auburn, the state's land-grant institution for whites. Even after black students enrolled at Alabama in June 1963, Auburn's governing board maintained its racial restrictions. As a result of a federal court order, the first African American graduate student enrolled in January 1964, and the first black undergraduates in September of that year. The Tigers hosted their first integrated home football game in 1966, but Coach Ralph "Shug" Jordan, a native of Selma, Alabama, was initially reluctant to consider black players for his team. Since the students at the university and the residents of the town of Auburn were almost entirely white, the school's football program seemed destined to be one of the last in the conference to drop its racial restrictions.[26]

These conservative racial attitudes changed quickly from 1968 to 1970, especially after basketball coach Bill Lynn signed an African American recruit, Henry Harris, in the spring of 1968. Several fans and trustees complained about the school's decision to accept African American players, but other Auburn supporters defended the use of black athletes as one means of strengthening the various Tiger teams. As one trustee explained at a board meeting, "The faster they run, the more touchdowns they make, the whiter they get!" Jordan's first black recruit, halfback James Owens, arrived on campus in 1969 and began his three-year varsity career in 1970. Thomas Gossom, an outstanding high school sprinter, enrolled one year after Owens and won a football scholarship in 1971. Since the number of African American football players grew slowly, the two pioneers, especially Owens, experienced much loneliness and social isolation on campus. For recreation, they frequently visited nearby Tuskegee Institute, where they were welcomed into social activities. Over the next ten years, the racial structure of the football team changed considerably. When popular halfback "Bo" Jackson, a future Heisman Trophy winner, helped lead the 1983 Tiger squad, nearly half of whom were African Americans, to the SEC championship—the team's first conference title in twenty-seven years—it was obvious that the Auburn football program had undergone a remarkable transformation.[27]

Mississippi State University also integrated its varsity team in 1970, surprising some observers. The school's small town location in Starkville, its historic role as an agricultural college, and the great influence exerted by the state's white segregationists worked against any liberal tendencies in race relations. In the late 1940s, the Maroons played several intersectional games against northern opponents but halted such scheduling when it became clear that the "gentleman's agreement" would no longer be honored. In fact, the school did not compete in football against an opponent from outside the former Confederacy again until 1970. During the state's integration crisis, Mississippi State escaped most of the national spotlight. Even after James Meredith's enrollment in Oxford in 1962, Mississippi State quietly refused to change its admission policy until 1965, when the school's first African American student attended summer school. The Maroons' initial integrated football game came in 1965 on the road against the University of Houston. Two years later, the Cougars visited Starkville and broke the color line at Mississippi State's Scott Field.[28]

During the 1950s and 1960s, the Mississippi State football team suffered in the shadow of its highly successful in-state rival, the Ole Miss Rebels. To make matters worse, from 1966 through 1969 Mississippi State failed to win even a single SEC contest. This dismal record may have made head coach Charley Shira (1966–72) more receptive to the recruitment of African Americans than successful coaches like Johnny Vaught of Ole Miss. In 1969, Shira succeeded in recruiting lineman Robert Bell and defensive halfback Frank Dowsing to the Maroon squad. Both had attended recently integrated white high schools and had participated in the previously all-white prep all-star game. The duo played on the Mississippi State varsity from 1970 through 1972. Bell became an occasional starter for the Maroons, while Dowsing twice earned all-conference honors and was named to one all-American team. Furthermore, Dowsing qualified for the SEC all-academic team three straight years. The National Football Foundation selected him as a scholar-athlete in 1972, the only SEC player to be so honored. In an even more remarkable development, his fellow students elected him "Mr. Mississippi State" in October of his senior year, the highest accolade that students could bestow on a male classmate. A growing number of African American recruits helped Mississippi State achieve winning records in 1975, 1976, and 1977, although the university later had to forfeit nineteen wins from those years when it finally lost a protracted legal battle with the conference over an ineligible player. In subsequent years, success usually proved elusive. However, in 2003 Mississippi State took an unprecedented action when it hired as its head coach Sylvester Croom, the first African American to hold such a position in the history of the SEC.[29]

Alabama, LSU, and Georgia Take Their Time

Noticeably missing from the list of the first six SEC schools to integrate their varsity football teams was the University of Alabama. Despite the popular myth that legendary Coach Paul "Bear" Bryant courageously took the lead in desegregating the conference, Alabama actually did not produce its first integrated squad until 1971. During the 1960s and 1970s, Bryant's teams dominated the SEC, winning an amazing twelve league championships and six national titles. However, the state's bitter resistance to federal efforts to end racial discrimination, led by Governor George C. Wallace, overshadowed Bryant's accomplishments during the 1960s. One black graduate student, Autherine Lucy, had briefly attended the University of Alabama in early 1956 before a white mob drove her from campus and the trustees permanently expelled her. Wallace's campaign to preserve black exclusion at the university, symbolized by his famous stand "in the schoolhouse door," delayed the permanent enrollment of African Americans until June 1963. Wallace's political maneuvers and racial violence inside the state stigmatized the Crimson Tide in the eyes of many fans and sportswriters outside the South. Moreover, the University of Alabama refused to schedule regular-season contests against integrated teams until the end of the 1960s. This absence from intersectional competition eventually endangered Alabama's national rankings, forcing Bryant and school officials to reconsider their policies.[30]

The obvious lack of African Americans on the Tide squad also attracted criticism, especially from black students and from several national sportswriters. In 1969, the Afro-American Association at the university voiced a number of complaints about campus racial problems, among them the absence of black players on the school's "white racist football team." Aided by the NAACP, the student group even filed a federal lawsuit accusing the university of practicing discrimination in its athletic program. These attacks declined after Wilbur Jackson of Ozark, Alabama, quietly enrolled at the university in September 1970 as the first African American recipient of a football scholarship. That same month, Alabama hosted the University of Southern California Trojans in Birmingham, in its first major intersectional home game since 1951. Led by several black stars, Southern Cal demolished the Tide, shocking southern white football fans. According to popular legend, this famous game supposedly convinced Bryant of the necessity to recruit black athletes. Actually, Bryant had already made this decision when he recruited Wilbur Jackson, but Alabama's humiliating defeat served to convince many white fans of the need for such a change in policy. In 1971, Jackson advanced to the Tide varsity, and junior college transfer John Mitchell joined him there. The following year three more African Americans—Sylvester Croom (future head coach at Mississippi State), Ralph Stokes, and Mike Washington—joined them. Beginning in 1971, Alabama resumed its domination of the SEC. The valuable contributions of Bryant's black recruits to this success made athletic integration at Tuscaloosa popular with most Tide fans and gave black athletes a new status on campus. The continued success of the Alabama teams, including national championships in 1973, 1978, and 1979, eventually obscured the fact that Bryant and Alabama had been followers, not leaders, in racial change within the SEC.[31]

Once Alabama abandoned Jim Crow, only three SEC schools were left with all-white teams—LSU, Georgia, and Ole Miss. In the fall of 1971, both LSU and Georgia handed out scholarships to African American recruits, who then competed on their freshman teams, setting the stage for the integration of their varsity squads the following year. Only Ole Miss still held the line against racial inclusion. In Louisiana, the Tiger football team enjoyed passionate support around the state. Starting in 1930, athletic department officials usually scheduled at least one attractive intersectional contest each year, and they attempted to continue to do so after the *Brown* ruling. In the spring and early summer of 1956, the board of supervisors confirmed a new series to begin the following year with the University of Wisconsin, which would have resulted in LSU's first integrated football games. Meanwhile, extreme segregationists gained control of the Louisiana legislature and in July passed a wave of statutes designed to reinforce white supremacy. One of these measures—the so-called sports segregation law—prohibited individuals, schools, or corporations from sponsoring any public athletic contests, social functions, or entertainment that included white and black participants. This law forced LSU to cancel the Wisconsin series, and the school did not schedule another regular season match against a northern or western opponent until 1970. Although the university had reluctantly accepted African American graduate and professional students since 1950 under a court order, the segregationist counterattack pressured school officials into rejecting black undergraduate applicants until the summer of 1964.[32]

The federal courts permanently struck down the Louisiana sports segregation law in 1959, and in the 1960s LSU administrators concluded that it had become politically safe to schedule teams with African American players. On January 1, 1965, the Tigers defeated Syracuse in the first integrated Sugar Bowl game held since the controversial 1956 Georgia Tech–Pittsburgh contest. The university did receive one formal complaint about its participation in the postseason classic, though. The southern Louisiana chapter of the White Citizens' Council wrote the athletic department to express its "trepidation and sincere concern for LSU's athletic future" over the game, since "LSU owes its greatness, academically and athletically, to its Anglo-Saxon heritage." When Coach Charlie McClendon failed to integrate his team's roster in the late 1960s, black LSU students conducted protests against this omission. In 1971, McClendon signed his first two African American recruits, Lora Hinton from Chesapeake, Virginia, and Mike Williams from Covington, Louisiana. Because Hinton suffered several injuries during his first two years at LSU, Williams became the first African American to play on the Tiger varsity, in the fall of 1972. Both players found their teammates to be unexpectedly supportive; in fact, the two roomed with white friends rather than with each other. In subsequent years, a steady stream of black players followed their example in proudly wearing the Tigers' purple and gold jerseys. LSU eventually tapped into a wealth of local football talent, which it had previously ignored. In fact, much of LSU's subsequent football success derived from its newly acquired African American heritage.[33]

The University of Georgia joined LSU in handing out its first football scholarships to African American freshmen in 1971 and integrating its varsity team in the fall of 1972. The Bulldogs had been one of the most active SEC members in promoting intersectional contests, although they had historically insisted that their opponents honor the "gentleman's agreement." Yet so anxious were

Georgia administrators to maintain the prestige and profits of intersectional matches that, starting in 1950, they actually permitted the Bulldogs to schedule integrated opponents, the first SEC member from the Deep South to do so. However, university officials refused to drop the color line for home games, since this would have been inconsistent with their fight to prevent African Americans from enrolling there. Despite the school's dogged resistance to desegregation, however, two black undergraduates, Hamilton Holmes and Charlayne Hunter, enrolled at the university under a federal court order in January 1961 and remained in school despite efforts by a mob to force them to withdraw.[34]

During the late 1960s, a few liberal white students and the Black Students Union at the University of Georgia complained about the all-white composition of the football team. The university did host its first integrated home football game in 1968, but that milestone only made critics more outspoken. Coach Vince Dooley apparently offered scholarships to several black high school prospects, but with competition for such athletes intensifying, all of the potential recruits turned him down. Finally, in the fall of 1971 five black freshmen joined the Bulldog football program. Three of these athletes, Horace King, Richard Appleby, and Clarence Pope, came from Clark Central High School in Athens, a new school created by the merger of the town's black and white high schools. Their ability, as well as their experience at an integrated high school and their local social network, made them attractive to the University of Georgia coaches. Two fellow Georgians—Chuck Kinnebrew of Rome and Larry West of Albany—joined them on the freshman squad that fall. More African American recruits followed them to Athens over the next decade. In 1980, after star halfback Herschel Walker helped Georgia win the national championship, one die-hard white Bulldog fan even exclaimed, in words that would have been blasphemous a decade earlier, "Thank God for Earl Warren!"[35]

Ole Miss Finally Surrenders

The University of Mississippi was the last SEC member to award an athletic scholarship to a black football player. No other member of the SEC, not even the University of Alabama, more fully embodied the cultural heritage of the Old South than did Ole Miss. Through the extensive use of such evocative symbols as the song "Dixie," the Confederate battle flag, the mascot "Colonel Rebel" (who resembled a plantation owner), and the team nickname of "Rebels," the university had created by the late 1940s a remarkable fusion of school traditions and Deep South imagery. Furthermore, the state government's extreme intransigence concerning public school integration in the 1960s; the deadly riot that accompanied the arrival of the school's first black student, James Meredith, in 1962; and periodic Ku Klux Klan violence all combined to make Mississippi the epicenter of southern white resistance to racial change. Moreover, race relations on the Oxford campus remained strained for the rest of the 1960s. It is therefore not surprising that Ole Miss was the last SEC school to drop the color line for its football program.

The University of Mississippi opened its doors in 1848 but temporarily suspended operations in 1861 when most of its students rushed to enlist in the Confederate army. The university formed its first football squad in 1893, and over the years the University of Mississippi teams acquired the nicknames of the "Red and Blue" and later the "Flood," before "Rebels" became the permanent designation in 1936. The figure of Colonel Rebel made his first appearance the following year, but he did not become a campus mainstay until the late 1940s. After the Dixiecrat Party made the Confederate battle flag its unofficial emblem in 1948, the use of the flag and the song "Dixie" increased considerably at the school.[36]

During the 1950s, these symbols became packed with even greater meaning, as Mississippi assumed a pivotal role in the "massive resistance" movement against school desegregation. In 1961, James Meredith, a native Mississippian and a U.S. Air Force veteran, began his fight to desegregate Old Miss. After numerous legal delays, the federal courts ordered Meredith's admission for the fall semester of 1962. On September 30, several hundred federal marshals escorted Meredith to the campus. As word about his presence spread, students and many whites from the Oxford area, as well as segregationists from other states, poured onto the campus, and a full-fledged riot broke out. Only the arrival of U.S. Army troops and a National Guard unit finally ended the disturbances and allowed Meredith to quietly register for classes on the following day.[37]

Struggling to keep the university operating, school administrators turned to football to provide a social outlet for its distracted students. Because of security concerns, federal officials forced the university to shift the upcoming October 6 homecoming game from Oxford to Jackson. Despite the move, the resumption of the football season did seem to calm down Ole Miss students and, according to Coach Johnny Vaught, "helped to ease tension throughout the state." Fan support for the Rebels soared, as the squad finished the season undefeated, captured the SEC championship, and earned a trip to the Sugar Bowl. The Rebels' outstanding success in 1962 and again in 1963 provided a source of great satisfaction to white Mississippians. Although the federal government had forced the university to accept African Americans in the classroom, the school's football field remained a special white space where white

Mississippians could demonstrate their athletic prowess and celebrate their cultural pride. Football thus represented an important symbol of an unchanging white Mississippi and its southern white heritage.[38]

This love affair between Ole Miss football and white Mississippians originated earlier in the century. In order to elevate its national profile, the university began scheduling in the 1920s one major intersectional game per season, provided that opponents understood its commitment to white supremacy and black exclusion. For example, when Ole Miss journeyed to Minneapolis to take on the University of Minnesota in 1932, in deference to the visiting southerners the home team automatically withheld its one African American player from the game. With the arrival of Coach Johnny Vaught in 1947, Ole Miss enjoyed over two decades of unprecedented success, capturing six SEC titles and one national championship. After an October 1954 contest against Villanova in Philadelphia, however, the university withdrew from intersectional competition in order to avoid northern teams, most of which now included African Americans, and it continued to abstain from such games until 1971.[39]

Following the Supreme Court's *Brown* decision, Mississippi segregationists demanded that the state's colleges and universities reaffirm their commitment to Jim Crow and avoid any activities even indirectly supporting desegregation, including sporting events. Jones County Junior College in Laurel ignored these warnings in late 1955, when its football squad met an integrated Compton (California) Junior College squad in the Junior Rose Bowl contest. This violation of segregationist principles infuriated state legislators, who threatened in early 1956 to adopt a law punishing college officials for any violation of Jim Crow. In order to head off legislative action, administrators at Ole Miss and other state colleges pledged to obey an "unwritten law" by the legislature prohibiting any interracial athletic competition, regardless of location. As a result of this policy, in late 1956 the University of Mississippi basketball team pulled out of a holiday tournament in Owensboro, Kentucky. Beginning in 1959, the Rebel baseball team declined several invitations to compete in the NCAA playoffs because of the possibility of meeting integrated opponents.[40]

The "unwritten law" survived until 1963. In early March of that year, Mississippi State president Dean W. Colvard successfully challenged the state's segregationist politicians by personally authorizing the university's basketball team, the SEC champions, to compete in the NCAA tournament. The Board of Trustees of State Institutions of Higher Learning, which governed all of the state's colleges and universities, declined to overrule Colvard's decision, despite a warning from one member that integrated competition "represented the 'greatest threat' to Mississippi's way of life since Reconstruction." However, establishing a replacement policy proved difficult, as the trustees could not reach a consensus. After over a year and a half of inconclusive bickering, board members finally threw up their hands in frustration and officially returned control of scheduling to university officials in December 1964.[41]

Ole Miss administrators forced the board's hand on the issue, since a few weeks before the trustees' vote they had reached the momentous decision to abandon the school's tradition of racial exclusion on the gridiron. After the end of the 1964 football season, university officials accepted an invitation to play in the upcoming Bluebonnet Bowl contest in Houston, the Rebels' eighth consecutive bowl visit. They took this action even though the opposing team from the University of Tulsa included several African Americans, among them star defensive lineman Willie Townes, a Mississippi native. The results of the university's first integrated contest disappointed Rebel fans, as Tulsa upset Ole Miss 14–7. Sportswriters selected Townes, who repeatedly tackled Rebel runners behind the line of scrimmage for losses, as the most valuable lineman in the game. Townes's outstanding performance inspired a widely circulated joke spoofing Ole Miss's switch to integrated competition. The joke came in the form of a question, which asked: "Who was the first Negro to integrate the Ole Miss backfield?" The answer: "Willie Townes!"[42]

The Ole Miss schedule for the next three years confirmed that the Tulsa game represented a permanent shift in athletic policy. In 1965, the Rebels continued their rivalry with the University of Houston squad, which featured sophomore halfback Warren McVea, the Cougars' first African American player. The decision not to cancel the series revealed that the university had rejoined the mainstream of college football. Rebel fans were distressed over the game's results, though, as McVea scored two touchdowns in a 17–3 upset win in Houston. The following year the Cougars met Ole Miss in Memphis, with the Rebels gaining revenge by a score of 27–6. In the fall of 1967, McVea and the Houston squad visited Oxford on October 28, the first occasion that an African American had been permitted to compete in Hemingway Stadium. This memorable game, a 14–13 victory for the Rebels, demonstrated that the university had abandoned racial exclusion on the gridiron at home, at least for visiting teams.[43]

This new flexibility on race by Ole Miss did not extend, however, to the recruitment of African Americans for the university's own teams. Coach Johnny Vaught initially ignored the issue, but as several SEC rivals pursued black prospects, Vaught and his staff reluctantly reevaluated their recruiting practices. In May 1969, Vaught surprised many fans when he announced that J. T. Parnell, a halfback from Jackson, had become the first African American to sign an SEC scholarship agreement with the Rebels. However, Parnell also accepted a scholarship to Southern Illinois University (permissible at the time under NCAA rules), and he eventually decided to enroll there rather than at Ole

Miss. Thus the unsuccessful effort to recruit Parnell actually focused further attention on the continued whiteness of the Ole Miss team.[44]

Beginning in the spring of 1969, African American students, a few white classmates, and several faculty members grew more outspoken about racial issues linked to the university's athletic program. They focused in particular on the continuing absence of black football players, the use of Confederate imagery, and the shouting of racial insults during Rebel football games. The newly formed Black Student Union took the lead in articulating black concerns, which included demands for the creation of a black studies program, the hiring of black faculty and staff, and the recruitment of black athletes. At the beginning of the fall semester, both Mississippi State and the University of Southern Mississippi enrolled their first African American football players, further highlighting the absence of black athletes at Ole Miss. During the winter and spring of 1970, black students voiced their disapproval of the Confederate battle flag as a symbol for the university's athletic teams, dramatically burning several of them on campus. Various letters to the student newspaper likewise condemned racially inflammatory language at football games, citing in particular the chant of "kill that nigger" heard during the Memphis State football game.[45]

These negative factors caused African American students to feel considerable alienation from the Ole Miss athletic program, especially the football team. Many skipped the Saturday games, and others who attended turned the stands into a forum for protest, periodically holding up signs reading "Racist Athletic Department" and "Ole Miss = Racism." For black students, the football team had come to symbolize the continued emphasis on "whiteness" at Ole Miss. The growing problem of Confederate imagery and its possible effect on recruiting was even noted by a white sportswriter for the *Jackson Clarion-Ledger* in the fall of 1970. After observing that "the real Ole Miss anthem is 'Dixie,'" the sportswriter went on to warn that "there will be no Negro flashes in the Ole Miss backfield, or lightning-fast black flankers in the flats or tough Negro troopers in offensive or defensive lines so long as the Stars and Bars of the Confederacy remains the true standard of the school."[46]

The issue of African American players continued to haunt the Rebel football team during the seemingly jinxed 1970 season. On October 17, Ole Miss hosted the University of Southern Mississippi. The victim of a 69–7 thrashing the previous year, Southern Mississippi stunned the previously undefeated Rebels with a shocking 30–14 upset, producing what one Southern Mississippi coach called "the greatest victory in Southern's football history." Worse yet, Willie Heidelburg, a five foot six inch halfback who was one of the first two black players for Southern Mississippi, scored two touchdowns on the Rebels. Critics of Ole Miss sports seized upon Heidelburg's performance as proof that the failure to integrate the Rebel squad was undermining its ability to compete.[47]

The loss to Southern Mississippi added to the athletic department's mounting woes. On Thursday before the game, Athletic Director Thad Smith suffered a heart attack. Three days after the upset, Coach Johnny Vaught also suffered a heart attack. Because of their health problems, both men soon retired from the university. After the end of the season, university trustees selected Billy Kinard as the Rebels' new coach. Since Kinard was considerably younger than Vaught, some observers assumed that his youthfulness would make him more flexible on race than his predecessor. Moreover, the basketball program had just recruited its first black player, Coolidge Ball, lessening the shock that football integration might deliver to older Ole Miss fans. Nonetheless, when the 1971 season opened in September, the Rebel varsity and freshman squads remained as white as ever. Worse yet, Ole Miss appeared to be isolated even within the SEC, since every other conference member had issued at least two football scholarships to African Americans.[48]

At the end of 1971, the Ole Miss football program finally attracted its first black recruits. The continuing desegregation of the public school system in Mississippi greatly aided this change. As African Americans entered previously all-white high schools and participated on their athletic squads, University of Mississippi scouts could easily evaluate their skills against possible white recruits as part of their normal recruiting duties. Integrated high school competition also lessened the social and cultural shock that a change in recruitment policies at Ole Miss might bring to the state's white football fans. Finally, on December 11, 1971, tackle Robert J. "Ben" Williams of Yazoo City, Mississippi, and halfback James Reed of Meridian, Mississippi, signed scholarship agreements with the Rebels, eventually becoming the first African Americans to compete for the Rebel squad.[49]

Williams and Reed were reasonably well prepared for the challenges that they would face at the university. Both athletes were serious students who had attended integrated high schools, and Williams had even served as the captain of his team. When the two arrived on campus, they shared a room in the athletic dormitory, although Williams had a white roommate on road trips that year. Because a new NCAA rule permitted freshmen to compete on varsity teams and because the Rebels were shorthanded in the defensive line, Ole Miss coaches quickly moved Williams up to the varsity. Meanwhile, Reed spent the fall on the newly created junior varsity, which had replaced the old freshman squad. Williams made his debut on September 16 at Memphis State. Two weeks later, on September 30, exactly ten years to the day after the infamous Ole Miss riot over James Meredith's arrival on campus, Williams took the field in Hemingway Stadium in Oxford against Southern Mississippi in the first home game of the season, to the cheers of most Rebel fans. Williams soon proved to be an outstanding performer, earning all-SEC honors during the next three seasons and all-American honors as a senior. Although James Reed attracted less publicity than Williams, he enjoyed a successful career for the Rebels, starting at the halfback position as a junior and for part of his senior year.[50]

It was difficult to overlook Ben Williams on the football field or on campus. The easy-going, relaxed young man soon became popular with white as well as black students. In the fall of his senior year, Ole Miss students even elected him to the honorary post of "Colonel Rebel," the highest honor available to a male student. To many white students, Williams's selection demonstrated that tremendous racial progress had taken place on campus. On the other hand, many African Americans feared that the honor would be used to exaggerate the level of racial acceptance on campus and bestow unwarranted praise on the football program, which had been one of the last bastions of white exclusiveness. The photograph of Williams and "Miss Ole Miss," Barbara Biggs, which later appeared in the yearbook, symbolically captured the ambiguous status of African Americans at the university in 1976. The photograph showed the couple posing in a rural setting, with Williams standing behind and slightly to the right of Biggs. Both were leaning on a wooden fence, which subtly but clearly separated the two from physical contact. Like blacks and whites on the Oxford campus, Williams and Biggs were so close, and yet so far away.[51]

The integration of the Old Miss football program expanded steadily during the remainder of the 1970s. By the fall of 1976, the football media guide listed sixteen African American players, and the university employed its first black assistant coach, Tommy Thompson. Despite these changes, the Rebels failed to gain much success on the gridiron after 1971. The school's small town location and distance from rapidly growing urban and suburban areas of the South no doubt hindered recruiting. By the early 1980s, another explanation gained prominence. University administrators and football coaches concluded that the school's Old South and Confederate traditions created a competitive disadvantage in recruiting, since most of the increasing number of outstanding black players across the Deep South, and especially their parents, did not identify with those symbols and often found them offensive.[52]

Campus controversies, erupting periodically over the role of these traditional images, harmed the football team's image. In the fall of 1982, Ole Miss's first black cheerleader refused to carry the Confederate flag onto the football field at home games, touching off a controversy that eventually forced the university to officially dissociate itself from the flag's use. Finally, in 1997 the school banned all dangerous items, including sticks and flagpoles, from university events, in an effort to make it difficult for die-hard Rebel fans to display the flag. When "Dixie" also came under attack in the 1980s, Ole Miss officials partially deflected such criticism by merging the song with "The Battle Hymn of the Republic" into a musical montage. In the early 1980s, school officials removed the iconic image of Colonel Rebel from the football team's helmets, but the durable colonel survived as the university mascot until the fall of 2003, when the university officially retired him from active duty, despite protests from some white students and alumni. The extent of the impact that these symbols and the controversies over them had on Ole Miss football is difficult to calculate. One result is clear, though—from the beginning of racial integration on SEC playing fields through the end of the twentieth century, the Rebels never again won a conference championship. Of all the SEC schools, the University of Mississippi appeared to have lost the most by its dogged resistance to integration, both in the classroom and on the gridiron.[53]

Eliminating the Color Line

Historically nonblack southern universities, especially those that eventually formed the prestigious SEC, maintained a rigid color line both in the classroom and on the athletic field for over seven decades. During those years, most of these colleges eagerly pursued the prestige and profits that could be acquired through high-profile intersectional football games against northern teams. After World War II, many SEC members modified their racial policies for intersectional competition and agreed to compete against integrated teams, provided that the games were staged outside the South. This modest liberal initiative was soon reversed, at least for universities in Alabama, Mississippi, and Louisiana, during the years of "massive resistance" to school desegregation following the *Brown v. Board of Education* decision in 1954. By the mid-1960s, once African Americans had won admission to the college classroom, SEC members became willing to host integrated games at home. Yet their football teams continued for a time to exclude black athletes, preserving the gridiron as an area of protected white space. Despite their modest numbers, African American students eventually protested the absence of black athletes from their school teams. Furthermore, many white coaches and fans began to fear that such all-white squads were becoming less competitive nationally. Finally, the desegregation of local public school systems, along with the accompanying integration of high school sports programs and state athletic associations, helped prepare white fans for the integration of college athletic teams.

Within the SEC, the ten member institutions pursued athletic integration at their own individual pace. The University of Kentucky, located in a border state, took the lead in recruiting black football players. Somewhat surprisingly, though, the university gained no long-term competitive advantage from its pioneering role in embracing athletic integration. The University of Mississippi achieved the dubious distinction of becoming the last SEC school to issue football scholarships to African Americans, as well as one of the last three to field an integrated varsity team. The fierce resistance of the state's political leaders to any racial change and the widespread prevalence of southern white symbols on campus proved to be heavy burdens for the Rebel squad. Most SEC schools experienced no long-term shift in their competitive standing because of athletic integration; Ole Miss was the main exception. After the league's integration, the Rebels never regained the lofty status they had enjoyed during the 1950s and 1960s when they had at times dominated the SEC.

The eventual recruitment and acceptance of African American players by southern college athletic teams in the late 1960s and early 1970s represented an important turning point in race relations on campus and in the region. Through their perseverance and hard work, such pioneering black athletes as Nat Northington at Kentucky, Lester McClain at Tennessee, James Owens at Auburn, and Ben Williams at Ole Miss, together with their counterparts elsewhere in the SEC, made integration work and opened the door for later generations of athletes. Their inclusion into a previously closed area of white space signaled a new acceptance of integration by whites and a new perspective on African Americans as valuable members of the university community. In the years that followed, the SEC's increasingly integrated football teams not only heralded a new era in athletic competition but also provided shared symbols around which white southerners and black southerners alike could finally unite and commence the process of racial reconciliation.

Notes

1. *Atlanta Constitution*, January 12, 1988.

2. SEC Football Media Guide, 1990, 1994. The current names of SEC schools—not necessarily those in use at earlier times—have been used throughout this essay.

3. Charles H. Martin, "Racial Change and 'Big-Time' College Football in Georgia: The Age of Segregation, 1892–1957," *Georgia Historical Quarterly* 80 (Fall 1996): 532–58.

4. *Atlanta Constitution*, December 3, 1955 (quotation); Martin, "Racial Change," 559–62. For a survey of racial problems at various postseason bowl games, see Charles H. Martin, "Integrating New Year's Day: The Racial Politics of College Bowl Games in the American South," *Journal of Sport History* 24 (Fall 1997): 358–77.

5. A 1904 state law prohibited integrated classes at any public or private school in the state, at all levels of instruction. David C. Roller and Robert W. Twyman, eds., *The Encyclopedia of Southern History* (Baton Rouge: Louisiana State University Press, 1979), 677–82; Charles Gano Talbert, *The University of Kentucky* (Lexington: University of Kentucky Press, 1965), 174. On antiblack violence in Kentucky, see George C.

Wright, *Racial Violence in Kentucky, 1865–1940* (Baton Rouge: Louisiana State University Press, 1990); and J. Michael Rhyne, "Rehearsal for Redemption: The Politics of Racial Violence in Civil War Era Kentucky" (paper presented at the C. Ballard Breaux Public Conference, Filson Institute, Louisville, Ky., May 19, 2001, copy in author's possession).

6. In one unusual case, an undergraduate transfer student, Holloway Fields, was able to gain entry to the engineering school under the 1949 court order and in 1951 earned a B.S. in electrical engineering. Fields's enrollment did not otherwise affect the University of Kentucky's undergraduate admissions policy. Talbert, *University of Kentucky*, 174–76; George C. Wright, *A History of Blacks in Kentucky: In Pursuit of Equality, 1890–1980*, vol. 2 (n.p.: Kentucky Historical Society, 1992), 170–183; *Lexington Leader*, October 13, 1954; *Lexington Herald*, May 5, 1981; *Fifty Years of the University of Kentucky African-American Legacy, 1949–1999* (Lexington: University of Kentucky, 1999), 6, 47, 49.

7. Numan V. Bartley, *The New South, 1945–1980* (Baton Rouge: Louisiana State University Press, 1995), 163, 196; Steven A. Channing, *Kentucky: A Bicentennial History* (New York: W. W. Norton, 1977), 203–4; Wright, *History of Blacks in Kentucky*, 193–205; *New York Times*, January 24, 1957.

8. In both 1948 and 1951, Adolph Rupp privately asked the rival coaches to leave their respective black players behind, but they refused to do so. Kevin Grace, "The Stargel Story: One Measure of Progress," *UC Currents*, October 23, 1992, 1–3; Paulette Martis, e-mail to author, July 16, 2004; Ron Thomas, *They Cleared the Lane: The NBA's Black Pioneers* (Lincoln: University of Nebraska Press, 2002), 116–24; *New York Times*, December 18, 1951; University of Kentucky *Kentucky Kernel*, December 14, 1951; *Lexington Leader*, December 18, 1951. The *Kernel* published a rumor that the Michigan State University football team had brought an African American player to Lexington in 1944, but neither university's records support this account.

9. *Kentucky Kernel*, December 15, 1961; Frank G. Dickey to the author, September 4, 1990.

10. *Kentucky Kernel*, March 22–27, April 22–27, 1963.

11. *Kentucky Kernel*, April 30, 1963; *Lexington Herald*, May 30, 1963; *New York Times*, April 30, May 30, 1963; *Jacksonville (Florida) Journal*, June 31, 1962; Minutes, Board of Directors Meeting, University of Kentucky Athletic Association, April 29, 1963, in Frank G. Dickey Papers, King Library, University of Kentucky, Lexington.

12. *Kentucky Kernel*, March 27, April 7, 1964; University of Texas *Daily Texan*, December 15, 1964, February 11, 1965; *New York Times*, April 9, December 20, 1965.

13. University officials assured Northington's parents that he would be fully protected on any trips to the Deep South. *Lexington Herald*, December 20, 23, 1965; *New York Times*, December 20, 1965; Mrs. William Northington to Edward T. Breathitt, December 22, 27, 1965, and Mrs. Edwin I. Baer to Breathitt, December 21, 1965, both in John W. Oswald Papers, King Library, University of Kentucky.

14. University of Kentucky Football Media Guide, 1967, 1968; *Kentucky Kernel*, September 5, 1967.

15. Two weeks after Page's accident, freshman football player Cecil New, who was

white, also suffered a broken neck in a scrimmage but escaped any permanent disability. *Kentucky Kernel*, October 29, 1964, September 8, 11, 13, 1967; *Atlanta Constitution*, September 7–14, 1986, series reprinted as "Run for Respect," 2; A. M. Coleman to Robert A. Page, October 3, 1967, copy in Oswald Papers, University of Kentucky.

16. *Kentucky Kernel*, October 2–4, 1967; "Run for Respect," 2.

17. *Kentucky Kernel*, October 23–24, 1967, February 18, 1971; "Run for Respect," 2; *Houston Informer*, June 15, 1968.

18. *Kentucky Kernel*, February 18, 1971; "Run for Respect," 2.

19. *Kentucky Kernel*, February 18, 1971. The University of Kentucky's pioneering change in football contrasted with the negative image of UK's basketball program derived from the school's 1966 NCAA tournament championship game against Texas Western College, as depicted in Frank Fitzpatrick, *And the Walls Came Tumbling Down: Kentucky, Texas Western, and the Game That Changed American Sports* (New York: Simon and Schuster, 1999).

20. James Riley Montgomery, Stanley J. Folmsbee, and Lee Seifert Green, *To Foster Knowledge: A History of the University of Tennessee, 1794–1970* (Knoxville: University of Tennessee Press, 1984), 199, 228–30, 267–69; University of Tennessee *Daily Beacon*, January 27, 1968.

21. *New York Times*, December 24, 1946; *Memphis Commercial-Appeal*, February 1, 1956; Richard Pennington, *Breaking the Ice: The Racial Integration of Southwest Conference Football* (Jefferson, N.C.: McFarland, 1987), 10; "Football Desegregation at UT," *Context*, December 2, 1994, 6–7; *Daily Beacon*, October 26–27, 1965, February 10, 1966; *Knoxville News-Sentinel*, February 5, 1966.

22. *Daily Beacon*, February 1, April 15, May 10, 1967, October 16, 1968; *Nashville Tennessean*, May 29, 1971; *Washington Post*, November 25, 1972; *Knoxville Journal*, May 22, 1989; Montgomery et al., *To Foster Knowledge*, 269.

23. Paul K. Conkin, *Gone with the Ivy: A Biography of Vanderbilt University* (Knoxville: University of Tennessee Press, 1985), 540–80, 641, 698–700; Melissa Fitzsimons Kean, "'At a Most Uncomfortable Speed': The Desegregation of the South's Private Universities, 1945–1964" (Ph.D. diss., Rice University, 2000), 363–89; Vanderbilt University *Hustler*, May 3, 1968, May 2, 16, 1969, January 9, February 25, September 18, 1970, February 9, 1971, January 23, 1973; "Concerned Students" to Alexander Heard, April 23, 1968, and unidentified memo, 1968, in Chancellors' Papers, Alexander Heard Papers, University Archives, Vanderbilt University, Nashville.

24. University of Florida Football Media Guide, 1993; *New York Times*, April 13, 1963; David T. Bruce, "The Desegregation of Intercollegiate Athletics in the State of Florida" (Honors' thesis, University of South Florida, 1996), 2–4, 29–30, 34; Peter Wallenstein's essay in this volume.

25. Bruce, "Desegregation of Intercollegiate Athletics," 31–48; Betty Stewart-Dowdell and Kevin M. McCarthy, *African Americans at the University of Florida* (Gainesville: University of Florida, 2003), 62–65; *Christian Science Monitor*, February 23, 1968; Norman Sloan, *Confessions of a Coach* (Nashville, Tenn.: Rutledge Hill, 1991), 143–44; *Washington Post*, November 25, 1972.

26. Auburn University *Plainsman*, September 25, 1964, February 26, 1981; Minutes

of Informal Board of Trustees Meeting, July 17, 1963, in Joseph B. Sarver Collection, University Archives, Auburn University, Auburn, Ala.; Harry M. Philpott Oral History Transcripts, University Archives, Auburn University, 244, 326, 333.

27. *Anniston (Alabama) Star*, December 24, 1991; Auburn University Football Media Guide, 1969, 1970, 1971, 1972, 1973, 1974; *Plainsman*, March 28, 1968, January 30, 1969; Philpott Oral History Transcripts, 28–29, 243–45, 326 (quotation).

28. John K. Bettersworth, *People's University: The Centennial History of Mississippi State* (Jackson: University Press of Mississippi, 1980), 343–52, 393; *New York Times*, November 5, 1946, January 19, 1956; Pennington, *Breaking the Ice*, 34–40, 46.

29. Bettersworth, *People's University*, 342–43, 432–34, 466; Mississippi State University *Reflector*, October 20, November 17, 1972, January 26, 1973; *Washington Post*, November 25, 1972; *New York Times*, December 2, 2003, July 18, 2004.

30. On Bryant's career, see Paul W. Bryant and John Underwood, *Bear: The Hard Life and Good Times of Alabama's Coach Bryant* (Boston: Little, Brown, 1974); and Keith Dunnavant, *Coach: The Life of Paul "Bear" Bryant* (New York: Simon and Schuster, 1996). On the integration of the university, see E. Culpepper Clark, *The Schoolhouse Door: Segregation's Last Stand at the University of Alabama* (New York: Oxford University Press, 1993).

31. Jim Murray of the *Los Angeles Times* was especially critical of Bryant over Alabama's racial policies. University of Alabama *Crimson-White*, October 27, November 10, 1969; *Birmingham Post-Herald*, July 23, 1969; *Anniston Star*, December 22–23, 1991; Andrew Doyle, "An Atheist in Alabama Is Someone Who Doesn't Believe in Bear Bryant: A Symbol for an Embattled South," in *The Sporting World of the Modern South*, ed. Patrick Miller (Urbana: University of Illinois Press, 2002), 247–58; Brent Wellborn, "Coach Paul Bryant and the Integration of the University of Alabama Football Team," *Southern Historian* 18 (Spring 1997): 70–71; University of Alabama Football Media Guide, 1972, 1973, 1974.

32. One black undergraduate briefly attended classes in 1953 until a federal court overturned his admission. Minutes, Board of Supervisors Meetings, February 18, April 7, May 28, 1956, in Louisiana Collection, Hill Memorial Library, Louisiana State University, Baton Rouge; *Kansas City Call*, November 10, 1950; *Baton Rouge Morning Advocate*, July 6, 16, 1956; Louisiana State University *Daily Reveille*, September 13, 1956; *Baton Rouge State Times*, June 9, 1964; Adam Fairclough, *Race and Democracy: The Civil Rights Struggle in Louisiana, 1915–1972* (Athens: University of Georgia Press, 1995), 165–66, 205–6, 219; SEC Football Media Guide, 1989.

33. *Daily Reveille*, April 27, 1968, December 8, 1970, February 16, March 18, September 28, October 13, 1971, January 21, 1972; *Baton Rouge States Times*, April 27, 1968; *New Orleans States-Item*, August 12, 1971; interview with Lora Hinton, September 1, 1993, in T. Harry Williams Center for Oral History, Louisiana State University; Ken Rappoport, *The Syracuse Football Story* (Huntsville, Ala.: Strode, 1975), 255 (quotation); Louisiana State University Football Media Guide, 1975.

34. *Los Angeles Mirror*, October 2, 1950; Thomas G. Dyer, *The University of Georgia: A Bicentennial History, 1785–1985* (Athens: University of Georgia Press, 1985), 323–34; Charlayne Hunter-Gault, *In My Place* (New York: Farrar Straus Giroux, 1992), 167–96;

Atlanta Journal, February 22–23, 1957; *Atlanta Journal and Constitution*, October 6, 1957. For a detailed account of the events leading up to 1961, see Robert A. Pratt, *We Shall Not Be Moved: The Desegregation of the University of Georgia* (Athens: University of Georgia Press, 2002).

35. University of Georgia *Red and Black*, November 12, 1968, February 4, 1969; *Athens Banner-Herald*, December 14, 1970; "Run for Respect," 5; Loran Smith and Lewis Grizzard, *Glory! Glory! Glory! Georgia's 1980 Championship Season* (Atlanta: Peachtree, 1981), 69–75.

36. Beginning in 1959, the university gave away free miniature Confederate flags at home games in order to encourage support for the Rebels. Kevin P. Thornton, "Symbolism at Ole Miss and the Crisis of Southern Identity," *South Atlantic Quarterly* 86 (Summer 1987): 254–59; Nadine Cohodas, *The Band Played Dixie: Race and the Liberal Conscience at Ole Miss* (New York: Free Press, 1997), 9–12, 20–21, 34, 41; David G. Sansing, *Make Haste Slowly: The Troubled History of Higher Education in Mississippi* (Jackson: University Press of Mississippi, 1990), 36–38, 53–57; University of Mississippi *Mississippian*, November 23, 1929, November 17, 1967; *Oxford Eagle*, October 15, 1953.

37. Two men, a French reporter and a white Oxford resident, were killed during the riot. Cohodas, *Band Played Dixie*, 57–87; James W. Silver, *Mississippi: The Closed Society* (New York: Harcourt, Brace, and World), 119–20; *New York Times*, September 30, 1962. On the Meredith admissions case, see Sansing, *Make Haste Slowly*, 142–95. A recent account of the Ole Miss riot is William Doyle, *An American Insurrection: The Battle of Oxford, Mississippi, 1962* (New York: Doubleday, 2001).

38. John Vaught, *Rebel Coach: My Football Family* (Memphis, Tenn.: Memphis State University Press, 1971), 113–23; Cohodas, *Band Played Dixie*, 89–90.

39. University of Mississippi Football Media Guide, 1993; Penelope Krosch, e-mail to author, October 5, 1998.

40. *New York Times*, January 13, 19, December 31, 1956; Russell L. Henderson, "The 1963 Mississippi State University Basketball Controversy and the Repeal of the Unwritten Law: 'Something More than the Game Will Be Lost,'" *Journal of Southern History* 63 (November 1997): 829–30; *Atlanta Daily World*, December 4, 7, 1955.

41. Minutes, Board of Trustees of State Institutions of Higher Learning, March 9, 21, April 18, 1963, September 17, December 17, 1964, in University Archives, University of Mississippi; Silver, *Mississippi*, 318–19; Sansing, *Make Haste Slowly*, 198–200.

42. Cohodas (*Band Played Dixie*, 114–15) incorrectly states that Ole Miss's first integrated game came in 1964 versus Memphis State; the visitors had no African Americans on their roster. *New York Times*, December 20, 1964; Silver, *Mississippi*, 321.

43. Pennington, *Breaking the Ice*, 37–42, 46–47; University of Mississippi *Daily Mississippian*, October 24, 26, 30, 1967.

44. *Houston Informer*, September 17, 1966; *Daily Mississippian*, May 6, 7, 1969, March 6, 1970; *Jackson Daily News*, September 17, 1970.

45. The BSU newsletter used a modified Confederate flag on its cover, with a raised black fist superimposed across the middle of the flag. *Daily Mississippian*, March 27, May 9, 1969, February 13, March 6, 9, 19, September 25, 1970; Cohodas, *Band Played*

Dixie, 135, 146, 151, 154; Anthony W. James, "A Demand for Racial Equality: The 1970 Black Student Protest at the University of Mississippi," *Journal of Mississippi History* 57 (1995): 97–120.

46. Cohodas, *Band Played Dixie*, 168–70; *Daily Mississippian*, February 5, November 18, 1970.

47. University of Southern Mississippi *Student Printz*, October 20, 1970; *Daily Mississippian*, October 19–21, 1970, April 23, October 15, 1971; *El Paso (Texas) Times*, December 11, 1988.

48. *Daily Mississippian*, October 21, November 5, 1970, January 27, April 23, 1971.

49. University of Mississippi Football Media Guide, 1993; *Memphis Commercial Appeal*, October 26, 1972, November 12, 1975; *Daily Mississippian*, February 9, 1972.

50. Warner Alford, interview by author, March 24, 1994, Oxford, Miss.; Ben Williams and James Reed Files, Department of Intercollegiate Athletics, University of Mississippi; Cohodas, *Band Played Dixie*, 170–72; *Memphis Commercial Appeal*, October 26, 1972; *Daily Mississippian*, September 19, 22, 25, 1972.

51. *Ole Miss 1976* (school yearbook); Cohodas, *Band Played Dixie*, 185–86.

52. University of Mississippi Football Media Guide, 1974, 1975, 1976, 1993; *Memphis Commercial Appeal*, February 11, 1975.

53. Cohodas, *Band Played Dixie*, 199–203, 213–20, 251–53; Thornton, "Symbolism at Ole Miss," 265–66; unidentified newspaper clipping, June 3, 1980, "Athletics" vertical file, University of Mississippi Library; William Nack, "Look Away, Dixie Land," *Sports Illustrated*, October 28, 1997, 114; *Oxford Eagle*, April 26, 1993.

7

African American Women Pioneers in Desegregating Higher Education

MARCIA G. SYNNOTT

Explorations of the movement for equal civil rights have too often focused on male leaders, black and white, to the exclusion of women and less visible leaders and grassroots activists. This essay seeks to rectify that imbalance by discussing why African American women willingly became plaintiffs in higher education lawsuits initiated by the National Association for the Advancement of Colored People (NAACP) between the 1930s and the 1960s. Black women, like black men, saw education as an avenue of individual and racial advancement. Moreover, the NAACP needed reliable plaintiffs to desegregate almost every white southern state university, and women as well as men responded to the opportunity to make a difference not only for themselves but for all black southerners.[1] The plaintiffs were represented by competent local attorneys and by skilled attorneys from the NAACP's Legal Defense Fund in New York City, notably Harvard law graduate Charles Hamilton Houston, Howard University Law School graduate Thurgood Marshall, and and Columbia University law graduate Constance Baker Motley.[2] By voluntarily serving as plaintiffs in many desegregation cases and then by enrolling in the early unwelcoming years, black women pursued both their own individual interests and the wider campaign to desegregate higher education across the South.[3]

Of the many African American women pioneers in the desegregation of higher education in the South, six women were particularly notable: Lucile Harris Bluford (University of Missouri), Ada Lois Sipuel Fisher (University of Oklahoma), Autherine Juanita Lucy and Vivian Juanita Malone (University of Alabama), Charlayne Alberta Hunter (University of Georgia), and Henrie Dobbins Monteith (University of South Carolina). While the first three sought professional training—Bluford in journalism, Sipuel in law, and Lucy in library science—Malone, Hunter, and Monteith sought to complete their undergraduate education. The inclusion of their life histories will significantly broaden the historical narrative of the civil rights movement.

The first African American woman pioneer to participate in any university lawsuit was Lucile Bluford, who began her quest to enter the University of Missouri's School of Journalism shortly after the U.S. Supreme Court ruling, in *Gaines ex rel. Canada v. Missouri* (1938), that states could not fulfill their obligations under the Fourteenth Amendment by sending black students out of state for higher education in fields offered to white students at in-state schools. A decade later, Ada Lois Sipuel Fisher's lawsuit to enter the University of Oklahoma law school resulted in her becoming the first plaintiff since Lloyd L. Gaines to bring a desegregation case to the Supreme Court. In Alabama, Autherine Lucy's aspirations to break the color barrier at a state flagship university were no doubt shared by other African American women pioneers. She longed, she said, "to reach the top" and to "become the best citizen for Alabama." Instead, in 1956 she was the first black student at any public university to experience a riot and, for criticizing the University of Alabama trustees, to be expelled. Religious faith sustained her throughout the ordeal, as it did the other women pioneers. In 1961, Charlayne Hunter joined Hamilton Holmes as a plaintiff in the second lawsuit against the University of Georgia, and the first successful one. They experienced a riot like Autherine Lucy had, but they stayed and graduated. In 1963, without a riot, the University of Alabama admitted Vivian Malone and James Alexander Hood. Hood, like Autherine Lucy, was subsequently expelled, but Vivian Malone graduated in 1965. As she later recalled, the school had at first refused to admit her, and "the only reason that I couldn't attend was because I happened to be black."[4] So she, like Autherine Lucy, relied on a federal court order to override the university's refusal to permit her to attend. South Carolina was the final holdout against any desegregation in higher education. There, in 1963, Henrie Monteith was the first black woman, and the second plaintiff after Harvey Gantt at Clemson College, to enroll at a historically white institution, in her case the University of South Carolina.

Not all of the pioneer women had to go to court to gain admission. Lucinda Brawley gained admission to Clemson after Harvey Gantt's court victory had already opened the doors to African Americans. Nevertheless, in what might be described as second-stage desegregation, Brawley stretched the boundaries of white acceptance of a black presence. The 1964 Civil Rights Act further expanded opportunities for black women by outlawing racial discrimination in public education and public places and by banning discrimination in employment on the grounds of race, color, religion, sex, or national origin (monitored by the Equal Employment Opportunity Commission). Black women could make personal choices and overcome obstacles that were based on gender as much as on race, as Cheryl Butler's experience reveals. In 1973, she was the first black woman to join the Corps of Cadets at Virginia Polytechnic Institute and State University in Blacksburg, which was the first institution to admit women to its military program, three years before the U.S. service academies. Thus these eight African American women, together with their families, were agents of change in the movement for equal civil rights. Their stories emerge through careful reading of court cases and university records, combined with oral histories, personal memoirs, autobiographies, and biographies.[5]

Lucile Bluford

The career aspirations of Lucile Bluford (B.A. University of Kansas, 1932, and news editor of the *Kansas City Call*) were nurtured by her college-educated parents and encouraged by Charles Hamilton Houston. Following the U.S. Supreme Court's 1938 ruling in *Gaines*, Lloyd Gaines had disappeared. Black men often had reason to fear for their lives when seeking admission to a historically white institution, since white men justified using violence against them on the assumption that they posed a physical and sexual threat to white females. Needing a new plaintiff to apply to the University of Missouri, Houston explained why he chose a black woman. By bringing "to the front the discrimination against Negro women," Houston wrote, Bluford's suit to enter its School of Journalism would keep "public attention focused on the University problem." Her "rejection . . . would have much more publicity value than a rejection of a man."[6] If Bluford could demonstrate to whites that black women were intelligent, academically qualified, and sufficiently proper, she could dispel in their minds the erroneous view that black females threatened to debase white women socially and intellectually by entering the same classrooms.

According to Houston, who had personally prepared Bluford's case, "her father had moved from North Carolina where she was born to Kansas City to give his children a better chance." A high school teacher in Kansas City, Bluford's father had graduated from Howard University and then studied at Cornell University; her mother was a graduate of Oberlin College. Bluford had earned "a B-plus average in journalism at K.U.," and her brothers had both received degrees from Kansas University. In addition, her brother Guion, a teacher at Alcorn College in Mississippi, had earned a master's degree in mechanical engineering from the University of Michigan. Bluford's recital of her family's educational history impressed the courtroom audience. The spectators, most of whom were white women students from Stephens College, "had never seen intelligent Negroes." When they cheered Bluford's answers, the judge had the courtroom cleared. During cross-examination, Registrar S. W. Canada admitted that "he never inquired of a qualified white girl her motive for wanting to enter the U. Mo."[7]

Losing admissions suits in Missouri courts and two civil suits for damages against the University of Missouri registrar in the federal courts, Bluford was "so blooming angry" that she was "tempted to go ... sit in classes until they put me out." She declined to register at the unequal journalism school operated at Lincoln University from 1942 to 1944 and made "a standing application" for graduate courses in journalism at the University of Missouri, which was closed from 1942 to 1944, due to low wartime enrollments. She wondered "what kind of democracy it is for which I am buying defense bonds" and for which her brothers were in uniform. Despite the stress of another trial, in view of "the most vicious appeals to race prejudice," she resolved to defend the "principle at stake" and carry "through to the end, win, lose or draw."[8]

Though never admitted to the University of Missouri's School of Journalism—the first black student to enroll was James Saunders, a male journalism instructor at Lincoln University, who earned a master's degree in journalism in 1955—Bluford became publisher and majority owner of the *Kansas City Call*. The University of Missouri awarded her, in 1984, a Missouri Honor Medal for Distinguished Service in Journalism and, in 1989, an honorary doctorate of humanities, which Bluford accepted "for the thousands of black students who suffered discrimination all those years."[9]

Ada Lois Sipuel Fisher

Ada Lois Sipuel, a Langston University honors graduate, was motivated, like Lucile Bluford, by a belief, as she later wrote, that segregation "was wrong." She readily agreed to become "a purple cow, a pioneer, the principal figure in a historic court case, a 'who does she think she is?'" Her life story showed how "family, community, faith, and conviction" came "together to make history."[10]

Both of Sipuel's parents influenced her. Her father, the Reverend Travis B. Sipuel, son of ex-slaves, was minister, business manager, and bishop in the Pentecostal Church of God in Christ; her housewife mother, daughter of a former slave and her white master, belonged to the local NAACP chapter, and was active in endorsing candidates for office. In the fall of 1945, the NAACP's regional director for southwestern Oklahoma told the Sipuel family about Thurgood Marshall's legal strategy to challenge segregated higher education. When her brother Lemuel, an army veteran, declined to be a plaintiff, Sipuel readily agreed to be the plaintiff.[11]

Sipuel's "scholastic credits are nearly perfect," admitted University of Oklahoma president George Lynn Cross, who assisted her lawsuit by stipulating that the law school rejected her because of her racial identity. She had married Warren W. Fisher, a soldier in the all-black 349th Field Artillery, in 1944, but she used her maiden name during the suit, so that her name on her law school application matched the name on her undergraduate transcript from Langston University. After a three-and-a-half-year fight, marked by a partial victory before the Supreme Court and the closing of Langston's law facility, she enrolled, in June 1949, as the only African American and only woman among over 300 white male law students.[12]

Fisher's "most humiliating" experience was "walking past my classmates in the law school classroom and climbing the levels up to the 'colored' chair," behind a rail, with its "large printed sign that said COLORED." Erected on orders of the state attorney general, hers was an ironic pedestal. Even if other black students had been with her, she would have felt "despair," because the chair "represented the laws and public policy of the state." "What were they thinking?" she wondered. "Was I walking erect and maintaining a calm demeanor? I must show no emotion. I had to be careful not to stumble." During her three years as a law student, Fisher "was usually too busy studying and commuting back and forth to be lonely," but she keenly felt her "aloneness." After the Supreme Court ruled, in *McLaurin v. Oklahoma State Regents for Higher Education* (1950), that segregation within the classroom, library, or cafeteria violated the Fourteenth Amendment's equal protection clause, she immediately took her "place" in a first-row seat.[13]

The instructor in her first class was Maurice Merrill, who had argued against her admission in both the Oklahoma courts and the U.S. Supreme Court. "Now it was Professor Merrill," thought a stunned Fisher, "who was going to lecture me on the meaning of the American Constitution." Fortunately, Merrill proved to be a supportive professor once he was no longer her legal adversary, and the law students were quite friendly. Some even welcomed her and wanted the rail removed, and they also helped her to catch up on the work that she had missed. Her husband, Warren, employed in personnel at the nearby Tinker Air Force Base, dropped her off and picked her up at the university on his way to and from work. She "always considered that Warren and I graduated together in August 1951."[14]

After graduating from law school, Ada Lois Sipuel Fisher practiced law. In addition, she earned an M.A. in history from the University of Oklahoma in 1968, and she served as professor and chair of social sciences at Langston University. In recognition of her accomplishments, the University of Oklahoma designated February 1, 1978, as Ada Lois Sipuel day. In 1991, the university received $100,000 from an anonymous donor to establish the Ada Lois Sipuel Scholarship. And on May 11, 1991, the university conferred on her an honorary Doctor of Humane Letters degree. Appointed a University of Oklahoma regent by Governor David Walters in 1992, Fisher questioned "why the state's flagship university does not have more tenured black faculty and why its retention rate for minority students is not higher."[15]

Autherine Lucy

Autherine Lucy, the tenth and youngest child of a farmer and a housewife, was perhaps unlikely to be a pioneer plaintiff. But in her personal longing to "become the best citizen for Alabama," she had been motivated by Pollie Anne Myers, a member of the NAACP Youth Council whom she had met in a public speaking class at Miles College in Birmingham, Alabama. Lucy thought her acceptance letter to the University of Alabama's library school service program "a miracle"; Myers was admitted in journalism. Arriving at the Tuscaloosa campus, they were denied admission because of their race. In July 1953, they brought suit in federal district court.[16]

When their lawsuit finally came to trial, on June 29–30, 1955, the judge ordered their admission, citing previous Supreme Court rulings and recognizing the existence of "a tacit policy" of excluding blacks. But he suspended his injunction until January 1956, pending appeal.[17] Trustee-sponsored background investigations eliminated Myers, who was pregnant before marriage, because "her conduct and marital record have been such that she does not meet the admissions standards of the University."[18] Although voting eleven to one to admit Lucy on February 1, the trustees unanimously denied her room and board, because her presence "might endanger the safety or result in sociological disadvantage of the students."[19]

Lucy's attendance at classes on February 3, 4, and 6 ended with a riot, as the University of Alabama became the first flagship state university to experience violent demonstrations against the admission of a black student. Crosses were burned near campus, and crowds, disrupting traffic, turned into mobs that sang "Dixie" and chanted "Hey, Hey, Ho, Ho, Autherine Must Go." One hundred state troopers were on stand-by, but they made no arrests except to protect state property from damage. A mob of about 1,000 students, rubber and foundry workers, and Klansmen shouted: "'Where is the Nigger?' 'Lynch her!' 'Kill her!' and 'Keep 'Bama White.'"[20]

During a day defined by fear and faith, Autherine Lucy recalled being "very much afraid" as she lay on the floor of a highway patrolmen's car taking her away from campus for her own safety. She prayed "to be able to see the time when I would be able to complete my work on the campus, but that if it was not the will of God that I do this, that he give me the courage to accept the fact that I would lose my life there."[21]

Because they did not have control of the campus, the trustees voted unanimously to exclude Lucy for her own protection.[22] After she accused them of conspiring with the mob and asked for damages, the trustees expelled her and a white student rioter, Leonard Wilson, a protégé of the Citizens' Council.[23] During a February 29 court hearing, trustee John Caddell blamed the NAACP and Lucy for her coming "in a Cadillac automobile; she had chauffeurs with her." Walking around campus, she was "obnoxious and objectionable and disagreeable." But the university had never offered any friendly advice about how she should behave on campus and handle the media. Moreover, admitted Caddell, "We very greatly underestimated the fury of the mob," which had been intensified by the contemporaneous Montgomery bus boycott.[24]

Lucy's reputation was smeared in Alabama for years. She moved to Texas in April 1956 to marry Hugh Lawrence Foster, a Baptist minister, and the family did not return to Birmingham until 1975.[25] The "case spelled disaster for the NAACP in Alabama," concluded historian E. Culpepper Clark, when a state court injunction forced the termination of its activities until 1964. However, Autherine Lucy Foster reclaimed her dignity as a woman, and "her natural reserve guaranteed that she would become the victim, not the perpetrator," observed Clark. Though becoming "a national symbol of virtue defiled," she saw herself as just one of many who contributed to the civil rights movement.[26]

In 1988, the board of trustees reversed her 1956 expulsion. Three years later, in August 1991, Autherine Lucy Foster completed the work for her M.Ed. in elementary education. At her graduation on May 9, 1992, at which she received a standing ovation, her portrait was unveiled in the Hill Ferguson Student Center. She is honored for "her initiative and courage" that "won the right for students of all races to attend the University." Her daughters attended the University of Alabama—Angela Foster attended in the 1980s, and Grazia Foster graduated in 1992 with a bachelor's degree in corporate finance. An endowed scholarship at the University of Alabama is named in honor of Autherine Lucy Foster.[27]

Vivian Malone

Vivian Malone, the fourth of eight children of parents who worked at Brookley Air Field near Mobile, wanted to transfer in 1963 from Alabama A&M to the University of Alabama to study personnel management. Malone and James A. Hood, who sought to transfer from Clark College in Atlanta, received assistance from the NAACP's Legal Defense Fund and approval from the Reverend Martin Luther King Jr. But their motivation was their own.[28]

Malone's reputation was "spotless." Even state detective Ben Allen, who never conducted a similar investigation of a white student, concluded: "Vivian was good people. She had made good grades . . . and I had the gut feelin' that here was the first person to break the color barrier in the state of Alabama."[29]

Realizing that Autherine Lucy's court order would admit Malone and Hood, the University of Alabama willingly cooperated with the John F. Kennedy administration to avoid the riot that had occurred when James H. Meredith entered the University of Mississippi the previous fall. University of Alabama officials had the campus sealed to outsiders, met with the two black students beforehand to "strategize," and sought to contain Governor George C. Wallace, Malone remembered. However, she never expected Governor Wallace to refuse to leave the doorway of Foster Auditorium, which gave their enrollment on June 11, 1963, "world-wide dimensions." The governor's stand embodied "an entangled reality of class and gender," according to scholar Rhoda E. Johnson, and reassured the countless southern whites who resented a black woman and a black man enrolling at a university that many of them could not afford to attend. To protect the "dignity" of Malone and Hood on national television, however, Deputy Attorney General Nicholas Katzenbach decided "not to take students up to the schoolhouse door," but left them in the car. He read President Kennedy's "cease and desist" proclamation to Wallace; the governor countered with his statement denouncing the federal government's interference.[30]

Within half an hour, President Kennedy federalized Alabama's National Guard, whose commander persuaded Wallace, after making a second, short speech, to step aside just after 3:30 p.m. Meanwhile, the students had been taken to their dormitories. Assigned to a single room in Mary Burke Hall, Malone ate lunch in the dining room, where white coeds joined her. Later, she and Hood quietly registered.[31] On national television that evening, President Kennedy defined civil rights as "a moral issue" and urged Congress to enact a broad civil rights bill.[32]

But violence continued to afflict the South—the June 12 assassination of Medgar Evers outside his Jackson, Mississippi, home by Byron de la Beckwith; the September 15 bombing of the Sixteenth Street Baptist Church in Birmingham that killed four black girls; the November 22 assassination of President Kennedy in Dallas. Despite being well protected for the rest of 1963 by a small number of National Guardsmen, nine U.S. marshals, Tuscaloosa motorcycle policemen, and the campus police, Vivian Malone was "alone," she said, as she weathered cross burnings, telephone threats, and five bomb explosions on or very near the campus that damaged its buildings. Indeed, Wallace, not seeing what historian Culpepper Clark has termed Malone's "introspective beauty," still tried to "get the nigger bitch out of the dormitory." Alabama's segregation laws also limited her activities. After she went one Saturday night to the Skyline Drive-in Theater with two white young women and a white young man in late September, Malone was told by a city policeman to return to campus, which she did, because it was unlawful in Alabama for a black to attend a white drive-in theater. Nor could she bring a date to a dance in her dormitory, but she did attend, under protection, the Florida-Alabama football game. Meanwhile, that August, Jimmy Hood had been compelled to withdraw, because he gave an off-campus political speech that violated university regulations. Caught between two worlds—one of being liked on campus and the other of making civil rights speeches—Hood "had almost forgotten who he was," said historian Culpepper Clark.[33]

In May 1965, Vivian Malone graduated with a management degree, the first known African American to graduate from a historically white public university in Alabama. "I felt very confident that I should be there," she later explained, since whites lacked "the ability to change what I was." A "lady" and "a loner," she "had no more desire to fraternize with everybody on that campus than they had any desire to fraternize with me." Socializing at nearby Stillman College, she met her future husband, Michael Jones.[34]

She first returned to campus in 1972 for the dedication in her honor of the university's Afro-American Cultural Center. In October 1996, when George C. Wallace awarded Vivian Malone Jones, a successful Atlanta businesswoman, the first Lurleen B. Wallace Award of Courage, she graciously forgave the former segregationist. "We all make mistakes," she said. In an appearance in Mobile, a year before she died on October 13, 2005, Vivian Jones discussed her meeting with former Governor Wallace in 1996: "'I asked him why did he do it,'" to which he replied: "'He did what he felt needed to be done at that point in time, but he would not do that today. At that point, we spoke—I spoke—of forgiveness.'" She recalled that she never felt "afraid" during her and Jimmy Hood's integration of the University of Alabama. "God was with me."[35]

Charlayne Hunter

Charlayne Hunter gained a sense of self from her mother, her "ideal woman—smart and strong, creative and feminine," who worked as a manager in a prominent black-owned real estate company, and from her grandmother. Her father, often absent before her parents' separation and divorce, taught her self-discipline and showed her, through his sermons as an African Methodist Episcopal (AME) minister and an army chaplain during the early years of army integration, how to reach across racial divisions. Allowed to develop as an independent person, Hunter, at age sixteen, converted, together with two girlfriends, to Catholicism, her "first serious act of defiance."[36]

Since the age of twelve, Hunter had desired to become a journalist like the adventurous and romantic comic-strip reporter Brenda Starr. Nurtured and "inspired" by her English teachers at Atlanta's Henry McNeal Turner High School, she became editor-in-chief of the student newspaper, the *Green Light*, and also assistant yearbook editor. Hunter talked with Hamilton Holmes, valedictorian and senior class president, about applying to the University of

Georgia. But he entered Morehouse College in Atlanta, and she attended Wayne University (later Wayne State University) in Detroit, with assistance from Georgia's tuition grant program since no in-state black college offered a journalism degree. There she found her black sisters in Delta Sigma Theta to be "soft and appealing, clear-headed and strong without being strident."[37]

During their lawsuit against the University of Georgia, Hunter and Holmes were advised: "Keep your mouth shut; that's how they got Autherine Lucy."[38] Under a federal district court order, they enrolled on January 9, 1961.[39] On the drive from Atlanta, Hunter resolved to "walk onto the campus at Georgia, loving myself a lot and demanding respect." For Georgia's "white sons and daughters," she observed, it was "their most apocalyptic moment since Sherman marched to the sea"; for the state's "Black sons and daughters their most liberating moment since the Emancipation Proclamation." But when white students rioted in front of her dormitory after their first day of classes, January 11, the dean of students ordered that Hunter and Holmes be returned to Atlanta. However, the federal district judge overturned the state law cutting off funds to state institutions that desegregated, and he ordered the University of Georgia to readmit them under protection.[40]

Like Vivian Malone, Hunter managed to cope with "a special kind of loneliness," said writer Calvin Trillin, as both "the best-known student on campus and a social undesirable at the same time." Because, as Hunter later wrote, she "had no problem being alone," having "always relished my solitude"—though in the past, "by choice"—she "really was the right one to desegregate the University of Georgia."[41] Writing of civil rights in her autobiography, *In My Place* (1992), she said that "the Movement had endowed me with a sense of mission that was bigger than myself, and I felt I had to lose my public self in order to find my place in that new world where other people's lives would be the focal point, no matter their color or status in life."[42]

On June 1, 1963, Hunter and Holmes became the first black undergraduates at flagship universities in the Deep South to earn bachelor's degrees. Hunter also chose to marry secretly a southern white journalism student, Walter Stovall, in violation of Georgia's miscegenation law.[43] Over the years, Charlayne Hunter-Gault (her later name) went on to develop a distinguished career in the national media as a journalist and television commentator.[44] In June 1988, twenty-five years after her graduation, she became the first African American to deliver the University of Georgia commencement address. She entitled it "In Our Place." Declaring that the South was America's "true melting pot," she urged greater recruitment of black students while applauding the hiring of new black faculty. Earlier, she and Holmes had both been honored by a university chair that brought in a lecturer each year on civil rights or race relations.[45]

Lucinda Brawley

South Carolina avoided violence, but it resisted desegregation just as strongly as other Deep South states by legal maneuvering and official repression. Few African Americans applied to the University of South Carolina (USC) after John Howard Wrighten III's 1947 suit to enter its law school resulted in the state establishing a Jim Crow law school at South Carolina State College in Orangeburg. Massive political resistance under Governor George Bell Timmerman Jr. and lack of support by the black community discouraged applicants until the early 1960s, when Harvey Gantt applied to Clemson College. Finally, in January 1963 Clemson peacefully admitted Gantt under a federal district court order.[46]

As chairman of the South Carolina Student Council's Student Public Relations Committee, Gantt traveled around the state meeting with black high school students. Committed to persuading other blacks to become applicants, he evidently reassured Lucinda Brawley, who had been accepted as a freshman both at Clemson and at Fisk University in Nashville, to enroll as Clemson's first black coed, in September 1963. Encouraged by her Hopkins High School principal, J. E. Brown, Brawley had graduated second in her class; she scored in the top 4 percent in a statewide algebra test. Concerned about her gender as well as her race at a historically white male military school—Clemson had voted in 1955 to give men civilian status and to admit women, but had just opened a women's dormitory in 1963—she wanted to know whether the women students, in particular, would be friendly. In contrast to Gantt, whom she met in person during her first day at Clemson, Brawley "had epithets hurled at her" by white students. But she and Gantt did attend all home football games—made their presence on campus very visible—without trouble.[47] Moreover, they were warmly welcomed by Clemson's African American employees, who invited them to church and to Sunday dinner.

Gantt graduated—with honors—in 1965. He and Brawley then married, and she left Clemson, which did not award its first degrees to African American women until 1969, when Dorothy Ashford, Delores Chymes Barton, and Laverne Williams White graduated. Lucinda Gantt finished her college education at the University of North Carolina at Charlotte and worked for the Charlotte-Mecklenburg School System and then as business manager for an assisted-living establishment in Charlotte. In March 2000, she and her husband returned to Clemson for the dedication of the Harvey and Lucinda Gantt Office of Multicultural Affairs in the Hendrix Student Center.[48]

Henrie Monteith

Harvey Gantt also met with Vivian Malone, who, he said, was "a very low key type person" able to distance herself from the pressures of integration. Henrie Monteith, he said, was a "very smart young lady, a lot like Vivian Malone," although he thought that she was "probably a little more cynical about the system than I was."[49] Henrie Monteith received strong support from her mother, R. Rebecca Monteith, a teacher who had earlier brought a salary equalization case and was sister of civil rights activist Modjeska Monteith Simkins.[50]

Rebecca Monteith complained, as a mother and taxpayer, to Governor Ernest F. Hollings, as chairman ex officio of the Board of Control for Southern Regional Education, that its scholarship plan was "fully undemocratic and unjust, in relation to colored students," who, "regardless of their ambitions, talents and previous training," had the choice of only South Carolina State College, if it offered the program they wanted, or paying to study out of state. "For me and my daughter," she wrote, "it means the severing of family ties and great additional expense, even though I live right in Columbia where the University of South Carolina is located."[51]

After USC rejected her because she was "a Negro," Henrie Monteith, the top 1962 graduate of St. Francis de Sales High School in Powhatan, Virginia, entered the College of Notre Dame in Baltimore. Ineligible for an out-of-state tuition grant because chemistry was offered at South Carolina State College, she received assistance from a Catholic Youth Scholarship, the National School Service Fund for Negro Students, and a federal government student loan. Meanwhile, Monteith and her mother filed a class action suit in federal district court.[52]

On July 10, 1963, the court ordered Monteith and "all others similarly situated" admitted to USC in September. USC also admitted Robert G. Anderson Jr., of Greenville, South Carolina, who had applied as a transfer student from Clark College in Atlanta. James L. Solomon, a teacher at Morris College in Sumter, South Carolina, was admitted as a graduate student in mathematics. These three were the first black students ever to enroll at USC, aside from a four-year interlude during Reconstruction between 1873 and 1877.[53]

On July 29, the USC Board of Trustees issued a statement directing "complete compliance" and the maintenance of law and order on campus, influenced in part by the May 20 demonstration during which over a thousand white students had burned a cross and hanged a black in effigy on one of the athletic fields before marching to the state capitol.[54] For Monteith, the greatest danger occurred during the night of August 27, 1963, when a dynamite explosion caused a five-foot-long crater in a field near her home and shattered a window in her uncle's home. This "cowardly act," said Rebecca Monteith, would not deter her daughter from enrolling at USC. No arrests were made.[55]

Monteith, Anderson, and Solomon did receive a friendly welcome at an informal meeting held September 8 by the South Carolina Student Council on Human Relations and chaplains at USC.[56] On September 11, the three registered in an atmosphere of "orchestrated calm." For security reasons, Monteith and Anderson were housed on campus in private rooms with private bathrooms, and they ate at different times from other students in the main dining hall of Russell House. Solomon commuted to campus from his home in Sumter. No campus police accompanied them to their classes the next day, but both undergraduates subsequently agreed "as a safety precaution" not to attend USC football games. Bob Anderson, who was from Anderson in upstate South Carolina, had been optimistic that, like Harvey Gantt, he would not experience "another Alabama or Mississippi," because "South Carolina has good leadership, far better than you'd find in Alabama or Mississippi." But he apparently felt such hostility that he wanted to leave the university; after earning a B.A. in political science in June 1966, he did not return to USC until 1988. Monteith had a less stressful experience, for though she also lived on campus, she had the support of a network of family and friends in Columbia. Moreover, she "didn't care" whether white students liked her. Deciding to wait and "see whether we would like each other," she eventually made friends at USC.[57]

After graduation in August 1965 in premedicine, Monteith earned a doctorate at Boston University and later chaired the biology department at Morris Brown College in Atlanta. When she returned in 1988 to USC as keynote speaker for the twenty-fifth anniversary of its desegregation, Henrie Monteith Treadwell was program director for the W. K. Kellogg Foundation.[58]

Cheryl Butler

In 1973 Cheryl Butler (McDonald), an African American sophomore, helped to make history at Virginia Polytechnic Institute and State University, or Virginia Tech, when she joined the school's Corps of Cadets. (Previously known as Virginia Polytechnic Institute, or VPI, in 1970 the school adopted the longer name to reflect the emergence of a comprehensive educational mission.) Virginia Tech admitted women to its Corps of Cadets a year before either Norwich University, in Northfield, Vermont, the first private military college to do so, or state-supported Texas A&M, which trains the largest number—some 2,000—of uniformed students. In 1976, under congressional order, the U.S. service academies began admitting women. Thus the first female members of the Virginia Tech Corps of Cadets, who formed its "L" Squadron, the women's unit for the U.S. Air Force, were true pioneers in overcoming gender barriers.[59]

In order for Cheryl Butler to be able to join the Corps of Cadets, the school—which had been established in 1872 for the agricultural and technical instruction of none but white male students—had to make major changes in both race and gender. Although five white women enrolled full-time in 1921, from 1944 to 1964 women were generally expected to attend the coordinate Radford College. Virginia Tech enrolled its first few African American students, all male undergraduates studying engineering, beginning in 1953, without a court order, though all the early black students at the school had to live off campus. Thus did the school become the first historically white land-grant institution in the former Confederacy to admit a black undergraduate. Then in 1958, when Charlie L. Yates (who graduated with honors in mechanical engineering) earned his degree, Virginia Tech became the first such school to graduate an African American. Virginia Tech widened the door for the enrollment of women undergraduates in 1964 when it separated from Radford College. That same year, it made the Corps of Cadets optional for all male freshmen and sophomores (it had been optional for juniors and seniors since 1924), though the corps remained closed to female students. In 1966, six African American women undergraduates enrolled at Virginia Tech; they were among around forty black students at the school, which then had an enrollment of 9,000. Two years later, one of them, Linda Adams, became its first black female graduate. Having reached double digits for the first time in 1966, Virginia Tech's black enrollment, though it remained small, soon reached triple digits.[60]

In 1973, Cheryl Butler and the other women cadets felt they were both pioneers and "specimens," who "were kind of put under a microscope," as she later described the experience. However, they did not face the male hostility that women like Shannon Faulkner did at The Citadel in 1995 or those at the Virginia Military Institute in 1997, both of which required all male students to be in their Corps of Cadets. Virginia Tech changed its policy and began to admit women to the Corps of Cadets in part because of the decline in male corps members, as most students were civilians. One reason a female student like Cheryl Butler might want to join the corps was the heightened discussion, in the 1970s, of women's issues. Butler supported "women's lib," she explained, because it allowed her "to push the boundaries" and be an individual. At the time, the only discrimination she felt was on account of her gender, not her race. She developed leadership skills as the 2nd commander of "L" Squadron in 1973 and its commander in 1974.[61]

Eldest daughter of an air force enlisted man and a housewife mother, both of whom had approved of her entering the Corps of Cadets, Butler had attended integrated schools on or near military bases. Having "always viewed myself as a female opposed to being a black female," she thought that the civil rights movement largely settled the racial issue; as she observed, "the race issue had been settled in my mind long before the gender issue." She experienced almost no racial discrimination until later, she said, when "I was stationed down South" in Florida. Indeed, the only segregation that she saw in the military "was between officer and enlisted not between black and white, or non-white and white." Serving in the air force from 1976 to 1994, Cheryl Butler McDonald was "one of the first officers in the family—the entire extended family."[62]

Black Women on Historically White Campuses

Like the pioneer black women plaintiffs, Cheryl Butler McDonald believed that neither race nor gender should be a barrier to women's educational aspirations and career goals. Though race, rather than gender, had defined the exclusion of black women and led to their legal action, gender was also a factor in their complete acceptance on campus. Viewing black women differently from black men, whites often assumed that black women were prone to "uppity," "obnoxious," and even "promiscuous" behavior. Thus black women were put in the position of having to prove that they were not doubly inferior because of race and gender. Testing the white norm of appropriate feminine behavior, often under intense publicity and harassment, black women made courage, intelligence, and moral superiority the attributes of "a lady."[63]

Their personal place was not the southern white lady's pedestal; but it was one, as several black female pioneers put it, of "aloneness." Black women did much to transform southern campuses—public places where whites continued at least well into the 1960s to memorialize the Lost Cause by waving Confederate flags and singing "Dixie"—into new spaces that recognized the value of racial diversity to all students. The institutional transformation they ultimately effected was the most important legacy that these eight African American women made to American higher education in general, and to black higher education and women's higher education in particular. Their compelling life stories opened doors and encouraged increasing numbers of black women to attend college as a means to upward mobility. A generation later, twice as many black women as black men were attending college.[64]

Notes

Some of the material in this essay appeared previously in "Race, Gender, and Personal 'Place' in the Desegregation of State Universities in the American South," in *Women and Higher Education: Past, Present and Future*, ed. Mary R. Masson and Deborah Simonton (Aberdeen, Scotland: Aberdeen University Press, 1996), 154–71.

1. Elizabeth L. Ihle, "Black Women's Education in the South: The Dual Burden of Sex and Race," in *Changing Education: Women as Radicals and Conservators*, ed. Joyce Antler and Sari Knopp Biklen (Albany: State University of New York Press, 1990), 69–80; Linda M. Perkins, "The Education of Black Women in the Nineteenth Century," 64–86, and Jeanne Noble, "The Higher Education of Black Women in the Twentieth Century," 87–106, both in *Women and Higher Education in American History: Essays from the Mount Holyoke College Sesquicentennial Symposia*, ed. John Mack Faragher and Florence Howe (New York: Norton, 1988). See also Linda M. Perkins, "The African-American Female 'Talented Tenth': A History of African-American Women in the Seven Sister Colleges," *Harvard Educational Review* 67 (Winter 1997): 718–57.

2. Contrary to segregationists' assumptions, they were not "tools" of NAACP Legal Defense Fund attorneys Charles Hamilton Houston, Thurgood Marshall, and Constance Baker Motley. Genna Rae McNeil, *Groundwork: Charles Hamilton Houston and the Struggle for Civil Rights* (Philadelphia: University of Pennsylvania Press, 1983). Motley's plaintiffs included Autherine Lucy and Vivian Malone and James Hood at the University of Alabama; Charlayne Hunter and Hamilton Holmes at the University of Georgia; James Meredith at the University of Mississippi in 1962; and Harvey Gantt at Clemson College in 1963. Several of the local NAACP attorneys were very good, notably Matthew J. Perry of South Carolina, who, in 1979, was appointed the first black federal judge in the Deep South. See Constance Baker Motley, *Equal Justice under Law: An Autobiography* (New York: Farrar, Straus and Giroux, 1998): 64, 65, 84, 120–25, 137–38, 145–46, 187–88. Motley had also helped write the NAACP briefs that Thurgood Marshall used in *Brown v. Board of Education* (1954) to argue that segregation denied black pupils equal protection of the laws. She won nine of her ten cases before the Supreme Court. The first woman Manhattan borough president and the first black woman in the New York State Senate, Motley was appointed by President Lyndon B. Johnson to the U.S. Court for the Southern District of New York in September 1966 and later became chief judge. She died September 28, 2005 ("Constance Baker Motley," infoplease at http://print.infoplease.com/ipa/A0900715.html).

3. Charles W. Eagles, "Toward New Histories of the Civil Rights Era," *Journal of Southern History* 56 (November 2000): 815–48. Eagles points out that no clearly defined interpretive historiographical field yet exists for the civil rights movement comparable to that which has developed for the contemporaneous Cold War. Although Eagles refers to various recent biographies of women activists and to such notable memoirs by women as Anne Moody's *Coming of Age in Mississippi* (New York: Dial Press, 1968) and Sara Evans's *Personal Politics: The Roots of Women's Liberation in the Civil Rights Movement and the New Left* (New York: Knopf, 1979), he says that "other valuable memoirs, too numerous to mention, are beyond the scope of this study" (819, n.6).

4. Autherine Lucy Foster, interviews by E. Culpepper Clark, March 13, 19, April 2, 1975, transcript in the William Stanley Hoole Special Collections Library, University of Alabama, Tuscaloosa, 6, 16–19, 21, 46. The starting point for research on civil rights oral histories is Howell Raines, *My Soul Is Rested: Movement Days in the Deep South Remembered* (New York: G. P. Putnam's Sons, 1977; reprint, New York: Penguin Group

Viking Penguin, 1983), which includes interviews with black female and male student pioneers (Vivian Malone Jones quoted, 332–33).

5. In addition to the eight pioneers featured in this essay, black women also played prominent roles in various other desegregation efforts—in litigation to gain entry into the University of Delaware's undergraduate programs in 1950; into junior colleges in Texas in the 1950s; and into regional universities in Louisiana (see Michael Wade's essay in this volume), also in the 1950s. Esther McCready had to bring suit to enter the University of Maryland's nursing program (*McCready v. Byrd*, 73 A.2d 8 [1950]), yet black women pioneers in some other states enrolled without litigation, as when Edith Mae Irby desegregated the University of Arkansas medical school in 1948 (see Peter Wallenstein's essay in this volume). In Texas, following the 1955 decree implementing *Brown* "with all deliberate speed," twelve out of thirty community colleges and nineteen public and ten private four-year colleges began admitting black men and women. The University of Texas at Austin admitted, in June 1955, John W. Hargis on transfer from Prairie View A&M University, but not until September 1956 did it admit a significant number, 110, of black men and women as freshmen and transfer students. Initially, black women were not permitted to live in dormitories, even off campus; later they were segregated in separate campus housing because the administration feared that black men coming to the women's dormitories to date black women would be offensive to the white women students and their parents. In April 1957, black music major Barbara Smith was not allowed to sing in the university's production of *Dido and Aeneas* (although Dido was queen of Carthage, located in North Africa, near modern Tunis). The next year, she performed her senior recital before a packed audience. In the more cosmopolitan climate of the 1980s, the University of Texas elected Barbara Smith Conrad a Distinguished Graduate and honored her by the establishment of a scholarship (Richard B. McCaslin, "Steadfast in His Intent: John W. Hargis and the Integration of the University of Texas at Austin," *Southwestern Historical Quarterly* 95 [July 1991]: 33–41; Logan Wilson, interview by David G. McComb, November 8, 1968, at the American Council of Education, Washington, D.C., Lyndon Baines Johnson Library, University of Texas, Austin). Women were also among the first black undergraduates to enroll at the University of Florida, in 1962. And of course black women pioneered the desegregation of such women's colleges as what later became James Madison University (in Virginia) and the University of North Carolina at Greensboro.

6. R. McLaren Sawyer, "The Gaines Case: The Human Side," *Negro Educational Review* 38 (January 1987): 4–14; Mark V. Tushnet, *The NAACP's Legal Strategy against Segregated Education, 1925–1950* (Chapel Hill: University of North Carolina Press, 1987), 36–37; [Charles H. Houston], Memorandum on the Gaines Case, January 12, 1940, Group II Legal Container List 1940–55, Box 197, File University of Missouri (*Bluford v. Missouri*) Correspondence 1940, and Charles H. Houston to Lucile Bluford, January 27, 1939, Legal File 1910–39, Group II Addenda Box L38, File University of Missouri, *Bluford v. Missouri* 1938–September 1939, in the Papers of the National Association for the Advancement of Colored People (NAACP), Library of Congress (hereafter cited as NAACP Papers). See also microfilm reels 12, 13, and 24, NAACP Papers,

Part 3, The Campaign for Educational Equality: Legal Department and Central Office Records, 1913–50, Series B: Legal Department and Central Office Records, 1940–1950, and Addendum File, all in *Black Studies Research Sources: Microfilms from Major Archival and Manuscript Collections*, August Meier and Elliott Rudwick, general editors; guide compiled by Martin Schipper, a Microfilm Project of University Publications of America (Frederick, Md., 1986).

7. Charles H. Houston, memorandum to Walter White, Roy Wilkins, and Thurgood Marshall in re *Lucile Bluford v. Univ. Missouri*, February 12, 1940, NAACP Papers, Group II Legal Container List 1940–55, Box 197, File University of Missouri Correspondence 1940. See also microfilm reels 12, 13, and 24, NAACP Papers, Part 3, Series B: Legal Department and Central Office Records, 1940–50.

8. Lucile Bluford to Thurgood Marshall, Charles H. Houston, and Sidney Redmond, enclosing report Re: Lincoln University School of Journalism, February 6, 1941; Houston, Memorandum for [Carl R.] Johnson, [L. Amasa] Knox, [Charles H.] Calloway, [James H.] Herbert, [Lucile] Bluford, [Sidney R.] Redmond, and [Thurgood] Marshall, February 17, 1941; Lucile Bluford to Thurgood Marshall, July 10, 1941, enclosing clipping, "M.U. Negro Bar Holds," *Kansas City Star*, July 8, 1941, and a draft of her statement; Houston to Bluford, July 15, 1941, NAACP Group II Legal Container List 1940–55, Box 197, File University of Missouri (*Bluford v. Missouri*), Correspondence 1941; Houston to Bluford, January 14, 1942; Houston, Memorandum for Carl, Lucile, Thurgood, March 26, 1942; "Missouri U. Cancels Journalism Courses to Bar Race Students," NAACP press release, March 27, 1942; Howard Flieger, "Missouri Now Battleground of Negro Issue," *Norfolk Virginian Pilot*, April 19, 1942, clipping enclosed in letter from Harold Wilkie to Bluford, May 1, 1942; Bluford to Houston, March 31, 1942, NAACP Group II Legal Container List 1940–55, Box 198, File University of Missouri (*Bluford v. Missouri*), Correspondence 1942–45.

Bluford also lost the trial before a three-judge federal district court, in which, after an hour's deliberation, the jury rejected her suit for three types of relief: $20,000 in damages, an injunction, and a declaratory judgment establishing "her right to take education in her calling under conditions equal to those afforded the whites." Charles H. Houston to Lucile Bluford, April 26, 1942, enclosing a copy of his report on the trial of *Bluford v. Canada*, Civil Action No. 128, U.S. District Court, Western Dist., Mo., before Judges Collet, Reeves, and Otis, April 23–24, 1942, in Jefferson City, Mo.; Houston, Memorandum to the office, April 30, 1942; Bluford to Dr. Scruggs and to S. W. Canada, April 28, 1942; Bluford to Governor Forrest C. Donnell, September 18, [1941]; "Missouri Discontinues Jim Crow School of Law and Journalism," NAACP press release, December 17, 1943; Lincoln University news release, January 29, 1944; "Majority Missouri U. Students Vote Admission to Negroes," *St. Louis American*, June 15, 1944, clipping, NAACP Group II Legal Container List 1940–55, Box 198, File University of Missouri Correspondence 1942–45. See also microfilm reels 12, 13, and 24, NAACP Papers, Part 3, Series B: Legal Department and Central Office Records, 1940–50; Tushnet, *NAACP's Legal Strategy*, 83–85.

9. Marianna W. Davis, ed., *Contributions of Black Women to America*, vol. 1: *The Arts, Media, Business, Law, Sports* (Columbia, S.C.: Kenday Press, 1982), 255; W. Augustus

Low and Virgil A. Clift, eds. *Encyclopedia of Black America* (New York: McGraw-Hill, 1981), 646; Delia Crutchfield Cook, "Shadows across the Columns: The Bittersweet Legacy of African Americans at the University of Missouri" (Ph.D. diss., University of Missouri–Columbia, 1996), 53–55; Bluford, quoted in Diane E. Loupe, "Storming and Defending the Color Barrier at the University of Missouri School of Journalism: The Lucile Bluford Case," *Journalism History* 16 (Spring–Summer 1989): 26, 29. Bluford was among "The Top 15" of "the 150 most influential Kansas Citians" (Brian Burnes and Jeffrey Spivak, *Kansas City Star*, "KC @150: Our City's Sesquicentennial. Into the 21st Century," wysiwyg://5/http://www.kestar.com/kc150/content/ file.21st-top15.htm). In 1961, Lincoln University recognized Bluford's achievements as a reporter and editor. In 1977, the National Newspaper Publisher's Association, formerly the Negro Newspaper Publishers Association, selected her as the first woman to be included in its Gallery of Distinguished Publishers. In 1983, the seventy-two-year-old Bluford greeted her nephew, Guion Stewart Bluford Jr., a Ph.D. in aerospace engineering from the Air Force Institute of Technology, when he returned to the Johnson Space Center in Houston from his first flight as an astronaut, August 30–September 5 (*Newsweek*, September 19, 1983, 49).

10. Ada Lois Sipuel Fisher, with Danney Goble, *A Matter of Black and White: The Autobiography of Ada Lois Sipuel Fisher* (Norman: University of Oklahoma Press, 1996), xvii–xviii, 185. According to legal scholar Mark V. Tushnet (*NAACP's Legal Strategy*, 149), plaintiffs like Bluford and Sipuel "had to be in the fight as a matter of principle, and people who undergo serious strains for matters of principle are likely to be rather aggressive sorts, both in initiating contacts with lawyers and in dealing with their attorneys once litigation begins.... [T]hey were women who knew what they wanted and surely would not have acquiesced in legal maneuvers with which they disagreed."

11. Fisher, *Black and White*, xiii, xvii–xviii, 6–12, 15, 17, 18, 24–25, 41, 44–69, 75–78. Sipuel, who was five feet eight inches tall and slender, played basketball and sang in the school choir.

12. Roscoe Dunjee to Thurgood Marshall, January 15, March 13, 1946, File University of Oklahoma Correspondence 1945–46, Box 198; Biographical sketch of Ada Lois Sipuel Fisher, July 15, 1948, File University of Oklahoma Correspondence June–December, 1948; "Ada Sipuel Fisher Begins Law Classes at Okla. U.," June 23, 1949, and "NAACP Youth to Honor Mrs. Ada Sipuel Fisher," October 27, 1949, NAACP press releases, File University of Oklahoma press releases 1946–49, Box 199, Group II Legal Container List 1940–55, NAACP Papers. See also microfilm reels 13 and 14, NAACP Papers, Part 3, Series B: Legal Department and Central Office Records, 1940–50. Class valedictorian at her senior high school in 1941, Sipuel attended the Agricultural, Mechanical, and Normal College at Pine Bluff, Arkansas, before transferring her sophomore year to Langston University, where she majored in English and earned a B.A. with honors in 1945. George Lynn Cross, *Blacks in White Colleges: Oklahoma's Landmark Cases* (Norman: University of Oklahoma Press, 1975); Fisher, *Black and White*, 64–69, 83–85, 119–32, 142–45; Tushnet, *NAACP's Legal Strategy*, 120–24, 192, 223 n.27; Jean Preer, *Lawyers v. Educators: Black Colleges and Desegregation in Public Higher Education* (Westport, Conn.: Greenwood Press, 1982), 64, 74–83, 106–9. On January 12,

1948, she won her case before the U.S. Supreme Court, which, citing the *Gaines* case, reversed the Oklahoma courts and ordered Oklahoma to provide legal education to Sipuel, under the Fourteenth Amendment's equal protection clause, at the same time that it provided such education to white students. Understandably, she would not accept admission into the three-room black Langston University College of Law that opened on January 26, 1948, in the state capitol with three white attorneys; it was later closed since only one black student ever enrolled. The University of Oklahoma admitted her to its law school after a three-judge federal district court panel, citing the *Sipuel* case, ruled that the University of Oklahoma had either to admit retired teacher George W. McLaurin, who sought a degree in school administration, or close its graduate program in education.

13. Fisher, *Black and White*, 143–53. See the fourth interview, July 28, 1986, 15–18, selected from the transcript of *W. Page Keeton: An Oral History Interview*, in Rare Books and Special Collections, Tarlton Law Library, the University of Texas at Austin, http:/www.law.du.edu/russell/lh/sweatt/docs/koh.htm; "Association Hails Setbacks to Bias," *New York Times*, June 28, 1950.

14. Fisher, *Black and White*, 146, 151.

15. Fisher was also an assistant vice president for academic affairs and directed the Langston University Urban Center in Oklahoma City. In 1981, the Smithsonian Museum included her among the 150 outstanding black women in American history. After retiring from Langston in 1988, she served, until 1991, as corporate counsel for Automation Research Systems, a large minority business in Alexandria, Virginia. In Oklahoma, she received numerous awards and recognitions: a major street in Chickasha is named Ada Sipuel Avenue, and the city honored her by Ada Sipuel Fisher Day on July 3, 1993. She was a member of the state advisory committee on civil rights. In April 1992, Ada Sipuel Fisher and attorney Melvin Hall became the second and third blacks to serve on the seven-member board of regents of the University of Oklahoma. Wayne Greene, "A Full Circle from Exclusion: Black Lawyer Rises to Regent," *New York Times*, June 5, 1992; Robert L. Johns, "Ada Fisher," in *Notable Black American Women*, ed. Jessie Carney Smith (Detroit: Gale Research, 1992), 344–46; William C. Matney, ed., *Who's Who among Black Americans*, 4th ed. (Lake Forest, Ill.: Educational Communications, 1985), 271; Fisher, *Black and White*, 155–93. Her husband, Warren, died in December 1987. Diagnosed with inoperable cancer, Ada Lois Sipuel Fisher died October 18, 1995.

16. Lucy Foster, interviews, 6, 16–19, 21, 46; E. Culpepper Clark, *The Schoolhouse Door: Segregation's Last Stand at the University of Alabama* (New York: Oxford University Press, 1993), 5–8, 71–113. Lucy attended Linden Academy (1945–47) in Linden, Alabama, and then enrolled at Selma University for two years. In 1949, she decided to live with her sister in Birmingham and attend Miles College, from which she graduated in May 1952. According to historian Culpepper Clark (*Schoolhouse Door*, 8), their "decision emerged from a combination of ambition and circumstances." The NAACP never specifically recruited Lucy and Myers, but they did receive encouragement from Emory Jackson, editor of the *Birmingham World*, where Myers worked, and from Ruby Hurley, regional director of the NAACP, for whom Myers worked part-time. Attorney Arthur D. Shores agreed to help Myers and Lucy because he thought that a desegrega-

tion lawsuit might very well succeed, although the NAACP later maintained that if it had been recruiting plaintiffs in Alabama, it would have preferred an outstanding recent high school graduate. Nor did the NAACP pay her tuition and fees; these were paid by the Jessie Smith Noyes Foundation.

17. Autherine Lucy and Polly Anne Myers, testimonies, Transcript of Record, *Autherine J. Lucy, and Polly Anne Myers, Plaintiffs v. Board of Trustees of the University of Alabama, et al., Defendants*, U.S. District Court, N.D. Alabama, W.D., June 29–30, 1955, transcript in the Hoole Special Collections Library; Lucy Foster, interviews, 19–20. See also *Autherine J. Lucy et al., Plaintiffs v. William F. Adams, Defendant*, No. 652, United States District Court, N.D. Alabama, W.D., August 26, 1955, 134 F.Supp. 235; Transcript of Record, United States Court of Appeals Fifth Circuit, *William F. Adams, Appellant, v. Autherine J. Lucy and Polly Anne Myers*, Appellees; Appeal from the District Court of the U.S. Northern District of Alabama, Western Division, at the Office of the Legal Defense Fund, New York City. Federal District Judge Harlan Hobart Grooms cited *Gaines ex rel. Canada v. Missouri* (1938), *Sipuel v. Oklahoma State Board of Regents* (1948), *Sweatt v. Painter* (1950), and *McLaurin v. Oklahoma State Regents for Higher Education* (1950). On December 30, 1955, the per curiam ruling of the Court of Appeals upheld Judge Grooms's injunction against Dean of Admissions Adams.

18. Clark, *Schoolhouse Door*, 3–5, 17–21, 54–57, 106. The younger of two children of Henry Myers, a cotton tie bundler in a Birmingham foundry, and Alice Lamb Myers, a housewife, Pollie Anne Myers had married Edward Hudson, her longtime beau, in October 1952. Having given birth to a son seven months later, she was vulnerable to a charge of having sexual relations before marriage, something that proper University of Alabama coeds simply did not do. To support herself, she was writing a society column for the *Birmingham World*, substitute teaching, and working periodically as a waitress.

19. Clark, *Schoolhouse Door*, 253; Lucy Foster, interviews, 21–23. Accompanying Lucy to campus on February 1, Myers relocated later that month to Detroit, where she earned two master's degrees from Wayne State University and taught in Detroit's public schools; she later taught in Nigeria. Hill Ferguson—son of a Confederate veteran, president pro tem of the board of trustees, and a trustee of the University of Alabama from 1929 to 1967, voted against Lucy because he believed that she was "undesirable" "on general principles," since detectives had reported that she and Myers "ran around in a sporty car to the various beer joints of Birmingham." Hill Ferguson to R. E. Steiner, June 10, 1955; Hill Ferguson, "One of the University of Alabama's Tragic Eras from Miss Lucy (1956) to Miss Vivian (1963)," September 1963, vol. 93, MS 976.149, Hill Ferguson Collection, Archives, Birmingham, Alabama, Public Library; J. Rufus Bealle, Action Taken by the Board of Trustees of the University of Alabama in Special Called Meeting at the University on January 21, 1956; copy of minutes of Meeting of the Board of Trustees of the University of Alabama, January 29, 1956, John A. Caddell, acting secretary, File #307 Race Question (statement to the press); O. C. Carmichael to Hill Ferguson, September 6, 1956, File #251 Negro Applications, and Carmichael to R. E. Steiner Jr., October 26, 1956, File #307 Race Question, Oliver Cromwell Carmichael Papers, Hoole Special Collections Library.

20. "First Alabama Negro Enrollment Brings 3-Day Demonstration," *Southern School News* 2 (March 1956): 6; "First in Alabama," *Time*, February 13, 1956, 53; Chronology of Events Concerning Efforts of Autherine Lucy and Pollie Ann Hudson Seeking Admission as Students in the University of Alabama and Notes on Demonstrations, File #307 Race Question, Carmichael Papers; J. Jefferson Bennett, interview by author, May 26, 1980, University of Alabama, Tuscaloosa; Sarah Healy Fenton, interview by author, November 7, 1981, Fairhope, Ala.; E. Culpepper Clark, interview by author, May 29, 1980, University of Alabama at Birmingham; E. Culpepper Clark, "The Autherine Lucy Episode: Life Histories in the Historical Moment" (paper presented at the American Studies Association Ninth Biennial Convention, Philadelphia, November 1983).

21. Autherine Lucy Foster, in Raines, *My Soul Is Rested*, 325–27.

22. Bennett, interview; Trustees and Carmichael, quoted in "3-Day Demonstration," 6–7.

23. Autherine Lucy, quoted in "3-Day Demonstration," 7. Among the four codefendants with the trustees was Robert Chambliss, who would later be convicted for bombing the 16th Street Baptist Church in Birmingham on September 15, 1963.

24. Clark, *Schoolhouse Door*, 112–13; "3-Day Demonstration," 7; Wayne Phillips, "Alabama Expels Student in Riots," *New York Times*, March 13, 1956; "Alabama's Scandal," *Time*, February 20, 1956, 40; "One-Way Ride," *Time*, February 27, 1956, 68; Statement of John A. Caddell, Member, Executive Committee, Board of Trustees, University of Alabama News Bureau, March 1, 1956, in File Alabama, University; Lucy, Autherine, Newspaper Clippings, Presented to the University of Alabama by Dean ten Hoor, Hoole Special Collections Library. For the trustees' defense of their expulsion and problem with protecting Lucy on campus, see *Transcript of Proceedings*, February 29, 1956, File ADS [Arthur D. Shores]/Lucy 1/4/1/2, Talledega College, 170–82. See also Judge Constance Baker Motley, interview by author, September 16, 1980, New York City; and Judge Constance Baker Motley, interview by Mrs. Walter Gellhorn, January 7, 1978, Interview #5, transcript, 281–92, Columbia University Oral History Research Office, New York. President Dwight D. Eisenhower was hesitant to send in federal troops to protect Lucy because he believed that the situation was one that state authorities should handle (Burke Marshall, interview by Anthony Lewis, June 14, 1964, Interview #4, transcript, 86–87, John F. Kennedy Library Oral History Program, Boston). In his January 18, 1957, ruling, Judge Grooms upheld the right of the trustees to discipline students by expulsion.

25. Clark, *Schoolhouse Door*, 106. As late as May 31, 1963, trustee John Caddell, then chairman of the executive committee of the board of trustees, denounced the NAACP and Lucy for attracting such "attention" that the "disturbances arose resulting in a near riot." Her arrival "in a Cadillac automobile" had now become "a caravan of Cadillac automobiles" (Caddell was interviewed in "Hopes to Win in Courts, University of Alabama Trustee Tells of Steps to Block Negroes," *Shreveport Times*, May 31, 1963, Reel No. 9 NK 2, Records of the Assistant Attorney General Civil Rights Division, January 1964).

26. Clark, *Schoolhouse Door*, 7–8, 15–18, 37, 71–90, 106, 109–13; Lucy Foster, interviews, 6, 16–19, 21, 46. For refusing to turn over membership lists, the NAACP

was fined $100,000. For a sweeping narrative of these tumultuous events, see Taylor Branch, *Parting the Waters: America in the King Years, 1954–63* (New York: Simon and Schuster, 1988), 222–24.

27. Thomas Hargrove, "Nightmare Now 'Seems Like a Dream,'" *Birmingham Post-Herald*, February 10, 1981; "36 Years after the Hate, Black Student Triumphs," *New York Times*, April 26, 1992; Clark, *Schoolhouse Door*, 253, 259–60. Into the 1980s, Autherine Lucy Foster was a high school English and world history teacher at a magnet high school in Birmingham; her husband is a retired minister. By 1990, black students were almost 10 percent of the university's enrollment (1,755, or 9.7 percent of the 18,096 students; 33.6 percent of Alabama's public school enrollment were minority students).

28. Clark, *Schoolhouse Door*, 174–77. Malone was also encouraged by John L. LeFlore, director of Case Work for the Citizens' Committee, an agency that carried on work similar to that of the NAACP after that group had been banned in Alabama. Hood was the eldest of six children of a tractor operator at the Gadsden Goodyear Tire Plant and a housewife.

29. Ben Allen and Vivian Malone Jones, in Raines, *My Soul Is Rested*, 328–31 (Allen quoted 328–29), 332–33; Vivian Malone Jones, interview by author, March 10, 1981, Atlanta; Clark, *Schoolhouse Door*, 174–77, 209 ("spotless"), 234–36. Al Lingo, head of the Alabama Department of Public Safety, told Allen that "all of 'em's backgrounds would prevent any of 'em from attendin' college" (Clark, *Schoolhouse Door*, 210).

30. Clark, *Schoolhouse Door*, 195–96, 208–9, 216–26; D. Robert Owen to Burke Marshall, June 6, 1963, Governor Wallace, University of Alabama, File Memoranda University of Alabama, Box 17, Burke Marshall Papers, John F. Kennedy Library; Bennett, interview; Malone Jones, interview; Nicholas Katzenbach, memorandum to Attorney General, May 31, 1963, File Civil Rights: Alabama, University of, Box 10, Robert F. Kennedy Attorney General's General Correspondence; Rhoda E. Johnson, "Making a Stand for Change: A Strategy for Empowering Individuals," in *Opening Doors: Perspectives on Race Relations in Contemporary America*, ed. Harry J. Knopke, Robert J. Norrell, and Ronald W. Rogers (Tuscaloosa: University of Alabama Press, 1991), 153–57, 163–64; Nicholas Katzenbach, in Raines, *My Soul Is Rested*, 337–42.

31. Bennett, interview; Malone Jones, interview; Nicholas Katzenbach, interview by author, June 22, 1981, Princeton, N.J.; Governor George C. Wallace, interview by author, November 10, 1980, Montgomery, Ala.; George Dan Jones Jr., "The Last Door Swings Open: A Historical Chronology of the Desegregation of the University of Alabama" (Ed.D. diss., University of Alabama, 1982), 177; "Races," *Time*, June 21, 1963, 13–18; "Nation's Crisis Crowds In on One Man," *Life*, June 21, 1963, 119; Clark, *Schoolhouse Door*, 171–74, 193–94, 226–31, 235–36, 254. Two days later, on June 13, David McGlathery—a sharecropper's son, navy veteran, honors graduate in mathematics from Alabama A&M, and NASA employee—registered, without incident, as a graduate student in engineering and applied mathematics at the University of Alabama's Huntsville Center.

32. President John F. Kennedy, televised speech to the nation, June 11, 1963; "Crisis: Behind a Presidential Commitment," ABC and Drew Associate Producer, ABC Narration James Lipscomb, IFP: 132, Audio-Visual Division, Kennedy Library; Anthony

Lewis, "A New Racial Era," *New York Times*, June 13, 1963; Clark, *Schoolhouse Door*, 220–22, 232–33.

33. Clark, *Schoolhouse Door*, 214, 240–54 (Wallace quoted, 246); Vivian Malone Jones, in Raines, *My Soul Is Rested*, 332–33; Jones, interview; John W. Cameron, Executive Office for U.S. Marshals, to Tuscaloosa File, September 23, 1963, Reel No. 36, NK 2, Records of the Assistant Attorney General Civil Rights Division, January 1964. Finally, trustee John Caddell persuaded Wallace to desist in his efforts to remove Malone. To preserve his image of still fighting the university's integration, Wallace had the papers filed for a final appeal of the May 16, 1963, desegregation order of Federal Judge Harlan Hobart Holmes, which a three-judge panel of the Court of Appeals affirmed on March 13, 1964 (Clark, *Schoolhouse Door*, 248, 251–52). Regarding Hood's forced withdrawal from the university, see Clark, *Schoolhouse Door*, 240–46, 250; for his later career, see 254. Hood returned to the University of Alabama in 1995 and earned a Ph.D. in interdisciplinary studies in 1997.

34. Jones, in Raines, *My Soul Is Rested*, 332–33; Jones, interview. The university hired Michael Jones to drive her. By the time Malone graduated, ten black students were enrolled.

35. Jones, in Raines, *My Soul Is Rested*, 333; Jones, interview; "33 Years Later, Opening Doors," *USA Today*, October 11, 1996. After graduation, Vivian Malone Jones worked for the Justice Department and then for the Veterans' Administration in Washington, D.C. In 1969, she moved to Atlanta; her husband, Michael (Mack) Jones, earned his medical degree in obstetrics and gynecology at Emory University. She worked for the U.S. Environmental Protection Agency (EPA) before heading the Voter Education Project, Inc. Then she served as director of the regional EPA's civil rights compliance division in Atlanta. She was founder of Real Estate Professionals, Inc., partner in the fast-food Chicken George franchise, and president of the medical equipment company, Metro Medical, Inc. Jones's two children did not follow in her footsteps to the University of Alabama, choosing instead to attend Howard University. Clark, *Schoolhouse Door*, 254; "Civil Rights Pioneer Vivian Jones Dies," Associated Press report contributing reporter Philip Rawls in Montgomery, Ala., October 13, 2005, earthlink.net/channel/news/print? guid=20051013/434ddbc0_3ca6_1552620051.

36. Charlayne Hunter-Gault, *In My Place* (New York: Farrar Straus Giroux, 1992), 93–94, 103, 116, and photograph caption opposite 116. She was drawn to the Catholic Church by its "ritual" and "mystery" and its outreach to blacks. The Catholic Church had opened its new hospital in Atlanta to blacks at a time when, except for three black private hospitals, only Grady Memorial Hospital accepted them as patients. During an interview, she emphasized her self-reflective nature by raising the question of whether her experiences are caused by her race, her gender, or circumstances. See also Brian Lanker's profile of Hunter-Gault, one of the women profiled in *I Dreamed a World: Portraits of Black Women Who Changed America*, rev. (New York: Stewart, Tabori and Chang, 1999).

37. Tall and slim, with hazel eyes, she was elected Miss Turner, homecoming queen, in 1958–59. President of the Senior Honor Society, she graduated third in her class that spring. Hunter-Gault, *In My Place*, 109, 118–29, 149.

38. Calvin Trillin, *An Education in Georgia: Charlayne Hunter, Hamilton Holmes, and the Integration of the University of Georgia* (1964; reprint, Athens: University of Georgia Press, 1991), 123. Drawing extensively on his *New Yorker* articles, written at the time of the events he described, Trillin thoroughly examined the personalities of these "student heroes" (*Education in Georgia*, 4) and their suit to desegregate the University of Georgia.

39. *Ibid.*, 23, 37–38, 84. After a hearing in September 1960 before Federal District Judge William A. Bootle in Macon, Georgia, Hunter and Holmes were told to present themselves, in November, at the University of Georgia for interviews. Registrar and Admissions Director Walter Danner found Hunter acceptable, but wrote that there was no room for her category of transfer student until the fall of 1961. After asking Holmes whether he had visited the red light district in Athens, Danner rejected him as unsuitable. Holmes believed that he had been rejected "because of the white Southern male's historic fear of the Black male, the fear that he would at some point 'mess with' white women, one way or another, and, maybe even deeper than that, a fear of turnabout as fair play," observed Hunter-Gault (*In My Place*, 223). The case came to trial in Athens, Georgia, on December 13, 1960. Ruling on January 6, 1961, that there was "a tacit policy" of excluding blacks on account of their race, Judge Bootle ordered that Hunter and Holmes be admitted immediately to the University of Georgia (*Holmes and Hunter v. Danner*). His subsequent granting of a delay to the state was immediately reversed by Judge Elbert Tuttle of the Fifth Circuit Court of Appeals.

40. Hunter-Gault, *In My Place*, 172, 176; Robert A. Pratt, *We Shall Not Be Moved: The Desegregation of the University of Georgia* (Athens: University of Georgia Press, 2002). In addition to government escorts, university faculty patrolled the campus, and the administration announced that it would suspend or expel any rioting students.

41. Trillin, *Education in Georgia*, 153; Hunter-Gault, *In My Place*, 203. In contrast to Hunter—who had eventually developed a social life for herself on campus, including friendships with whites—Holmes did not use the campus dining hall, the library, or the gymnasium. He lived with a black family in Athens and returned home to Atlanta every weekend. For Holmes, observed journalist Calvin Trillin (*Education in Georgia*, 84), attending the University of Georgia was "simple combat." Although his classmates respected him academically, Holmes said that "they think that outside the classroom I'm just another nigger" (quoted in ibid., 88). Through hard study, he was elected to the Phi Kappa Phi scholastic honorary society and then graduated Phi Beta Kappa. He acknowledged to Trillin (ibid., 167) that he "matured a lot here. I had to mature or just die out." In the fall of 1963, Holmes became the first African American to enroll in the Emory University Medical School, a step that he might not have taken had he remained at Morehouse. He became a prominent orthopedic surgeon in Atlanta, the medical director of Grady Memorial Hospital, and associate dean of the Emory University School of Medicine. Dr. Holmes died in 1995; by then a second generation of a black family had enrolled at the University of Georgia when his son, Hamilton Jr. ("Chip"), did so in the 1980s.

42. Hunter-Gault, *In My Place*, 240.

43. Trillin, *Education in Georgia*, 175–78; Hunter-Gault, *In My Place*, 232–33, 235–

42; Peter Wallenstein, *Tell the Court I Love My Wife: Race, Marriage, and Law—An American History* (New York: Palgrave Macmillan, 2002), 205–6. Their marriage so deeply offended University of Georgia president Omer Clyde Aderhold that he stated that neither of them would be permitted back on campus. Hunter and Stovall had a daughter, Susan, but they subsequently divorced. In 1971, Hunter married Ronald Gault, a black Chicagoan and a vice president of First Boston Corporation. They have a son, Chuma Gault.

44. Hunter-Gault has received numerous awards, among them three *New York Times* Publishers Awards: 1970 (shared with a *Times* colleague, Joseph Lelyveld, on a twelve-year-old who died of a heroin overdose); 1974 (on Mayor Abraham Beame's selection of Paul Gibson Jr. as New York City's first black deputy mayor); and 1976 (on crime among blacks and the renaming of Harlem's Muslim Mosque for Malcolm X). She continued to pioneer by reporting for public television, becoming national correspondent for the *MacNeil/Lehrer NewsHour* in 1983. She received the University of Georgia's Henry W. Grady School of Journalism's 1986 George Foster Peabody Award for Excellence in Broadcast Journalism for her five-part documentary on "apartheid's people" in South Africa. The National Association of Black Journalists honored her as the 1986 Journalist of the Year. Traveling widely in the 1990s, she reported on the Middle East, famine in Somalia, and the U.S. mission in that African country. Marcia G. Synnott, "Charlayne Hunter-Gault," in *Great Lives from History: American Women*, ed. Frank N. Magill, 5 vols. (Pasadena, Calif.: Salem Press, 1995), 947–51. As of January 2001, when she spoke at the University of Georgia on the fortieth anniversary of her admission, Hunter-Gault was a CNN bureau chief.

45. Hunter-Gault, *In My Place*, 253–55. Her graduation address is the last chapter in her book. Black students numbered 300 out of the 1988 graduating class of 6,200 and 1,200 among the whole student body of 26,000. As of 2000, the number of black students enrolled at the University of Georgia remained "stagnant at 6 percent, less than half the percentages at the universities of Alabama, Mississippi and South Carolina." Black enrollment had risen by 24 percent in Georgia's four-year public institutions since the 1993 inauguration of the merit-based Hope Scholarships, funded by the State Lottery, which pays all in-state tuition and fees for Georgia residents who maintain a B average or better. But these black students were not attending, and perhaps not even applying to, the University of Georgia, the system's capstone. David Firestone, "Hope Reinvents University," *The State* (Columbia, S.C.), February 4, 2001.

46. *Wrighten v. Board of Trustees of University of South Carolina et al.* 72 F.Supp. 948 (1947); Tushnet, *NAACP's Legal Strategy*, 87; "Clemson Enrolls a New Student," *San Francisco Chronicle*, January 30, 1963, clipping, South Carolina Council on Human Relations (SCCHR) Papers, Box 23 Education, File 1963; Bert Lunan, "Harvey Gantt: A Step into the Unknown," A Special Report, *The State and the Columbia Record*, January 20, 1963, clipping in SCCHR, Box 40, File Colleges and Universities: Clemson University, South Caroliniana Library (SCL), University of South Carolina, Columbia.

47. Harvey B. Gantt, interview by author, July 14, 1980, Charlotte, N.C.; Elizabeth C. Ledeen to Mrs. E. G. Grimes, June 25, 1963, and Elizabeth C. Ledeen to Harvey B. Gantt, June 24, 1963, SCCHR, Box 3, File May–June 1963; South Carolina Student

Council on Human Relations Report on the Enrollment of Negro Students in Recently Desegregated Colleges of the State, First Semester 1964–65, SCCHR, Box 10, File Student Council, 1964; Supplement, Student Council Report on the Enrollment of Negro Students in recently desegregated colleges of South Carolina, SCCHR, Box 3, File January 22–February 1965, SCL. Brawley, who had three brothers and two sisters, had worked in New York City during the summer to earn money for college. Her father, Ernest—like Gantt's father—was a federal employee, working at the Veterans' Hospital in Columbia.

48. "Ten Years Later," *Charlotte Observer*, May 11, 1975, Clemson University Archives; "Clemson's Hendrix Student Center to include suite named for Harvey and Lucinda Gantt," *CLEMSONews*, March 31, 2000, http://clemsonews.clemson.edu/WWW_releases/2000/March2000/Gantt_Ste_Hendrix_Ctr.html; Leslie Skinner, "Sibling Institutions, Similar Experiences: The Coeducation and Integration Experiences of South Carolina's Clemson and Winthrop Universities" (Ph.D. diss., University of South Carolina, 2002). Lucinda and Harvey Gantt had four children. After earning a master's degree in city planning from MIT in 1970, Harvey Gantt became a partner in a successful biracial firm, Gantt Huberman Architects, in Charlotte; served on the city council; and ran three times for mayor, winning in 1983 and 1985. He then lost two races for the U.S. Senate, in 1990 and 1996, against Republican incumbent Jesse Helms.

49. Gantt, interview.

50. South Carolina was defeated in three teachers' salary equalization cases: *Duvall v. Seignous* [School Board of Charleston] (1944); *Monteith v. Cobb* [County Board of Education of Richland County] (1944); and *Thompson v. Gibbes* [County Board of Education of Richland County] (1945). File Teachers' Salaries—South Carolina, Richland County 1944–45, Box 180, NAACP Legal File 1940–55, Group II B. See also microfilm reel 9, NAACP Papers, Part 3, Series B: Legal Department and Central Office Records, 1940–50.

51. R. Rebecca Monteith to Governor Ernest F. Hollings, February 5, 1962, Papers of Governor Ernest F. Hollings, File Education, State Dept. of, South Carolina Department of Archives and History, Columbia.

52. Direct examination of Henrie Dobbins Monteith by Matthew J. Perry and cross-examination of Monteith by David W. Robinson, in transcript of *Henri Dobbins Monteith v. The University of South Carolina et al.*, hearing before Judge J. Robert Martin, June 21, 1963, CA/1005 in the District Court of the United States for the Eastern District of South Carolina (DCEDSC), Files of the Legal Defense Fund 1000–1495, New York City. See also President Thomas F. Jones Papers, 1963–64, Box 5, Record Group 2 (President), File Integration, University of South Carolina Archives and Special Collections.

53. *[Henrie Dobbins] Monteith, a Minor, by Her Mother and Next Friend, Mrs. R. Rebecca Monteith, Plaintiff v. The University of South Carolina et al.* (1963), Civil Action No. AC-1005, in DCEDSC, Columbia Division, Files of the Legal Defense Fund 1000–1495. Monteith's lead attorneys in South Carolina were Matthew J. Perry and Lincoln Jenkins of Columbia, who were joined by Constance Baker Motley and Jack Greenberg of the Legal Defense Fund. Direct examination of Rollin E. Godfrey by Matthew J. Perry and cross-examination of Godfrey by David W. Robinson, in transcript

of *Henri Dobbins Monteith v. The University of South Carolina et al.*, hearing before Judge J. Robert Martin, June 21, 1963, CA/1005, DCEDSC, Columbia, S.C.; Thomas F. Jones, interview by author, July 29, 1980, MIT, Cambridge, Mass., where former USC president Jones was then vice president for research; Thomas F. Jones, sound portion of videotape interview by Albert T. Scroggins, Dean of the USC College of Journalism, March 10, 1980, USC; Daniel R. McLeod, interview by author, May 15, 1980, Office of the Attorney General, Columbia, S.C.; Minutes of the Board of Trustees, January 1, 1961–January 1, 1962, No. 11, University of South Carolina; Daniel R. McLeod to Rutledge L. Osborne, Chairman, Board of Trustees, and Thomas F. Jones, President, July 23, 1963; David W. Robinson to Thomas F. Jones, August 27, 1963, President Thomas F. Jones Papers, 1963–64, Box 5, Record Group 2 (President), File Integration. USC gained an extension until November 10, 1963, from Judge Martin in which to file an appeal. WIS-TV News, July 11, 1963, 11:05 P.M.; WIS-TV News, July 20, 1963, 11:05 P.M., report by Charles Caton, transcript courtesy of Joe Wieder, Ways and Means Corporation, 1231 Lincoln Street, Columbia, S.C. (WIS-TV film footage has been donated to USC).

54. Thomas F. Jones, interview; Thomas F. Jones, sound portion of videotape interview by Scroggins; Daniel W. Hollis, conversation with the author, July 23, 1981, USC, about the role of President Jones at USC and his remembrance of Howard H. Quint, former USC history professor; Robinson to Jones, August 27, 1963; Report of Meeting on Security Plan, President's Office, August 20, 1963; Confidential Internal Plan, August 21, 1963, President Thomas F. Jones Papers, 1963–14, Box 5, Record Group 2 (President), File on Final Plan for Integration; Maxie Myron Cox, "1963—The Year of Decision: Desegregation in South Carolina" (Ph.D. diss., University of South Carolina, 1996), 78–101; Henry H. Lesesne, *A History of the University of South Carolina, 1940–2000* (Columbia: University of South Carolina Press, 2001), 138–50.

55. Rebecca Monteith quoted by WIS-TV News, August 27, 1963, 1:00 P.M.; WIS-TV News, August 27, 1963, 6:30 P.M.; WIS-TV News, August 28, 1963, 1:00 P.M. and 6:30 P.M.; and WIS-TV News, August 30, 1963, 1:00 P.M., transcripts courtesy of Joe Wieder. Anticipating the possibility of violence against his niece, Dr. Henry Monteith had sat on his porch the previous nights with a rifle; the night of the explosion he had retired due to illness. The next day, Dr. Monteith's secretary received an anonymous telephone call, warning him to leave Columbia. The FBI and county law enforcement assisted Columbia police in the investigation, and Richland County sheriff Strother Sligh offered a $250 reward for reliable information, which was matched by Dr. Monteith.

56. M. Hayes Mizell, "The Impact of the Civil Rights Movement on a White Activist" (paper presented at the 65th annual meeting of the Southern Historical Association, Fort Worth, Tex., November 1999); [M. Hayes Mizell] to Miss Henri Monteith, December 5, 1962, M. Hayes Mizell Collection, Box 10, Papers ca. 1960–69, Corres., by personal name and with grandparents misc., SCL. Monteith wrote a letter to the campus *Gamecock*, published May 10, 1963, thanking USC students for their encouraging letters that offered "personal support" and anticipating that they would accept

her peacefully if the court ordered her admission. [Elizabeth C. Ledeen, Program Director], Student Program, June and July 1963 Report, South Carolina Student Council on Human Relations, SCCHR, Box 10, File Student Council 1963, SCL. Harvey Gantt and other Clemson students participated as resource leaders in the September 8, 1963, informal conference.

57. The three at USC, together with marine sergeant James H. Hollins, who enrolled at the University Center in Beaufort, were four African Americans among about 6,000 white students. Henrie Monteith Treadwell, quoted in *The State*, November 11, 1988; Henrie Monteith Treadwell, interview by author, November 14, 1980, Atlanta; Robert Anderson, quoted by WIS-TV News, August 6, 1963, 11:05 P.M.; and WIS-TV News, September 11, 1963, 7:00 P.M. and 11:05 P.M., reports by Charles Caton; WIS-TV News, September 12, 1963, 7:00 P.M. report by Charles Caton, transcripts courtesy of Joe Wieder; Lesesne, *History of the University of South Carolina*, 147–48. In his videotaped interview with Dr. Grace Jordan McFadden, November 18, 1988 (Dr. McFadden's oral history collection), Anderson remembered being the only one of the three students to live on campus, although Monteith roomed in a women's dormitory. The only black male student on campus, Anderson was threatened by a white student who pointed a broomstick at him and yelled: "Nigger, we got you now!" Henrie Monteith Treadwell, keynote speech at "The Origins of Contemporary Desegregation at the University of South Carolina, a Twenty-five Year Retrospective 1963–1988," November 18–19, 1988, USC, videotape, McFadden's oral history collection. Robert Anderson and Henrie Monteith Treadwell recalled their experiences at USC in the *Gamecock*, November 21, 1988, and in Carolyn B. Matalene and Katherine C. Reynolds, eds., *Carolina Voices: Two Hundred Years of Student Experiences* (Columbia: University of South Carolina Press, 2001), 178–81. After integration, a small number of alumni/ae disassociated themselves from USC (President Thomas F. Jones Papers, File on Integration).

58. Treadwell, interview; Papers of President Thomas F. Jones Papers, File on Integration; Treadwell, keynote speech.

59. "Black Women at Virginia Tech History Project," http://spec.lib.vt.edu/archives/blackwomen/; Marcia G. Synnott, "Surviving the Company of Men—in the Company of Women: Lessons from the Corps of Cadets at Virginia Tech, The Citadel, and the Virginia Military Institute," in *Proceedings of the South Carolina Historical Association, 2003* (March 2003): 63–80. See also Web pages on Norwich University, "An Organization's Legacy Is Defined by What the Organization Contributes to Society over Its Lifetime," http://www.norwich.edu/about/lrgacy.html; and on the Texas A&M's Corps of Cadets, "Celebration Set for 30th Anniversary of Women in the Corps," http://www.tamu.edu/univrel.aggiedaily/news/stories/04/082604-4.html.

60. Peter Wallenstein and Tamara Kennelly, "Time Line of the History of Virginia Tech," http://spec.lib.vt.edu/archives.125th/timeline.htm; Peter Wallenstein, "The First Black Students at Virginia Tech, 1953–1963," http://spec.lib/vt/edu/archives/blackhistory.timeline.blackstu.htm; "Black Women at Virginia Tech History Project," http://spec.lib.vt.edu/archives/blackwomen/; Warren H. Strother and Peter Wallenstein,

From VPI to State University: President T. Marshall Hahn Jr. and the Transformation of Virginia Tech, 1962–1974 (Macon, Ga.: Mercer University Press, 2004), 114–15, 151–68, 292–96.

61. Cheryl Butler McDonald, interview by Tamara Kennelly, November 28, 1998, Transcript, Part 1 [of 3], Black Women at Virginia Tech Oral History Project, First Black Woman in the Corps of Cadets, http://spec.lib.vt.edu/bwhp/cheryl/cheryl1.htm; Part 2, http://spec.lib.vt.edu/bwhp/cheryl//cheryl2.htm.

62. McDonald, interview, Parts 1 and 3. She married but had no children.

63. Beverly Guy-Sheftall, *Daughters of Sorrow: Attitudes toward Black Women: 1880–1920*, vol. 11 of *Black Women in United States History Series* (Brooklyn, N.Y.: Carlson, 1990), 13–28, 39–43, 46–49, 130–40, 157, 163–69; Paula Giddings, *When and Where I Enter: The Impact of Black Women on Race and Sex in America* (New York: Bantam Books, 1985). Black women "were perceived to be the intellectual inferiors of black men and white men and women and the moral inferiors of white women," said Guy-Sheftall (*Daughters of Sorrow*, 168).

64. Walter R. Allen, "The Color of Success: African-American College Student Outcomes at Predominantly White and Historically Black Public Colleges and Universities," *Harvard Educational Review* 52 (Spring 1992): 25–44.

Afterword

Unfinished Business

During the Age of Segregation, black southerners dissented throughout the region. They made the civil rights movement happen, and, as an integral part of that movement, they assaulted the citadels of white supremacy and black exclusion wherever they found them, including so-called public, so-called white, institutions of higher education. They persisted in making application to schools that made it clear they did not want to admit them. Qualified on every ground but their racial identity, they often went to court, where they sometimes won.

At many schools, black students found that, though admitted to take classes, they were still unwelcome visitors with limited rights. Some institutions, among the early ones to admit black applicants, separated them for a time into particular spaces in classrooms, libraries, and cafeterias. Some institutions, having admitted black undergraduates to take classes, did so only in restricted curricular areas, unavailable at a black school in the state, especially engineering. Such students might find that they were not allowed to change their major to some other discipline, could not live on campus, and could not eat in the cafeteria. Segregation, exclusion, and other discriminatory practices often persisted well beyond the first glimmers of "desegregation"—through the 1950s and, though in fewer areas of campus life, well into the 1960s.

By the time the Civil Rights Act of 1964 became law, the major hurdles had been leveled. The formal obstacles to admission were largely gone. Yet as black southerners often found, obstacles continued to loom. Full participation in such activities as intercollegiate sports provided a particularly visible object not yet attained. Renovating an institution so that the culture, the institutional identity, as well as the formal administration of the place welcomed them to a home that they, too, could fully share—that task often remained incompletely accomplished for a very long time.

Desegregation of Higher Education as a Process

The era of predesegregation was by definition unsuccessful, in that it consisted of failed efforts to break through the walls of exclusion. Yet even those failed efforts often forced change. For one thing, the early efforts led to enactment of state laws that, to some degree, funded black southerners' access to out-of-state programs. For another, such efforts brought about enhanced facilities and programs at in-state black schools. Moreover, such efforts led the way, blazed a path, and encouraged other black southerners to press again, press harder, attempt once more to gain access to all institutions of higher education.

Desegregation itself, as we have seen, was a process, not an event. Or at least it was, as a rule, a whole series of events. The University of Maryland provides a good example. Under court order, Donald Murray gained admission to the law school in Baltimore in 1935. He graduated in 1938, and other black Marylanders followed him. At midcentury, he was the lead lawyer in court cases that opened the doors to black enrollment at the nursing school in Baltimore, in the master's program in sociology at the College Park campus, and in the undergraduate engineering curriculum at College Park. The years that followed brought further change, including a policy of admitting black students to all university programs.

Chapter 1 in this book reviewed the process, from the 1930s through the mid-1960s, of desegregation at twenty-four schools across the South, all of them public institutions that drew on statewide populations but had historically excluded African Americans. Limited desegregation occurred at black schools as well as nonblack institutions. At the end of the twentieth century, the University of South Carolina had the highest black enrollment among the twenty-four schools, 19 percent, and Clemson University was at 8 percent, but the state's population was 30 percent black, and South Carolina State University was 95 percent black. Compared with the Virginia population as a whole, which was 20 percent black, Virginia Tech's undergraduate enrollment was only 4 percent African American, while Virginia State University's was 94 percent.[1]

In the Border South states, with their heavily white populations, desegregation led to small black percentages at previously nonblack schools and, in some cases, sharp percentage declines of black students at previously black schools. In the late 1990s, Oklahoma State University had a black enrollment of about 3 percent, Langston University 61 percent. West Virginia University was 4 percent black, and West Virginia State College, which had shifted from all-black to mostly white, was only 13 percent black. One question that could arise in such Border South states was whether, having lost, or largely lost, a school with a black identity, black residents had gained proportionately in claiming an integral part of the identity of the historically nonblack school.[2]

Today, in various ways and for various reasons, the surviving black pioneers of desegregation at state universities in the South are by no means uniformly convinced that, decades later, their schools have done all they could or should have done to push the process along. Nor are they agreed that all change resulted in net benefits. But they can see remarkable change over the past half-century—far beyond the beginnings that they themselves propelled. For a glimpse of that change, let's return to North Carolina for a postscript to the story of desegregation and a few final words from one of the black pioneers.

Who Would Have Believed?

In the 1990s, the president of a black student group at the University of North Carolina at Greensboro—the old Woman's College—pushed to establish a memorial to the two students who had begun the school's desegregation back in 1956. The idea gained approval, and in 1992 dedication of the Tillman-Smart Parlor in Shaw Hall took place in front of the dormitory. Bettye Tillman had died; JoAnne Smart Drane was the main speaker at the ceremony. "I only wish Bettye was here to share it," she told her audience, which included the university chancellor, the student government president, and representation from the board of trustees.[3]

She reflected on how much had changed since her time as an undergraduate. "Who in my class, the class of 1960," she asked, ". . . would have believed that there would be black faculty and black administrators teaching and overseeing programs and policies at this university? And who in my class would have envisioned that this university would name any place on this campus in honor of persons of African descent?"[4]

Four years later, in 1996—forty years after a car trip from Raleigh to Greensboro so that JoAnne Smart, class of 1960, could go to college and help end the school's long and absolute exclusion of African Americans—she was made a member of the Board of Trustees of the University of North Carolina at Greensboro. Joining her on the board the very next year was Claudette Graves Burroughs-White, class of 1961, who had gone to Woman's College as part of her black high school's senior class project.[5] Like their undergraduate years, their terms on the board overlapped. Members of the first two integrated classes, they became members of the school's board of trustees. Indeed, who would have thought?

Unfinished Business: Displaying a School's Social and Cultural History

The selection of pioneer black students to a university's governing board—exemplified by JoAnne Smart Drane and Claudette Graves Burroughs-White at the University of North Carolina at Greensboro—was one key way that schools in the 1990s connected with their past, recognized the contributions and the leadership of black pioneers, and commemorated a set of events that, at the time they occurred, elicited resistance and evasion rather than celebration.

In other ways, too, various campuses have taken pains to grant some visibility to their racial histories across the moment when desegregation began. The Tillman-Smart Parlor in Greensboro provides one example, and other examples are mentioned in the essays, among them Silas Hunt Hall, dedicated in 1993 at the University of Arkansas. But there are many other examples as well. In March 2003, as one of the events of that year's Black Alumni Reunion, Virginia Tech dedicated a new campus residence hall, Peddrew-Yates, named for the school's first black student to enroll, Irving L. Peddrew, in 1953, and the first to graduate, Charlie L. Yates, in 1958.

The University of Texas has named its main library after two men, each an outstanding academic in his own right, who represent large racial or ethnic minorities in Texas—Hispanics and African Americans. The Perry-Casteñeda Library was dedicated in 1977. Carlos Eduardo Casteñeda taught Latin American history at Texas for many years before his death in 1958. Ervin Sewell Perry was the first African American to earn a Ph.D. at the University of Texas—in 1964, in civil engineering. Moreover, he was the first African American to gain appointment to the faculty there when he was named an assistant professor, also in 1964.[6]

Other schools (or their black students and alumni) have taken other actions. At the University of Kentucky, the Lyman T. Johnson Alumni Group, named in 1991 for the school's first African American student, is a black subset of the university's alumni association, organized with a view to increasing black graduates' participation in alumni affairs. Similarly, the Hulon Willis Alumni Association commemorates a pioneer African American student at the College of William and Mary. At the University of Virginia, the Walter N. Ridley Scholarship Fund seeks alumni support for minority scholarships. The University of Georgia has a speaker series named after the school's first two black students and alumni, Hamilton Holmes and Charlayne Hunter-Gault.

The University of Oklahoma took two notable actions in the late 1980s and 1990s to render its history visible and explicit and to reshape the moral order and the campus culture. One was de-naming a building that had long honored a racial antediluvian. The time came when that professor's positive contributions to the school's development were perceived as offset by his antipathy to racial equality, including his leadership in the Ku Klux Klan, and the school erected a marker that detailed the action and the rationale for changing the name of the building. The school's other notable act regarding its racial history was the construction of a lovely courtyard to commemorate Ada Lois Sipuel Fisher, the African American woman from Chickasha, Oklahoma, who found herself appealing all the way to the Supreme Court the university's refusal to admit her to law school in 1946. A prominent plaque supplies a frank, eloquent explanation of the historical significance of the action that the university took in the 1990s to redeem its behavior half a century earlier.

The essays in this book have looked back at the beginnings of a partial transformation of college campuses, as traditionally nonblack schools enrolled their first generation or two of African Americans, in most cases in the 1950s or 1960s. The pioneer black students on historically nonblack campuses permitted those institutions eventually to redefine themselves. A plaque in the library at Clemson University, for example, proclaims Clemson to be a coeducational, multiracial research university, something—a collection of things—it surely was not until long into the twentieth century. Similar identities have been adopted by schools across the South, institutions that were founded to serve a much more narrowly defined student constituency. Without the courage and steadfastness of the pioneer African American students, self-definitions like Clemson's could not have undergone such change.

Many historically "white" campuses in the South have yet to honor their African American pioneers in permanent, public ways. Indeed, not all have so much as correctly ascertained the names of those pioneers. Publicly naming these individuals from yesterday can reveal to students of today and tomorrow—students of all racial and ethnic identities—the black pioneers' part in each institution's history. Such public expressions of respect and commemoration render the institution's history more complete and more visible. Such commemoration helps shape the campus culture, helps create an institutional identity that is more inclusive. And it appropriately ascribes agency to the people who, by fostering significant institutional change, made history happen. Categorical exclusion of African Americans ended decades ago. Full inclusion is still in process.

Unfinished Business: Reconstructing the History of Desegregating Higher Education

These essays make considerable headway in reconstructing the process of desegregation at public, historically white institutions of higher education, but they leave much undone or merely begun. Every facet of desegregation requires further exploration: (1) the participation in an institution by people who were identified as neither white nor black, such as Chinese Mississippians after World War II at Ole Miss or Mississippi State; (2) enrollment of the first black students into exceptional programs, made available on the basis that no such curriculum could be pursued at a black school in the state; (3) the enrollment of black students who were permitted to take classes but were excluded from such dimensions of college life as campus housing and varsity sports; (4) the breakthroughs into such areas as those; and (5) such subsequent developments as the active recruitment of black students, the recruitment of black faculty, and the development of courses, for black and nonblack students alike, that reflected a broader historical experience than what were, in effect, implicitly white studies. The presence of black students on otherwise nonblack campuses had important implications for all groups.

Another direction of inquiry must address the presence—or absence—of black construction workers who built a campus in the first place, but who could not, because of the exclusion of black students, send their children to the school. Another significant group consists of black cafeteria workers, who preceded the first black students on a campus and, certainly in some cases, were vitally important in the success of black pioneers in social and academic environments that were, otherwise, at best indifferent and often overtly hostile to their presence. The impact was reciprocal. By the late 1960s, black students often played important roles in efforts to upgrade the pay and benefits of black workers on campus.[7] In addition, desegregation as related to student enrollment led, sooner or later, to opportunities for employment as clerical staff, as faculty, and as administrators—as deans, provosts, and presidents, as well as members of boards of visitors or regents.

Much else remains to be done, work that must be done before those facets can be very fully reconstructed. Some schools have developed a considerable body of interview materials, especially with pioneer black students but also with such other people as administrators and faculty involved in promoting or curtailing the process of desegregation. Until many other schools do something along the lines of what has been accomplished at the University of Florida, at the University of North Carolina at Greensboro, or at Virginia Polytechnic Institute and State University, far too much will remain unknown and unknowable about the experiences of many individuals and institutions. Even at those three schools, the task remains incomplete. Given the distance in time since the beginnings of desegregation, there is some urgency about pursuing an agenda that would make such materials available. People who were eighteen years old in 1945, 1955, or 1965 turned sixty, seventy, or even eighty in the year 2007.

Although the essays in this volume have explored various facets of the desegregation of higher education, they have mostly explored only the history of schools that are public and that at one time excluded black students. Such an approach leaves out three important broad categories of schools. One such category includes schools that are private and at one time were nonblack, such as Johns Hopkins, Vanderbilt, Duke, Emory, Rice, and Tulane.[8] The other two categories include schools that are private and historically black, among them Hampton and Fisk; and those that are public and historically black, chief among them Howard University and the "colleges of 1890."[9] Each category of schools, and each individual school, has a story that historians and other interested people should seek to reconstruct.

The emergence of desegregation bears comparison to the emergence of coeducation. Efforts to press change from single-sex education, together with opposition to any such change—or efforts to contain the change—can be seen at many times and places. Public institutions of higher education, if at one time they excluded women, went through a process of change, whether at northern state universities, typically in the second half of the nineteenth century, or at their southern counterparts, typically in the first half of the twentieth. Moreover, the two processes were related when, given the prospect that black men might otherwise enroll, southern white women's schools either kicked out their few male students or postponed decisions to go coeducational.[10]

Another dimension of the history of higher education in the 1950s and 1960s must relate developments in the South to what was happening outside the region. This broad category of inquiry might include a comparative investigation of how black citizens of Indiana fared in the 1930s through the 1960s at Purdue, for example, or black citizens of Iowa at Iowa State. It would illuminate the opportunities for black athletes—from the South or the North—at northern schools, and the recruitment of such athletes by those schools, as well as the practices of schools in the South that played schools from the North. It would ask how black southerners fared when they went north to gain admission into programs that were unavailable to them in their home states. And it would compare southern patterns with hiring practices and curricular developments in northern schools at each step of the way. What was it like to be a black student, or prospective student, a black faculty member, or prospective member of the faculty, at a northern school?[11]

Unfinished Business: Pushing the Process of Desegregation Farther Along

At no point, whether in 1935 or 1965, did any school under discussion in this book achieve anything approaching full desegregation. Black students, black faculty, and black administrators can be found at work on the campus of perhaps any institution of higher education, across the entire South, in the twenty-first century, but most would hesitate before affirming—and, in many cases, not hesitate at all before disputing—the thesis that full desegregation had yet emerged. The process, already under way in the 1960s, remains under way decades later.

College desegregation did not leave the federal courts once the process had begun everywhere by around 1970. To the contrary, through the end of the century, the federal government played some role in the unwinding of historical patterns. For one thing, litigation took place to obtain enhanced funding and programs at historically black schools. For another, questions of "affirmative action" ended up in the courts, inside and outside the South—in California, Texas, Michigan, and other states. This book does not explore these matters, although it provides background to understanding what remained to be accomplished after the first generation of black pioneers had succeeded in enrolling at each historically nonblack school.[12]

The black pioneers forced the big questions, and their efforts led to big changes. They left it to future generations to work out the details.

Notes

1. See appendix 10.
2. Ibid.
3. Anubha Anand, "Parlor Re-named to Honor Alumni," University of North Carolina at Greensboro *Carolinian*, April 27, 1992; Dedication Program, April 20, 1992, in "Tillman-Smart Parlor" file, University Archives, University of North Carolina at Greensboro.
4. "Remarks—Dedication Tillman-Smart Parlor," in "Tillman-Smart Parlor" file, University Archives, University of North Carolina at Greensboro.
5. Press release, "JoAnne Smart Drane of Raleigh Named to UNCG Board of Trustees," University Archives, University of North Carolina at Greensboro; University of North Carolina at Greensboro *Alumni News* (Fall 1997), 21.
6. Peter Wallenstein, "Naming Names: Identifying and Commemorating the First African American Students on 'White' Campuses in the South, 1935–1972," *College Student Affairs Journal* 20 (Fall 2000): 131–39.
7. For one example, see Delia Crutchfield Cook, "Shadows across the Columns: The Bittersweet Legacy of African Americans at the University of Missouri" (Ph.D. diss., University of Missouri–Columbia, 1996), 114–32.
8. A particularly notable study along these lines is Melissa Fitzsimons Kean, "'At a Most Uncomfortable Speed': The Desegregation of the South's Private Universities, 1945–1964" (Ph.D. diss., Rice University, 2000), summarized in Melissa F. Kean, "Guiding Desegregation: The Role of 'the Intelligent White Men of the South,' 1945–1954," *History of Higher Education Annual* 19 (1999): 57–83. Another such work is Clarence L. Mohr and Joseph E. Gordon, *Tulane: The Emergence of a Modern University, 1945–1980* (Baton Rouge: Louisiana State University Press, 2000), with the portion relevant here summarized in Clarence Mohr, "Opportunity Squandered: Tulane University and the Issue of Racial Desegregation during the 1950s," *History of Higher Education Annual* 19 (1999): 85–119. Regarding a smaller school, with a different time line, see Charles S. Padgett, "'Without Hysteria or Unnecessary Disturbance': Desegregation of Spring Hill College, Mobile, Alabama, 1948–1954," *History of Education Quarterly* 41 (Summer 2001): 167–88, drawn from his "'Schooled in Invisibility': The Desegregation of Spring Hill College, Mobile, Alabama, 1948–1963" (Ph.D. diss., University of Georgia, 2000).

9. Robert Muckel enrolled at Alabama A&M in June 1963, the first white student there, just before Governor Wallace took his defiant stand at Tuscaloosa (Bruce Lowery, "Integration at Alabama's Historically Black Colleges and Universities," *Southern Historian* 19 [Spring 1998]: 35–59). For the broader phenomenon of black colleges in the aftermath of desegregation, see Zella J. Black Patterson, with Lynette L. Wert, *Langston University: A History*, 2 vols. (Norman: University of Oklahoma Press, 1979), especially 2:302; Edgar Toppin, *Loyal Sons and Daughters: Virginia State University, 1882 to 1992* (Norfolk, Va.: Pictorial Heritage, 1992); Ralph D. Christy and Lionel Williamson, eds., *A Century of Service: Land-Grant Colleges and Universities, 1890–1990* (New Brunswick, N.J.: Transaction, 1992); Julian B. Roebuck and Komanduri S. Murty, *Historically Black Colleges and Universities: Their Place in American Higher Education* (Westport, Conn.: Praeger, 1993); and Albert L. Samuels, *Is Separate Unequal? Black Colleges and the Challenge to Desegregation* (Lawrence: University Press of Kansas, 2004).

10. Three notable examples from the literature are Cathryn T. Goree, "Steps toward Redefinition: Coeducation at Mississippi State College, 1930–1945" (Ph.D. diss., Mississippi State University, 1993); Amy Thompson McCandless, *The Past in the Present: Women's Higher Education in the Twentieth-Century American South* (Tuscaloosa: University of Alabama Press, 1999), especially chapter 3; and Leslie Miller-Bernal and Susan L. Poulson, eds., *Going Coed: Women's Experiences in Formerly Men's Colleges and Universities, 1950–2000* (Nashville, Tenn.: Vanderbilt University Press, 2004).

11. Two books on subjects such as these are Clarence G. Williams, *Technology and the Dream: Reflections on the Black Experience at MIT, 1941–1999* (Cambridge, Mass.: MIT Press, 2001), and Elizabeth Higginbotham, *Too Much to Ask: Black Women in the Era of Integration* (Chapel Hill: University of North Carolina Press, 2001). An illuminating essay is Linda M. Perkins, "The African-American Female 'Talented Tenth': A History of African-American Women in the Seven Sister Colleges," *Harvard Educational Review* 67 (Winter 1997): 718–57. Multifarious voices speaking of segregation and desegregation in U.S. higher education—male and female; black, white, and beyond; outside the South as well as inside; from before, during, and after the 1950s and 1960s—are encountered in such sources as Meyer Weinberg, *A Chance to Learn: The History of Race and Education in the United States* (Cambridge: Cambridge University Press, 1977), chapters 7–8, and Jay M. Rochlin, *Race and Class on Campus: Conversations with Ricardo's Daughter* (Tucson: University of Arizona Press, 1997).

12. William A. Link, *William Friday: Power, Purpose, and American Higher Education* (Chapel Hill: University of North Carolina Press, 1995), chapters 9–12; McCandless, *Past in the Present*, chapter 7. For a survey through the Supreme Court's twin decisions in *Gratz v. Bollinger*, 539 U.S. 244 (2003), and *Grutter v. Bollinger*, 539 U.S. 306 (2003), see Marcia G. Synnott, "The Evolving Diversity Rationale in University Admissions: From *Regents v. Bakke* to the University of Michigan Cases," *Cornell Law Review* 90 (January 2005): 463–504.

Appendix 1

Federal Initiatives on Race and Higher Education, 1890–1965

A. The Morrill Act of 1890 stated that segregation was permissible, but these new funds for higher education must benefit black citizens as well as white citizens. As most southern states did not have black colleges at the time, the "colleges of 1890" soon resulted from the measure. Later acts of Congress developed new programs, particularly in training teachers to offer high school courses in agriculture and home economics, and these resulted in enhanced programs at many of the seriously underfunded black schools.

B. *Missouri ex rel. Gaines v. Canada, Registrar of the University of Missouri* (1938; see appendix 3).

C. The President's Commission on Civil Rights issued its report, *To Secure These Rights*, in October 1947.

D. The President's Commission on Higher Education completed its report, *Higher Education for American Democracy*, in February 1948 (see appendix 4).

E. *Sipuel v. Board of Regents of the University of Oklahoma*, 332 U.S. 631, decided January 12, 1948:

> On January 14, 1946, the petitioner, a Negro, concededly qualified to receive the professional legal education offered by the State, applied for admission to the School of Law of the University of Oklahoma, the only institution for legal education supported and maintained by the taxpayers of the State of Oklahoma. Petitioner's application for admission was denied, solely because of her color.
>
> Petitioner then made application for a writ of mandamus in the District Court of Cleveland County, Oklahoma. The writ of mandamus was refused, and the Supreme Court of the State of Oklahoma affirmed the judgment of the District Court. 199 Okla. 36, 180 P. 2d 135. We brought the case here for review.
>
> The petitioner is entitled to secure legal education afforded by a state

institution. To this time, it has been denied her although during the same period many white applicants have been afforded legal education by the State. The State must provide it for her in conformity with the equal protection clause of the Fourteenth Amendment and provide it as soon as it does for applicants of any other group. *Missouri ex rel. Gaines v. Canada*, 305 U.S. 337 (1938).

The judgment of the Supreme Court of Oklahoma is reversed and the cause is remanded to that court for proceedings not inconsistent with this opinion.

F. *Sweatt v. Painter* (1950; see appendix 6).

G. *Board of Trustees of the University of North Carolina v. Frasier*, 350 U.S. 979 (March 5, 1956), which affirmed *Frasier v. Board of Trustees* (see appendix 8), applied *Brown v. Board of Education* to undergraduate education.

H. *Florida ex rel. Hawkins v. Board of Control of Florida*, 350 U.S. 413, decided March 12, 1956:

On May 24, 1954, we issued a mandate in this case to the Supreme Court of Florida. 347 U.S. 971. We directed that the case be reconsidered in light of our decision in the Segregation Cases decided May 17, 1954, *Brown v. Board of Education*, 347 U.S. 483. In doing so, we did not imply that decrees involving graduate study present the problems of public elementary and secondary schools. We had theretofore, in three cases, ordered the admission of Negro applicants to graduate schools without discrimination because of color. *Sweatt v. Painter*, 339 U.S. 629; *Sipuel v. Board of Regents of the University of Oklahoma*, 332 U.S. 631; cf. *McLaurin v. Oklahoma State Regents for Higher Education*, 339 U.S. 637. Thus, our second decision in the *Brown* case, 349 U.S. 294, which implemented the earlier one, had no application to a case involving a Negro applying for admission to a state law school. Accordingly, the mandate of May 24, 1954, is recalled and is vacated. In lieu thereof, the following order is entered:

The petition for writ of certiorari is granted. The judgment is vacated and the case is remanded on the authority of the Segregation Cases decided May 17, 1954, *Brown v. Board of Education*, 347 U.S. 483. As this case involves the admission of a Negro to a graduate professional school, there is no reason for delay. He is entitled to prompt admission under the rules and regulations applicable to other qualified candidates.

I. The Civil Rights Act of 1964, Title VII, restricted federal funds to programs that did not discriminate on the basis of race.

J. The Higher Education Act of 1965, in view of the Civil Rights Act of 1964, spurred the beginnings of desegregation at historically white private institutions of higher education by offering as new inducements a variety of new federal programs.

Appendix 2

University of Maryland v. Murray (Maryland, 1936)

An early case regarding black exclusion from a public institution of higher education proved a victory for the African American plaintiff, Donald G. Murray, who won in 1935 in Baltimore City Court and then on January 15, 1936, on appeal in the Maryland Court of Appeals. The case is sometimes styled *University of Maryland v. Murray*, sometimes *Pearson v. Murray*, 169 Md. 478, 182 A. 590 (1936). So the first major victory for Charles Hamilton Houston, Thurgood Marshall, and the NAACP in a higher education case came in state court, and the arguments they framed convinced the court that the Fourteenth Amendment, even if it permitted segregation, did not condone exclusion from the only law school available in a state. Murray, who had already been admitted the previous fall under the lower court order, could stay in school. He graduated in 1938, and other black law students followed him there, as enrollment in one program at a public institution of higher education was desegregated, for the first time anywhere in the South since Reconstruction. In the version printed below, which is nearly complete, some citations have been removed or abridged.

The officers and governing board of the University of Maryland appeal from an order for the issue of the writ of mandamus, commanding them to admit a young negro, the appellee, as a student in the law school of the university. The appellee and petitioner, Murray, graduated as a bachelor of arts from Amherst College in 1934, and met the standards for admission to the law school in all other respects, but was denied admission on the sole ground of his color. He is twenty-two years of age, and is now, and has been during all his life, a resident of Baltimore City, where the law school is situated. He contests his exclusion as unauthorized by the laws of the State, or, so far as it might be considered authorized, then as a denial of equal rights because of his color, contrary to the requirement of the Fourteenth Amendment of the Constitution of the United States. The appellants reply, first, that by reason of its character and organization the law school is not a governmental agency, required by the amendment to give equal rights to students of both races. Or, if it is held that it is a state agency, it is replied that the admission of negro students is not required because the amendment permits segregation of the races for education, and it is the declared policy and the practice of the State to segregate them in schools, and that, although the law school of the university is maintained for white students only, and there is no separate law school maintained for colored students, equal treatment has at the same time been accorded the negroes by statutory provisions for scholarships or aids to enable them to attend law schools outside the state. A further argument in defense is that, if equal treatment has not been provided, the remedy must be found in the opening of a school for negroes, and not in their admission to this particular school attended by the whites.

The University of Maryland Law School was a private institution until the year 1920, when by statute, Acts 1920, ch. 480, it was consolidated with the Maryland State College of Agriculture, then an institution of the state government.... The agricultural college, during most of its career since the middle of the last century, had been a private institution, but later in that century, and during the early part of the present one, it was supported entirely from state funds, and the State owned an undivided half of its property, and after 1902 held a mortgage on the other half. A legislative enactment for the foreclosure of the mortgage of the college, "so that it become entirely a State institution," was passed in 1914 (chapter 128), and an Act of 1916 (chapter 372) provided a new corporation, to be known as the Maryland State College of Agriculture, to take the college over. All former property and powers were bestowed on the new corporation, and in accordance with the governmental character of it, the trustees were thenceforth to be appointed by the Governor of the State, by and with the advice and consent of the Senate, powers were given and duties were prescribed by the act for them and their officers, and they were required to make to the General Assembly at each session a report of the condition of the college and the property, and of their receipts and expenditures. The Attorney General of the State was designated as their adviser and attorney. That the corporation thus created is an instrumentality or agency of the State is plain, and we do not understand it to be disputed. "When the corporation is said, at the bar, to be public, it is not merely meant, that the whole community may be the proper objects of the bounty, but that the government have the sole right, as trustees of the public interests, to regulate, control and direct the corporation, and its funds and its franchises, at its own good will and pleasure"....

The consolidating Act of 1920, chapter 480, made the University of Maryland, with its law school, and the College of Agriculture, one corporation, which under the name of the University of Maryland was to be governed by the board of trustees provided for the College of Agriculture by the act of 1916.
...

The consolidation was completed. And from the fact of consolidation with a state agency, under one and the same board of trustees, appointed and controlled by the State, it would seem to follow inevitably that the law school maintained is a state agency, or part of one. The one corporation could not be both a public and a private one. It is argued that the school is "in the nature of a private corporation" because it receives the greater part of its support from the students' tuition fees, and therefore its freedom of selection and accommodation of students is not subject to the restriction by the Fourteenth Amendment. But a distinction between agencies which do and those which do not collect fees from individual users of their facilities would not support a distinction between private and public character. It is common practice for unquestionably public corporations to collect pay. Hospitals, and the various municipal corporations or agencies which make charges for utilities supplied, often with a margin of profit over expenses, remain none the less public in character. . . . There is no escape from the conclusion that the school is now a branch or agency of the state government. The State now provides education in the law for its citizens. And in doing so it comes under the constitutional mandates applicable to the actions of the states. The fact that the school, in its career as a private institution, was maintained for white students exclusively, would have no bearing on a question of compliance at this time. With respect to constitutional mandates it is in the situation of a new institution opened by the State. . . .

As a result of the adoption of the Fourteenth Amendment to the United States Constitution, a state is required to extend to its citizens of the two races substantially equal treatment in the facilities it provides from the public funds. "It is justly held by the authorities that 'to single out a certain portion of the people by the arbitrary standard of color, and say that these shall not have rights which are possessed by others, denies them the equal protection of the laws.' . . . Such a course would be manifestly in violation of the fourteenth amendment, because it would deprive a class of persons of a right which the constitution of the state had declared that they should possess." *Clark v. Maryland Institute*, 87 Md. 643, 661. Remarks quoted in argument from opinions of courts of other jurisdictions, that the educational policy of a state and its system of education are distinctly state affairs, have ordinarily been answers to demands on behalf of non-residents, and have never been meant to assert for a state freedom from the requirement of equal treatment to children of colored races. "It is distinctly a state affair. . . . But the denial to children whose parents, as well as themselves, are citizens of the United States and of this state, [of] admittance to the common schools solely because of color or racial differences without having made provision for the education equal in all respects to that afforded persons of any other race or color, is a violation of the provisions of the Fourteenth Amendment of the Constitution of the United States." *Piper v. Big Pine School Dist.*, 193 Cal. 664, 226 P. 926, 928; *Board of Education v. Foster*, 116 Ky. 484, 76 S.W. 354; *Ward v. Flood*, 48 Cal. 36.

The requirement of equal treatment would seem to be clearly enough one of equal treatment in respect to any one facility or opportunity furnished to citizens, rather than of a balance in state bounty to be struck from the expenditures and provisions for each race generally. We take it to be clear, for instance, that a state could not be rendered free to maintain a law school exclusively for whites by maintaining at equal cost a school of technology for colored students. Expenditures of this State for the education of the latter in schools and colleges have been extensive, but, however they may compare with provisions for the whites, they would not justify the exclusion of colored citizens alone from enjoyment of any one facility furnished by the State. The courts, in all the decisions on application of this constitutional requirement, find exclusion from any one privilege condemned....

Equality of treatment does not require that privileges be provided members of the two races in the same place. The State may choose the method by which equality is maintained. "In the circumstances that the races are separated in the public schools, there is certainly to be found no violation of the constitutional rights of the one race more than of the other, and we see none of either, for each, though separated from the other, is to be educated upon equal terms with that other, and both at the common public expense...."

Separation of the races must nevertheless furnish equal treatment. The constitutional requirement cannot be dispensed with in order to maintain a school or schools for whites exclusively. That requirement comes first.... And as no separate law school is provided by this State for colored students, the main question in the case is whether the separation can be maintained, and negroes excluded from the present school, by reason of equality of treatment furnished the latter in scholarships for studying outside the state, where law schools are open to negroes.

In 1933, an Act of Assembly, chapter 234, provided that the Regents of the University of Maryland might set aside part of the state appropriation for the Princess Anne Academy, an institution of junior college standing for negro students, now an eastern branch of the university, to establish partial scholarship at Morgan College in the state, or at institutions outside the state, for negroes qualified to take professional courses not offered them at Princess Anne Academy, but offered for white students in the university. Morgan College has no law school. None of the money necessary was appropriated for distribution under that act. By an Act of 1935, chapter 577, a commission on higher education of negroes was created and directed to administer $10,000 included in the state budget for the years 1935–1936 and 1936–1937, for scholarships of $200 each to negroes, to enable them to attend colleges outside the state, mainly to give the benefit of college, medical, law, and other professional courses to the colored youth of the state for whom no such facilities are available in the state. The allowance of $200 was to defray tuition fees only. This latter act went into effect on June 1st, 1935, and it appeared from evidence that by June 18th, when this case was tried below, three hundred and eighty negroes had sought blanks for applying for the scholarships, and one hundred and thirteen applications had been filled in and returned. Only sixteen had then sought opportunities for graduate or professional study, only one of them for study of the law. Applications were to be received during twelve more days. That any one of the many individual applicants would receive one of the fifty or more scholarships was obviously far from assured. For a large percentage of them there was no provision. And if the petitioner should have received one there would have been, as he argues, disadvantages attached.

Howard University, in Washington, District of Columbia, provides the law school for negroes nearest to Baltimore. The yearly tuition fee there is $135, as compared with a fee of $203 in the day school of the University of Maryland, and $153 in its night school. But to attend Howard University the petitioner, living in Baltimore, would be under the necessity of paying the expenses of daily travel to and fro, with some expenses while in Washington, or of removing to Washington to live during his law school education, and to pay the incidental expenses of thus living away from home; whereas in Baltimore, living at home, he would have no traveling expenses, and comparatively small living expenses. Going to any law school in the nearest jurisdiction would, then, involve him in considerable expense, even with the aid of one of the scholarships, should he chance to receive one. And as the petitioner points out, he could not there have the advantages of study of the law of this state primarily, and of attendance on state courts, where he intends to practice.

The court is clear that this rather slender chance for any one applicant at an opportunity to attend an outside law school, at increased expense, falls short of providing for students of the colored race facilities substantially equal to those furnished to the whites in the law school maintained in Baltimore. The number of colored students affected by the discrimination may be comparatively small, but it cannot be said to be negligible in Baltimore City, and moreover the number seems excluded as a factor in the problem. In a case on discrimination required by a state between the races in railroad travel, the Supreme Court of the United States has said: "This argument with respect to volume of traffic seems to us to be without merit. It makes the constitutional right depend upon the number of persons who may be discriminated against, whereas the essence of the constitutional right is that it is a personal one.... It is the individual who is entitled to the equal protection of the laws, and if he is denied by a common carrier, acting in the matter under the authority of a state law, a facility or convenience in the course of his journey which, under substantially the same circumstances, is furnished to another traveler, he may properly complain that his constitutional privilege has been invaded." *McCabe v. Atchison, T. & S. F. R. Co.*, 235 U.S. 151, 160. Whether with aid in any amount it is sufficient to send the negroes outside the state for like education is a question never passed on by the Supreme Court, and we need not discuss it now.

As has been stated, the method of furnishing the equal facilities required is at the choice of the State, now or at any future time. At present it is maintaining only the one law school, and in the legislative provisions for the scholarships that one school has in effect been declared appropriated to the whites exclusively. The officers and members of the board appear to us to have had a policy declared for them, as they thought. No separate school for colored students has been decided upon and only an inadequate substitute has been provided. Compliance with the Constitution cannot be deferred at the will of the State. Whatever system it adopts for legal education now must furnish equality of treatment now. "It would, therefore, not be competent to the Legislature, while providing a system of education for the youth of the State, to exclude the petitioner and those of her race from its benefits, merely because of their African descent, and to have so excluded her would have been to deny her the equal protection of the laws within the intent and meaning of the Constitution." And as in Maryland now the equal treatment can be furnished only in the one existing law school, the petitioner, in our opinion, must be admitted there.

We cannot find the remedy to be that of ordering a separate school for negroes. In the case of *Cumming v. Board of Education of Richmond County*, 175 U.S. 528, cited by the appellant, the question was whether a board with authority to establish separate schools, but with a limited fund available, could establish a high school for white children while expending the portion for colored children on primary schools, of which the people of that race were in greater need, suspending the erection of a separate high school for them. The Supreme Court denied the remedy of suppressing the white school meanwhile, and added: "If, in some appropriate proceeding instituted directly for that purpose, the plaintiffs had sought to compel the board of education, out of the funds in its hands or under its control, to establish and maintain a high school for colored children, and if it appeared that the board's refusal to maintain such a school was in fact an abuse of its discretion and in hostility to the colored population because of their race, different questions might have arisen in the state court." But in Maryland no officers or body of officers are authorized to establish a separate law school, there is no legislative declaration of a purpose to establish one, and the courts could not make the decision for the State, and order its officers to establish one. Therefore the erection of a separate school is not here an available alternative remedy. We do not understand that the Supreme Court was expressing any opinion on the problem as it is presented by the petitioner. See *Gong Lum v. Rice*, 275 U.S. 78.

The case, as we find it, then, is that the State has undertaken the function of education in the law, but has omitted students of one race from the only adequate provision made for it, and omitted them solely because of their color. If those students are to be offered equal treatment in the performance of the function, they must, at present, be admitted to the one school provided. . . .

Order affirmed.

Appendix 3

The U.S. Supreme Court and Segregation in Missouri (1938)

The U.S. Supreme Court addressed segregated public higher education in 1938, when Lloyd Gaines appealed a Missouri court decision that went against him. A majority of the Supreme Court concluded that promises to supply black citizens a program in the future, or offering to provide financial assistance for them to study in a neighboring state, did not satisfy the Fourteenth Amendment's requirement of equal protection of the laws, if an in-state program was available to white citizens. The Supreme Court decision—*Missouri ex rel. Gaines v. Canada, Registrar of the University of Missouri*, 305 U.S. 337, decided December 12, 1938—drew upon the Maryland appellate court's decision from two years earlier. But in contrast to the Maryland case, it did not direct the state university to admit a black student. Rather, the state could select among admitting Gaines into the historically white program, immediately creating a parallel program for him at the state's black college, or closing down the white program. Gaines disappeared before he enrolled, and states continued to establish and maintain scholarship programs to support black residents at out-of-state institutions, but the ruling provided a basis on which subsequent litigation was brought. The abridged version printed below deletes large portions, together with some cites, and also the dissenting opinion.

Petitioner Lloyd Gaines, a negro, was refused admission to the School of Law at the State University of Missouri. Asserting that this refusal constituted a denial by the State of the equal protection of the laws in violation of the Fourteenth Amendment of the Federal Constitution, petitioner brought this action for mandamus to compel the curators of the University to admit him. . . .

Petitioner is a citizen of Missouri. In August, 1935, he was graduated with the degree of Bachelor of Arts at the Lincoln University, an institution maintained by the State of Missouri for the higher education of negroes. That University has no law school

The clear and definite conclusions of the state court in construing the pertinent state legislation narrow the issue. The action of the curators, who are representatives of the State in the management of the state university, must be regarded as state action. . . .

In answering petitioner's contention that this discrimination constituted a denial of his constitutional right, the state court has fully recognized the obligation of the State to provide negroes with advantages for higher education substantially equal to the advantages afforded to white students. The State has sought to fulfill that obligation by furnishing equal facilities in separate schools, a method the validity of which has been sustained by our decisions. *Plessy v. Ferguson*, 163 U.S. 537, 544; *McCabe v. Atchison, T. & S. F. Ry. Co.*, 235 U.S. 151, 160; *Gong Lum v. Rice*, 275 U.S. 78, 85, 86. Compare *Cumming v. Board of Education*, 175 U.S. 528, 544, 545. Respondents' counsel have appropriately emphasized the special solicitude of the State for the higher education of negroes as shown in the establishment of Lincoln University, a state institution well conducted on a plane with the University of Missouri so far as the offered courses are concerned. It is said that Missouri is a pioneer in that field and is the only State in the Union which has established a separate university for negroes on the same basis as the state university for white students. But, commendable as is that action, the fact remains that instruction in law for negroes is not now afforded by the State, either at Lincoln University or elsewhere within the State, and that the State excludes negroes from the advantages of the law school it has established at the University of Missouri.

It is manifest that this discrimination, if not relieved by the provisions we shall presently discuss, would constitute a denial of equal protection. That was the conclusion of the Court of Appeals of Maryland in circumstances substantially similar in that aspect. *University of Maryland v. Murray*, 169 Md. 478. It there appeared that the State of Maryland had "undertaken the function of education in the law" but had "omitted students of one race from the only adequate provision made for it, and omitted them solely because of their color"; that if those students were to be offered "equal treatment in the performance of the function, they must, at present, be admitted to the one school provided." A provision for scholarships to enable negroes to attend colleges outside the State, mainly for the purpose of professional studies, was found to be inadequate and the question, "whether with aid in any amount it is sufficient to send the negroes outside the State for legal education," the Court of Appeals found it unnecessary to discuss. Accordingly, a writ of mandamus to admit the applicant was issued to the officers and regents of the University of Maryland as the agents of the State entrusted with the conduct of that institution.

The Supreme Court of Missouri in the instant case has distinguished the decision in Maryland upon the grounds—(1) that in Missouri, but not in Maryland, there is "a legislative declaration of a purpose to establish a law school for negroes at Lincoln University whenever necessary or practical"; and (2) that, "pending the establishment of such a school, adequate provision has been made for the legal education of negro students in recognized schools outside of this State."

... The basic consideration is not as to what sort of opportunities other States provide, or whether they are as good as those in Missouri, but as to what opportunities Missouri itself furnishes to white students and denies to negroes solely upon the ground of color. The admissibility of laws separating the races in the enjoyment of privileges afforded by the State rests wholly upon the equality of the privileges which the laws give to the separated groups within the State. The question here is not of a duty of the State to supply legal training, or of the quality of the training which it does supply, but of its duty when it provides such training to furnish it to the residents of the State upon the basis of an equality of right. By the operation of the laws of Missouri a privilege has been created for white law students which is denied to negroes by reason of their race. The white resident is afforded legal education within the State; the negro resident having the same qualifications is refused it there and must go outside the State to obtain it. That is a denial of the equality of legal right to the enjoyment of the privilege which the State has set up, and the provision for the payment of tuition fees in another State does not remove the discrimination.

The equal protection of the laws is "a pledge of the protection of equal laws." *Yick Wo v. Hopkins*, 118 U.S. 356, 369. Manifestly, the obligation of the State to give the protection of equal laws can be performed only where its laws operate, that is, within its own jurisdiction. It is there that the equality of legal right must be maintained. That obligation is imposed by the Constitution upon the States severally as governmental entities,—each responsible for its own laws establishing the rights and duties of persons within its borders. It is an obligation the burden of which cannot be cast by one State upon another, and no State can be excused from performance by what another State may do or fail to do. That separate responsibility of each State within its own sphere is of the essence of statehood maintained under our dual system. It seems to be implicit in respondents' argument that if other States did not provide courses for legal education, it would nevertheless be the constitutional duty of Missouri when it supplied such courses for white students to make equivalent provision for negroes. But that plain duty would exist because it rested upon the State independently of the action of other States. We find it impossible to conclude that what otherwise would be an unconstitutional discrimination, with respect to the legal right to the enjoyment of opportunities within the State, can be justified by requiring resort to opportunities elsewhere. That resort may mitigate the inconvenience of the discrimination but cannot serve to validate it.

Nor can we regard the fact that there is but a limited demand in Missouri for the legal education of negroes as excusing the discrimination in favor of whites. We had occasion to consider a cognate question in the case of *McCabe v. Atchison, T. & S. F. Ry. Co.* There the argument was advanced, in relation to the provision by a carrier of sleeping cars, dining and chair cars, that the limited demand by negroes justified the State in permitting the furnishing of such accommodations exclusively for white persons. We found that argument to be without merit. It made, we said, the constitutional right "depend upon the number of persons who may be discriminated against, whereas the essence of the constitutional right is that it is a personal one. Whether or not particular facilities shall be provided may doubtless be conditioned upon there being a reasonable demand therefor, but, if facilities are provided, substantial equality of treatment of persons traveling under like conditions cannot be refused. It is the individual who is entitled to the equal protection of the laws, and if he is denied by a common carrier, acting in the matter under the authority of a state law, a facility or convenience in the course of his journey which under substantially the same circumstances is furnished to another traveler, he may properly complain that his constitutional privilege has been invaded...."

Here, petitioner's right was a personal one. It was as an individual that he was entitled to the equal protection of the laws, and the State was bound to furnish him within its borders facilities for legal education substantially equal to those which the State there afforded for persons of the white race, whether or not other negroes sought the same opportunity.

Appendix 4

President Truman's Commission on Higher Education (1946–1948)

President Harry S. Truman's years in the White House brought a sea change in racial policy in American higher education. Congress proved unreceptive to any efforts to undermine or whittle down the structure of segregation in southern higher education. But the Supreme Court handed down three important decisions regarding "separate but equal" in higher education—one in January 1948 in a case from Oklahoma, two more in June 1950 in cases from Texas and Oklahoma. And the executive branch embarked on three key initiatives on the racial front in higher education. One was the President's Committee on Civil Rights. Another brought the U.S. Department of Justice into constitutional litigation—those three Supreme Court cases—on the side of plaintiffs against black exclusion from professional and graduate programs at historically white institutions. The third, the President's Commission on Higher Education, in addressing higher education in a comprehensive fashion, expressly critiqued racial discrimination in southern colleges and universities. Appointed in July 1946, the commission issued its reports in six slim volumes between December 1947 and February 1948.

The commission's findings and recommendations were wide-ranging—exhilaratingly so for some, deeply troubling for others. Addressing state as well as federal policy, the commission paid considerable attention to the distribution of opportunities among Americans to gain access to higher education and to secure real benefits from such access. In its summary volume 1, *Establishing the Goals*, the commission stated in a section on "racial and religious barriers" to individual or group opportunity, "the outstanding example of these barriers to equal opportunity is, of course, the disadvantages suffered by our Negro citizens." And it quoted the 1938 Supreme Court decision in *Gaines v. Missouri*: "If a state furnishes higher education to white residents, it is bound to furnish [within the state] substantially equal advantages to Negro students." In more detail, though often still without a lot of elaboration, volume 2 addressed the need for "equalizing and expanding individual opportunity."

In attacking racial segregation, the commission quoted from the President's Committee on Civil Rights:

The separate but equal doctrine stands convicted on three grounds. It contravenes the equalitarian spirit of the American heritage. It has failed to operate, for history shows that inequality of service has been the omnipresent consequence of separation. It has institutionalized segregation and kept groups apart despite indisputable evidence that normal contacts among these groups tend to promote social harmony.

In a section titled "To End Racial Discrimination," the commission asserted its conclusion: "There will be no fundamental correction of the total condition until [state] segregation legislation is repealed." The commission recognized that no executive order could dispatch states' segregation requirements, but it called for sustained work to achieve the outcome it was prescribing. Meanwhile, it urged that "separate educational facilities for Negroes be made truly equal in facilities and quality to those for white students."

Refusing to restrict itself to public higher education in its observations, the commission noted the crucial role that segregated black elementary and secondary schools, as well as private black colleges, would have to play: "Until Negro young people have available the opportunity to attend elementary and secondary schools which properly prepare their graduates for college, segregation works as a virtual nullification of the opportunity for higher education everywhere," in black colleges or white ones, within the South or elsewhere. Given the improbability that access to white institutions (public or private) could address the needs of many black southerners anytime soon, the commission went on: "The seriousness of the limitations upon Negro education makes it necessary to strengthen the private Negro colleges of the South which are now serving Negro youth in large numbers."

Caught as it was between strong prescriptions for expanded opportunity for all Americans and the current situation within which any immediate change regarding race must take place, the commission took a pragmatic approach. The report recognized that its "recommendation" regarding shoring up black colleges was "inconsistent with the Commission's position that segregation should be eliminated," but "the immediate practical fact is that with such meager opportunity for Negro youth for education, every current program to alleviate this situation should be encouraged." Addressing the expedient of establishing regional centers, an approach very much under consideration in the post–World War II South, the commission noted that such an approach to black education could hardly satisfy the *Gaines* rule requiring equal in-state opportunities, but it had "immediate practical merit," and—here the commission betrayed its optimism that such centers might be integrated rather than another ploy to maintain segregation—the centers might begin the development of integrated higher education in the South.

What might the federal government do? Whether the Congress would adopt any of the proposals that the commission broached was uncertain. But before Congress could even consider them, the commission had to point out what it saw as required for a new dispensation, with the federal government building on generations of assistance to higher education, expanding its role, and redirecting its efforts to equalize opportunities across the black-white racial boundary. In expanding the federal role, Congress must, the commission insisted, "clearly specify that there may be no [racial] discrimination in the channeling of such funds," whether among individuals or among institutions. As long as segregation remained the law of southern states, "the Negro institutions should by law receive their full proportionate share of all Federal and State funds destined for the support of college instruction."

Four members appended a "statement of dissent" to the commission's findings regarding race and opportunity. Writing in response to a section titled "Racial Discrimination," these four members were all from one or another among the seventeen segregated states—physicist and Washington University (St. Louis, Missouri) chancellor Arthur H. Compton, Virginia historian and journalist Douglas Southall Freeman, University of Arkansas president Lewis W. Jones, and Emory University president Goodrich C. White. Their dissenting statement follows:

> The undersigned wish to record their dissent from the Commission's pronouncements on "segregation," especially as these pronouncements are related to education in the South. We recognize that many conditions affect adversely the lives of our Negro citizens, and that gross inequality of opportunity, economic and educational, is a fact. We are concerned that as rapidly as possible conditions should be improved, inequalities removed, and greater opportunity provided for all our people. But we believe that efforts toward these ends must, in the South, be made within the established patterns of social relationships, which require separate educational institutions for whites and Negroes. We believe that pronouncements such as those of the Commission on the question of segregation jeopardize these efforts, impede progress, and threaten tragedy to the people of the South, both white and Negro. We recognize the high purpose and the theoretical idealism of the Commission's recommendations. But a doctrinaire position which ignores the facts of history and the realities of the present is not one that will contribute constructively to the solution of difficult problems of human relationships.

This "statement of dissent," penned by four men representing segregated states, endorsed the removal of racial "inequalities" but insisted that any such initiatives be pursued in a manner consistent with "the established patterns of social relationships, which require separate educational institutions for whites and Negroes." The quartet did not explicitly call on the authority of *Plessy v. Ferguson*, and their rhetoric conceded that black southerners should experience the "equal" as well as the "separate," but they saw no way or reason to soften the dominant regional stance against any racial integration in higher education. Maryland and West Virginia might address "inequalities" by integrating one or more programs, but, the four spokesmen for the white South were saying, no federal commission should stipulate that approach. The dissenters did not directly address the commission's proposals to inaugurate new ground rules for a vastly more equal dispensation in the world of "separate but equal."

The regional fault line on race and higher education in early post–World War II America was clear. The commission's report did not immediately result in any vast change, but it did reflect a new federal language on racial identity, public policy, and educational opportunity. As for the three leading cases decided between 1948 and 1950 on segregated higher education, their significance was vast, not only in terms of identifying the path that the NAACP promptly followed with regard to elementary and secondary education—the road that took the nation to *Brown v. Board of Education*—but also in propelling state after state to embark on modest beginnings in the process of desegregating its institutions of higher education. Then, in turn, the rulings in *Brown* propelled still farther change.

The commission's findings, which were first produced in six volumes in 1947-48, also appeared in full (though still in six sections, separately paginated) in *Higher Education for American Democracy: A Report of The President's Commission on Higher Education* (New York: Harper and Brothers, 1948) and subsequently in part in Gail Kennedy, ed., *Education for Democracy: The Debate over the Report of the President's Commission on Higher Education* (Lexington, Mass.: D. C. Heath, 1952). The passages quoted here are from *Higher Education for American Democracy*, 1:32, 34, and 2:29, 31, 35–36.

Appendix 5

McCready v. Byrd (Maryland, 1950)

In 1949, Esther McCready applied to the University of Maryland's nursing school in Baltimore. In Maryland state court, she sued university president Harry C. Byrd to obtain admission. When she lost in Baltimore City Court, she appealed the decision. The Maryland Court of Appeals handed down its ruling (195 Md. 131, 73 A.2d 8) on April 14, 1950. The ruling revealed the importance of a 1935 Maryland case, and it revealed, too, the significance of court rulings by the U.S. Supreme Court in 1938 and 1948, even before the two decisions the Court handed down in June 1950. In editing the opinion below, some citations have been removed or shortened.

This is an appeal from an order dismissing a petition for mandamus to require the governing board of the University of Maryland and officers of the university and its school of nursing to consider and act on petitioner's application, made on February 1, 1949, for admission as a first year student in the school of nursing, without regard to race or color, and admit her to the school upon her complying with the uniform lawful requirements for admission. No material facts are in dispute. Petitioner is a negro. She has all the educational and character requirements for admission. She was refused admission solely because of her race. The school of nursing is a branch or agency of the state government. It has been so held as to the law school. *University of Maryland v. Murray*, 169 Md. 478, 483.

In 1948 the State of Maryland and other southern states, without the consent of Congress under section 10 of Article I of the Constitution, entered into a regional compact, which was subsequently amended and, as amended, is set out in and was ratified by Chapter 282 of the Acts of 1949, effective June 1, 1949, relating to the development and maintenance of regional educational services and schools in the southern states in the professional, technological, scientific, literary and other fields, so as to provide greater educational advantages and facilities for the citizens of the several states who reside within such region. By arrangement pursuant to the regional compact the State of Maryland has sent a number of white students to study veterinary medicine in a school in another state and has sent, or is willing to send, negro students for the same purpose to a different school in another state. No instruction in veterinary medicine is offered by the University of Maryland or any other state agency in Maryland. Pursuant to the regional compact a contract for training in nursing education, dated July 19, 1949, was made between the Board of Control for Southern Regional Education, "a joint agency" created by the regional compact, and the State of Maryland, relating to nursing education of three first year students from the State of Maryland in Meharry Medical College, School of Nursing, at Nashville, Tennessee. Meharry Medical School and its school of nursing receive negro students only. In August, 1949 the University of Maryland offered petitioner a course in nursing at Meharry Medical College at a total over-all cost to her, including living and traveling expenses, which would not exceed the cost to her of attending the school of nursing at the University of Maryland. Petitioner declined the offer.

From the uncontradicted testimony, in ample detail, of Doctor Pincoffs, since 1922 Professor of Medicine in the University of Maryland Medical School and chief physician at the University Hospital, and other witnesses called by respondents, it seems clear that in educational facilities and living conditions the nursing school at Meharry College is not only equal but superior to the University of Maryland nursing school. The offer to petitioner of a course in nursing at Meharry Medical College therefore included every advantage except the one she now insists upon, viz., education in a state institution within the State of Maryland. Respondents stress the regional compact and the contract for training in nursing education. The terms and details of these agreements are not now material. Neither agreement mentions race. We may assume, without deciding, that the compact is valid without the consent of Congress. Under the contract the Board are only agents—or ambassadors—to negotiate a contract for nursing education between the State of Maryland and Meharry Medical College. Obviously no compact or contract can extend the territorial boundaries or the sovereignty of the State of Maryland to Nashville.

In *University of Maryland v. Murray*, the court affirmed an order for the issue of the writ of mandamus, commanding the officers and governing board of the University of Maryland to admit the petitioner, a negro, as a student in the law school. It was contended, among other things, that the State had discharged its obligation to the petitioner by providing certain scholarships at Howard University in Washington. This contention was rejected because the petitioner had a "rather slender chance" of getting a scholarship and, if he got one, would be subject to traveling or living expenses to which he would not be subject at the University of Maryland law school. The court, in its opinion by Chief Judge Bond, remarked, "And as the petitioner points out, he could not there have the advantages of study of the law of this state primarily, and of attendance on state courts, where he intends to practice." As has been indicated, this was not the ground of decision. In its opinion the court also said,

"Whether with aid in any amount it is sufficient to send the negroes outside the state for like education is a question never passed on by the Supreme Court, and we need not discuss it now."

The statement last quoted from the opinion, by Judge Bond, in the *Murray* case left open the question whether it is sufficient to send negroes outside the state for education like that given white students in Maryland, and the remark first quoted left it arguable that in this respect there may be a difference between the study of law and the study of nursing. Law in Tennessee is not the same as law in Maryland; presumably a sound education in nursing is the same in Tennessee as in Maryland. The statement last quoted from the *Murray* case was of course correct when made, but it would not be correct if made now. Since the *Murray* case the question there left open has been "passed on by the Supreme Court" and has been foreclosed in a way that permits no distinction between the study of law and the study of nursing.

In *State of Missouri, ex rel. Gaines v. Canada*, 305 U.S. 337, the court reversed a judgment of the Supreme Court of Missouri which denied a writ of mandamus to compel admission of a negro to the University of Missouri law school. One of the grounds of the decision of the state court was that "adequate provision [had] been made for the legal education of negro students in recognized schools outside of this State." The court, in its opinion by Mr. Chief Justice Hughes, referred at some length to the *Murray* case, quoted the above question specifically left open in that case, and referred to the remark first above quoted and to similar contentions made in the Missouri case. After mentioning these contentions, the opinion brushed them aside and decided the question left open in the *Murray* case on broad grounds which are no less applicable to a school of nursing than to a school of law.

We think that these matters are beside the point. The basic consideration is not as to what sort of opportunities other States provide, or whether they are as good as those in Missouri, but as to what opportunities Missouri itself furnishes to white students and denies to negroes solely upon the ground of color. The admissibility of laws separating the races in the enjoyment of privileges afforded by the State rests wholly upon the equality of the privileges which the laws give to the separated groups within the State. The question here is not of a duty of the State to supply legal training, or of the quality of the training which it does supply, but of its duty when it provides such training to furnish it to the residents of the State upon the basis of an equality of right. By the operation of the laws of Missouri a privilege has been created for white law students which is denied to negroes by reason of their race. The white resident is afforded legal education within the State; the negro resident having the same qualifications is refused it there and must go outside the State to obtain it. That is a denial of the equality of legal right to the enjoyment of the privilege which the State has set up, and the provision for the payment of tuition fees in another State does not remove the discrimination.

The equal protection of the laws is "a pledge of the protection of equal laws." *Yick Wo v. Hopkins*, 118 U.S. 356, 369. Manifestly, the obligation of the State to give the protection of equal laws can be performed only where its laws operate, that is, within its own jurisdiction. It is there that the equality of legal right must be maintained. That obligation is imposed by the Constitution upon the States severally as governmental entities,—each responsible for its own laws establishing the rights and duties of persons within its borders. It is an obligation the burden of which cannot be cast by one State upon another, and no State can be excused from performance by what another State may do or fail to do. That separate responsibility of each State within its own sphere is of the essence of statehood maintained under our dual system. It seems to be implicit in respondents' argument that if other States did not provide courses for legal education, it would nevertheless be the constitutional duty of Missouri when it supplied such courses for white students to make equivalent provision for negroes. But that plain duty would exist because it rested upon the State independently of the action of other States. We find it impossible to conclude that what otherwise would be an unconstitutional discrimination, with respect to the legal right to the enjoyment of opportunities within the State, can be justified by requiring resort to opportunities elsewhere. That resort may mitigate the inconvenience of the discrimination but cannot serve to validate it. [*State of Missouri, ex rel. Gaines v. Canada*, 305 U.S. 337, 349–350.]

It would be bold indeed to suggest that the late Chief Justice ever used words without due regard for their meaning. His words might be subsequently overruled or qualified by the court. But the words quoted have not been overruled or qualified. On the contrary, a case from Oklahoma, essentially the same as the Missouri case, was argued on Thursday, January 8, 1948, and was reversed on the following Monday, with the following *per curiam* opinion:

> On January 14, 1946, the petitioner, a Negro, concededly qualified to receive the professional legal education offered by the State, applied for admission to the School of Law of the University of Oklahoma, the only institution for legal education supported and maintained by the taxpayers of the State of Oklahoma. Petitioner's application for admission was denied, solely because of her color.
>
> Petitioner then made application for a writ of mandamus in the District Court of Cleveland County, Oklahoma. The writ of mandamus was refused, and the Supreme Court of the State of Oklahoma affirmed the judgment of the District Court. [*Sipuel v. Board of Regents of University of Oklahoma*, 199 Okl. 36]. We brought the case here for review.

The petitioner is entitled to secure legal education afforded by a state institution. To this time, it has been denied her although during the same period many white applicants have been afforded legal education by the State. The State must provide it for her in conformity with the equal protection clause of the Fourteenth Amendment and provide it as soon as it does for applicants of any other group. *State of Missouri, ex rel. Gaines v. Canada*, 1938, 305 U.S. 337.

The judgment of the Supreme Court of Oklahoma is reversed and the cause is remanded to that court for proceedings not inconsistent with this opinion.

"The mandate shall issue forthwith." *Sipuel v. Board of Regents of University of Oklahoma*, 332 U.S. 631, 632–633. We cannot subtract anything from what the Supreme Court has said. It would be superfluous to add anything.

Order reversed. . . .

Appendix 6

Sweatt v. Painter (1950)

The U.S. Supreme Court handed down two very important rulings on June 5, 1950, George McLaurin's case from Oklahoma (see appendix 1) and this one by Heman Sweatt. The version printed here of the Court's ruling (339 U.S. 629) is trimmed of footnotes, some citations, and a bit more.

This case and *McLaurin v. Oklahoma State Regents* present different aspects of this general question: To what extent does the Equal Protection Clause of the Fourteenth Amendment limit the power of a state to distinguish between students of different races in professional and graduate education in a state university? Broader issues have been urged for our consideration, but we adhere to the principle of deciding constitutional questions only in the context of the particular case before the Court. . . .

In the instant case, petitioner filed an application for admission to the University of Texas Law School for the February, 1946 term. His application was rejected solely because he is a Negro. Petitioner thereupon brought this suit for mandamus against the appropriate school officials, respondents here, to compel his admission. At that time, there was no law school in Texas which admitted Negroes.

The state trial court recognized that the action of the State in denying petitioner the opportunity to gain a legal education while granting it to others deprived him of the equal protection of the laws guaranteed by the Fourteenth Amendment. The court did not grant the relief requested, however, but continued the case for six months to allow the State to supply substantially equal facilities. At the expiration of the six months, in December, 1946, the court denied the writ on the showing that the authorized university officials had adopted an order calling for the opening of a law school for Negroes the following February. While petitioner's appeal was pending, such a school was made available, but petitioner refused to register therein. The Texas Court of Civil Appeals set aside the trial court's judgment and ordered the cause "remanded generally to the trial court for further proceedings without prejudice to the rights of any party to this suit."

On remand, a hearing was held on the issue of the equality of the educational facilities at the newly established school as compared with the University of Texas Law School. Finding that the new school offered petitioner "privileges, advantages, and opportunities for the study of law substantially equivalent to those offered by the State to white students at the University of Texas," the trial court denied mandamus. The Court of Civil Appeals affirmed. Petitioner's application for a writ of error was denied by the Texas Supreme Court. We granted certiorari, because of the manifest importance of the constitutional issues involved.

The University of Texas Law School, from which petitioner was excluded, was staffed by a faculty of sixteen full-time and three part-time professors, some of whom are nationally recognized authorities in their field. Its student body numbered 850. The library contained over 65,000 volumes. Among the other facilities available to the students were a law review, moot court facilities, scholarship funds, and Order of the Coif affiliation. The school's alumni occupy the most distinguished positions in the private practice of the law and in the public life of the State. It may properly be considered one of the nation's ranking law schools.

The law school for Negroes which was to have opened in February, 1947, would have had no independent faculty or library. The teaching was to be carried on by four members of the University of Texas Law School faculty, who were to maintain their offices at the University of Texas while teaching at both institutions. Few of the 10,000 volumes ordered for the library had arrived; nor was there any full-time librarian. The school lacked accreditation.

Since the trial of this case, respondents report the opening of a law school at the Texas State University for Negroes. It is apparently on the road to full accreditation. It has a faculty of five full-time professors; a student body of 23; a library of some 16,500 volumes serviced by a full-time staff; a practice court and legal aid association; and one alumnus who has become a member of the Texas Bar.

Whether the University of Texas Law School is compared with the original or the new law school for Negroes, we cannot find substantial equality in the educational opportunities offered white and Negro law students by the State. In terms of number of the faculty, variety of courses and opportunity for specialization, size of the student body, scope of the library, availability of law review and similar activities, the University of Texas Law School is superior. What is more important, the University of Texas Law School possesses to a far greater degree those qualities which are incapable of objective measurement but which make for greatness in a law school. Such qualities, to name but a few, include reputation of the faculty, experience of the administration, position and influence of the alumni, standing in the community, traditions and prestige. It is difficult to believe that one who had a free choice between these law schools would consider the question close.

Moreover, although the law is a highly learned profession, we are well aware that it is an intensely practical one. The law school, the proving ground for legal learning and practice, cannot be effective in isolation from the individuals and institutions with which the law interacts. Few students and no one who has practiced law would choose to study in an academic vacuum, removed from the interplay of ideas and the exchange of views with which the law is concerned. The law school to which Texas is willing to admit petitioner excludes from its student body members of the racial groups which number 85% of the population of the State and include most of the lawyers, witnesses, jurors, judges and other officials with whom petitioner will inevitably be dealing when he becomes a member of the Texas Bar. With such a substantial and significant segment of society excluded, we cannot conclude that the education offered petitioner is substantially equal to that which he would receive if admitted to the University of Texas Law School.

It may be argued that excluding petitioner from that school is no different from excluding white students from the new law school. This contention overlooks realities. It is unlikely that a member of a group so decisively in the majority, attending a school with rich traditions and prestige which only a history of consistently maintained excellence could command, would claim that the opportunities afforded him for legal education were unequal to those held open to petitioner. That such a claim, if made, would be dishonored by the State, is no answer. "Equal protection of the laws is not achieved through indiscriminate imposition of inequalities." *Shelley v. Kraemer*, 334 U.S. 1, 22 (1948).

It is fundamental that these cases concern rights which are personal and present. This Court has stated unanimously that "The State must provide [legal education] for [petitioner] in conformity with the equal protection clause of the Fourteenth Amendment and provide it as soon as it does for applicants of any other group." *Sipuel v. Board of Regents*, 332 U.S. 631, 633 (1948). That case "did not present the issue whether a state might not satisfy the equal protection clause of the Fourteenth Amendment by establishing a separate law school for Negroes." *Fisher v. Hurst*, 333 U.S. 147, 150 (1948). In *Missouri ex rel. Gaines v. Canada*, 305 U.S. 337, 351 (1938), the Court, speaking through Chief Justice Hughes, declared that "petitioner's right was a personal one. It was as an individual that he was entitled to the equal protection of the laws, and the State was bound to furnish him within its borders facilities for legal education substantially equal to those which the State there afforded for persons of the white race, whether or not other negroes sought the same opportunity." These are the only cases in this Court which present the issue of the constitutional validity of race distinctions in state-supported graduate and professional education.

In accordance with these cases, petitioner may claim his full constitutional right: legal education equivalent to that offered by the State to students of other races. Such education is not available to him in a separate law school as offered by the State. We cannot, therefore, agree with respondents that the doctrine of *Plessy v. Ferguson*, 163 U.S. 537 (1896), requires affirmance of the judgment below. Nor need we reach petitioner's contention that *Plessy v. Ferguson* should be reexamined in the light of contemporary knowledge respecting the purposes of the Fourteenth Amendment and the effects of racial segregation.

We hold that the Equal Protection Clause of the Fourteenth Amendment requires that petitioner be admitted to the University of Texas Law School. The judgment is reversed and the cause is remanded for proceedings not inconsistent with this opinion.

Reversed.

Appendix 7

"Desegregation" at the University of Missouri (1950)

These two documents are from the University Archives, University of Missouri. Most court action by black southerners to gain entrance into segregated nonblack universities took place in federal courts, but sometimes black prospective students sued instead in state court. The Circuit Court of Cole County, Missouri, decided a case in June 1950 that determined whether the University of Missouri could continue to exclude black residents of the state from programs that, unavailable at Lincoln University, were offered at either of the university's two nonblack campuses.

A. Black Citizens Bring Litigation in Missouri, 1950

JUDGMENT

Now on this 27th day of June, 1950, this cause comes on regularly for trial before the Court without a jury, all parties appearing by their respective attorneys of record and the defendants Elmer Bell, Jr., George Everett Horne and Gus T. Ridgel appearing in person; and the evidence is heard and the cause is submitted to the Court.

Now upon the pleadings and the evidence the Court finds the undisputed and admitted facts to be as stated in plaintiff's petition: that defendants Bell and Horne, Negro residents of Missouri, applied for admission as first-year engineering students in the School of Mines and Metallurgy of plaintiff and defendant Ridgel, a Negro resident of Missouri, applied for admission as a student in the Graduate School of plaintiff to pursue the course of study leading to a master's degree in Economics; that each of the said three defendants Bell, Horne and Ridgel is scholastically qualified to pursue the course of study for which he so applied; that plaintiff rejected each of said applications because of the state law and public policy of the State of Missouri requiring segregation of the white and Negro races for the purpose of higher education and because the laws of Missouri require the Board of Curators of Lincoln University to afford to the Negro people of the state the opportunity for higher education in all branches of instruction equal to that available at the University of Missouri; that there is not now available to defendants Bell, Horne and

Ridgel in Lincoln University, and Lincoln University does not offer, any of the aforesaid courses of study in engineering and Graduate Economics, inasmuch as no demand for the establishment of any of such courses of study in Lincoln University has ever been made by any resident Negro, and the General Assembly of Missouri has never appropriated, and the defendant Board does not have available necessary funds to enable the defendant Board to establish any of said courses of study; and that there is no reasonable probability that defendant Board will establish or be able to offer any of such courses of study in Lincoln University at any time in the near future.

WHEREFORE, upon the facts so found, it is by the Court ordered, declared and adjudged:

1. That this Court has jurisdiction of the parties and of the subject matter of this cause and has jurisdiction by declaratory judgment to declare and adjudge the rights and obligations of the parties as prayed in the petition and in the answers;

2. That while plaintiff in rejecting each of the aforesaid applications of defendants Bell, Horne and Ridgel has acted in accordance with the state law and public policy of Missouri requiring segregation of white and Negro races for the purpose of higher education, said state law and public policy have been and are restricted and modified by and must yield to the higher law, namely, the equal protection clause of the Fourteenth Amendment to the Constitution of the United States and Section 2 of Article I of the Constitution of Missouri, to the extent that plaintiff and other state-supported institutions of higher learning in Missouri are legally obligated to admit scholastically qualified Negro students to those divisions and curricula in which instruction is not immediately available in Lincoln University;

3. That under the facts as this Court has found them plaintiff's aforesaid refusal to admit each of the defendants Bell, Horne and Ridgel is a denial to each of said defendants of the equal protection clause of the Fourteenth Amendment to the Constitution of the United States, and is a denial of their respective equal rights and opportunity under the law, in violation of Section 2 of Article I of the Constitution of Missouri; and that therefore plaintiff's aforesaid refusal to admit each of said defendants Bell, Horne and Ridgel is not legally justified by the aforesaid state law and public policy;

4. That regardless of the aforesaid state law and public policy, each of the defendants Elmer Bell, Jr., and George Everett Horne has the right to be admitted as a first-year engineering student in the School of Mines and Metallurgy of the University of Missouri at Rolla, Missouri, and that

defendant Gus T. Ridgel has the right to be admitted as a student majoring in Economics in the Graduate School of the University of Missouri at Columbia, Missouri;

5. That the General Assembly of Missouri has by statute imposed upon the defendant Board of Curators of Lincoln University the mandatory duty to so organize Lincoln University that it shall afford to the Negro people of the state the opportunity for training up to the standard furnished in the University of Missouri, and has authorized said Board to open and establish any new school, department or course of instruction which may be required in order to enable said Board fully to perform its said mandatory duty; but that inasmuch as there never has been any demand heretofore made upon the defendant Board of Curators of Lincoln University by any resident Negro for the establishment in Lincoln University of any of the aforesaid courses of study for which defendants Bell, Horne and Ridgel have applied, and inasmuch as the General Assembly has never appropriated, and said defendant Board does not have available, the necessary funds to enable said defendant Board to establish said courses of study at Lincoln University, the defendant Board is legally excused for its failure thus far to have established said courses of study in Lincoln University as required by aforesaid mandatory statute.

And now plaintiff voluntarily agrees to, and does pay the costs of this suit.

(Signed)   S. C. Blair
Judge

B. To what degree was the University of Missouri "desegregated" when Gus Ridgel began classes in 1950? In the aftermath of this state court decision, officials at the University of Missouri puzzled over whether it applied to other applicants than the three named in the case. In addition to Gus Ridgel, eight African Americans had sought admission at the Columbia campus for classes that fall. Were they residents of Missouri? Was the program of study they sought available at Lincoln University? In the list below, a school officer's penciled comments are rendered in quotation marks:

APPLICATIONS FOR ADMISSION (NEGRO)
University of Missouri, Columbia
Fall 1950
1. Gus Tolver Ridgel—924 Benton, Poplar Bluff, Mo. Graduate School—major Economics—Has B.S. from Lincoln University. "In."
2. Marie Jefferson—2662 Lucas Ave., St. Louis, Mo. Graduate School—major—Home Economics. "Is it offered at Lincoln?"

3. Raymond J. Collins, Jr.—Cyrus Barracks, Lincoln University, Jefferson City, Mo. He did not indicate the division he wanted. "Must let us know."
4. Mrs. Jettie L. Lawson—South Masters School, Bell City, Mo. Graduate School—no major indicated. "Is it offered at Lincoln?"
5. Arthurine W. Reason—4520 Kennerly, St. Louis, Mo. Graduate School—major Home Economics—Has B.S. degree from Lincoln. "Is it offered at Lincoln."
6. Dolores Clinton—217 Bennett Hall, Lincoln University, Jefferson City, Mo. Wanted information concerning Graduate and Undergraduate work—Major—Speech Science. "Is it offered at Lincoln."
7. Robert L. Hurst—Lincoln University, Jefferson City, Mo. Graduate School (Probably a teacher at Lincoln as letter was on Lincoln University paper, Department of Agriculture). "Must let us know."
8. Hazel McDaniel Teabeau—Lincoln University, Jefferson City, Mo. Graduate School—major—English and Speech. Professor of English at Lincoln University. "Is it offered at Lincoln?"
9. Doris T. Figaro—413 Southwest Street—Lafayette, La. Wants admission to the College of Arts and Sciences as a Freshman. Ranked 6 out of 23 in high school graduating class. "No (a) Non-resident (b) Not covered by judgment."

Appendix 8

Frasier v. Board of Trustees of the University of North Carolina (1955)

In 1955, the year after the U.S. Supreme Court handed down its first ruling in *Brown v. Board of Education,* three classmates at all-black Hillside High School in Durham, North Carolina, among them Leroy Benjamin Frasier Jr., sought admission as freshmen at the University of North Carolina's nearby Chapel Hill campus. Turned down on grounds of their racial identity, they went to federal court, where they argued that the 1954 ruling in *Brown* ought to be interpreted to benefit them, even though the specific facts in *Brown* had to do with elementary and secondary schools. Their attorneys included Floyd McKissick, an African American who had been admitted to the University of North Carolina law school after a court victory four years earlier (later, McKissick became a leader in the Congress of Racial Equality). The case was argued on September 10, 1955; the decision came a mere six days later. Here is the district court ruling (134 F.Supp. 589), demonstrating that the law of the land in higher education might have been as thoroughly changed by *Brown* as for lower levels of public schooling. Some citations have been shortened as presented here.

This suit seeks a declaratory judgment that certain orders of the Board of Trustees of the Consolidated University of North Carolina, which deny admission to the undergraduate schools of the institution to members of the Negro race, are in violation of the equal protection clause of the 14th Amendment of the Constitution of the United States. The plaintiffs also ask for an injunction restraining the University and its trustees and officers from denying admission to the undergraduate schools to Negroes solely because of their race and color. The plaintiffs pray for relief under Rule 23(a) of the Federal Rules of Civil Procedure, 28 U.S.C.A., not only for themselves but also for all other Negro citizens of North Carolina as a class who possess the qualifications for entrance to the University.

The plaintiffs are three Negro youths who are citizens and residents of North Carolina and graduates of the Hillside High School of Durham, which is accredited by the Southern Association of Secondary Schools and Colleges and by the State Department of Public Instruction of the State. The plaintiffs made formal application for admission to the undergraduate school of the University on April 19, 1955, and accompanied their application with a record of their academic achievements, character and personal references, as required by the rules of the University. On April 27, 1955 they received identical letters from the Director of Admissions in which they were told that the Trustees of the University had not changed the policy of admission of Negroes who were eligible to make application for graduate and professional studies not offered at a Negro college in the state, but were not eligible at that time to apply for admission to the undergraduate schools. Thereupon the plaintiffs requested the University to reverse its policy of discrimination against Negroes and the Board of Trustees in reply, on May 23, 1955, reaffirmed its policy by passing the following resolution:

> The State of North Carolina having spent millions of dollars in providing adequate and equal educational facilities in the undergraduate departments of its institutions of higher learning for all races, it is hereby declared to be the policy of the Board of Trustees of the Consolidated University of North Carolina that applications of Negroes to the undergraduate schools of the three branches of the Consolidated University be not accepted.

The University of North Carolina is recognized both in Article IX, section 6 of the Constitution of the State, and in Article 1, Part 1, section 116–1, of the General Statutes of the State. These enactments provide that the General Assembly of the State shall have power to provide for the election of trustees of the University of North Carolina in whom shall be vested all the rights and privileges granted to the University, and the General Assembly is empowered to make laws and regulations for the management of the University. The General Statutes in Article 1, Part 1, section 116–2, provide for the merger and consolidation of the University of North Carolina, the North Carolina State College of Agriculture and Engineering, and the North Carolina College for Women into the Consolidated University of North Carolina. Section 116–10 of the General Statutes empowers the trustees to make such rules and regulations for the management of the University, as they may deem necessary and expedient, not inconsistent with the laws of the state.

The resolution of the Board of Trustees of May 23, 1955, above set out was passed under the authority of these constitutional and statutory provisions. The complaint rests upon the invalidity of this order. There is no constitutional or statutory provision which expressly requires the segregation of the races in the University; and the plaintiffs do not challenge the assertion of the defendants that North Carolina has provided adequate and equal educational facilities for all races in the undergraduate departments of its institutions of higher learning.

Having been refused admission to the University, the plaintiffs brought the present suit, and prayed that a three judge District Court be convened under 28 U.S.C.A. §§ 2281 and 2284; and the present court was accordingly established. The defendants contend that the case is not one for a three judge court because there is no constitutional or statutory provision which denies the admission of Negroes to the University or requires the segregation of persons admitted to the University on account of their color.

We hold, however, that jurisdiction exists in the Court, as now set up, because the statute 28 U.S.C.A. § 2281, requires a three judge court not only when it is sought to restrain the enforcement of an unconstitutional statute, but also the enforcement of an unconstitutional order of an administrative board or commission, clothed with authority and acting under the law of the State. The jurisdiction of a three judge court was sustained under circumstances precisely similar to those in the case at bar in *Wilson v. Board of Supervisors*, D.C.E.D.La., 92 F.Supp. 986, which was affirmed without opinion in 340 U.S. 909, and Id., 340 U.S. 939. The decision was based on the ground that a three judge court is required when an injunction is sought because of the unconstitutionality of the order of a State administrative board. It is beyond dispute that the State of North Carolina, both by constitution and by statute, has clothed the Board of Trustees of the University with authority to make such rules and regulations for the management of the institution as they deem necessary and expedient, and it follows that the regulation now under attack must be considered a "statute" to which the State has given its sanction within the meaning of the jurisdictional provisions of 28 U.S.C. § 2281. . . . In *McCormick & Co. v. Brown*, 4 Cir., 52 F.2d 934, 937, it was said: ". . . it is settled that a court of three judges is required not only when the constitutionality of the state statute is involved, but also when the constitutionality of an order of a state administrative board or commission, purporting to be authorized by state statute, is drawn into question. . . . "

It will have been noticed that the resolution of the Board of May 23, 1955, excluding Negroes from the undergraduate schools of the University, was promulgated after the decision of the Supreme Court in *Brown v. Board of Education of Topeka, Kansas*, 347 U.S. 483. In that case on May 17, 1954, the Supreme Court held that "in the field of public education the doctrine of 'separate but equal' has no place," and that the segregation of white and Negro children in the public schools of a State solely on the basis of race denies to Negro children the equal protection of the laws guaranteed by the 14th Amendment.

The only answer to this far reaching decision, and the only defense on the merits of the cases offered by the defendants in this suit is that the Supreme

Court in *Brown v. Board of Education of Topeka, Kansas,* decided that segregation of the races was prohibited by the 14th Amendment only in respect to the lower public schools and did not decide that the separation of the races in schools of the college and university level is unlawful. We think that the contention is without merit. That the decision of the Supreme Court was limited to the facts before it is true, but the reasoning on which the decision was based is as applicable to schools for higher education as to schools on the lower level. Chief Justice Warren, speaking for the Court, said:

> Today, education is perhaps the most important function of state and local governments. Compulsory school attendance laws and the great expenditures for education both demonstrate our recognition of the importance of education to our democratic society. It is required in the performance of our most basic public responsibilities, even service in the armed forces. It is the very foundation of good citizenship. Today it is a principal instrument in awakening the child to cultural values, in preparing him for later professional training, and in helping him to adjust normally to his environment. In these days, it is doubtful that any child may reasonably be expected to succeed in life if he is denied the opportunity of an education. Such an opportunity, where the state has undertaken to provide it, is a right which must be made available to all on equal terms. . . .
>
> We conclude that in the field of public education the doctrine of "separate but equal" has no place. Separate educational facilities are inherently unequal.

In view of these sweeping pronouncements, it is needless to extend the argument. There is nothing in the quoted statements of the court to suggest that the reasoning does not apply with equal force to colleges as to primary schools. Indeed it is fair to say that they apply with greater force to students of mature age in the concluding years of their formal education as they are about to engage in the serious business of adult life. We find corroboration for this viewpoint in the decision of the late Chief Justice Vinson in *Sweatt v. Painter,* 339 U.S. 629 at page 634, where, in commenting upon the inequality which inheres in the segregation of the races in graduate schools maintained for the teaching of law he said.

> Moreover, although the law is a highly learned profession, we are well aware that it is an intensely practical one. The law school, the proving ground for legal learning and practice, cannot be effective in isolation from the individuals and institutions with which the law interacts. Few

students and no one who has practiced law would choose to study in an academic vacuum, removed from the interplay of ideas and the exchange of views with which the law is concerned. The law school to which Texas is willing to admit petitioner excludes from its student body members of the racial groups which number 85% of the population of the State and include most of the lawyers, witnesses, jurors, judges, and other officials with whom petitioner will inevitably be dealing when he becomes a member of the Texas Bar. With such a substantial and significant segment of society excluded, we cannot conclude that the education offered petitioner is substantially equal to that which he would receive if admitted to the University of Texas Law School.

Finally, the defendants contend that the pending suit should not be sustained as a class action and the judgment should be confined to those who have appeared and asserted their rights. The representatives of the University seem to be apprehensive that a judgment in favor of all Negroes in North Carolina who may apply for admission to the University may deprive the Board of Trustees of their power to pass upon the qualifications of the applicants. Such is not the case. The action in this instance is within the provisions of Rule 23(a) of the Federal Rules of Civil Procedure because the attitude of the University affects the rights of all Negro citizens of the State who are qualified for admission to the undergraduate schools. But we decide only that the Negroes as a class may not be excluded because of their race or color; and the Board retains the power to decide whether the applicants possess the necessary qualifications. This applies to the plaintiffs in the pending case as well as to all Negroes who subsequently apply for admission.

A judgment and an injunctive order in accordance with this opinion will be issued.

The state appealed the ruling to the U.S. Supreme Court. Attorneys for the three black students included Conrad O. Pearson, Floyd McKissick, and Thurgood Marshall. In a terse, unsigned declaration (*Board of Trustees of the University of North Carolina et al. v. Frasier et al.*, 350 U.S. 979) on March 5, 1956, the high Court upheld the district court decision: "The motion to affirm is granted and the judgment is affirmed."

Appendix 9

Interview with Theotis Robinson Jr., of the University of Tennessee

Theotis Robinson Jr., who enrolled as a pioneer black undergraduate at the University of Tennessee in January 1961, was interviewed by Robert Epling on October 7, 1992, in Knoxville, Tennessee, as part of the Desegregation of Football of the University of Tennessee Oral History Project. The typed transcript, located in the university archives at the University of Tennessee, is presented here in part, with minor changes in punctuation and paragraphing.

Went to school here in Knoxville, graduated from Austin High School, and enrolled in Knoxville College in 1960, left there and came to the University of Tennessee in January of 1961....

Jackie Robinson ... was playing with the Brooklyn Dodgers when I was a kid, had broken the color line in major league baseball when I was five years old. I grew up very much aware of what he had done and his performance on the field, what all he had to go through and pave the way. Of course, there were many other people that I looked up to, particularly athletes. But, if I had a hero as such, if there was one who was premiere in my thinking, it would be Jackie Robinson.

... [I]n September of 1959, the school systems in Knoxville and in Knox County were still segregated.... I lived in east Knoxville, very near what was then East High, and had to leave the area where East was, I guess three or four blocks from my home, and travel two miles to get to school at Austin High. There were several black kids in that same circumstance, so we had decided to attempt enrolling at East. We went to East High, when school began that fall, and were turned away, and proceeded to file a lawsuit against the Knoxville City Schools to desegregate the system. So, I was becoming involved. I was already aware of what was going on, the racial discrimination, things of that nature.

The following spring, sit-ins began here in Knoxville at lunch counters. They began after a rather lengthy process where people tried to resolve the problems through negotiations, but those negotiations failed. The people, the managers of the stores that had lunch counter facilities, did not bargain in good faith, made promises which they broke upon the dates when desegregation was to take place, and so the sit-ins began. They began in June of 1960, and I was involved in those, going down and sitting at lunch counters.... In July of 1960, the leadership group, which was known as the Associated Council for Full Citizenship, took out an ad in a Sunday edition of the *Knoxville News Sentinel* listing a number of grievances that black people had here in the city of Knoxville. One of those was that the undergraduate school here at the University of Tennessee did not accept black undergraduate students. The graduate school had been desegregated ten years prior through a court order, initiated by, and on behalf of, a man Gene Gray who had wanted to pursue, I think, a master's program here. That ruling did not affect the undergraduate school. It was still segregated.

After reading the list of grievances and coming upon that particular one that Sunday night at home, I was all prepared to go to college at Knoxville College. I had a scholarship to attend Knoxville College. I looked at that and said this is something I can deal with because really what I wanted to do, I wanted to pursue a degree in political science. I could not do so at Knoxville College because they didn't have a program in political science that you could major in. You could minor in it. I sat down that night and wrote a letter to the university saying that I wanted to apply and wanted to attend school here. I did not mention where I had attended high school. I did not mention that I was black. I simply sent the letter saying I was interested in enrolling at UT. I got a response back from the university saying that it was not their policy to admit black undergraduate students. It has always been a bit of a mystery to me just how they knew that I was in fact black because there was no mention. The address that I had in the letter was in a mixed neighborhood. Regardless of that, I then contacted the people here at the university and set up a meeting to come over and talk with the people in admissions with my parents, my mother and my dad.

We came over and met with a man named John Smythe who was in undergraduate admissions, and another man by the name of Grady Atkinson who was in admissions, as far as graduate school, and apparently handled the applications of black graduate students who wanted to come to the university. They reaffirmed what the letter had said, that they could not alter the policy. It could only be changed by someone higher up than they and suggested that perhaps I might want to talk with the president of the school, Dr. Andy Holt. We indicated yes, we certainly would like to do that, so immediately set up to meet with Dr. Holt. My parents and I came over and met with him and he was very congenial, but very firm in saying that this was the school policy. It could only be changed by the trustees. If I would like, or we would like, he could present it to them....

We told him certainly we would like for him to present the matter to the Board of trustees, which he said that he would do, but that he should also understand, and they should understand, that unless action was forthcoming, so far as changing the policy, we did plan to file suit against the university. We made that very clear. Dr. Holt took the matter in the hands of one of the university's vice presidents, a Dr. Herman Spivey, who prepared the presentation for the Board of Trustees. They met in November of that year [1960]. . . . They evidently met just to consider this one matter, and did vote to change the policy, and I enrolled on January 3, 1961, along with two other students who came after the policy had been changed. . . .

[UT administrators Smythe, Atkinson, Holt, and Spivey] were congenial, helpful, but their hands were tied in terms of what they could do. Regardless of what they may have wanted to do, they couldn't change the policy but they did do those things that they could do to bring about the change necessary. Dr. Holt certainly could have proceeded along a different path than what he did. From everything that I know, he proceeded along a path to bring about change, rather than to obstruct that change which was obviously coming. . . .

It was obvious that they could not win a lawsuit. These things were falling everywhere. Courts were ruling across the country that you could not deny a person admission to an institution of higher learning, particularly state supported institutions, on the basis of race. They chose the path of conciliation, they chose the path of cooperativeness as opposed to one of obstruction, which we did see in other parts of the country [such as at the University of Alabama]. . . .

I really acted as an individual. I didn't even tell my parents I had sent the letter. It wasn't a matter of my going to them and talking to them about it. I made the decision to do so and I imagine I informed them as I was doing it, but it wasn't even a matter of seeking their counsel at that point. When it came time to come over to meet with the people here at the university, they were supportive of me and also spoke. I guess it was, I don't know what you would call it, the impetuousness of youth on my part that I just took the matter and went on with it. I did not go seek counsel, either from my family or anyone else. As the situation developed, of course, people [in the black community] were supportive. They let me know that if this has to be taken to court, that we will assist in helping to raise funds and things of this nature. . . .

[January 3 was the day] that I first enrolled here at the university, very pleasant winter day. No problems, very much unlike the University of Georgia at Athens where students enrolled in the undergraduate school on that same day and people rioted on campus, tried to burn down dormitories, had to call out the National Guard, all of that kind of turmoil. It simply didn't exist here. I arrived at the university that morning. I'm sure that there was security precautions taken that I was not aware of, but they were not visible. You couldn't see anything that was out of the norm. . . .

Part of my experiences here, the reason it went smoother than some other people's experiences, I was married, I lived in Knoxville and I lived at home. I did not live on campus. I did not depend upon the university environment for social life. I simply came to my class and I left class and went about my business. I did not spend any time on the strip, except to get off a bus on my way to school or to get on to a bus as I was leaving. I did not take my meals anywhere along the strip, and I just did not have any contact with that side of university life. My contact all came in a classroom and did also come in playing basketball pick up games in the old Alumni Gym. I had no problems in there whatsoever. I do understand that there were students who came after me, and who lived in dormitories on campus, that caught hell in those dormitory situations. . . . As I said, I didn't depend upon the university, or the people I met here, for my social life.

. . . [Y]ou know racism exists. There is no question about that. It existed then, it exists today. It will exist tomorrow. It will exist in the next century. Not everything that happens to a person is because of racism just like everything that happens to a person is not because they are not deserving of better. There are those situations in life where a person is qualified, does everything they need to do, ought to do, should do, and can do, and yet racism stands in the way of their progress. There are other situations where people don't do those things, or can't do, due to their own limitations, those things that they are expected to do, and it gets blamed on racism. And one has to be very careful to make sure that you aren't leveling blame in the wrong place, but you need to also be sensitive that it is not racism rearing its head.

. . . [T]he university had an athletic director who was very much a racist. He also was very powerful, was a legend. His name was Gen. Robert R. Neyland, for whom the stadium was named, and the drive to the stadium is named after him, and he just, you know, looms over the university, like Bear Bryant at Alabama. So much tradition within the football program springs from the days when Neyland was the football coach. But Neyland was a racist. And had a real problem with the idea of blacks and whites playing on the same athletic teams here at the university.

I remember a track meet that was scheduled in the spring, in the early 60s. I don't remember what year, but this would have been like '61, '62, one of those two years. The squad coming in to compete with the university had some black athletes, and when Neyland found out that there were black athletes on the squad, he called his track coach and told him to approach the opposing track coach and see if he would agree not to use his black athletes. Well, the man was a principled man and he took the position that "hey, I brought my track squad to compete and they will compete" which meant "no" as far as sitting his black athletes . . . whereupon Neyland cancelled the track meet on the basis that that there could be "trouble." Like what trouble? Nobody attended a track meet. The guys' girlfriends didn't even go to a track meet, you know? . . .

Another incident that I recall, a friend of mine named Avon Rollins walked on to try out for the men's basketball team, and had practiced with the squad, two or three days. This would have been like in the fall of '61 because Avon came to school in September of '61. When Neyland found out about it, he came down to the gym and saw Avon in there scrimmaging with the rest of the team. Cussed Avon out, cussed the coach out, and ran Avon out of the gym, wasn't going to have any of that. Those are things that stand out in my mind from those days.

Appendix 10

Model Universities and Racial Diversity

Universities continue, as they must, to discuss matters of diversity. Public universities speak, as they must, of obligations to their states. Virginia Tech president Paul E. Torgersen spoke in the 1990s of the school's aspiration to be a "model land-grant university for the twenty-first century."

One interpretation of this statement, generalized to public higher education across the South, is that a public university—surely a public institution that draws from the entire state, and perhaps especially a land-grant school—ought to serve a student population that more or less reflects the state's population. That premise is reflected in the method used in this appendix. The numbers presented here permit a quick systematic survey of roughly how well, at around the end of the twentieth century, each of twenty-four public universities in the South were performing in recruiting and retaining undergraduate student populations that reflected their state's population.

African Americans are the only social group investigated here, though a similar method could be applied to the study of other groups. The use of an index, relating campus enrollment to state population, adjusts the campus figures to accommodate widely differing racial compositions of various states. The results point toward schools that seem to be doing particularly well or, alternatively, particularly poorly. The latter group might explore what more successful institutions have tried and found to work.

The higher the index, the stronger the performance according to this approach. A black undergraduate enrollment percentage figure of 6 percent ranks higher—has a higher "index of dissimilarity"—in a state with a black population of 11 percent (the University of Missouri) or even 16 percent (the University of Arkansas) than in one with 26 percent (Auburn University). Yet an enrollment figure of 6 percent looks low for any of these schools. To the degree that the student population figure falls short of the population figure for the state, the school could be said to fail to meet an important obligation. To that extent, it continues to reflect the past, to demonstrate that the dead hand of the past is not so dead after all. One might argue that a model land-grant school, a model university, should approach the statewide figures—that it should approach an index of 100. (If, it might be said, one worked instead from the premise that at present roughly the same numbers of students attend

Table 10.1. Black Proportions: State Population, School Enrollment, and Index of Dissimilarity

State	% Black	School	% Black	Index
AL	26.0	Alabama	13	50
		Auburn	6	23
AR	15.7	Arkansas	6	38
DE	19.2	Delaware	5	26
FL	14.6	Florida	7	48
GA	28.7	Georgia	7	24
KY	7.3	Kentucky	5	68
LA	32.5	LSU	9	28
MD	27.9	Maryland	14	50
MS	36.3	Miss. State	16	44
		Ole Miss	11	30
MO	11.2	Missouri	6	54
NC	21.6	NCSU	10	46
		UNC	11	51
OK	7.6	Okla. State	3	39
		Oklahoma	7	92
SC	29.5	Clemson	8	27
		USC	19	64
TN	16.4	Tennessee	5	30
TX	11.5	Texas A&M	3	26
		Texas	4	35
VA	19.6	Virginia	10	51
		Virginia Tech	4	20
WV	3.2	WVU	4	125

the leading black institution in a state and the leading white one, one might adopt a lower index to measure effectiveness.)

The index of dissimilarity compares each school's enrollment of undergraduate African Americans with the state's racial composition. It does not compare motivation or effort. Rather, it compares results—a school's effectiveness in serving the state, in reflecting the state's population—wherever the explanation might lie. (Geography no doubt plays a role, as does reputation; so does the effectiveness of public schools in preparing candidates for college; and so does institutions' sustained effort at deploying creative, targeted measures to recruit and retain.)

In some states, the state university does much better than the historically white land-grant school in enrolling African Americans. Alabama has twice the black percentage of Auburn (thus twice the index), South Carolina twice Clemson's, and Virginia twice Virginia Tech's. Yet the North Carolina figures are nearly identical, and Mississippi State has a percentage of 16, while the University of Mississippi's is 11. It is not self-evident that the nature of the school, or differences in a land-grant school's past, can account for differences in the index of effectiveness.

Among the twenty-four schools, the University of South Carolina has the highest reported African American percentage (19), Texas A&M and Oklahoma State the lowest (3). Yet measured in terms of state population, West Virginia has the highest index (129) and Virginia Tech the lowest (20). In the middle are Oklahoma State (39) and Mississippi State (44).

Methodological Explanations

1. Definition of "the South": the seventeen states (Deep South, Upper South, and Border South) that entered the second half of the twentieth century with segregated institutions of higher education, thus two land-grant schools, one "white" and one "black" (one "college of 1862" and one "college of 1890").

2. Selection of schools: For each of the seventeen southern states, figures are supplied for (1) the historically white land-grant school (the "college of 1862") and (2) the flagship campus of the state university. Seven states have such separate institutions, one designated the state university and the other a land-grant university—Alabama, Mississippi, North Carolina, Oklahoma, South Carolina, Texas, and Virginia—and ten states designate the state university as a land-grant school. Thus we have twenty-four schools.

3. Source for school figures: *Peterson's Guide to Four-Year Colleges* 29th ed. (Princeton, N.J.: Peterson's, 1999), although if missing there, figures (rounded off) were obtained from the 1998 edition. The percent-black figures from the schools are increasingly dated. Around the year 2000, one school after another stopped reporting data. One reason is that fewer students were self-reporting their racial identity.

4. The U.S. Census actually reported two figures for 2000—one (the lower figure) called "Black or African American alone" and the other "Black or African American alone or on combination." Aggregate national figures were 12.3 percent and 12.9 percent, respectively. Traditionally, one might have expected to use the higher figures, but the census itself used the lower figures, for example, in the "Quickfacts from the US Census Bureau" posted on-line for each state. Thus those lower figures are listed here.

5. Method of determining the "index of dissimilarity" of black enrollment: The black enrollment percentage is divided by the state population figure and rounded off to a whole number.

Contributors

Hayward "Woody" Farrar is associate professor of history at Virginia Polytechnic Institute and State University. His publications include *The Baltimore Afro-American, 1892–1950* (1998) and chapters in *Black Conservatism* (Peter Eisenstadt, ed.) and *The Blackwell Companion to African American History* (Alton Hornsby, ed.).

Charles H. Martin is associate professor of history at the University of Texas at El Paso. His publications include *The Angelo Herndon Case and Southern Justice* (1976) and numerous articles on race and sports.

Robert A. Pratt, professor of history and department chair at the University of Georgia, is the author of *The Color of Their Skin: Education and Race in Richmond, Virginia, 1954–89* (1992), which received the Gustavus Myers Award for Human Rights, and *We Shall Not Be Moved: The Desegregation of the University of Georgia* (2002).

Marcia G. Synnott is professor emerita of history at the University of South Carolina. Her many publications include *The Half-Opened Door: Discrimination and Admissions at Harvard, Yale, and Princeton, 1900–1970* (1979) and "The Evolving Diversity Rationale in University Admissions: From *Regents v. Bakke* to the University of Michigan Cases," *Cornell Law Review* 90 (January 2005): 463–504.

Michael G. Wade, professor of history and former chair of the department at Appalachian State University, is the author of *Sugar Dynasty: M. A. Patout and Son, Ltd., 1791–1995* (1995) and the editor of *Education in Louisiana* (1999).

Peter Wallenstein is professor of history at Virginia Polytechnic Institute and State University. His previous books include *Tell the Court I Love My Wife: Race, Marriage, and Law—An American History* (2002), *From VPI to State University: President T. Marshall Hahn Jr. and the Transformation of Virginia Tech, 1962–1974* (coauthored with Warren H. Strother, 2004), *Blue Laws and Black Codes: Conflict, Courts, and Change in Twentieth-Century Virginia* (2004), and *Cradle of America: Four Centuries of Virginia History* (2007).

Joy Ann Williamson is associate professor in the College of Education at the University of Washington. Her previous publications include *Black Power on Campus: The University of Illinois, 1965–75* (2003), and she is currently finishing "Education for Liberation: Black Students, Black Colleges, and the Black Freedom Struggle."

Index

Abel, Glynn, 69
Adams (later Hoyle), Linda, 40, 212
Aderhold, Omer Clyde, 94, 96, 101, 106, 114n42, 224n43
Adkins, Arthur, 138, 140
Affirmative action, 159, 236
African Methodist Episcopal Church, 217
Alabama Agricultural and Mechanical Institute (A&M), 1, 205, 221n31, 237n9
Alcorn Agricultural and Mechanical College (Alcorn State University), 50, 118, 119, 201
Allen, Ben, 205
Allen, W. George, 42–43
Alpha Phi Alpha, 43, 76
Alumni associations, 81, 232
American Association of University Professors (AAUP), 130
American Baptist Home Mission Society, 118
American Missionary Association (AMA), 117–18, 120, 131
Amherst College, 27
Anderson, Robert G., Jr., 35, 210, 211, 227n57
Appleby, Richard, 185
Arceneaux, Claudette, 68
Arceneaux, Clayton, 76
Armstrong, W. O., 33
Arthur, Mary, 54n18
Ashford, Dorothy, 209
Asian or Asian-American students, 7–8, 16n13, 69
Association of American Universities, 30
Athletics. *See individual institutions; individual sports;* scholarships
Atkinson, Grady, 276–77
Atlanta University, 64, 93, 101
Auburn University: enrollment figures, 280, 281; football, 168, 180–81; pioneer black students, 35, 36
Austin, Carolyn, 145
Authement, Raymond, 82

Baker, Vaughan Burdin, 68
Baker v. Francis T. Nicholls State College (1963), 74
Ball, Coolidge, 190
Baltimore City College High School, 145
Banneker scholarship program (Md.), 159
Baptists, 118
Barbour, Jeptha, 133n6
Barkley Brown, Elsa, 159
Barksdale, Don, 171
Barnett, Herman A., 58
Barnett, Ross, 125, 126
Barton, Delores Chymes, 209
Basketball, 170, 171, 187; Kentucky and Texas Western, 195n19; Maryland, 139; Southwestern Louisiana Institute, 77–78, 81; Tennessee, 278, 279; Vanderbilt, 179
Bates, Daisy, 54n17
Battle, Huey Jefferson, 26
"Battle Hymn of the Republic," 192
Beittel, Adam D., 119–21, 124, 127, 131
Bell, Elmer, Jr., 266–68
Bell, Robert, 182
Bender, William Albert, 121
Berry, Mary Frances, 148, 153, 162, 163
Berry (later Saunders), Cora, 30
Bethune-Cookman College, 43
Biggs, Barbara, 191
Black enrollment, 50, 280–82. *See also under individual institutions*
Black Explosion (student newspaper), 145, 159, 164n28
Black faculty, 33, 81, 203, 231, 234; at Georgia, 208; at Maryland, 154, 158–59, 164n14; at Texas, 232; at University of North Carolina–Greensboro, 233
Black Muslims, 142
Black Panther Party, 142
Black Power, 131, 138, 139
Black Power (Stokely Carmichael and Charles Hamilton), 143

Black schools, historically or predominantly. *See* HBCUs
Black student unions or associations, 161; Florida, 180; Georgia, 185; Illinois, 163n8; Maryland, 140–60; Mississippi, 189, 197n45; University of North Carolina–Greensboro, 231
Black studies programs, 81, 234; black students' call for, at Mississippi, 189; Illinois, 165n30; Maryland, 148, 153–54, 159
Blackwell, Jackie. *See* Butler, Jackie
Blair, Charles Edgar, 35
Blair, Ezell, Jr., 10
Blair, S. C., 268
Blandford, Robert, 146
Blassingame, John, 148, 153, 162, 163–64
Bloch, Charles, 102
Blue, Carlton, 151, 152
Blue and White Flash (student newspaper), 121
Bluebonnet Bowl, 188
Bluford, Guion Stewart, Jr., 217
Bluford, Lucile Harris, 200, 201–2, 216–17nn8–9
Board of Control for Southern Regional Education, 28, 55n29, 210, 257–58
Board of Trustees of the University of North Carolina v. Frasier (1956), 34, 274. See also *Frasier v. Board of Trustees*
Bonanza (TV program), 129
Bonnet, James Stewart, 66, 68, 71, 84n10, 86n31
Booker T. Washington High School (Norfolk, Va.), 37
Booker T. Washington Papers project, 153
Bootle, William A., 106–7, 223
Borah, Wayne G., 64, 65, 85n14
Borinski, Ernst, 121–22
Boston University, 211
Bowie State College, 139
Bowling, Richard H., 11
Boxer Indemnity, 16n13
Boxer Rebellion, 16n13
Boycotts, in Mississippi, 128, 129
Boyd, William Madison, 93
Bradford, Sam, 124
Bradshaw, Charlie, 173, 174, 177
Brandon, John Lewis, 34
Brawley, Lucinda, 200, 209, 225nn47–48
Breathitt, Edward T., Jr., 173, 175

Breaux, Paul, 83n1. *See also* Paul Breaux High School
Brookley Air Field, 205
Brooks, Glenwood C., 148, 152–53, 163
Broutin, Charlotte, 68
Brown, Calvin, 129
Brown University, 131
Brown v. Board of Education (1954), 10, 16n13, 60–61, 170–71; and higher education generally, 12, 34, 41, 44, 60, 66; mightily resisted in the Deep South, 49–50, 74–76, 90n42, 122, 187; spurs desegregation of state universities in the Border South, 12, 26, 33, 45–50, 137, 170
Brown v. Board of Education (1955), 10, 12, 41, 45–50; leads to black undergraduate enrollment, without curricular restriction, 26, 33–34, 44, 45
Bryant, Darryl, 145, 154, 155
Bryant, Paul "Bear," 172, 182–83
Burroughs-White, Claudette Graves, 10, 11, 231
Burton et al. v. Northwestern State College, 83n3
Busbee, George, 108
Butler (later McDonald), Cheryl, 211–13
Butler (later Blackwell), Jackie, 40
Byrd, Daniel, 84n10
Byrd, Harry C., 27, 137
Byrd, Harry F., Jr., 115n57

Caddell, John, 204–5, 220n25, 222n33
Cafeterias, campus: access by black students to, 24, 26, 37, 38, 39, 44, 76, 203; black workers in, 234
Caillier, Jim, 81
Cajuns, 66, 72–73, 79
Caldwell, Harmon, 93, 94–95, 98–99, 102–3, 106, 107, 114n42
California Institute of Technology, 38
Callaway, Howard, 114n42
Cambre, Roland J., 88n36
Campbell College, 128
Campus Coalition Against Racism (Univ. of Maryland), 155–56, 157
Canada, S. W., 201
Carlson, William S., 30
Carson, Edward, 34
Carter, Dan, 153

Carter, Jimmy, 107–8, 109, 115n51
Carter, Robert L., 63, 96
Case Work for the Citizens' Committee (Ala.), 221n28
Casteñeda, Carlos Eduardo, 232
Catholic Church, 31–32, 69, 73, 207, 222n36; desegregated campus facilities, 71, 75, 87n30; official stance against racism, 67, 75, 86n22
Catholic University, 31–32
Catholic Youth Scholarship, 210
Center for Louisiana Studies, 68
Certificates of good moral character (La.), 75–76
Chambliss, Robert, 220
Chandler, Albert B. "Happy," 170
Chaplains: army, 207; campus, 137, 211
Charles, Roderick E., 29
Chase, John S., 44
Chen, Chunjin C., 7, 16n13
Chennault Air Base, 67
Cherry, Lindsay, 37, 38
China, 6, 7, 16n13
Chinese Mississippians, 7, 233
Chisholm, Andrew, 138
Christenberry, Herbert, 74, 76
Christian, Marcus, 70
Christiana G. Smith Alumni Chapter, 81
Citadel, The: early Chinese cadets, 6, 16n13; first female cadet, 212; pioneer black cadets, 36
Citizens' Council, 70, 122, 184, 204
Civil Rights Act of 1964, 12, 200, 229, 241
Civil rights movement, 9–11, 82, 132, 213
Clark, E. Culpepper, 205, 206, 207, 218n16
Clark Central High School (Athens, Ga.), 185
Clark College, 205, 219
Classrooms, segregated and desegregated: 22, 25, 28, 42, 58n64, 203
Clemson University, 35, 209, 230, 233; enrollment figures, 281
Clinton, Dolores, 269
Cohen, Robert, 115n54
Coleman, A. M., 174
College of Notre Dame, 210
College of the Sacred Heart, 67
College of William and Mary, 7, 232
Colleges of 1862, 4–5, 37, 38, 50; black enrollment figures, 281

Colleges of 1890, 4–5, 10, 235, 239; black enrollment figures, 281
Collins, Raymond J., Jr., 269
Columbia University, 136n39, 158, 199
Colvard, Dean W., 19, 187
Combre v. John McNeese State College, 73–74
Compton, Arthur H., 255
Compton (Calif.) Junior College, 187
Confederate battle flag, 40, 70, 139, 185, 186, 189, 191–92, 197n36, 197n45, 213
Congress of Racial Equality (CORE), 137, 138, 140, 143
Conner, Douglas L., 17
Conrad, Glenn, 68
Constantine, Clara Dell, 60, 63, 64
Constantine, Helma, 60, 80, 82
Constantine v. Southwestern Louisiana Institute (1954), 60, 63–66, 79
Conway, Martha Jane, 63, 64
Cook, Eugene, 99
Cooper, Terence, 160; student leader, 141, 142, 144–45, 147, 150, 152, 154, 155, 158; later career, 164
Coppin State College, 139
Cornell University, 151, 158, 201
Coulter, E. Merton, 94, 113n7
Courtney, James Louis, 45
Crisler, Robert, 71, 73, 79
Crockett, Manuel, 11, 34
Croom, Sylvester, 182, 183
Cross, George Lynn, 202
Curricular restrictions, 45, 49–50, 51; Arkansas, 23–24, 33, 48; Delaware, 29–32; Florida, 41, 179–80; Kentucky, 33, 34, 170, 177, 194n6; Louisiana State, 34, 35; Maryland, 26–29, 32, 33, 48, 137; North Carolina, 34, 49; North Carolina State, 34; Oklahoma, 25, 33, Oklahoma State, 25–26, 33; Tennessee, 34, 35, 177; Texas, 33, 44, 58n64; Virginia, 46; Virginia Polytechnic Institute, 36–40, 46; West Virginia, 33

Danner, Walter N., 93–94, 99, 101, 105, 107, 223
Dansby, David Mozart, Jr., 11
Dashiki Players, 78
Davidson, Julia, 148, 163
Davis, Albert, 178
Davis, Nancy Randolph, 25

Davis, Thurston N., 87n30
Davis, Tommy, 146, 160, 163
Dawkins, Benjamin C., Jr., 64, 74, 84–85n14
Dawkins, Benjamin C., Sr., 85n14
Dean, Jesse James, 44
Dearsley, Ann, 10
DeBlanc, Bertrand, 67, 75–76
Deferrari, Roy J., 31–32
de la Beckwith, Byron, 206
Delaware State College, 30, 31
Delta Sigma Theta, 208
Desegregation, in higher education: creating a literature of, 47–50, 233–35; as a process, 11–14, 40–41, 50–52, 229–33, 235–36; use of the term, 49, 51; within campuses, 21–22, 32–33, 42, 45, 50–52, 62, 203, 233–34; without black students, 21. *See also* basketball; cafeterias; classrooms; curricular restrictions; dormitories; football; libraries; track
DeVane, Dozier A., 41–42
Diamondback (student newspaper), 146, 157
Dichmann, Mary, 80
Dickey, Doug, 178, 180
Dickey, Frank G., 171–72
Dissent, the South's dual tradition of, 2–4, 18, 92
"Dixie," 40, 185, 186, 189, 192, 204, 213
Dixiecrat Party, 20, 186
Dixon, Clarence, Jr., 45
Donald, Cleveland, Jr., 21
Dooley, Vince, 185
Dormitories, segregated and desegregated: Florida, 42, 44; Georgia, 105–6; Maryland, 29; Mississippi, 190; Oklahoma State, 25, 26; Southwest Louisiana Institute, 76–77; Tennessee, 278; Texas, 45, 215n5; Virginia Polytechnic Institute, 37, 39–40, 46
Dormon, James H., 78
Dowsing, Frank, 182
Drane, JoAnne Smart, 11, 34, 231
Dudley High School (Greensboro, N.C.), 10, 11
Duke University, 234
Dunn, Arthur Lee, 45
Dutton, Ken, 139
Duval, Daphne, 42
Dyson, Luther H., 74

Ebron, Roy, 77
Edmonds (later Turner), Linda, 40
Edwards, Cheryl, 146
Eisenhower, Dwight D., 86
Elkins, Wilson H.: president of University of Maryland, 140, 143, 147, 148, 149–52, 157, 164; reevaluated, 162
Elliott, Edward, Jr., 45
Ellison, Jane, 25
Elster, Susie Jones, 33
Emancipation Proclamation, 121, 208
Emory University, 222, 223, 234, 255
Engineering programs, 36; Delaware, 29–30; Kentucky, 33, 170, 194n6; Maryland, 28–29; Missouri, 266–68; Oklahoma State, 26; University of Virginia, 46; Virginia Polytechnic Institute, 36–40
Equal Employment Opportunity Commission, 200
Erich, Mark, 147
Evans, Bernest Charles, 45
Evers, Medgar, 123, 126, 206

Farm Security Administration, 118
Farrar, Hayward "Woody": as black student leader, 141–58; reflections of, 158–62; subsequent career of, 164–65n28
Favor, George, 151–52
Federal funds, 19, 67, 241. *See also* Morrill Land-Grant Acts of 1862 and 1890; National Defense Education Act; National Science Foundation
Ferguson, Hill, 219
Fields, Uriah, 129
Figaro, Doris T., 269
Finney, Essex E., Jr., 38, 39
First Baptist Church (Middlesboro, Ky.), 175
Fisher, Ada Lois Sipuel, 25, 29, 200, 202–3, 217–18n12; commemorated, 203, 232–33; later career, 203, 218n15; urges recruitment of more black faculty, 203
Fisher, Warren W., 203, 218n15
Fisk University, 165, 209, 234
Fletcher, Joel Lafayette, 66, 71–72, 73, 80, 85n19, 88n32
Florida A&M University, 42, 44
Florida ex rel. Hawkins v. Board of Control of Florida (1956), 41, 240. *See also* Hawkins, Virgil D.
Florida Supreme Court, 41
Floyd, Henry W., 25

Fontenot, Mary Alice, 86n22
Football: early varsity players of Asian ancestry, 6–7, 39, 40; pioneer black students' attendance at games, 42–43, 206, 209, 211; transition from exclusion to inclusion of black players, 39, 139, 166–93. *See also* Confederate battle flag; "Dixie"; *individual institutions*
Ford Foundation, 131
Foster, Angela, 205
Foster, Autherine Juanita. *See* Lucy, Autherine Juanita
Foster, Autherine Lucy. *See* Lucy, Autherine Juanita
Foster, Grazia, 205
Foster, Hugh Lawrence, 205
Fourteenth Amendment. *See individual court cases;* "separate but equal"
Francis, Willie, 67, 86n22
Franklin, Harold A., 35, 36
Franklin, John Hope, 162, 165
Frasier, Leroy Benjamin, Jr., 34, 49, 270
Frasier, Ralph, 34, 49
Frasier v. Board of Trustees of the University of North Carolina (1955), 34, 46–47, 85, 270–74
Fraternities and sororities, 76, 139, 208. *See also individual organizations*
Frazier, Lethar, 74
Frederick Douglass High School (Baltimore, Md.), 28, 154
Freedman, Morris, 153
Freedmen's Bureau, 117
Freedom Riders, 120, 128
Freedom Summer, 129
Freeman, Douglas Southall, 255
Frostburg State, 140

Gaines, Ernest J., 81
Gaines, Jerry, 40
Gaines, Lloyd, 21, 200, 201. See also *Missouri ex rel. Gaines v. Canada*
Gandy, Samuel L., 90n42
Gantt, Harvey, 1, 35, 209, 210, 225nn47–48
Garrett, James, 161
Gartin, Carroll, 130
Gassner, Julius, 69, 72, 75, 76
Gault, Chuma, 224n43
Gault, Ronald, 224n43

General Education Board, 118
Genovese, Eugene D., 78
Gens de couleur libres, 68
"Gentleman's agreement" re benching black players, 168, 171, 184
George, Leonard, 180
Georgia Bar Association, 95
Georgia Institute of Technology, 168
Georgia State University, 105
Gold, Mike, 147, 149, 156
Goldwater, Barry, 20
Gong, Dong Jung, 7
Gordon, Helen Reaux, 82
Gordon, Oliver, 44
Gossom, Thomas, 181
Grady Memorial Hospital, 222n36, 223n41
Grambling College, 64, 76, 83n3
Gratz v. Bollinger (2003), 237n12
Graves, Claudette, 10, 11, 231
Graves, Ray, 180
Gray, Gene Mitchell, 34, 177, 276
Green, James, 174, 175–76
Green, Rose, 44
Greene, Leon James, 45
Gremillion, J.P.F., 75
Griffin, Marvin, 168
Grutter v. Bollinger (2003), 161, 237n12
Guy-Sheftall, Beverly, 228n63

Haber, Francis C., 147, 148, 153, 159, 162
Hackett, Wilbur, 174, 175–77
Hahn, T. Marshall, Jr., 40
Haley, Alex, 78
Hall, Melvin, 218
Halliday, Kene, 139
Hamilton, Ken, 78
Hampton Institute, 38, 234
Handy (later Powell), Helen, 31
Hardy, Joseph, 69
Hare, Nathan, 139
Hargis, John W., 44, 215n5
Harley, Sharon, 159
Harper (later Scott), Marguerite, 40
Harris, Henry, 181
Harvard University, 199
Harvey and Lucinda Gantt Office of Multicultural Affairs (Clemson), 209
Hatfield, Charles, 61–62
Hawkins, Virgil D., 23, 41–42, 43, 49

Hazeur, Catherine J. See Young, Catherine J.
HBCUs (historically black colleges and universities), 62–63, 116, 139, 151–52. See also individual schools
Heard, Alexander, 179
Heath, Horace Lincoln, 58n64
Hegert, G. Caldwell, 61
Heidelburg, Willie, 189
Held, John, 134n11
Helms, Jesse, 225
Henry McNeal Turner High School (Atlanta), 105, 207, 222n37
Heymann, Maurice, 67, 73
Higginbotham, A. Leon, Jr., 115n51
Higher Education Act of 1965, 241
High schools, desegregation of: Georgia, 185; Mississippi, 190; Virginia, 38, 46
Hill, Darryl, 139
Hillside High School (Durham, N.C.), 270
Hinton, Lora, 184
Hirzel, Robert, 153
Hispanics, 69, 232
Hocutt, Thomas, 61
Hogg, Houston, 174, 175–77
Holland, Roy E., Jr., 31
Hollier, Velma, 63
Hollings, Ernest F., 210
Hollowell, Donald, 100, 104, 106, 107, 112
Holmes, Hamilton: commemorated, 208, 232; later career, 223n41; pioneer black student at Georgia, 19, 35, 71, 105–7, 110, 185, 207–8, 223nn38–41
Holmes, Hamilton, Jr., 223n41
Holmes, Harlan Hobart, 222
Holmes, Irwin, 11
Holmes, Richard E., 17–18
Holmes Cultural Diversity Center (Mississippi State Univ.), 18
Holmes v. Danner (1961), 106–7
Holt, Andrew, 276–77
Hong, Jefferson D., 7
Hood, James Alexander, 1, 19, 35, 205–7, 221n28, 222n33
Hooper, Frank, 96, 103–4
Horne, George Everett, 266–68
Hosch, J. Alton, 94, 97
Houston, Charles Hamilton, 214n2, 216n8; architect of the NAACP's legal strategy against segregated higher education, 27, 92, 201; Harvard law graduate, 199;
Howard University, 30, 234–35; students at or graduates of, 26, 29, 106, 199, 201, 222n35
Hoyle, Linda (Adams). See Adams, Linda
Hudson, Edward, 219
Hull, Foster, 154–155
Hulon Willis Alumni Association, 232
Hunt, Silas, 23–24, 25
Hunter (later Hunter-Gault), Charlayne A.: background, 207–8, 222nn36–37; commemorated, 208, 232; enrollment at Georgia, 19, 71, 105–7, 185, 232nn38–41; interracial marriage, 208, 224n43; subsequent career, 208, 224nn44–45; urges enhanced recruitment of black students, 208
Hunter, Edwin F., Jr., 64, 65, 73
Hunter-Gault, Charlayne. See Hunter, Charlayne
Hurley, James, 179
Hurley, Ruby, 218
Hurst, Robert L., 269
Hutcheson, Edward, 64

Illinois Institute of Technology, 118
Index of dissimilarity, 280–82
In loco parentis, 73
Inscoe, John C., 115n54
Irby, Edith Mae, 24–25, 54nn17–18, 215n5

Jackson, "Bo," 181
Jackson, Emory, 218
Jackson, Hurchail, 61
Jackson, Levi, 168
Jackson, Miss.: Ole Miss football games in, 176; student protest in, 120–39;
Jackson, Shelby M., 66
Jackson, Vernell, 45
Jackson, Wilbur, 183
Jackson, Willie B., 180
Jackson State College: historical background, 117, 118–19, 121; as a movement center, 123–27, 129–30, 132; presidential leadership style, 118–19, 120–21, 125–27; shooting deaths, 157
James, Kenneth, 33
James Madison University, 215n5
Jamieson, Mary E., 83n3

Japan, 7
Jeanmard, Jules, 73
Jefferson, Marie, 268
Jefferson High School (Louisville), 173
Jehovah's Witnesses, 29
Jesse Smith Noyes Foundation, 219n16
Jews, 67, 122
Johns Hopkins University, 38, 234
Johnson, Albert, 174–76
Johnson, Erastus, 146
Johnson, John Henry, 168
Johnson, Junious "Pete," 139
Johnson, Lyman T., 33, 170, 232
Johnson, Lyndon B., 20, 214n2
Johnson, Paul, 130
Johnson, Rhoda E., 206
Johnson, Viola, 61–62
Joint Legislative Committee on Segregation (La.), 75
Jones, Billy, 139
Jones, Edith Mae Irby, 24–25, 54nn17–18, 215n5
Jones, Ernest J., 45
Jones, Lewis W., 255
Jones, Michael "Mack," 207, 222nn34–36
Jones, Nathaniel, 115n51
Jones, Ralph Waldo Emerson, 83n3
Jones, Robert R., 78
Jones, Vivian Malone, 1, 19, 35, 205–7, 210, 222n35
Jones County Junior College (Laurel, Miss.), 187
Jordan, Ralph "Shug," 181
Jordan, Vernon, 106, 114n42
Julius Rosenwald Fund, 118
Junior Rose Bowl, 187

Kappa Alpha, 139
Katzenbach, Nicholas, 206
Keeney, Barnaby, 131
Keeton, Page, 96
Kennedy, John F., 205–6
Kennon, Robert, 66, 85n19
Kent State University, 157
Kentucky Kernel (student newspaper), 172, 194n8
Kentucky State University, 170
Kinard, Billy, 190

King, Ed, 120
King, Horace, 185
King, Martin Luther, Jr., 9, 137, 144, 205; assassination of, 140–41
Kinnebrew, Chuck, 185
Kirk, W. Astor, 58n64
Kirwan, Albert D., 80
Kishi, Taro, 6–7
Kit, Daniel, 155
Klarman, Michael, 48–49
Kluger, Richard, 48, 62, 63
Knapp, Charles B., 111, 115
Knoxville College, 275, 276
Korea: U.S. soldiers in, 76, 94, 99
Ku Klux Klan, 78, 98, 186, 232
Ku Klux Klan Act of 1870, 63
Ku Klux Klan Act of 1871, 63–64
Kysor, John, 89n38

Ladner, Dorie, 135n22
Ladner, Joyce, 135n22
Lafayette, La.: history of, 66–68. *See also* Southwestern Louisiana Institute
Lamar, Dwight, 77
Langston University, 25, 26, 203, 217–18n12, 230
Lapeyre, Odile, 67, 86n22
Lawson, Jettie L., 269
Leblanc, Leroy "Happy Fats," 78–79
Lee, Anthony Tilford, 36
Lee, Cato, 6, 7
LeFlore, John L., 221
LeNormand, Marin, 68
Leo XIII (pope), 86n22
Leverett, Freeman, 100
Libraries, segregated and desegregated, 22, 42, 203
Liddell, Colia, 123
Lincoln High School (Gainesville, Fla.), 42
Lincoln University, 202–3, 266–69
Lingo, Al, 221
Longwood College, 36
Louisiana State University: black undergraduates, 23, 35, 50, 184; football, 168, 183–84; at New Orleans, 74; struggle to desegregate graduate and professional programs, 34, 61–62, 184
Louisiana Tech, 74, 83

Louisiana Weekly (newspaper), 62
Louistall, Victorine, 33
Lucy, Autherine Juanita (Foster): first black student at Alabama, 1, 19, 35, 182, 200, 204–5, 208, 218–19n16; later life and career, 205, 221n27
Lurleen B. Wallace Award of Courage, 207
Lyman T. Johnson Alumni Group, 232
Lynn, Bill, 181
Lyons, Tycine Marie, 26

Major, Gerri, 146
Malcolm X, 78, 144
Malone, Vivian Juanita, 1, 19, 35, 205–7, 210, 222nn33–34; commemorated, 207; later life and career, 222n35
Mangram, John, 122
March on Washington for Jobs and Freedom, 9
Marshall, Thurgood, 63, 112, 202; argues for desegregated undergraduate programs, 274; earns law degree at Howard, 26; reflects on his rejection by Maryland law school, 26–27; seeks desegregation of programs, 27–28, 55n29, 62, 96–97;
Martin, J. Winston, 141, 147, 159, 162
Martin, Michael, 81
Maryland Court of Appeals, 27, 28, 55n29
Maryland State College for Negroes (Univ. of Maryland–Eastern Shore), 137, 139, 151, 152
Massive resistance, 39, 61, 80, 168, 186, 192, 209
Matsu, Art, 7
Matthews, Josetta B., 36
Mays, Benjamin E., 93, 104
McCain, Franklin, 10
McClain, Lester, 178, 193
McClendon, Charlie, 184
McClendon, Edessie V., 45
McCready, Esther, 27, 28, 137, 215n5, 257–61
McCready v. Byrd (Md., 1950), 27, 28, 257–61
McDonald, Cheryl Butler. *See* Butler, Cheryl
McDowell, Cleve, 21
McFeely, William S., 115n54
McGlathery, David, 221
McKissick, Floyd, 34, 270, 274
McLaurin, George W., 25, 62, 218n12
McLaurin v. Oklahoma State Regents for Higher Education (1950), 62, 203
McLeod, Bob, 138, 141, 142, 160
McNair, Michael, 146, 160, 163

McNeal, Valerie, 145
McNeese State University, 61, 73–74, 75
McNeil, Joseph, 10
McVea, Warren, 188
McWhorter, Robert L., 94
Medical schools, 17; Arkansas, 24–25, 215n5; Emory University, 222n35, 223n41; Florida, 52; Georgia, 8–9; Louisiana State, 62; Maryland, 27–28, 29; North Carolina, 48; Texas, 58n64; Virginia, 23, 46. *See also* veterinary schools
Meharry Medical College, 28
Memory, 159–62, 231–33
Memphis State University, 189, 190
Meredith, James: application to and enrollment at Mississippi, 11, 19, 35, 125, 126–27, 186–87, 205–6; student at Jackson State, 124, 125, 126–27;
Merrill, Maurice, 203
Michigan State University, 17, 171, 194n8
Mickle, Stephan, 43–44
Middle States Association of Secondary Schools and Colleges, 30, 32
Miles College, 204, 218n16
Millsaps College, 122
Miner, Luella, 133n4
Minus, Homer W., 31
Miscegenation, 7, 208, 223n39, 224n43
Mississippi Improvement Association of Students (MIAS), 124, 126
Mississippi Sovereignty Commission, 122, 127, 129
Mississippi State University: Chinese Mississippians at, 7, 233; enrollment figures, 17, 281, 282; first black student, 17–18, 19, 35, 181; football, 168, 181–82
Mississippi Vocational College, 118
Missouri ex rel. Gaines v. Canada, Registrar of the University of Missouri (1938), 27, 200, 249–52; delayed effect in Missouri and elsewhere, 27, 61–62, 201–2; early impact in West Virginia, 33; results beginning in 1948, 218n12, 259–61
Mitchell, John, 183
Mitchell, Parren J., 28, 137
Monteith, Henrie Dobbins, 1, 2, 35, 210–11, 225n53, 226–27n56
Monteith, Henry, 226n55
Monteith, R. Rebecca, 210, 211

Montgomery Bus Boycott, 129, 205
Montgomery Improvement Association, 129
Moore, Austin, 129
Morehouse College, 93, 101, 105, 208
Morgan State College, 28, 29, 139
Morrill Land-Grant College Act of 1862, 4–5
Morrill Land-Grant College Act of 1890, 5, 239
Morris, Aldon, 116
Morris Brown College, 211
Morris College, 210
Moss, Alfred A., Jr., 159
Mote, C. D., 160
Motley, Constance Baker, 100, 103, 106, 107, 199, 214n2, 225n53
Movement centers, 116, 132
Muckel, Robert, 237n9
Murphy, B. D., 100, 103
Murphy, William H., Jr., 151–52
Murray, Donald, 55n27, 230; civil rights attorney, 27, 28, 29; pioneer black law student at Maryland, 2, 27, 61, 242
Murray, Jim, 196n31
Murray v. Maryland (1935), 27, 137, 242
Myers, Pollie Anne, 204, 218–19n16, 219n18

Napper, George, 143
National Association for the Advancement of Colored People (NAACP), 9–10, 92, 116, 121, 133n8; applicants said to be tools of, 94, 214n2; banned in Alabama and Louisiana, 74, 220–21n26, 221n28; and direct action, 127–28; field secretaries, 84n10; and higher education lawsuits, 31–32, 60–65, 92, 93, 137, 199, 218–19n16; Legal Defense Fund, 60, 199, 205; regional directors, 202, 218n16; state and local chapters, 60, 62, 93, 123–24, 126, 128, 180, 202; youth councils, 123, 204. *See also* Houston, Charles Hamilton; Marshall, Thurgood; Motley, Constance Baker; Tureaud, A. P.
National Association of Intercollegiate Athletes (NAIA), 77
National Collegiate Athletic Association (NCAA): baseball tournament, 187; basketball tournament, 77, 171, 187, 195n19; penalties, 77, 81; rules, 188, 190
National Defense Education Act (NDEA), 78
National Football Foundation, 182
National Guard, 186, 206

National Medical Association, 24–25
National School Service Fund for Negro Students, 210
National Science Foundation (NSF), 42, 45
National Youth Administration, 67
Native Americans, 6
Negro History Week, 121
Newby, Betty Richardson, 33
New England School of Law, 42
Neyland, Robert R., 278–79
Nicholls State College, 74
Nonblack, as preferred term to "all-white," 6–9
North Carolina Agricultural and Technical College (A&T), 10, 11, 122
North Carolina State University: early black students, 11, 34; enrollment figures, 281
Northeast Louisiana College, 74
Northington, Nathaniel "Nat," 166, 173–75, 193
Northwestern State College (La.), 73, 74, 83
Northwestern University, 103, 105, 106, 110, 168
Norwich University, 211
Notre Dame. *See* College of Notre Dame
Nunn, Sam, 108–9
Nursing school. *See* McCready, Esther
NYAMBURU cultural center (Univ. of Maryland), 159. *See also* University of Maryland

Oberlin College, 119, 201
Oklahoma State University: black enrollment, 25–26, 33; Native American enrollment, 6; total enrollment figures, 230, 282;
Olympics, 171
Omnibus Judge Act of 1978, 114–15n49
Onley, Charles, 146
Original Hootenanny U.S.A., 129
Oswald, John W., 173–74
Otis, Jesse, 119
Owens, George, 131, 132, 136n39
Owens, James, 181, 193

Pace, Bill, 179
Page, Greg, 174–75
Parker, Brooks M., 30
Parker v. University of Delaware (1950), 31
Parnell, J. T., 188
Paul Breaux High School, 70, 76, 80, 81, 83n1; strike regarding, 60

Payne, Lutrill Amos, 34, 62
Pearson, Conrad, 274
Peddrew, Irving L., III, 36–37, 38, 83n2, 232
Peddrew-Yates Residence Hall (Virginia Tech), 232
Peltason, Jack, 148
Pentecostal Church of God in Christ, 202
Peoples, John A., 133n8
Perez, Leander, 63
Perinbam, B. Marie, 164
Perrault, W. C., 66
Perry, Ervin Sewell, 232
Perry-Casteñeda Library (Univ. of Texas), 232
Pettijohn, Samuel Lamar, Jr., 36
Phi Beta Kappa, 164, 223
Piper, Don, 153
Pi Tau Sigma, 38
Plessy v. Ferguson (1896), 5, 47, 60–61, 92, 112n1
Pope, Clarence, 185
Population, state, racial composition of, 20, 230, 280–82 (table, 281)
Powell, Helen. *See* Handy, Helen
Prater, Jonathan L., 139
Prather, H. Lee, 89n38
Pratt, Robert A., 115n54
Predesegregation, 2, 229
Presidents, college and university. *See* Aderhold, Omer Clyde; Beittel, Adam D.; Elkins, Wilson H.; Fletcher, Joel Lafayette; Hahn, T. Marshall, Jr.; Reddix, Jacob L.
Protodesegregation, 29, 32

Quakers, 119

Rabinowitz, Howard N., 5
Racial identity: defined by 2000 census, 282n4; fewer students self-reporting, 282n3; indeterminate, 68, 70; laws defining and redefining, 6, 70; rhetoric of, 6, 8
Rainach, Willie, 75
Raney, Everett Pierce, 36
Ransdell, Joseph E., 72
Ray, John, 177
Reason, Arthurine W., 269
Rebel, Johnny, 78
Reb Rebel Records, 78
Reconstruction, 2, 4, 5, 14–15n3, 187, 210
Redding, Louis L., 30, 31

Reddix, Jacob L., 118–19, 120–21, 125–27, 133n8, 135n24
Reed, James, 190
Reference letters: required of black applicants, 95–96. *See also* certificates of good moral character
Reserve Officers' Training Corps (ROTC), 42, 70, 75
Rice University, 234
Richmond, David, 10
Rickels, Milton, 72
Rickels, Patricia, 72, 79
Ridgel, Gus Tolver, 22, 266–68
Ridley, Walter N., 232
Riehl, Joseph A., 69, 70–71, 72
Robinson, Armstead, 82
Robinson, Jackie, 275
Robinson, Stuart, 155, 156
Robinson, Theotis, Jr., 35, 275–79
Rockefeller Foundation, 40
Rogers, Robert, 148
Rollins, Avon, 279
ROTC. *See* Reserve Officers' Training Corps
Roman, Francisco, 164
Rupp, Adolph, 171, 194n8
Rutledge, Steven, 129

Sacred Heart Normal School, 75
Salary equalization cases, 210, 225n50
Salter, Eldri, 123
Salter, John, Jr., 123
San Francisco State College, 149, 151, 158
Saunders, Cora. *See* Berry, Cora
Saunders, James, 202
Scholarships, 159, 210, 219n16; athletic, 40, 173–74, 178–81, 183–85, 188, 190; named in honor of pioneer black students, 203, 205, 215n5, 232; out-of-state, 61, 93, 99, 100, 208, 210. *See also* National Defense Education Act; National Science Foundation; Rockefeller Foundation
Scott, Marguerite. *See* Harper, Marguerite
Searcy, Barbara, 45
Sedlacek, William E., 147, 156, 159, 160, 164
Segregation, on campus. *See* basketball; cafeterias; classrooms; curricular restrictions; dormitories; football; libraries; track
Seibert, L. R., 93, 100–101

Seitz, Collins J., 31
"Separate but equal," 20, 253–56; and the 1890 Morrill Act, 5; altered meanings of, 31, 32; and black exclusion, 5, 27–28; calls for enhance equality under the formula, 27–28, 31, 32, 62–63, 255; and *Plessy v. Ferguson*, 5, 60–61, 62; repudiated in *Brown v. Board*, 39
Shabazz, Amilcar, 48
Sheffield, James E., 115n51
Shipley, Beryl, 77
Shira, Charley, 182
Shores, Arthur D., 218
Shropshire, Jackie L., 24
Sigur, Alexander, 73
Sigur, Gwen, 77
Silas H. Hunt Hall (Univ. of Arkansas), 24, 232
Simkins, Modjeska Monteith, 210
Simpson, Amos, 72, 76
Simpson, Anne, 76
Simpson, Thetis, 76–77
Singleton, Charles Vincent, 63, 64
Sipuel, Ada Lois. *See* Fisher, Ada Lois Sipuel
Sipuel, Lemuel, 202
Sipuel, Travis B., 202
Sipuel v. Board of Regents of the University of Oklahoma (1948), 25, 218, 239–40, 260–61
Sit-ins, 39; Mississippi, 124; North Carolina, 11, 122; Tennessee, 275–76
Sixteenth Street Baptist Church (Birmingham), 206, 220n23
Skinner, Roy, 179
Slaughter, John, 159
Smart, JoAnne, 11, 34, 231
Smith, Barbara, 215n5
Smith, Christiana G., 75, 81, 89
Smith, Horace, 171
Smith, Thad, 190
Smith, W. D., 76
Smothers, Eric, 152
Smythe, John, 276–77
Solomon, James L., 35, 210, 211
Son of Mississippi, 78
South, definition of, 4, 282n1
South Carolina State College, 209, 210, 230
South Carolina Student Council on Human Relations, 211
Southeastern Conference (SEC): formed, 168; segregated and desegregated football, 166–93. *See also individual universities*

Southeastern Louisiana College, 61, 73–74, 75
Southern Association of Colleges and Secondary Schools (SACS), 101, 118, 130
Southern Christian Leadership Conference (SCLC), 116
Southern Conference, 168
Southern Illinois University, 188
Southern Manifesto, 80
Southern Regional Education, Board of Control for, 28, 55n29, 210, 257–58
Southern University, 60, 61–62, 64, 90
Southwestern Louisiana Institute (SLI), 13, 67; basketball, 77–78, 81; black students, 68–69, 70–71,75, 76–77, 79, 81–82; commemoration of desegregation, 81–82; circumstances of early black enrollment, 66–73, 79–81, 85n19; experiences of pioneer; lawsuit to desegregate, 60, 61, 63–66, 69
Southwest Louisiana Industrial Institute, 67
Speaker ban (Miss.), 129–30
Spelman College, 165
Spicer, Leonard, 139
Spivey, Herman, 276–77
Sports. *See* scholarships; *individual institutions; individual sports*
St. Francis de Sales High School (Powhatan, Va.), 210
St. John's University, 171
St. Mary's College, 168
Stargel, Willard, 171
Starke, George H., Jr., 42
State Board of Trustees of Institutions of Higher Learning (Miss.), 118–19, 129–30, 187
State funds, threatened cutoff to desegregated universities: in Georgia, 9, 96, 100, 208; in Mississippi, 126
Stephens College, 201
Sterling, A. Leroy, 45
Stewart, Donald W., 29
Stewart, Janice, 146
Stillman College, 207
Stokes, Ralph, 183
Stokes, Taylor, 179
Stovall, Walter, 208
Stovall, Wayne, 141, 142, 144–45, 147, 150–51, 152, 154, 160
Student Government Association (SGA):

Jackson State, 124–26; Maryland, 139, 147, 149, 150, 155–57
Student Nonviolent Coordinating Committee (SNCC), 116, 122–23, 138
Students for a Democratic Society (SDS), 138
Sugar Bowl, 169, 184, 186
Sullivan, Patricia, 82
Sutton, George Douglas, 45
Swanson, Gregory, 23
Sweatt, Heman Marion, 44, 62
Sweatt v. Painter (1950), 62, 66, 179, 262–65, 273–74
Syracuse University, 184

Talladega College, 119, 136n39
Talmadge, Eugene, 92
Talmadge, Herman, 92, 100, 102, 108–9
Tate, U. Simpson, 63, 64, 65
Tau Beta Pi, 38
Taylor, John Harold, 68
Taylor, John Henry, 30
Taylor, Shirley, 63, 64
Teabeau, Hazel McDaniel, 269
Texas A&M University: early Japanese-American football player, 6–7; enrollment figures, 282 first female in the Corps of Cadets, 211; pioneer black students, 45
Texas Southern University, 62
Texas Western College, 195n19
Thibeaux, Juanita Jackson, 82
Third Party (Univ. of Maryland), 147, 155
Thomas, Walter, 145–146, 163
Thompson, Charles H., 30
Thompson, Tommy, 191
Thurmond, Strom, 20
Tillman, Bettye Anne Davis, 11, 34, 231
Tillman-Smart Parlor (Univ. of North Carolina–Greensboro), 231
Tillotson College, 58n64
Timmerman, George Bell, Jr., 209
Tinker Air Force Base, 203
Tolson, Arthur Lincoln, 25–26
Tolson, Melvin B., Jr., 25
Torgersen, Paul E., 280
Tougaloo College, 117–18, 119–22, 123–25, 127–29, 130–32, 136n39
Tougaloo Nine, 124
Townes, Willie, 188
Towson State College, 140

Track: Kentucky, 174, 175–76; Tennessee, 178, 278–79; Virginia Polytechnic Institute, 7, 40
Treadwell, Henrie Monteith. *See* Monteith, Henrie Dobbins
Trillin, Calvin, 71, 208, 223n38, 223n41
Trotter, C. S., 73
Truman, Harry, 85n14, 98; President's Commission on Civil Rights, 239; President's Commission on Higher Education, 239, 253–56
Trumpauer, Joan, 128
Tulane University, 234; football, 168
Tureaud, Alexander Pierre, Jr., 23, 63, 196n32
Tureaud, A. P. (Alexander Pierre) 62, 63, 64, 74, 83
Turner, Linda. *See* Edmonds, Linda
Tushnet, Mark V., 217
Tuskegee Institute, 181
Tuttle, Elbert, 223

U.S. Air Force, 37–38, 186, 212
U.S. Army, 42, 97, 178, 186
U.S. Census Bureau, 40
U.S. Department of Agriculture, 38, 118
U.S. Department of Defense, 97
U.S. Department of Health, Education, and Welfare (HEW), 148, 154
U.S. Military Academy, 7
United Church of Christ, 130
University of Alabama: black enrollment figures, 221n27, 281; football, 168, 182–83; Huntsville Center, 221n31; pioneer black students, 1, 19, 35, 61, 204–7, 222nn33–35
University of Arkansas, 23–25, 29, 48, 232, 255; enrollment figures, 280
University of California at Berkeley, 151, 158
University of California at Los Angeles (UCLA), 171, 178
University of Chicago, 118, 119, 164–65
University of Cincinnati, 171
University of Delaware, 29–33, 63, 215n5; board of trustees, 30
University of Florida: football, 42–43, 168, 179–80; graduate and professional desegregation, 41–43; interviews at, 42–44, 234; undergraduate desegregation, 43–44, 215n5
University of Georgia, 8–9, 19, 208, 223nn39–41; black enrollment figures, 110, 224n45, 281; board of regents, 93, 95–97, 99–101,

102–3, 104; football, 110, 168, 183, 184–85. See also Holmes, Hamilton; Hunter, Charlayne; Ward, Horace Taliaferro
University of Houston, 178, 188
University of Illinois, 148, 158
University of Kansas, 201
University of Kentucky, 33, 232; contrasting images regarding resistance to change on race, 195n19; football, 166, 168, 169–77, 192–93
University of Louisiana at Lafayette, 81–82.
University of Maryland: black enrollment figures, 138, 148, 158, 163n9; black faculty, 148, 154, 158–59, 164n14; Black Student Union, 140–60; black studies program, 153–54, 164n21; board of regents, 29, 137, 149; early Asian students on the College Park campus, 7; first black football players, 139; first black students at College Park, 28–29; law school, 2, 26–27, 137, 151, 242–48; misleading history of, 47–48; nursing school, 27–28; recruitment of black students, 158, 159. See also Campus Coalition Against Racism; Elkins, Wilson; McCready, Esther; Murray, Donald; NYAMBURU cultural center
University of Maryland Baltimore County (UMBC), 151, 152
University of Maryland–Eastern Shore, 152, 165
University of Maryland v. Murray (1936), 27, 242–48, 257–59. See also Murray, Donald
University of Michigan, 153, 169, 170, 201
University of Minnesota, 187
University of Mississippi: Black Student Union protest, 189, 197n45; Chinese Mississippians, 7, 233; "desegregated" yet no black students, 21; enrollment figures, 281; football, 166, 168, 185–93; pioneer black students, 11, 19, 21, 35, 126–27; violence, 11, 19, 61, 185–86, 205–6
University of Missouri, 22, 201–2; enrollment figures, 280; litigation against, 266–69; partial desegregation at, 268–69
University of North Carolina at Chapel Hill: board of trustees, 270–74; and the consolidated university, 270–71; early football, 167; enrollment figures, 281; graduate and professional programs, 34, 48, 61; undergraduate admission to, 11, 34, 48, 49, 270–74
University of North Carolina at Charlotte, 209

University of North Carolina at Greensboro: board of trustees, 231; commemoration, 231; interviews, 234; pioneer black students, 10–11, 34, 215n5;
University of Oklahoma: black enrollment, 25, 33, 45; Native American enrollment, 6. See also Fisher, Ada Lois Sipuel
University of Pittsburgh, 168–69
University of South Carolina, 2, 35, 209, 210–11, 230; board of trustees, 210; enrollment figures, 14–15n3, 281, 282; University Center, Beaufort, 227
University of Southern California, 183
University of Southern Mississippi: Chinese Mississippians enrolled, 7; football, 189–91
University of Southwestern Louisiana, 76. See also Southwestern Louisiana Institute
University of Tennessee: board of trustees, 276–77; football, 168, 177–78; graduate admission, 34, 177, 276; undergraduate admission, 35, 177, 275–79
University of Texas, 97, 215n5, 232; black graduate students at, 44; black undergraduates at, 34, 44–45, 215n5; medical school, 58. See also *Sweatt v. Painter*
University of the South (Sewanee), 168
University of Tulsa, 188
University of Virginia, 23, 46, 232; enrollment figures, 281
University of Wisconsin, 184
"Unwritten law" (banning interracial sports competition), 187
Upward Bound, 139

Vanderbilt University, 234; football, 168, 179
Vaught, Johnny, 182, 186, 187, 188, 190
Veterinary schools, 26, 45, 55n29
Vietnam War, 157–58
Villanova University, 187
Virginia Military Institute, 7, 36, 212
Virginia Polytechnic Institute and State University (Virginia Tech), 234, 280; board of visitors, 37, 38; Corps of Cadets, 37, 40, 200–1, 211–13; early Chinese students, 6, 7; enrollment figures, 230, 281, 282; pioneer black female students, 40, 211–12; pioneer black male students, 36–41, 83n2, 84n9
Virginia State College (Virginia State University), 36, 38, 39, 46, 230

Vista Community College (Calif.), 161
Voter registration, 136n39

Wake Forest University, 167
Walden, Austin Thomas, 94, 96, 100, 102
Walker, Herschel, 185
Walker, Irvin, 21
Walker, Sol, 171
Wallace, George C., 19, 137, 182, 206, 207, 222, 237n9
Walter N. Ridley Scholarship Fund, 232
Walters, David, 203
Walters, Ronald, 159
Ward, Horace Taliaferro, 113n17; appointed to judgeships, 108–9; assists in litigation against the University of Georgia, 105–7, 114n42; commemorated, 110––12; earns law degree at Northwestern, 103, 105; serves in state legislature, 107–8; tries to enroll at the University of Georgia, 23, 49, 93–105
Ward, Ruth, 115n59
Ward v. Regents of the University System of Georgia (1957), 100–104
Warren, Earl, 185
Washington, D.C., 113n7, 139–40, 142, 154
Washington, Mike, 183
Washington University (Mo.), 255
Wayne State University, 105, 208, 219n19
W. B. Vennard Academy, 78
Wells, Robert G., 39, 40
Wells v. Luther H. Dyson (1955), 74
West Virginia State College, 230
West Virginia University, 33, 230; enrollment figures, 282
West, E. Gordon, 83n3
West, Larry, 185
Westminster School District of Orange County v. Mendez (1947), 85n18
Wetherby, Lawrence, 170
Wharton, Dolphin Al, Jr., 26
Wharton, Glenn Bernarr, 26
Wharton, Vernon Lane, 88n34
Whisner, Elbert C., 30
White, Goodrich C., 255

White, Laverne Williams, 209
Whitehurst, James L., 39–40
Whittle, Hiram, 28–29, 137
Wichita Falls Junior College District v. Battle (1953), 85n17
Wiley College, 17, 25
Wilkerson, Philip L., 36
Williams, J. Otis, 159
Williams, Johncyna, 44
Williams, Linda Faye, 159
Williams, Mike, 184
Williams, Robert J. "Ben," 190–91, 193
Williams, Walter, 125, 133n8, 135n24
Williams et al. v. Northwestern State College, 83n3
Williamson, Joy Ann, 158, 162
Willis, Hulon, 232
Wilson, Floyd, 37–38
Wilson, Roy S., 62
Wilson, Shawn, 81
Wilson, Thaddus, 76
Wilson v. Board of Supervisors of Louisiana State University (1950), 62
Wingo, Hin Luck, 7
Winn, Phail, 25
Winston, Matthew M., Sr., 38, 39
Woman's College. *See* University of North Carolina at Greensboro
World War II, 7, 67, 72, 121, 202; veterans of, 24, 28, 171, 202
Wrestling, 31
Wright, J. Skelly, 63, 76
Wrighten, John Howard, III, 209
Wyatt, Karl, 145, 155
Wynn, Earl, 138, 140

Xavier University, 63

Yale University, 168
Yates, Charlie L., 37, 38, 212, 232
Young (later Hazeur), Catherine J., 30
Young, Chris, 145
Young Men's Christian Association (YMCA), 38

SOUTHERN DISSENT
Edited by Stanley Harrold and Randall M. Miller

The Other South: Southern Dissenters in the Nineteenth Century, by Carl N. Degler, with a new preface (2000)

Crowds and Soldiers in Revolutionary North Carolina: *The Culture of Violence in Riot and War,* by Wayne E. Lee (2001)

"Lord, We're Just Trying to Save Your Water": Environmental Activism and Dissent in the Appalachian South, by Suzanne Marshall (2002)

The Changing South of Gene Patterson: Journalism and Civil Rights, 1960–1968, edited by Roy Peter Clark and Raymond Arsenault (2002; first paperback edition, 2020)

Gendered Freedoms: Race, Rights, and the Politics of Household in the Delta, 1861–1875, by Nancy D. Bercaw (2003)

Civil War on Race Street: The Civil Rights Movement in Cambridge, Maryland, by Peter B. Levy (2003)

South of the South: Jewish Activists and the Civil Rights Movement in Miami, 1945–1960, by Raymond A. Mohl, with contributions by Matilda "Bobbi" Graff and Shirley M. Zoloth (2004)

Throwing Off the Cloak of Privilege: White Southern Women Activists in the Civil Rights Era, edited by Gail S. Murray (2004)

The Atlanta Riot: Race, Class, and Violence in a New South City, by Gregory Mixon (2004)

Slavery and the Peculiar Solution: A History of the American Colonization Society, by Eric Burin (2005; first paperback edition, 2008)

"I Tremble for My Country": Thomas Jefferson and the Virginia Gentry, by Ronald L. Hatzenbuehler (2006; first paperback edition, 2009)

From Saint-Domingue to New Orleans: Migration and Influences, by Nathalie Dessens (2007)

Higher Education and the Civil Rights Movement: White Supremacy, Black Southerners, and College Campuses, edited by Peter Wallenstein (2008; first paperback edition, 2009)

Burning Faith: Church Arson in the American South, by Christopher B. Strain (2008; first paperback edition, 2020)

Black Power in Dixie: A Political History of African Americans in Atlanta, by Alton Hornsby Jr. (2009; first paperback edition, 2016)

Looking South: Race, Gender, and the Transformation of Labor from Reconstruction to Globalization, by Mary E. Frederickson (2011; first paperback edition, 2012)

Southern Character: Essays in Honor of Bertram Wyatt-Brown, edited by Lisa Tendrich Frank and Daniel Kilbride (2011)

The Challenge of Blackness: The Institute of the Black World and Political Activism in the 1970s, by Derrick E. White (2011; first paperback edition, 2012)

Quakers Living in the Lion's Mouth: The Society of Friends in Northern Virginia, 1730–1865, by A. Glenn Crothers (2012; first paperback edition, 2013)

Unequal Freedoms: Ethnicity, Race, and White Supremacy in Civil War–Era Charleston, by Jeff Strickland (2015)

Show Thyself a Man: Georgia State Troops, Colored, 1865–1905, by Gregory Mixon (2016)

The Denmark Vesey Affair: A Documentary History, edited by Douglas R. Egerton and Robert L. Paquette (2017)

New Directions in the Study of African American Recolonization, edited by Beverly C. Tomek and Matthew J. Hetrick (2017)

Everybody's Problem: The War on Poverty in Eastern North Carolina, by Karen M. Hawkins (2017)

The Seedtime, the Work, and the Harvest: New Perspectives on the Black Freedom Struggle in America, edited by Jeffrey L. Littlejohn, Reginald K. Ellis, and Peter B. Levy (2018; first paperback edition, 2019)

Fugitive Slaves and Spaces of Freedom in North America, edited by Damian Alan Pargas (2018; first paperback edition, 2020)

Latino Orlando: Suburban Transformation and Racial Conflict, by Simone Delerme (2020)

Slavery and Freedom in the Shenandoah Valley during the Civil War Era, by Jonathan A. Noyalas (2021)